An Injury Law Constitution

AN INJURY LAW
CONSTITUTION

Marshall S. Shapo

OXFORD
UNIVERSITY PRESS

Oxford University Press, Inc., publishes works that further Oxford University's objective of excellence
in research, scholarship, and education.

Oxford   New York
Auckland   Cape Town   Dar es Salaam   Hong Kong   Karachi   Kuala Lumpur   Madrid   Melbourne
Mexico City   Nairobi   New Delhi   Shanghai   Taipei   Toronto

With offices in
Argentina   Austria   Brazil   Chile   Czech Republic   France   Greece   Guatemala   Hungary   Italy
Japan   Poland   Portugal   Singapore   South Korea   Switzerland   Thailand   Turkey   Ukraine
Vietnam

Published by Oxford University Press, Inc.
198 Madison Avenue, New York, New York 10016

Oxford is a registered trademark of Oxford University Press
Oxford University Press is a registered trademark of Oxford University Press, Inc.

Library of Congress Cataloging-in-Publication Data

Shapo, Marshall S., 1936–
An injury law constitution / Marshall S. Shapo.
   p. cm.
Includes bibliographical references and index.
ISBN 978-0-19-989636-3 ((hardback) : alk. paper)
1. Personal injuries—United States. 2. Damages—United States. 3. Workers'
compensation—Law and legislation—United States. 4. Torts—United States.
5. Actions and defenses—United States. I. Title.
KF1257.S53 2012
346.7303'23–dc23   2011036205

Note to Readers
This publication is designed to provide accurate and authoritative information in regard to the subject matter
covered. It is based upon sources believed to be accurate and reliable and is intended to be current as of the time it
was written. It is sold with the understanding that the publisher is not engaged in rendering legal, accounting,
or other professional services. If legal advice or other expert assistance is required, the services of a competent
professional person should be sought. Also, to confirm that the information has not been affected or changed by
recent developments, traditional legal research techniques should be used, including checking primary sources
where appropriate.

*(Based on the Declaration of Principles jointly adopted by a Committee of the
American Bar Association and a Committee of Publishers and Associations.)*

You may order this or any other Oxford University Press publication
by visiting the Oxford University Press website at www.oup.com

For Helene
Always, the nonpareil

And for

Nat and Robin
Ben and Jackie
Noah, Michaela, Joshua, Jonathan, Gabrielle, Aaron

To the memory of my parents
Mitchell Shapo and Norma Shapo

PREFACE

This book frames a group of our nation's responses to the problem of injuries, a problem that almost everyone encounters at one time or another.

It arises from my study of the subject over forty-six years. That study, which I still continue, owes much to many people whom I have encountered and whose work I have read during that time. I can mention only a few of them.

Libraries are seedbeds of inquiry. I am indebted to a succession of librarians at the schools where I have taught—Texas, Virginia, and Northwestern. I have had indispensable help during my thirty-three years at Northwestern, from a number of fine professionals. In the front rank of these people is Marcia Lehr, ever selfless and helpful. I am thankful also to her colleagues, Pegeen Bassett, Irene Berkey, and Heidi Kuehl, and I have appreciated the efforts of Jim McMasters, who most recently has served as law librarian at Northwestern. A generation and more of student assistants at Northwestern have reinforced my research; on a highly selective basis, I mention Lauren Daniel, Leighton Leib, Jonathan David Shaub, and Cristina Carmody Tilley.

Northwestern has provided research support that has made this book possible. I thank the deans under whose tenures those funds have been dispensed: David Ruder, Bob Bennett, and David van Zandt.

Mike Sobczak, my faculty assistant, has been invaluable in bringing this book to fruition—not only in his tireless retyping of the manuscript, but his plumbing of the intricacies of the computer world and his personal patience.

The research that has fueled this book has included the reading of tens of thousands of primary materials and secondary sources. My footnotes give credit to dozens of these sources, but they do not mention many others that I have absorbed over the years.

I have had the pleasure of association with many fine minds in the community of torts teachers across the country, and was privileged to serve as chair of the Torts Round Table Council and of the Torts-Compensation Systems Section of the Association of American Law Schools. I have been a speaker and panelist at meetings of those organizations over a period spanning five decades. Those experiences made special contributions to my knowledge of my subject. I shall not try to name at length the many excellent educators in my area of scholarship who have challenged me with their ideas and deepened my knowledge of the subject. But I must note my exceptional luck in being associated at the beginning of my career with Page Keeton and Leon Green, who were among the greatest contributors to legal education of their generation. Another important educational experience has been my membership in the American Law Institute. My participation in many plenary meetings of that organization has often involved the cut and thrust of debate of a sort that sharpens the mind.

In participating in exchanges with many colleagues abroad, I have imbibed from them ideas that appear in this book, either directly or indirectly. These encounters have occurred in places including Wolfson College, Cambridge, and the Center for Socio-Legal Studies at Wolfson College, Oxford; Observatori de Dret Privat Europeu I Comparat, Universitat de Girona; Kobe University, the Osaka Bar Association, and Ritsumeikan University; Universitat Pompeu Fabra, Barcelona; University LUISS Guido Carli, Roma; Facoltà di Giurisprudenza, Università di Pisa; Juristiches Seminar, University of Gottingen; Fachbereich Rechtswissenschaften, Universitat Bremen; Ius Gentium Conimbrigae, University of Coimbra; the Brazilian Bar Association.

My family is my extraordinary good fortune. Their love, companionship, and intellect have inspired my work and my life generally. I had countless lessons from my father, Mitchell Shapo, and my mother, Norma Shapo, that bore on law as well as life. I especially remember words that my father wrote to me toward the end of his life: "When I studied law, my ambition was to fight injustice." My sons Benjamin and Nathaniel are constant sources of penetrating analysis, as well as personal joy. Much joy also comes from their spouses, Ben's wife Jackie and Nat's wife Robin, and from their children—Aaron, Gabrielle, Joshua, Jonathan, Michaela, and Noah. I already have recorded Gabrielle's words and actions in other published work.

Helene Shapo is a nonpareil. A doyenne of the craft of legal writing and an investigator on various scholarly frontiers, she is the most acute of critics—distinguished for her intellectual courage, her sense of style, her common sense, and her opposition to all forms of cant.

Chicago and Evanston
August 2011

CONTENTS

Introduction　　*xi*

1. An Injury Law Constitution　　*1*
2. Injury Law and Power　　*25*
3. Rights　　*37*
4. Injuries　　*71*
5. Mechanisms of the Law　　*85*
6. Legal Doctrine　　*101*
7. Functional Elements of the Law　　*123*
8. Social and Individual Goods, Sometimes in Competition　　*179*
9. The Rationales of Injury Law　　*213*
10. Remedies and Sanctions　　*235*
11. The Supreme Court and Injury Law　　*243*
Conclusion　　*263*

Index　　*273*

INTRODUCTION[1]

From the carnage on the highways to many thousands of silent deaths attributable to hospital care to the gusher in the Gulf, the problem of injuries is always with us. Injuring events destroy lives, rend families, and sometimes ravage whole communities.

Over many decades, even centuries, society has developed a great body of law to deal with these problems—sometimes quite incrementally, sometimes in bursts of judicial and legislative creativity. This book develops the idea that this body of law has developed into what I call an injury law constitution. It reaches across the spectrum of legal institutions and societal mechanisms to encompass basic ideas of responsibility for injuries and prevention of injuries. With respect to that subject, it provides a fundamental set of principles that govern relations between human persons and corporate and governmental institutions.

Giving colorful point to the ideas I explore here are headline stories about lawsuits for personal injury during the last half century of American life. Many of these stories come to the public heavy with social and political content. Here is just a set of examples, decade by decade:

- In the 1960s, a young consumer activist named Ralph Nader sued General Motors for a slew of activities, ranging from wiretapping to sicing prostitutes on him, which he alleged invaded his privacy and caused severe emotional distress. After a ruling favorable to Nader by the highest court of New York on at least the privacy issues,[2] GM settled the case.[3]

1. I appreciate suggestions from several colleagues that have led me to sources mentioned here: Robert Burns, Steven Calabresi, Michael Green, John McGinnis, James Pfander, Stephen Presser, Marty Redish. I am particularly grateful to Professor Redish for comments and conversation about the topic and to Professor Green for comments.

2. Nader v. General Motors, 255 N.E.2d 765 (1970).

3. Nader's lawyer explains the tactical reasons for settlement in Stuart Speiser, Lawsuit 101–04 (Horizon Press 1980).

- In the 1970s, a dramatic lawsuit involving the first implantation of an artificial heart in 1969 resulted in a federal appellate decision in Texas favoring a famous cardiovascular surgeon.[4]
- Also in the 1970s, an injury victim sued the Ford Motor Company, contending that it had manufactured a rolling bomb for civilian transportation, a car which burst into flames when it was hit from the rear. In a litigation that extended into the eighties the jury awarded more than one hundred million dollars in punitive damages. A California appellate court approved the granting of punitive damages, although it reduced the award considerably.[5]
- In a case stemming from the Lockerbie disaster in 1988 that involved damages awards in the millions of dollars, Pan American World Airways acknowledged that survivors of three victims should be able to recover for their loss of financial contributions and services of the victims, and a majority of a federal appellate court issued a nuanced set of holdings on damages for loss of society and parental care sought by plaintiffs who were adult children.[6]
- In the first decade of the new century, juries and judges across the nation delivered split decisions on the question of whether hormonal drugs caused breast cancer.[7]

These litigations, and hundreds of thousands of others—the great majority of which never progress to trial—present a highly charged element of American life. The very fact that someone goes to a lawyer about a grievance usually is a marker of vexation; often it betokens rage. When a defendant does not settle a claim and the dispute progresses into litigation, that very fact may show a substantial dispute about the facts. Sometimes it may indicate that both parties have reasons for pursuing the litigation that are not just "about the money."

Alongside the private law of personal injuries—the tort suit by individuals against alleged injurers—has grown up a formidable body of public law: legislation passed to enhance safety generally. These statutes range from the Food Drug & Cosmetic Act, which also regulates devices, to the

---

4. Karp v. Cooley, 493 F.2d 408 (5th Cir. 1974).

5. Grimshaw v. Ford Motor Co., 174 Cal. Rptr. 348 (App. Ct. 1981).

6. Air Disaster at Lockerbie Scotland on Dec. 21, 1998, 37 F.3d 804 (2d Cir. 1994).

7. *Compare*, e.g., Rush v. Wyeth, 514 F.3d 825 (8th Cir. 2008)(affirming verdict for manufacturer) *with* Rowatt v. Wyeth, 36 Prod. Safety & Liab. Rep. 166 (Feb. 18, 2008) (reporting Nevada district court's refusal to give manufacturer a new trial on jury award of $134.5 million, including $99 million in punitive damages, to three plaintiffs). In the *Rowatt* case, the Nevada Supreme Court affirmed the judgment for the plaintiffs, as reduced by the trial court to a total of $35 million for the three claimants. Wyeth v. Rowatt, 244 P.3d 765, 786 (2010).

Occupational Safety and Health Act and the National Traffic and Motor Vehicle Safety Act. They have responded to data on occurrence of injuries and illness and in some cases to public perceptions stoked as much by anecdotes about sympathetic victims as by large numbers of injuries.

Recently, public concern about clusters of illnesses from various foods has resulted in Congressional advocacy of larger budgets for food safety, including increases in the number of inspectors. At the same time, legislators have pressed for more resources for the analysis of both new drugs and drugs already on the market with an eye to protecting people from injurious side effects. And, in an ironically simultaneous development, some sufferers have complained that the government has been too restrictive about allowing them access to experimental drugs they desire.

In the background of these developments has been the emergence of markets for consumer goods made possible by nanotechnology, a technology posing much uncertainty about the risks it may pose to consumers and workers exposed to the substances it creates. At this writing, there has been a remarkable lack of regulatory action aimed at the collection of data on risk in this area, let alone specific rules designed to minimize risk.

The interaction between safety regulation statutes and tort law is complex. One important set of issues concerns the effects in civil litigation of violations of safety statutes. In tort cases, the law on this subject varies from state to state, with results often differing according to the type of statute that is involved. If a statute clearly targets a particular group of vulnerable people for protection—child labor laws are a good example—courts usually will decide that a violation of the statute effectively shows that the defendant was at fault and should be liable, whatever the individual facts of the case (including the carelessness of the plaintiff, objectively viewed) may indicate. In other cases, which involve statutes of more general application, some courts conclude that a statutory violation (for example, breaking a rule of the road) can serve as evidence of negligence, but may be excused.

A quite separate set of issues, which raise important questions about the nature of our federal system, arise when the defendant argues that what otherwise might be held a defective or negligently made product cannot be the subject of a tort suit because Congress has "occupied the field" of that particular kind of safety problem. The Supreme Court has decided several cases on this issue of "federal preemption." That roster of cases has included decisions for plaintiffs in one litigation involving a prescription drug,[8] a case involving a pesticide,[9] a case involving the lack of a propeller guard on

---

8. Wyeth v. Levine, 555 U.S. 555 (2009).
9. Bates v. Dow AgroSciences LLC, 544 U.S. 431 (2005).

a motorboat,[10] and a case involving allegedly deceptive advertising for light cigarettes.[11] It has also included split holdings in another cigarette case, with a fault line following different provisions in two statutes. Other decisions in this group are differing holdings in two cases involving medical devices, with the variation depending largely on different regulatory processes administered by the Food and Drug Administration.[12] Additionally, the Court has favored an auto manufacturer's preemption argument in a case involving the lack of an air bag on a vehicle.[13] Some of these cases have been decided by one-vote margins; that in itself reflects differences of opinion about the nature of the federal system as well as Congress' intent in passing the statutes at issue. This body of law, although often technical in its superstructure, generates basic foundational issues about our injury law constitution that run like a thread through this book.

The way that the private law and safety statutes overlap, and sometimes generate legal conflict, underlines an observation by a great teacher of mine, Leon Green, that "private law is public law in disguise."[14] Some most ordinary lawsuits for personal injuries may bring into play questions of culture and politics. Judicial decisions in such everyday matters as injuries caused to workers by various kinds of machines may involve ideological premises about the nature of individual responsibility—as well as both behavioral and philosophical assumptions about how much freedom we have to make choices about personal safety.

The development of our injury law has indeed been, in significant measure, an effort to fix responsibility for injuring events. Sometimes the law does so on individuals—including injured persons. Sometimes it fixes responsibility on corporations. And on occasion it does so with damage awards against government officials and even governments. On occasion, governments accept responsibility for injuries through legislation, for example in the form of grants of money. The United States has even provided compensation for injuries inflicted by malevolent third parties, as in the case of the September 11th attacks. In certain cases, our law divides or spreads responsibility among multiple parties.

---

10. Sprietsma v. Mercury Marine, 537 U.S. 51 (2002).

11. Altria Group, Inc. v. Good, 555 U.S. 70 (2008).

12. Medtronic v. Lohr, 518 U.S. 470 (1996); Riegel v. Medtronic, 552 U.S. 312 (2008).

13. Geier v. American Honda Motor Co., 529 U.S. 861 (2000). However, the Court later distinguished this decision in a case arising from an auto maker's failure to install a lap-and-shoulder belt in the rear inner seats of a vehicle. Williamson v. Mazda Motor of Am., Inc. 131 S. Ct. 1131 (2011).

14. See Leon Green, Tort Law Public Law in Disguise: I, 38 Tex. L. Rev. 1 (1959); II, 38 Tex. L. Rev. 257 (1960).

The word accountability has become a mantra in the last decade, its usage increasing by leaps and bounds with the emergence of the financial crisis in 2008. In the end, though, that term has the ring of an entry in a ledger sheet. The idea of responsibility, by contrast, connotes a societal judgment, often one with moral overtones. And it includes not only the obligation of those tagged as injurers but the responsibility for self-protection of those labeled victims.

Much of our injury law—tort law as well as legislation—seeks to control conduct, sending signals about what is permitted and what is prohibited. There are many arguments about the clarity of the signals. Business persons, in particular, would like the rules to be as crisp as possible: Exactly how high should the guardrail be? Certainty about the rules—including about the decisions that will interpret the rules—is desirable. Law and order do run together, in general public perception as well as in the title of a group of long-running television shows. Yet, particularly when people expose others to risk in ways that are reckless or even more culpable, there is something to be said for preserving a broad zone of conduct into which one ventures at his peril. In a Missouri case a century ago, the court said that those bent on fraud

> would like nothing half so well as for courts to say they would go thus far and no further in its pursuit. . . . Accordingly definitions of fraud are of set purpose left general and flexible, and thereto courts match their astuteness against the versatile inventions of fraud-doers.[15]

It is often useful to analyze society's efforts to control risky conduct from an economic perspective. But running through the social judgments that are made on risk-generating behavior are moral notions of reparation, sometimes of punishment, often of vindication. All of these ideas partake of custom and culture, and the jagged profile of injury law reflects the fact that we are a land of competing cultures and many customs. Mirroring these complexities are the different intensities of signals that the law sends out. Sometimes it says what is permitted, with various degrees of enthusiasm. Illustratively, it may in effect endorse different models of products with different levels of risk because of the way that a variety of products serves consumers. In other cases, the signal is not so much about what is permitted but what is condoned. Thus, we may morally condemn sellers who do not reveal important details about their products, but we provide a broader zone of condonation for nondisclosure than for explicit misrepresentations.

---

15. Stonemets v. Head, 154 S.W. 108, 114 (Mo. 1913).

The inner life of the American public reveals itself in many forms of our injury law: by media reports of verdicts in tort cases as well as officially reported decisions in those cases, and through various forms of government regulation as represented by statutes and regulations, as well as in Congressional hearings and debates. It is worth remembering that each judicial decision as well as each statute analyzed here is an historical event, emerging from battles in courts by advocates and parties who have been willing to invest substantial resources in a dispute and in the case of statutes by contending forces in the legislature. Thus, our injury law is framed by, and contributes to, the history of our times.

From the 1960s to the present the United States has seen a great set of struggles, ideological and cultural, about what we mean by the ordinary rights of Americans, and about the very definition of injury—that is, the kind of injury the law will recognize. These struggles have included debates, not only in Congress and the courts, but among scholars. Commentators have approached the subject of liability for injuries from a variety of perspectives, often combining substantial intellectual power with a narrowness that ultimately beggars analysis. Economic analysts have focused on one strand of the topic, that of achieving efficiency through market transactions. In some cases they have aided the examination of legal problems; in others, their commentaries have an Oz-like quality, putting reality to one side in favor of elegant theory and mathematical formulas that do not even pretend to get down to the solution of specific cases or sets of legal problems.

From another side of the academic groves there sounds a powerful commitment to the idea that justice in the area of injury law, at least in private litigation, should be viewed principally as a matter of corrective justice, a concept that goes back to Aristotle. As interpreted today, this idea stresses justice between private litigants without reference to "instrumental" considerations, for example, the question of what effects a decision in a particular case will have on society—including, but not limited to, the efficiencies it may achieve in the buying and selling of goods and services.[16] This idea provides a stimulating challenge to our definition of justice. But it also ignores the role that courts routinely play—and express themselves as playing—in making judgments about such social impacts as the effects of their decisions on the allocation of resources or on the spreading of losses that otherwise would fall on single individuals.

16. See generally, e.g., Ernest J. Weinrib, The Idea of Private Law (Harvard University Press 1995); Symposium, Corrective Justice and Formalism: The Care One Owes One's Neighbors, 77 Iowa L. Rev. No. 2 (1992).

By the turn of the last century, several visions had emerged about the function and structure of American injury law. I advanced a pluralistic model in a thousand-page monograph I wrote for an American Bar Association committee in the 1980s. This analysis set tort law in a framework that included safety regulation and no-fault compensation systems like workers' compensation—the third major element of the injury law triad along with tort and regulation.[17]

In this connection, I must note the impossibility of achieving even-handed justice across the spectrum of injuries with respect to both prevention of injury and compensation. In the realm of prevention, there is an enormous range of dollar figures that different government agencies have assigned to the value of a human life. In the realm of compensation for workplace injuries in particular, there are great differences between workers' compensation and tort law with respect to the chance of receiving any money at all. Tort law may bar workers entirely from compensation on the grounds that they "assumed the risk" of injury. By contrast, workers injured on the job are very likely to get at least some money under workers' compensation, a no-fault system that generally precludes an employee from bringing a tort claim, based on fault, against her employer.

People who could look only to the tort system for other injuries—for example those caused by slips and falls, in the course of medical practice, and by consumer products—might have very different chances of receiving any money, and there is a broad range of the amounts they might recover if they do receive something. Some tort claimants for workplace injuries who are successful may receive considerably more than they would get for the same injuries if they were limited to workers' compensation. However, among those who settle tort cases with alleged injurers, the amount they receive in settlement would probably be substantially less than what a jury might find their injuries were worth. And under tort law, the small percentage of people who wind up going to trial face a significant chance of complete failure. Moreover, many people who sincerely believe that someone else was responsible for their injuries will never even enter the tort liability system. This might be because technical legal rules pose insuperable obstacles. For example, in some states, one may not recover under tort law for negligent infliction of emotional distress without a showing of physical impact on the body.

17. Am. Bar Ass'n, Spec. Comm. on the Tort Liability System, Towards a Jurisprudence of Injury: The Continuing Creation of a System of Substantive Justice in American Tort Law (Marshall S. Shapo Rptr. 1984).

Another reason people might not get into the tort system is that socially defined norms would cause juries to value their damages in a way that would make it unprofitable to pursue the case. Research by Professor Lucinda Finley has shown that juries award different percentages of "noneconomic loss"—for example pain and suffering and other kinds of intangible harms—in different tort cases involving injuries to children during the birth process: 93 percent of damages are noneconomic loss when the baby dies, but only 14 percent are noneconomic loss when the baby lives. There also are differing percentages, although the difference is not so pronounced, between personal injury plaintiffs who are men and women.[18] An important practical impact of such differences occurs in states where the legislature has put caps on the amount recoverable for noneconomic damages. If most of the damages of a prospective claimant are noneconomic—although many people would consider them quite real—a cap may cause it to be prohibitive for a contingency fee attorney to invest time in the case.

The profile of valuation of life and limb is a jagged one when one compares society's ways of compensating as well as preventing injuries. Commentators have viewed this landscape in different ways. A committee of scholars, working on a project funded by the American Law Institute (ALI), presented an analysis that focused on various social "institutions" that deal with the injury problem. These institutions included loss insurance and private contract as well as tort law, regulation and no-fault compensation systems. The authors suggested that instead of "using only one policy instrument—tort law—to serve multiple goals that are often conflicting . . . we might employ a variety of devices, each tailored to the particular role that is parceled out to it."[19] In a comment on this project, I noted the unreality of the image of "parceling out" of various social functions to particular "institutions." I suggested that the only way this could be facilitated would be by a super-institution—essentially, a "Tsar," a "tireless administrator with a file-cabinet mind, superior intelligence, and a computerized grip on dangerous activity . . . sitting at a great control board at which he adjusts risks twenty-four hours a day."[20]

The metaphor of a Tsar who "parcel[s]" out injury law tasks to various entities and processes is thus pretty theoretical. Where the ALI authors and I agree, at least at a very general level, is that given our political process and

18. See Lucinda Finley, The Hidden Victims of Tort Reform: Women, Children and the Elderly, 53 Emory L. J. 1263, e.g., at 1299, 1294, 1300.

19. 1 Am. Law Inst., Enterprise Liability for Personal Injury 34 (1991).

20. Marshall S. Shapo, Tort Reform: The Problem of the Missing Tsar, 19 Hofstra L. Rev. 185, 188, quoting Marshall S. Shapo, The Duty to Act: Tort Law, Power, and Public Policy 116 (University of Texas Press 1977).

our culture, we will always be dealing with—to use their phrase—a "pluralistic personal injury universe."[21] It should be noted, however, that the ideal
of some commentators would be to "do away with the core of modern tort
law."[22] This was done, more or less, in New Zealand, which in 1972 virtually
eliminated tort law in favor of an accident compensation scheme,[23] which
has since gone through various reworkings of its system for dealing with
personal injuries.[24]

Criticisms of tort law have come from around the ideological spectrum.
A self-identified socialist legal scholar attacked the capitalist basis for our
tort law. He concluded a thoroughgoing critique of the tort system by arguing that the only way to "fully realize the widely shared values of autonomy,
equality, and community in the encounter with risk" is to "embrac[e] democratic socialism: worker ownership and management, consumer coopera-
tives, equalization of benefits (resources) and burdens (risk), and a state
sufficiently powerful to regulate environmental pollution."[25] A very different idealization of how society should respond to the injury problem came
from feminist-oriented scholars who suggested that tort law should promote human "flourishing."[26] From yet another vantage point, the corporate
lawyer Philip Howard has inveighed against an environment of "litigation
anxiety" in which "Americans are . . . scared" of the possibility of having to
defend injury suits.[27] He declares that "[d]oing something wrong is not

21. See ALI study, *supra* note 19, at 33.

22. See, e.g., Stephen D. Sugarman, Doing Away with Personal Injury Law 212 (Quorum
Books 1989). Sugarman's "first step" would be to "promptly remove the bulk of the personal
injury claims from the tort system and provide those victims with generous and efficiently paid
benefits for their economic losses." The "longer-run solution" would include the payment of
benefits "to tort victims" "as part of our regular social insurance and employee benefit system,"
with deterrence being "the domain of administrative agencies concerned exclusively with safety,
the market, self-protection, and private morality." Under Sugarman's model, "[a]ctions in tort
for punitive damage would remain for cases of egregious wrongdoing" and "private injunction
remedies would still be available to stop unreasonably dangerous activities." *Id.* at 211–12.

23. For commentary on the early versions of this legislation, see Geoffrey Palmer,
Compensation for Personal Injury: A Requiem for the Common Law in New Zealand, 21
Am. J. Comp. L. 1 (1973); Donald Harris, Compensation in New Zealand: A Comprehensive
Insurance System, 37 Mod. L. Rev. 361 (1974).

24. See, e.g., Richard Miller, An Analysis and Critique of the 1992 Changes to New Zealand's
Accident Compensation Scheme, 52 Md. L. Rev. 1078 (1993).

25. Richard Abel, A Critique of Torts, 37 UCLA L. Rev. 785, 831 (1990).

26. See, e.g., Heidi Li Feldman, Harm and Money: Against the Insurance Theory of Tort
Compensation, 75 Tex. L. Rev. 1567, 1585–94 (1997).

27. See Philip K. Howard, The Lost Art of Drawing the Line: How Fairness Went Too
Far 30–31 (Random House 2001), later published as The Collapse of the Common Good
(Ballantine Publishing Co. 2001), which refers to the first title as "in slightly different form"
(quotations in this text at same pages in The Collapse of the Common Good).

what scares most Americans. What we're afraid of is someone claiming we did."[28]

What is clear is the limits of all idealized approaches to the injury problem. Many people's minds probably hold an image of a system of personalized justice in which injured persons confront alleged injurers in a process through which decision makers make speedy decisions that define justice between the parties in an individualized way. The limitations of this vision are evident in the fact that most payments on behalf of injurers come from liability insurance, which has a tendency to minimize the personalization of injury. Moreover, the realities of various kinds of injury law make it clear that the game is mostly a defensive one—trying to achieve as much before-the-fact safety as possible and to set a level of compensation that will provide some financial support, and a little balm, for victims. It would require a much more affluent society than ours for the legal system to produce positive results for human flourishing.

*** ***

In part, this book seeks to explain the links between our injury law and the views and attitudes of ordinary people. The importance of that linkage is the way it ties in with our faith in democratic institutions. For the law depends on ordinary people for perceptions of the justice it metes out, and thus for its integrity. It is perhaps not surprising that in an area of legal conflict so riven with social tension and often literally filled with blood and pain, our injury law as it has developed has taken on constitutional dimensions.

After analyzing the concept of an injury law constitution, this book delves into the idea of legal rights, an idea that springs easily to the minds of citizens and residents of a nation born from a strong conception of rights. We examine the concept of injury itself, noting that some events that many people would view as harms are not considered to be injuries by the law. We place these concepts in the context of legal doctrines and legislative definitions that have developed over more than two centuries of national existence, and of the structure of law through which those concepts are defined and interpreted. All these topics may be viewed as layers of a system that are piled on top of each other and that sometimes exchange genetic information.

One of the principal elements of the injury law constitution is tort law. Another is the set of statutory compensation schemes which pay out more money each year than do tort recoveries. Its third major dimension resides

28. *Id.* at 12.

in our broad array of safety statutes and regulations. The injury law constitution also includes various informal guides to conduct embedded in
national culture and various subcultures. These are a cluster of ideas, principles, attitudes, and perceptions—often notions derived from ideologies
not articulated—that are literally constitutive of our society.

The injury law constitution embraces the strictures against the use of
arbitrary power by officials and governments that generated Magna Carta.
It includes the prohibitions in our Federal Constitution and our state constitutions against denials of due process and equal protection of the laws,
provisions that have been litigated many times in "constitutional tort" cases.
Yet it also includes a body of principles that have developed over the years,
in thousands upon thousands of decisions in our tort law and in our many
safety statutes—principles which, taken together, define in significant measure our rights to be free from misuse and abuse of power possessed by
private persons. And on the opposite side of injury litigation, I note,
American lawyers attacking tort liability judgments will sometimes mount
their challenges on the basis that to impose liability on their clients would
be arbitrary or irrational.

I observe that the idea of an injury law constitution explored here runs
parallel to transAtlantic concepts in the developmental stage. As I shall
explain, some of these ideas are evolving in Britain, their roots in both opinions of the European Court of Human Rights and the domestic Human
Rights Act. And I shall refer to a particularly fascinating development that
appears in an opinion of the Italian Court of Cassation that speaks of "an
inviolable right of the individual."

*** ***

The legal system constantly presents an experiment in progress, testing
out what we mean by justice, in the setting of injury. It is especially representative of our culture because of the dramatic, often tragic settings in
which it works itself out. The resolution of injury problems in the legal
system, through both judge-made rules and policy choices reflected in legislation, reflects our views of the human condition.

CHAPTER 1

An Injury Law Constitution

A foundational premise of this book is that the body of law Americans have developed concerning responsibility for injuries and prevention of injuries has some of the qualities of a constitution—a fundamental set of principles that govern relations between human persons and corporations and governments. I have derived this idea, which I call an injury law constitution, from my forty-six year study of judicial decisions, legislation and administrative regulations, as well as many cultural standards that help to shape our moral landscape.

To be sure, the basic idea of a constitution, as understood by scholars who specialize in the law of our world famous federal Constitution, has focused on the division of power among branches of government, the control of governmental power, and the rights of individuals against the state, and in significant measure on the assessment of the validity of legislation claimed to clash with constitutional principles. Yet I speak here of a set of ideas that are fundamental enough to be constitutional. The injury law constitution I describe here embraces rules and guidelines for decision created by courts, legislatures, and agencies. These constitutive documents do not have the binding status of the U.S. Constitution, nor do they provide an authoritative basis for courts to invalidate common law rules or statutes. Indeed, like its older cousin the British constitution, the injury law constitution can be and is subject to change by legislation. Derived partly from unwritten codes, norms, and precepts that are literally constitutive of our society, it provides a normative framework, and a set of moral standards, by which we measure existing and proposed rules for society's response to injuries. I shall use the term "injury law constitution," but I recognize that this description may cause some readers to prefer the phrase "a constitutive injury law."

The principles and ideas embodied in this constitution have evolved from both political consensus and conflict, over time, concerning the governance of the American community. They include a definition and ranking of personal interests worthy of valuation, and they are composed of a mixture of generalities and specifics. In that sense, they reflect the history of constitutions that reach back to the sixth century B.C. At that time, an early creator of a constitution was the aristocratic Athenian leader Solon. As was so with other constitutions of the era that became the greatness of Athens, Solon's laws addressed the structure of government, in part by "establish[ing] a constitution in which input into the political process was allotted in accord with income."[1] For this purpose, he used "[p]roperty classes that had been in being for some time ... to divide the citizens into tiers, with the addition of a special class at the very top," and with "[c]lasses ... ranked according to agricultural wealth."[2] Membership in a class determined eligibility to fill particular offices, but "[c]itizen men from all classes could serve in the *he liaia*, a body of prospective jurors."[3]

Solon's first laws "address[ed] the sufferings of the poorest people." As Aristotle summarized it, Solon "not only made loans on the security of a person's freedom illegal," but also "carried out the cancellation of debts."[4] Indeed, he "tracked down as many Athenians as he could who, because they could not pay their debts, had been sold as slaves outside of Attica," and "bought them back, setting them up as free Athenians once more."[5] Solon also revised "measures, weights and coinage."[6]

Aristotle said that what seemed to be "the three most popular features of Solon's constitution" were: "first and most important, that nobody might borrow money on the security of anyone's freedom; ... that anyone might seek redress on behalf of those who were wronged; ... [and] the right of appeal to the *dikasterion*," the jury court, remarking that "when the people have a right to vote in the courts they control the constitution."[7]

Apparently in the background of Solon's measures related to the political process was a desire to damp down the "outrage" of the hoplite middle class at the "monopoly on privilege" of a governing class from wealthy families.[8]

1. Sarah B. Pomeroy et al., Ancient Greece; A Political, Social, and Cultural History 188 (Oxford University Press 2d ed. 2008).

2. *Id.*

3. *Id.*

4. See Steven Everson, ed., Aristotle: The Politics and the Constitution of Athens 214, para. VI; 217, para. X (Cambridge University Press 1996).

5. See Pomeroy, *supra*, at 187.

6. See Everson, *supra*, at 217, para. X.

7. See *id.* at 216, para. IX.

8. See Pomeroy et al., Ancient Greece: A Political, Social and Cultural History 167, 162 (1st ed. 1999).

The hoplites originally were a military class, and we are told that beginning with ancient Sparta, in war there emerged a "reality of strict equality in the ranks, where aristocrats and nonaristocrats fought side by side," which made it "increasingly difficult" for the aristocrats "to maintain their exclusivity and their hold on political power."[9] This development lay in the background of the structural features of the Athenian constitution as it developed.

A striking feature of Solon's approach, as summarized by Aristotle, appeared in a poem in which "he champions both sides against the other, and argues their position and then recommends an end to the prevailing rivalry."[10] This approach, which describes a society's constitution as an ongoing effort to achieve consensus from conflict—is central to my idea of an injury law constitution.

The idea that Aristotle put forth in his work *The Constitution of Athens* did emphasize the structure of government. Aristotle had collected a total of 158 constitutions, of which he may have written some or all, and of which he made use in writing his *Politics*.[11] In his summary of "[t]he primitive constitution before the time of Draco," whose code has been dated to 621 B.C., Aristotle focuses on political offices and eligibility for them and on the power of the officials known as archons to decide cases.[12] In summarizing the legislation introduced by Draco, which he describes as "this constitution," he also focuses on the choice of officers by "those who provided their own armour," and becomes so specific as to identify a set of particular fines on members of a governing body, the Boule, if they failed to attend a sitting of the body. One specific item in Draco's code was that "[l]oans were made on the security of the person of the borrower."[13]

Beyond that, though, Aristotle's summary of constitutions before his time and in his time also included substantive legislative details. For example, the governing body known as the Thirty "made it legal for a man to leave his property to anyone he wished without restraint."[14] Later, in the Archonship of Eucleides, rules were adopted that allowed Athenians who wished to leave the city to live in Eleusis, "where they should retain full citizen rights, have complete self-government and enjoy their incomes," whereas generally speaking, "[t]hose living at Eleusis were not allowed to visit the city of Athens, nor were those living in Athens allowed to visit

9. See Pomeroy et al., *supra* note 1 (2d ed.), at 122.
10. See Everson, *supra*, at 213, para. V.
11. See *id.* at xii.
12. See *id.* at 211–212, para. III.
13. See *id.* at 213, para. IV.
14. See *id.* at 237, para. XXXV.

Eleusis." An example of the specificity of these rules is that if a person leaving Athens "took over a house of Eleusis, they were to do it with the agreement of the owner" and "if agreement proved impossible, each was to select three assessors, and the owner was to accept the price they fixed."[15] The rules in the constitution at the time of Aristotle were specific enough to prescribe the election of two trainers for men who took up guard duties who would "teach them to fight in armour, and to use the bow, the javelin and the catapult," and even prescribed the compensation "for their maintenance."[16]

The constitution at that time included specific consumer protection provisions, under which market superintendents selected by lot were "required by law to supervise goods for sale to ensure that merchandise is pure and unadulterated." Additionally, commissioners were to "ensure first that there is no sharp practice in the selling of unprepared corn in the market, secondly that the millers should sell their barley flour at a price corresponding to that of unmilled barley, and thirdly that the bakers should sell loaves at a price corresponding to the price of wheat and containing the full language which the commissioners have laid as the law requires them to do."[17] The rules were also quite precise about the penalties for embezzlement, bribe taking, and maladministration—for example imposing a penalty on bribe takers of ten times the amount of the bribe.[18]

Thus, this material from two papyri, written by the greatest of political scientists, tells us that constitutions span a great spectrum of principles and rules, ranging from structural provisions to detailed substantive prescriptions and prohibitions. It is true that the idea of a constitution in Archaic and Classical times begins at an abstract level—the concept of a "mixed constitution" includes "monarchical, oligarchical, and democratic elements."[19] However, it is worthy of note that when the constitution makers Aristotle summarizes got down to business—even the business of structure—they tended to be quite specific.

To be sure, the most traditional meaning given to the term constitution in America is an idea associated with Magna Carta—as Professor Howard has summarized it, "a fundamental law by which other laws should be

15. See *id.* at 240, para. XXIX.
16. See *id.* at 243, para. XLII.
17. See *id.* at 249–50, para. LI.
18. See *id.* at 252, para. LIV. Cf. Stuart Madden, Integrating Comparative Law Concepts Into the First Year Curriculum: Torts, 56 J. L. Legal Edu. 560, 567–73 (2006) (a summary of ancient Greek and Roman law on injuries, featuring statute-like references to quite specific penalties imposed for particular offenses).
19. See Pomeroy et al., *supra* note 1 (2d ed.), at 170, 173.

tested."[20] The principal idea that drove "rebellious barons"—Professor Howard described them as "rude, mostly unlettered, and generally selfish," yet having won the Charter "for generations yet unborn" as well as for themselves[21]—to thrust Magna Carta "upon an unwilling king" was anger at "the accumulation and abuse of royal power."[22] While Magna Carta "was not in the main concerned with the distribution of governmental powers or with the shape of governmental machinery"—subjects of intense of intense debate in our current constitutional law—"it was very much concerned with individual rights and liberties against the state."[23]

One of the most famous provisions of Magna Carta has found its way into American positive law and case law on torts. This is chapter 40, which declared "To no one will We sell, to none will We deny or delay, right or justice." Many American state constitutions have adopted this idea in what are known as "open courts" provisions. Just one illustration is the Ohio constitutional provision that says that "[a]ll courts shall be open, and every person, for an injury done him . . . shall have remedy by due process of law and shall have justice administered without denial or delay."[24] The Ohio Supreme Court has employed this provision, for example, to invalidate a statute of repose that applied to improvements to real property, where an improvement had been constructed twenty-eight years before an accident that injured a plaintiff who sued within one year of the event. The court said that the statute "deprived the plaintiffs of the right to sue before they knew or could have known about their or their decedents' injuries."[25]

Although Magna Carta was aimed at the power of the king, language that descended from it in the American colonies spoke quite broadly of the "liberties, franchises and immunites" that would attach to colonists "as if they had been abiding and borne within this our realme of Englande or anie other of saide dominions."[26] Beyond the generalities of Magna Carta were quite specific provisions in such colonial charters as that of Virginia. That charter, given in 1606, specified rights to "landes, woods, soile, groundes, havens, courts, rivers, mines, mineralls, marshes, waters, fishinges,

20. A. E. Dick Howard, The Road from Runnymede: Magna Carta and Constitutionalism in America 373 (University Press of Virginia 1968).

21. A.E. Dick Howard, Magna Carta: Text & Commentary 3 (University Press of Virginia 1998).

22. Howard, Road from Runnymede, *supra*, at 6–7.

23. *Id.* at 220.

24. Ohio Constitution, Art. I, §16.

25. Brennaman v. R. M. I. Co., 639 N.E.2d 425, 430, amended by 643 N.E.2d 138 (Ohio 1994).

26. Three Charters of the Virginia Co. of London 9 (Samuel M. Bemiss, ed., Williamsburg 1957), quoted in Howard, *supra* note 20, at 15.

commodities and hereditamentes," and even specified the fractions of gold and silver that the adventuring colonists must give to the Crown.[27] The source of the rights of colonists, and the revolutionaries who followed them, was viewed by many as arising from natural rights—as defined by John Locke, the rights of life, liberty, and property.[28]

Beginning in the early seventeenth century there emerged a group of formidable natural law scholars led by Hugo Grotius, who referred to "[i]nalienable things"—"things which belong so essentially to one man that they could not belong to another, as a man's life, body, freedom, honour."[29] Commentators have insisted that Grotius therefore considered it impossible to sell the "right in one's person,"[30] but presumably one could vindicate rights in these "things."

Surely Locke, whose work was one of the most important texts in the mental and physical libraries of the American founders, confirmed that there were natural rights protectable against others. In his Second Treatise on Government, published in 1690, he had written that "[m]an being born . . . with a title to perfect freedom, and an uncontrouled enjoyment of all the rights and privileges of the law of nature, equally with any other man, or number of men in the world, hath by nature a power . . . to preserve his property, that is, his life, liberty and estate, against the injuries and attempts of other men," in addition to discussing the power to judge and punish criminal conduct.[31]

A century later, Kant, insisting that one "cannot give himself away for any price," premised that "[h]umanity itself is a dignity," that "a human being cannot be used merely as a means by any human being . . . but must always be used at the same time as an end." He wrote that "[i]t is just in this that his dignity (personality) consists, by which he raises himself above all other beings in the world that are not human beings and yet can be used, and so over all things."[32] And more than another century and a half afterward, with Germany just emerging from the nightmare of Nazism, the German Supreme Court—in the summary of one scholar—"endorsed (or created)

---

27. See Howard, Road from Runnymede, *supra* note 20, at 14–15.
28. See, e.g., *id.* at 232.
29. Matthew W. Finkin, Menschenbild: The Conception of the Employee as a Person in Western Law, 23 Comp. Lab. L. & Pol'y J. 577, 599 (2002), quoting R.W. Lee, ed., Introduction to the Jurisprudence of Holland, II.I.41., 42.
30. See *id.* at 598.
31. Locke, Second Treatise on Government, sec. 87.
32. Finkin, *supra*, at 606, quoting Mary Granger translation, Cambridge Texts in the History of Philosophy 6:462 (1996).

the general right of personality," with its president later declaring "that the roots of the concept lay in natural law."[33]

Contemporaneously with Kant, natural rights ideas permeated the thinking of the architects of revolution in the American colonies. As David Ramsay, who published a *History of the American Revolution* in 1789, viewed it, the revolutionaries "looked, not to Magna Carta, but to God":[34] "Many of them had never heard of Magna Charta . . . they looked up to Heaven as the source of their rights, and claimed, not from the promises of Kings, but, from the parent of the universe."[35] Just as the Revolution was brewing, an English commentator denied that "Magna Charta is the great foundation of English liberties," saying that "the original and only real foundations of liberty were, by the Almighty architect, laid together with the foundations of the world, when this right was engrafted into the nature of man at his creation."[36] Certainly the idea of protecting the enjoyment of "life, liberty and property" was fundamental in the thinking of the revolutionaries and creators of the new nation; that language, appears, for example, in the Massachusetts Constitution of 1780 largely drafted by John Adams.[37]

Over many years, paralleling such particulars as those in the Virginia charter and the generalities of early state constitutions, there arose one of the greatest of bodies of law, the common law. A plaque put up by the Virginia State Bar Association at Jamestown refers to "the Common Law" as "the cornerstone of individual liberties, even as against the Crown."[38] However, when the first settlers of Virginia landed in 1607, it was "doubtful if the colonists had any precise idea what was meant by the 'common law' or similar phrases."[39] Indeed, later in that century, the Recorder at the London trial of William Penn in 1670 condescendingly responded to a question by Penn at his trial for "tumultuous assembly" as to what the

33. *Id.* at 625 (summarizing precedent and commentary). German law features a concept "of the human being,"*Menschenbild,* which finds analogies in our own injury law. This concept has prism-like qualities, being subject to both "reductionist" and "communitarian" interpretations. *Id.* at 579 n.11 (summarizing authorities). But one manifestation of the idea in modern German law appears to reside in a right of personality, or a recognition of "personhood" as a protectable interest, and indeed the German constitution gives each person "the right to the 'free development of personality.'" See *id.* at 580–81, quoting German Basic law Art. II(1). A subset of a protectable "right to personality" lies in the idea of privacy, recognized not only in Germany but in such countries as France, England, and Canada, see *id.* at 628 (citing authorities) as well as in various American decisions and statutes.

34. Howard, Road from Runnymede, *supra* note 20, at 189 (characterizing Ramsay).

35. *Id.,* quoting 1 Ramsay, History of the American Revolution 31.

36. *Id.* at 192, quoting John Cartwright, American Independence, The Interest and Glory of Great Britain 76–77 (Philadelphia 1776).

37. See *id.* at 209.

38. *Id.* at 23.

39. *Id.* at 102.

common law was on which his indictment was based, saying that "you must not think I am able to run up so many years, and over so many adjudged cases, which we call common-law, to answer your curiosity."[40] The great New York jurist, James Kent, who became known as Chancellor Kent, recalled that when he became a judge on the Supreme Court of New York, "there were no reports or State precedents . . . . We had no law of our own, and nobody knew what it was."[41] By 1812, Thomas Jefferson was "derid[ing] . . . the ordinary doctrine, that we brought with us from England the *common law rights.*" Acknowledging that "[t]his narrow notion was a favorite in the first moment of rallying to our rights against Great Britain," Jefferson declared that "[t]he truth is, that we brought with us the *rights of men* . . . ."[42]

There are two other chapters, literally from our Constitutional history, which deserve mention in placing a frame around the injury law constitution. The first of these is the clause in Article IV, section 2 of the original Constitution that declares that "[t]he Citizens of each State shall be entitled to all Privileges and Immunities of Citizens in the several States." In an 1823 opinion, Justice Bushrod Washington, sitting as a circuit justice, addressed the meaning of that provision. In a case involving the seizure of an oystering vessel for violation of a New Jersey law that prohibited nonresidents from gathering oysters in the waters of the state, he "confine[d] these expressions to those privileges and immunities which are, in their nature, fundamental; which belong, of right, to the citizens of all free governments."[43] The "general heads" of these privileges and immunities were "[p]rotection by the government; the enjoyment of life and liberty, with the right to acquire and possess property of every kind, and to pursue and obtain happiness and safety." Some of the "particular privileges and immunities" included the right "to institute and maintain actions of any kind in the courts of the state."[44] Justice Washington gave no citations of authority for these propositions, which may be taken as representing a distillation of a group of rights that the general history of the young nation, and perhaps natural law antecedents, indicated were fundamental.

The Fourteenth Amendment, passed in 1868, contains another privileges and immunities clause. Section 1 of the Amendment says that "[n]o State shall make or enforce any law which shall abridge the privileges or

<hr/>

40. See *id.*, quoting 6 Howell's State Trials 951, 958 (1670).

41. *Id.* at 256, quoting William Kent, Memoirs and Letter of James Kent 117 (Boston 1898).

42. Thomas Jefferson to John Tyler, June 17, 1812, quoted by Howard, *supra*, at 259, from Lyon G. Tyler, Letters and Times of the Tylers 265 (Richmond 1884).

43. Corfield v. Coryell, 6 F. Cas. 546, 551 (1823).

44. *Id.* at 551–52.

immunities of citizens of the United States." There has been considerable controversy about the scope and meaning of this clause.[45] As one writer summarized some of these views, they include the first eight amendments of the Bill of Rights and various versions of natural rights, primarily rights of liberty and property.[46] He writes of the oystering case mentioned above as the "leading authority on the substance of privileges and immunities," referring in this connection to "[t]he saliency of state private law rights" that include not only property and contract rights but rights to "personal security, and access to governmental mechanisms that protect those primary rights," which he associates with the Civil Rights Act of 1866.[47] One primary view of the "concept of privileges and immunities of United States citizens" is "a concept that is not just vague at the edges, but that has no discernible core of meaning,"[48] one that "'proceeds by purporting to extend to everyone a set of entitlements.'"[49] I do not try here to unravel the complex arguments about the meaning of the Fourteenth Amendment clause but only to note the range of interpretations about rights, potentially including rights with respect to injuries, that may reside in an important constitutional provision.

Interesting collateral data appears in an examination of the text of state constitutions at the dawn of the Reconstruction period for evidence of the recognition of "fundamental rights."[50] The authors, Steven Calabresi and Sarah Agudo, identify at least one tort right—the right to sue for libel—that many state constitutions specifically recognized at that time.[51] They also indicate that the constitutions of 34 of the 37 states existing at the time provided for rights against "unreasonable searches and seizures"—today a staple of constitutional tort litigation for police misconduct—although noting that no state constitutions then even provided for exclusion of evidence thereby obtained.[52]

Quite interesting is their finding that 27 state constitutions at the time, in states including 71 percent of the population, "declared as a matter of positive state constitutional law the existence of natural, inalienable, inviolable,

---

45. See generally John Harrison, Reconstructing the Privileges or Immunities Clause, 101 Yale L.J. 1385 (1991).

46. See id. at 1393–94.

47. See id. at 1416.

48. See id. at 1473.

49. See id., quoting John Hart Ely, Democracy and Distrust 22 (1980).

50. Steven G. Calabresi and Sarah E. Agudo, Individual Rights Under State Constitutions When the Fourteenth Amendment was Ratified in 1868: What Rights Are Deeply Rooted in American History and Tradition?, 87 Tex. L. Rev. 1 (2008).

51. See id. at 45–46.

52. See id. at 57–58.

or inherent rights."[53] They cite as "typical" the California provision which declares that among people's "inviolable rights" "are those of enjoying life and liberty, acquiring, possessing and protecting property, and pursuing and obtaining safety and happiness."[54] the authors comment that "[t]hese references to unenumerated rights, and particularly to natural and inalienable rights . . . could be read to indicate a belief that certain rights—including, perhaps, the right to defend life, liberty, and property—exist in and of themselves as preexisting entitlements." They add that this "suggests that our constitutions and bills of rights do not *create* rights but simply *declare* or *recognize* their existence."[55]

Two millennia after Aristotle's summary of constitutions, and a century after Locke, Jefferson had, in Gordon Wood's summary, expressed a "concern with separating fundamental principles and 'the natural rights of mankind' from ordinary statutory law."[56] And Madison had written to Jefferson just after the Constitutional Convention that the document "had actually created a political system 'so novel, so complex and intricate' that writing about it would never cease."[57] Although not "so complex and intricate" as its elder sibling, the injury law constitution has many knots and tangles. Surely it continues to reflect what Professor Wood has called the "basic ambiguity in the American mind about the nature of law that was carried into the Revolution."[58] This constitution has multiple roots, but ultimately it is rooted in the people—as the opening words of the great Constitution, "We the People" indicate. Certainly, as with the great Constitution, the injury law constitution reflects a "community . . . filled with different, often clashing combinations of interests."[59] Within its broad boundaries, it reflects the will of the people at large—and with the need to bring all of the conflicting interests of the people under one roof, it has the characteristics of a kind of social contract.[60]

The need to bring together all factions in the effort to control injuries and respond to them when they happen has been complicated by what Wood has described as "the Americans' ambivalent attitude toward law"

53. *Id.* at 88.
54. *Id.*, quoting Cal. Const. of 1849, Art. I, §1.
55. *Id.*
56. Gordon S. Wood, The Creation of the American Republic, 1776–1787, at 275 (University of North Carolina Press 1998).
57. *Id.* at 593, citing sources on letter of Madison to Jefferson, Oct. 24, 1787.
58. *Id.* at 295.
59. *Id.* at 58.
60. Cf. *id.* at 283, describing the pre-Constitutional period as including a recognition that "[o]nly a social agreement among the people, only such a Lockeian Contract, seemed to make sense of their rapidly developing idea of a constitution as a fundamental law designed by the people to be separate from and controlling of all the institutions of government."

when they confronted the circumstances of the period leading up to the adoption of the Constitution.[61] These views were confected from many sources, including a commitment to justice and equity,[62] to the idea of "righteousness" being "the basis of law,"[63] and even to the application of "common sense as between man and man."[64]

To this day, the injury law constitution has had to house the gloomy scene that Professor Wood attributes to John Adams of an America that is "a ceaseless scrambling for place and prestige, a society without peace, contentment, or happiness, a society in which 'the awful feeling of a mortified emulation' ate at everyone's heart and made failure unbearable."[65] This evolving constitution has been a continuing modern attempt to delineate what Professor Wood has termed the "evolving relationships among" the American people "themselves and with the state."[66] In large part, it refers to relationships of individuals "among themselves" but some of its most salient features have to do with their relationship with the state and its officials.

A mixture of ideas about the societal fiber of constitutions appears in Professor Grey's references, focusing on judicial review, to the "broad textual provisions" of the Constitution being "seen as sources of legitimacy for judicial development and explication of basic shared national values." These values, he said, "may be seen as permanent and universal features of human social arrangements—natural law principles—as they typically were in the 18th and 19th centuries." Alternatively, they might "be seen as relative to our particular civilization, and subject to growth and change, as they typically are today."[67] Surely, as battles constantly rage among Justices and commentators about the meanings of the federal Constitution, those values must be gleaned, in part, from a variety of informal sources. Despite sallies from defenders of the idea that we can only derive those meanings from the written text of the Constitution, it seems evident that they must be derived

61. See *id.* at 303.
62. See, e.g., *id.* at 262, 301, 305.
63. See *id.* at 295 (characterizing James Otis).
64. See *id.* at 297, quoting "a legally untrained judge," a New Hampshire justice, although emphasizing that "colonial adjudication was not simply a matter of applying some kind of crude, untechnical law to achieve common-sense 'frontier' justice" and referring to evidence suggesting "that even as early as the late 17th century in new back-country counties the quality of legal procedures was remarkably sophisticated."
65. See *id.* at 574.
66. See *id.* at 283.
67. Tom Grey, Do We Have an Unwritten Constitution? 27 Stan. L. Rev. 703, 709 (1975) ("[o]ur characteristic contemporary metaphor is 'the living Constitution'—a constitution with provisions suggesting restraints on government in the name of basic rights, yet sufficiently unspecific to permit the judiciary to elucidate the development and change in the content of those rights over time").

from what Professor Tribe has called "invisible constitutional principles," "nontextual foundations and facets [of] the Constitution," which he somewhat poetically describes as an "ocean of ideas, propositions, recovered memories and imagined experiences" on which the "visible Constitution" "floats."[68]

As Professor Powell has observed in a book focused on the requirements of conscience for judges deciding constitutional issues, political conflict in a free society is inevitable and persistent,[69] and indeed, "decisions about the best human outcome depend, much of the time, on substantive and highly contestable accounts about what is, in fact, the human good."[70] In fact, although people, "especially human beings organized into political societies, typically do not like disagreement," the U.S. Constitution begins from the premise that "disagreement on matters of great importance is ineradicable."[71] One thing that judge-made law provides as a lubricant is "technical argument," "a means of communication which transcends the heated disagreements which it serves to express."[72] Central to constitutional argument are "virtues" that I believe may be said to apply to the judicial process generally—"[c]onfidence in the possibility of dialogue, recognition of the inescapability of judgment, humility in the imposition of one's own opinions, acquiescence in decisions that seem wrong to one's judgment but have persuaded others."[73] Powell's description of "the moral dimension of constitutional decision—the demand it places on the conscience of the judge"[74]—may apply equally to decisions on crucial matters of private law. This process of argument, ubiquitous and continuous across fifty states in both state and federal courts, is an element of the constitutional dimensions of the judge-made portion of our injury law.

THE PUZZLE OF THE BRITISH CONSTITUTION

A useful parallel to the ideas presented here appears in the British Constitution, which is truly a conceptual conglomerate—and indeed a puzzle that has been the subject of scholarly argument over centuries that continues to this day.

68. See Laurence H. Tribe, The Invisible Constitution, e.g., at 38, 11, 9 (Oxford University Press 2008).
69. H. Jefferson Powell, Constitutional Conscience: The Moral Dimensions of Political Decision 7 (University of Chicago Press 2008).
70. Id. at 36.
71. Id. at 92.
72. Id. at 73–74.
73. Id. at 101. For an analogous summary, see id. at 107.
74. Id. at 10.

First it should be noted that there is debate over the fundamental definition—even the existence—of the British Constitution. In an article more than a half century ago, George Catlin declared that "the most remarkable and Lewis Carroll quality of this eminent Constitution," as described by an English justice in the eighteenth century, "was that it did not exist; and this remains its quality."[75] Another writer quoted Prime Minister Robert Peel as telling the House of Commons in 1841, "I presume I shall hardly be asked to define what I mean by the 'spirit of the Constitution.'"[76] Writing in 1997, a commentator said that it was "perhaps reasonable to ask with Tocqueville" and a fictional character who said that "[a]nything is constitutional or anything is unconstitutional, just as you choose to look at it," "whether there is really any constitution to reform."[77] And Anthony King, in the most positivistic sense, has said that the British Constitution "is not in any sense a benchmark, it is simply for better or worse, a state of affairs—'what happens.'"[78]

To be sure, one feature of the British Constitution on which there appears to be wide agreement is the way that it checks governmental power. In his classic 1881 work, *Introduction to the Study of the Law of the Constitution*, A. V. Dicey referred to the principle that "no man is punishable or can be lawfully to be made to suffer in body or goods except for a distinct breach of law established in the ordinary legal manner before the ordinary courts of the land." Dicey said that "[i]n this sense the rule of law is contrasted with every system of government based on the exercise by persons in authority of wide, arbitrary, or discretionary powers of constraint."[79] In more modern times, constitutionalism in both Britain and America has as its "most fundamental" factor a "commitment to democratic and accountable government."[80]

75. George Catlin, Considerations on the British Constitution, 70 Political Science Quarterly 481, 481 (1955).

76. William Huse Dunham Jr., The Spirit of the British Constitution: Form and Substance, 21 U. Toronto L. J. 44, 46 (1971), quoting 1 Emden, Selected Speeches on the Constitution 67 (London 1939).

77. Eric Barendt, Is There a United Kingdom Constitution?, 17 Oxford J. of Legal Studies 137, 137 (1997) (referring to Anthony Trollope, The Prime Minister, referenced to World Classics 260 (Oxford University Press 1983)).

78. Anthony King, The British Constitution 9 (Oxford University Press 2007). See also *id.* at 10 ("[a] constitution merely describes a state of affairs, which state of affairs may be good, bad, or indifferent").

79. A. V. Dicey, Introduction to the Study of the Law of the Constitution 188 (10th ed. 1959).

80. Lord Irvine of Lairg, Human Rights, Constitutional Law and the Development of the English Legal System 250 (Hart Publishing 2003).

Quite broadly, the Oxford English Dictionary has defined a constitution as "[t]he system or body of fundamental principles according to which a nation, state, or bodily politic is constituted and governed."[81] It was clear in the eighteenth century that the constitution constrained the powers of the king, who "was not merely a monarch but a 'constitutional monarch.'"[82] Beyond that, "[t]he word 'constitution'" has been said to refer to "the set of the most important rules and common understandings in any given country that regulate the relations among that country's governing institutions and also the relation between that country's government institutions and the people of that country."[83] Thus, in the traditional way of looking at constitutions, they define the relationship between institutions of government, but they also seek to "ensure that individuals and organizations are protected against arbitrary and intrusive action by the state."[84]

The basic conception of the British Constitution has included the long tradition of parliamentary sovereignty in Britain, but counterposed to this is the idea of the rule of law. J. W. F. Allison has referred to Sir Edward Coke's "contradictory or paradoxical descriptions of a controlling common law alongside a transcendent Parliament."[85] Dicey, as interpreted by Allison, wrote of "twin pillars of the rule of law and parliamentary sovereignty."[86] And the writings of Coke suggest a sympathy for a "law of nature" that is "immutable,"[87] although this sympathy or receptiveness "to natural law thought"[88] has been challenged, with Allison summarizing "the semantic reluctance of English lawyers to invoke the law of nature as such" as being "one reason for not simply viewing Coke's common law as an emanation of European natural law."[89]

The elements of the British Constitution have been described in many ways. Writing in the 1950s, Catlin opined that "we can say with assurance . . . that, under the British Constitution, there is no difference in law, as touching change and repeal, between 'ordinary' and 'constitutional' laws."[90] He referred to the British Constitution as being, by contrast with the American one, "so largely a matter of habit, morals, and *responsa juris*

---

81. King, *supra*, at 11 (quoting Oxford English Dictionary, 2d ed., Vol. 3, at 790 (Oxford University Press 1989)).
82. *Id.*
83. *Id.* at 3.
84. *Id.* at 12.
85. J.W.F. Allison, The English Historical Constitution: Continuity, Change and European Effects 132 (Cambridge University Press 2007).
86. *Id.* at 187.
87. *Id.* at 139.
88. See *id.* at 140.
89. *Id.* at 135.
90. Catlin, *supra* note 75, at 483.

prudentium."[91] He also wrote of "a constitutional morality which declines to sacrifice the fundamentals, beyond the limits of a shrewd common sense, to the pleasures of tactics."[92]

William Dunham has written of "the spirit of the constitution" as "a synonym for constitutional and political morality, one that has provided authority for constitutional law and an emotional drive, conscience if you will, for law observance."[93] Dunham wrote that "the constitution's spirit," "[a]s an inspiring, animating principle," became in the nineteenth century "a receptacle of men's emotions," into which "they poured their desires and sentiments, their opinions and prejudices, and their attitudes and moods." Although describing the idea as having "been useful," he cautioned that "the spirit also may be a dangerous one, for it is volatile, nebulous, amorphous, fluid, slippery, and seldom tangible" and declared that "[a]t times, the constitution's spirit has seemed a mere will-o'-the-wisp, a mirage, an hallucination or illusion, perhaps only a bit of ectoplasm."[94] Yet, he also opined that the "spirit of the constitution" has "proved to be a political imperative and has produced a code of conduct consisting of rules, ethics and beliefs that constitutes Britain's political morality."[95] For Dunham, "[t]he fair, the reasonable, and the balanced have been the most stable components of this fickle spirit."[96] Illustrations supporting this point of view include precedents from both the nineteenth and twentieth centuries embodying several variations on the term "reasonable," including "the duty of taking reasonable care," and "this test of a lack of reasonable care, or negligence."[97]

A remarkable development in the history of the British Constitution resides in the concept of human rights as it developed in "the rulings of the European Court of Human Rights," which, "like the rulings of European Court of Justice, came to be seen as an important source of British law."[98] Cases arising in those tribunals included injury law-type issues involving "the inhuman treatment of terrorist suspects in Northern Ireland, corporal punishment in schools and by stepparents," and "parental access to children."[99]

A domestic legislative development was the Human Rights Act 1998, which among other things "provide[d] remedies such as injunctions and

91. *Id.* at 495.
92. *Id.* at 497.
93. Dunham, *supra* note 76, at 44–45.
94. *Id.* at 46.
95. *Id.* at 45.
96. *Id.* at 54.
97. See *id.* at 56 (quoting various authors).
98. King, *supra* note 78, at 128.
99. *Id.*

the payment of damages for administrative wrongdoings," with "administrative authorities" being defined to "include not just ministers, civil servants and local authorities but 'any person certain of whose functions are functions of a public nature.'" Under this broad definition, "[t]he courts themselves are covered. So are administrative tribunals. So are private companies that run public services."[100] In a striking metaphor, one commentator has said that "the Act weaves [European] Convention rights into the warp and woof of the common law and statute law."[101]

Just after the Human Rights Act 1998 was passed, one commentator said that most of the rights in the European Convention on Human Rights "are to be found in our common law; indeed, most of them may be said to have been derived from the common law of this country."[102] J.W.F. Allison, quoting another writer, suggests that "'the Convention will be interwoven in the common law' through the common law's incremental method."[103] Although there was recognition of "the high degree of deference to be accorded to Parliament," there were differing emphases on the degree of deference.[104] Analyzing this notable new development, Allison says that the interpretation and application of the 1998 Act by the courts "illustrate[s] the English historical constitution." He refers to the judicial interpretation of the Act as "mandating an explicit human rights jurisprudence and a more substantive rule of law through an incorporation of Convention rights."[105]

In summarizing the evolution of the rule of law, Allison says that "[w]hatever balance is achieved evolves historically and is drawn pragmatically." He comments that "[a]lthough widely supposed, if not to function as a constitution, to be a central constituent, a principle at the center of the constitution, the rule of law is itself the object of a debate raising issues of change and continuity and thus illustrating a lasting eclipse of principle by pragmatism in the English historical constitution." He says that that constitution "has been open, not adamant" and predicts that "[t]hrough its openness or flexibility, it can be expected to adapt and react to whatever be

100. *Id.* at 132–33.

101. King, *supra*, at 133, quoting Lord Lester of Herne Hill and Lydia Clapinska, Human Rights and the British Constitution, in Jeffrey Jowell and Dawn Clover, eds., The Changing Constitution, 5th ed. (Oxford University Press), at 82.

102. Sydney Kentridge, "The Incorporation of the European Convention on Human Rights," Inaugural Conference of the Cambridge Center for Public Law, Faculty of Law, University of Cambridge, in University of Cambridge Centre for Public Law, Constitutional Reform in the United Kingdom: Practice and Principles 69 (Oxford: Hart Publishing, 1998), quoted in Allison, *supra* note 85, at 223.

103. Allison, *supra*, at 224, quoting Sir John Laws, The Limitations of Human Rights [1998] PL 254, "especially at 265."

104. See *id.* at 226–27.

105. *Id.* at 228.

the present and future European developments, as it has in formative periods in the past."[106] As Allison sums it up, "[t]he invocation of substantive
values under the rule of law, the tenability of the more contentious bi-polar
sovereignty, the enactment and resumption of the Human Rights Act
1998—innovative in substance but 'reassuringly orthodox' in form—all
illustrate the rough workings of the English historical constitution."[107]

This constitutional work in progress has a strong judicial component.
Anthony King has declared that the Human Rights Act "gives the courts,
in principle at least, unprecedented power under the UK constitution."
He says that "British judges are now legally entitled to confront both the
government of the day and the once-sovereign parliament in a way that they
never were before" and that "[a]side from the specific circumstances of the
'war on terror,' British ministers, civil servants and other public authorities
now have every incentive to adapt their behaviour so as not to run the risk
of falling afoul of both the Human Rights Act and the judges charged with
interpreting it." Giving special point to this analysis is King's reference to a
British judge's "fear that one consequence of the coming into force of the
1998 act might be the growth in the practice in the UK of 'preventive
administration' akin to the practice in U.S. of 'defensive medicine,' with
public officials going to extreme lengths to do nothing that might get them
into trouble or, alternatively, going to extreme lengths to do an exceedingly
large number of things in the first place to avoid getting themselves into
trouble."[108]

Lord Irvine has referred to a 1999 decision of the House of Lords in
a case he summarizes as involving a successful challenge by prisoners to
"a government policy of preventing visits by professional journalists," which
he says represents a judicial assertion of "common law constitutional
rights."[109] The result, it seems, is that the "rough workings of the English
historical constitution"[110] parallel the development of judicial remedies
against officials in the United States.[111] More broadly, interpretations of the
European Convention and the Human Rights Act by British judges appear
to have produced a subconstitution of injury law—one that parallels

106. *Id.* at 235.
107. *Id.* at 236.
108. King, *supra* note 78, at 135, quoting quotation of Lord Woolf by Duncan Fairgrieve,
The Human Rights Act 1998, Damages and Tort Law, Public Law (Winter 2001), at 701.
109. Irvine, *supra* note 80, at 215.
110. Allison, *supra*, quoted text accompanying note 107.
111. See, e.g., Monroe v. Pape, 365 U.S. 167 (1961) (expansive interpretation of 42 U.S.C.
§1983, a section of the Civil Rights Act of 1871); Bivens v. Six Unknown Agents of Federal
Bureau of Narcotics, 403 U.S. 388 (1971) (allowing suit for violation by federal officials of
Fourth Amendment rights).

European conceptions of human rights with various branches of American tort law, including constitutional tort law.

A CONSTITUTIONAL FRAMEWORK FOR ITALIAN INJURY LAW

A very recent parallel appears in a remarkable opinion by the Italian Supreme Court of Cassation,[112] which places an important wedge of injury law in a constitutional framework. This opinion ties together the country's constitution and its civil code, referencing the European Convention on Human Rights, and describing a process of legal evolution. It presents a comprehensive map of the law on noneconomic damages, a subject which as the court says "is regulated by art. 2059 of the Italian Civil Code ('Non-economic damage'), according to which 'Non-patrimonial damage can only be refunded in the hypotheses established under Law.'"[113] The court described the issue as "a case of compensation of non-economic damage defined by the law at its highest level."[114]

The Supreme Court opinion responded to decisions of the Court of Cassation that seem to add a category of "existential" damage to the categories of biological damage and "moral damage." Those decisions distinguished the "existential" damage categories—"consist[ing] in any prejudice caused to the activities, by which an individual realises their personality (e.g., a threat to the family's serenity, or to the healthiness of one's environment"— from the "inner, subjective suffering" of "moral damage."[115]

The Court recognized a class of damages that were relational in nature. It referred to a definition of "existential damage" in a prior decision as "any prejudice (not having just emotion and interior nature, but objectively assessable) affecting the non-profit making activities of a person, and which alters their life habits and relational organization, thus forcing them to adopt different choices for their life, with regard to the expression and real-ization of their personality in the external world."[116] The Court went so far as to declare that "the compensation of non-economic damage is possible

---

112. Chronol. No. 26974, Nov. 11, 2008.

113. *Id.* at paragraph 2 [subsequent citations to this opinion only use paragraph numbers]. In an English translation of the Code published in the United States, this provision is trans-lated, "Non-patrimonial damages shall be awarded only in cases provided by law." The Italian Civil Code & Complementary Legislation, Book Four: Obligations, Art. 2059 (Release No. 2008-1, Booklet 6, Issued June 2008; most recent supplementation and translation by Susanna Beltramo).

114. *Id.* at 2.1.

115. *Id.* at 1.

116. *Id.* at 33.

even in matters relating to liability in contract,"[117] specifying, among other things, that this applies to employment contracts.[118]

At the same time, the Court excluded trivialities from "the grounds of existential damage," referring to "inconveniences, discomforts, disappointments, anxiety and other dissatisfaction concerning the most varied aspect of the daily life of each individual in their respective social environment."[119] It elaborated on this idea with a reference to cases "in which the consequential damage is trifling or absurdly low, or, although objectively serious, it is, according to the social conscience, insignificant or irrelevant in relation to the entity reached."[120] Still again, the Court stressed that "[t]he right must be affected beyond a minimum threshold, causing a serious prejudice" and that "[t]he infringement must exceed a certain offensiveness standard, so that the prejudice is serious enough to deserve protection in a system that requires a minimum level of tolerance."[121]

In developing this taxonomy, the Court emphasized that there were "no distinct sub-classes in the general category of 'non-economic damage,' but only the occurrence of specific cases of repair of non-economic damage as defined by the highest law, i.e., the Constitution."[122] Defining the issue as "whether the so-called existential damage can be included as an

---

117. *Id.* at 4.1: "Now, the interpretation given to art. 2059 It. Civil Code on the basis of the Constitution permits to affirm that the compensation of non-economic damage is possible even in matters relating to liability in contract.

It derives from the principle of the necessary application, for inviolable rights of the individual, of the minimum protection given by the compensation relief, that the breach of an inviolable right of the individual, which has determined a non-economic damage, will imply the obligation to compensate such damage, regardless of whether the source of the liability is a contract or a tort." *Id.*

118. See *id.* at 4.5: "This is the case for employment contracts. Art. 2087 It. Civil Code ('The entrepreneur shall, in the exercise of his business, adopt all such measures which, depending on the peculiarity of the activity, and according to expertise and technique, are required to protect the physical integrity and moral personality of workers') included within the scope of employment relationships interests that were not liable to be measured in monetary terms (physical integrity and moral personality): thus it already implied that, in any event of a default affecting them, compensation was also due for any non-economic damage.

"The inclusion of such interests of the individual among inviolable rights under the Constitution has then strengthened their protection. The effect of this is that the breach of such rights may result in the repair of the damage-consequence, under the profile of the impairment of psycho-physical integrity (Art. 32 It. Constitution), subject to compensation according to the forms of biological damage, or of the prejudice caused to the personal dignity of the worker (Arts. 2, 4 and 32 It. Constitution), as in the case of downgrading to lower-skilled occupations, which imply a worsening of the worker's expectations on the development of their personality as it is expressed in the social organization coinciding with the enterprise."

119. *Id.* at 3.9.

120. *Id.* at 3.10.

121. *Id.* at 3.11.

122. See *id.* at 2.13. See also *id.* at 3.13 ("it is to be reaffirmed that non-economic damage is a general category, not liable to be divided into variously named subclasses").

autonomous category in the context of the compensation relief given to non-economic damage,"[123] the Court emphatically declared that

> it is to be reaffirmed that non-economic damage is a general category, not liable to be divided into variously named subclasses. In particular, it is not acceptable to refer to a generic subclass named "existential damage," because this results in attributing an atypical character even to non-economic damage; although this is done through the apparently typical category of existential damage, the latter, however, includes cases that are not always indicated by the provision for purposes of refund of such type of damage.[124]

The Court stressed that "[t]he mention of certain types of damage, variously named (moral damage, biological damage, damage from loss of parental relationship) meets descriptive needs, but it does not imply the admission of distinct damage categories."[125]

However, the Court clearly did accept the category of "existential damage" as a term of description. It emphasized that

> within the general category of non-economic damage, the expression moral "damage" does not identify an independent subclass, but it describes, among the various, possible types of non-economic damage, the prejudice consisting in the subjective suffering caused by the offence, taken in itself. The intensity and duration in time of such suffering have no relevance to establish the existence of the damage, but only for the quantification of the refund.[126]

A by-product of the Court's unified vision of damages was its opposition to "double compensation" for duplicative damages. One of several examples it gave of "double compensation" was the "case of the associated attribution both of the moral damage in its new definition, and of the damage from loss of parental relationship, because the sufferings incurred at the time in which the loss is perceived and those that will accompanying the damaged person during their life, are but components of the same, complex damages, which must be refunded to its entirety and unity."[127] It gave as a further example "[d]amages of existential nature, concerning relational aspects of life, and consequent to infringements of the psycho-physical integrity of an individual,"

123. *Id.* at 3.
124. *Id.* at 3.13.
125. *Id.* at 4.8. Applying this approach to its remand of a specific case, the court said that "[i]n particular, the judge shall consider: that the so-called existential damage is no autonomous category of non-economic damage." *Id.*, Application No. 11749/2004, at 2.1.
126. *Id.* at 2.10.
127. *Id.* at 4.9.

which it said "can only be construed as 'items' of biological damage in its dynamic aspect, which, according to an opinion now generally accepted by courts, includes the so-called damage to relational life, so that a distinct repair of both would result in double compensation."[128] Overarching this doctrinal roadmap was a constitutional framework; the rights protected, the Court declared, were those "of constitutional importance, regarding inviolable positions of each human being."[129] It said that "[a]part from the cases defined under law, compensation relief for non-economic damage is given only when the breach of an inviolable right of the individual is ascertained; that is, a constitutionally qualified injustice is necessary."[130] The potential sources of law were continent wide: the Court referred to "the breach, at least, of a constitutionally protected interest, inferred from positive law, including international conventions (such as the . . . European Convention for the protection of human rights . . . .)" At the same time, it pointed out that "such rights have not the status of constitutionally protected rights because, although the Convention's nature differentiates it from the obligations deriving under other international Treaties, it has not the status of a constitutional source pursuant to art. 11 It. Constitution and it cannot be equalised, for such purposes, to the effectiveness of the EU sources of law in our domestic system."[131] The Kantian language of inviolable rights is a leitmotif:

> For other damages of existential nature, relating to the relational life of the individual, but which do not derive from a psycho-physical injury and do not, therefore, fall under the category of biological damage (which, according to an opinion now shared by large part of judges, includes both the "aesthetic damage" and the so-called "damage to relational life") the refund will be possible provided that they result from the breach of an inviolable right of the individual, other than the right to psycho-physical integrity.[132]

128. *Id.*

129. *Id.* at 2.14.

130. *Id.* at 2.12. See also a reference to prior cases involving employees in which the court says that "the compensation was connected with a constitutionally qualified injustice," *Id.* at 3.2, and another summary of prior decisions to the effect that "the unjust character of the damage must be constitutionally qualified." *Id.* at 3.3. See also *id.* at 3.5 ("From what has been said above, existential damage can therefore be refunded only within the limit given by the unjust nature, qualified under the It. Constitution, of the damage event. If no inviolable, constitutionally protected rights are breached, there will be no compensation relief." Yet another iteration of this idea is the court's statement that "there must be an unjust infringement of a constitutionally protected interest, because otherwise it is radically impossible (except for the cases regulated under law) to invoke Art. 2059 of the Italian Civil Code" [which deals with noneconomic loss], *id.* at 3.10.

131. *Id.* at 2.11.

132. *Id.* at 3.4.2. See also *id.* at 3.13: ". . . and it is not even necessary on the basis of an interpretation of art. 2059 It. Civil Code in line with the Constitution: to satisfy this latter it is sufficient to give compensation relief to specific values of the individual that are at the basis of

The Italian Court was articulate on the point that "[t]he protection is not limited to the cases of inviolable rights of the individual expressly recognized by the Italian Constitution at this historical time but, as art. 2 of the same Constitution is open to an evolution process, the interpreter should be considered allowed to find, within the constitutional system in its whole, the suitable indexes to verify whether certain new interests emerged in the social reality are—not just generically relevant under law but—of constitutional importance, regarding inviolable positions of each human being."[133] The practical result of this reasoning appears to be that the principles the court sets out on noneconomic damages shall be a measuring rod for future decisions on the legal validity of court decisions, and even legislation, on that topic.

*** ***

For more than two and one half millennia, the Western world has generated a broad and ever-developing framework of injury law. This framework, with what I view as constitutional dimensions, has evolved from the time of Solon through the era of America's founding minds, and now arches over the trenches of current litigation. Today, we see its influence across a transatlantic landscape, with features that include—among other elements— the American law of torts and "constitutional torts," European conceptions of human rights, and Italian constitutional law.

The rules and guidelines embedded in our injury law constitution, and indeed the customs and mores on which they depend, provide a treatise, always in the process of development, which is frequently consulted by judges, legislators and members of the community. They are not only students of that constitution as a result of their different roles, but they are contributors to it. Its social significance is great because it is born in perceived violations of interests that are close to all of us—most personally our bodies and our minds, but also our pocketbooks. Often it literally is born in blood. And the marrow of the subject involves fierce debates about its very definition, and about attitudes toward risk and various kinds of loss. Thus the injury law constitution embraces the fundamental controversies about

inviolable rights pursuant to the It. Constitution." At the same time, in excluding trivial harms, the Court says that "[a]part from the hypotheses defined by ordinary law, only the breach of an inviolable right of the individual, actually identified, is a source of liability for compensation of non-economic damage." *Id.* at 3.9.

133. *Id.* at 2.14.

human nature and the control of power that are at the root of our institutions that deal with injuries.

The law of this constitution governs the day-to-day interactions in which most of us engage that sometimes threaten others with various kinds of risks. Largely based in case law and statutes, it includes rules and quasi-rules announced by private organizations, and custom of a sort that is on occasion spelled out in all of those sources. It assumes, as the Supreme Court said more than 130 years ago, that state laws and "the laws of the United States" "form one system of jurisprudence."[134] A social constitution, it embodies a large set of perceptions that govern our everyday activities and relationships. My use of the term constitution, therefore, depends on a cluster of ideas that define the social fiber, making up a dynamic document that, as I have suggested, is literally constitutive of American society.

One dimension of the American injury law constitution resides in the statutory compensation schemes that pay out more money each year than do tort recoveries. Another resides in our broad array of safety regulation statutes. This system of law also surely embraces the strictures against the use of arbitrary power by officials, and governments, that generated Magna Carta. It includes the prohibitions in our Federal Constitution and our state constitutions against denials of due process and equal protection of the laws, provisions that have been litigated many times in "constitutional tort" cases. And it also includes principles that have developed over the years, in thousands of decisions in the body of our tort law and in our many safety statutes, which, taken together, in large measure define our rights to be free from misuse and abuse of power possessed by private persons. I further note that on the opposite side of injury litigation, American lawyers attacking tort liability judgments will sometimes mount their challenges on the basis that to impose liability on their clients would be arbitrary or irrational.

Our injury law constitution is a reflector of, and vehicle for, change. It perches atop a cauldron of controversy, involving battlegrounds of ideology, culture and policy. As I have observed, this constitution does not provide an authoritative basis for invalidation of legislation or the reversal of common law decisions. But over time, particular laws and various kinds of social phenomena build up by accretion a set of standards for courts—and indirectly legislators—to assess the social legitimacy of their decisions on particular issues. This broad constitution constantly sends out messages about right and wrong, and indeed provides an evolving, living guide to some of the moral foundations of society, especially as regards the uses of

---

134. Claflin v. Houseman, 93 U.S. 130, 137 (1876).

private and official power. Among its principal elements are a sense of human dignity, a concern with decency and compassion, and the idea of economy in the use of resources.

As we shall see, these ideas will provide tools for the definition of rights in areas ranging from discrimination on the basis of personal characteristics to police behavior. They will superintend the risks of many kinds of products and activities—a topic including the ability of individuals to choose the level of risks they prefer. They will provide a beginning point for the assessment of compensation schemes for injuries defined in both broad and narrow ways. And they will force decision makers to a disinterested examination of their own presuppositions—including the application of an acid bath to their own prejudices—about what is best for society as a whole.

CHAPTER 2

Injury Law and Power

An important component of justice is how the law responds to power, particularly to the ability of individuals, firms, and government officials to exercise control over people in many aspects of their lives, including control of people's exposure to a variety of risks, both physical and economic.[1] Much of our modern law of injuries manifests an effort on the part of judges and legislators to check the use, including misuse and abuse, of power. The law manifests its concern with the ability to exercise power in areas ranging from simple assaults to the sale or use of dangerous products and processes, and including the actions of mass media in the areas of defamation and invasion of privacy.[2]

Graphic illustrations of judicial concern with abuses and defaults in the use of power appear in cases in which one person sues another for failing to provide aid that would prevent serious harm to the claimant.[3] A good example of such a situation appears in a case in which Scott Tiedeman was a guest in the home of his girlfriend, Nichole Morgan. Tiedeman's parents alleged that knowing of his history of serious heart problems, Nichole's parents were slow to get assistance for him when he became ill. This delay, the parents claimed, led to permanent brain damage. One provision of a Minnesota statute, labeled a "Good Samaritan" law, immunized from suit people who volunteer to render emergency care. However, a state appellate court did not think the statute applicable, observing that such laws

---

1. I have defined power in this sense to include "physical force and the ability to use various forms of energy in ways that exercise effective control of people's destinies in particular transactions or circumstances." Marshall S. Shapo, The Duty to Act xiii (University of Texas Press 1978).

2. See, e.g., *id.* at xv.

3. See generally *id.* (thesis summarized at xii).

"are aimed at inducing voluntary acts by those who do not have a preexisting duty." In reversing a summary judgment granted by the trial court to the Morgans, the appellate court referred to prior Minnesota decisions that imposed liability in situations in which the defendant arguably had a "preexisting duty of care." The court said it could not conclude that there were no factual issues concerning the defendants' alleged violation of their duty to the plaintiff.[4] This is only one of many decisions that impose a duty on persons who stand in a position of temporary power over the fate of others.

The general point of view that informs such decisions based on the common law carries over into situations in which the plaintiff grounds her claim on legislation. An example is a case in which the plaintiff asserted that a hospital wrongfully discharged her daughter, who had come there for diagnosis, failing to diagnose spinal meningitis. The daughter's symptoms included fever, a rash, a stiff neck with a tilt of her head to one side and a combination of irritability and lethargy.[5] At issue was a section of the federal Emergency Medical Treatment and Active Labor Act, which in effect required hospitals to render "such treatment as may be required to stabilize the medical condition" of a patient who "the hospital determines . . . has an emergency medical condition." After construing language of the statute defining "emergency medical condition" and "to stabilize,"[6] the court rejected the argument that the history of the statute required a patient to prove that she had been "dumped" because of inability to pay. The court emphasized that the legislation "nowhere mentions indigency, an inability to pay, or the hospital's motive." Moreover, it declared that the legislation did not solely cover "outright refusals to treat."[7]

This decision, while based on what the court viewed as the "plain meaning" of the statute, reveals a judicial inclination toward the view that when one party, especially an institution, is in a position to control the medical fate of another whose reliance is manifest and unavoidable, justice requires compensation for a failure to act carefully. The defendant had argued that the plaintiff was doing no more than asserting a malpractice claim under state law, and thus could not be held to have violated the statute,[8] but the point here is that the same concerns with power that drive common law decisions for plaintiffs in this area will support statutory interpretations that take into account the power relationships of the parties.

4. Tiedeman v. Morgan, 435 N.W.2d 86, 89 (Minn. Ct. App. 1989).
5. Deberry v. Sherman Hosp. Ass'n, 741 F. Supp. 1302 (N.D. Ill. 1990).
6. See id. at 1305.
7. Id. at 1305–06.
8. See id. at 1303.

Courts also have refused to find that parties not realistically in a position to make a deal have dealt themselves out of a legal remedy for injuries. Just one example in the broad field of torts is a case involving a fee-paying guest in a fitness center who drowned in a swimming pool. The defendant sought to bar a suit on the basis of an exculpatory clause that mentioned the world "fault." Rejecting this defense, the Wisconsin Supreme Court said that the clause was "overly broad and all-inclusive," and that the document "never makes clear what type of acts the word 'fault' encompasses." Besides saying that the waiver clause "was not distinguishable enough" on the guest registration and waiver form, the court declared that "there was no opportunity for [the plaintiff's decedent] to bargain over the exculpatory language." Although she "had an opportunity to read the form and ask questions" and "was told that the form included a waiver, and allegedly took her time reading the card," the court said this was "not sufficient to demonstrate a bargaining opportunity."[9]

The workers' compensation laws, mostly passed in the first two decades of the twentieth century, were in part a response to the power exercised by employers over their employees. That power had gone essentially unchecked by the law, because employees who sued for workplace injuries were often barred from recovering tort damages by legal doctrines that rejected liability when an employee had carelessly taken chances with his own safety or could be shown, at least theoretically, to have accepted the hazards of a dangerous job. Where employers thus were at liberty to impose the most hazardous conditions on their workers with little fear that they would have to pay for resulting injuries, the workers' compensation legislation required at least some payment, if not directly mandating an improvement in the level of workplace safety. It took another generation for Congress to give employees the right to organize, with at least secondary results favoring workplace safety. And it took more than another generation for Congress to legislate directly in favor of workplace safety with the Occupational Safety and Health Act.

In many other areas of human activity, the regulatory law of injuries developed slowly. Legislatures did regulate drugs to some extent since pre-Revolutionary times.[10] Congress entered the picture in 1906 with the Pure Food and Drugs Act, at a time when drugstore customers could routinely buy cocaine, holding up one finger for "a 'five-cent powder'; two fingers ten

9. Atkins v. Swimwest Family Fitness Ctr., 691 N.W.2d 334, 340–42 (Wis. 2005).
10. See, e.g., Abigail Alliance for Better Access to Developmental Drugs v. Von Eschenbach, 495 F.3d 695, 703–04 (D.C. Cir. 2007) (summarizing historical beginnings with Virginia colonial statute in 1736).

cents worth; three, fifteen cents, and so on."[11] But it took a public scare—the deaths of more than a hundred people from the drug sulfanilamide—to drive Congress to enact the Food, Drug, and Cosmetic Act of 1938. And it took another scare—evidence that the drug thalidomide, for which one use was the treatment of nausea in pregnancy, caused birth defects in children—to motivate a new set of amendments to the food and drug legislation. Interestingly, a major provision of those 1962 amendments required proof of efficacy, rather than safety, in medical drugs.

It was not until 1965, and the decade that followed, that Congress passed a major cluster of "consumer protection" statutes, dealing with motor vehicles, cigarettes, flammable fabrics, toxic chemicals, and a catch-all category of "consumer products." These statutes responded to various kinds of power exercised by companies: the power inherent in knowledge, often proprietary information, and the power resident in modern techniques of product promotion and advertising. In the case of the Occupational Safety and Health Act, passed in 1970, this meant the power directly exercised by employers over their workers, as well as power that employers indirectly exercised in the political process.

In quite another area, that of the relationship of citizens to the federal government, the enactment of the Federal Tort Claims Act in 1946 provided at least a small legal symbol of the rights of free people for which World War II had been fought. In some areas of governmental activity, that statute reversed the general rule of governmental immunity for torts committed by employees of the United States in favor of a rule of liability.

Bursts of judicial activity beginning in the early years of the twentieth century responded to various uses of power by private power holders, both individuals and corporations. One area of activity, which came more and more into focus later in the century, was the manufacture and sale of injury-causing products. A 1912 opinion by a federal trial judge, in a case involving trichinosis caused by a pork product, declared that the ability of consumers to sue parties with whom they did not have a direct contract should not "depend upon the intricacies of the law of sales,"[12] which had barred suits by those who could not show a contractual relation with a defendant. The court's recognition of the importance of power relationships was evident in its declaration that "[t]he obligation of the manufacturer . . . should rest . . . upon 'the demands of social justice.'"[13]

11. Richard Ashley, Cocaine: Its History, Uses and Effects 65 (1975), quoted in Marshall S. Shapo, Freud, Cocaine, and Products Liability, 77 Bost. U. L. Rev. 421, 424 (1997).
12. Ketterer v. Armour & Co., 200 F. 322, 323 (S.D. N.Y. 1912).
13. Id.

A famous decision by Judge Cardozo in 1916 sharpened the point in a case brought against the Buick Motor Company for injuries caused by a negligently manufactured wheel on a car, when the plaintiff did not have a direct contract with the manufacturer. In his decision favoring the plaintiff, Cardozo stressed that the basis for consumer remedies lay not in contract, but "in the law."[14] But it was not until the early 1960s that an opinion by another distinguished judge, Roger Traynor, confirmed on behalf of his court that liability could be imposed on the maker of a defective product that had no direct contract with a consumer even though the alleged problem lay in the product itself and not in the manufacturer's conduct.[15] This was a landmark in the development of "strict liability" for defective consumer goods.

Meanwhile, judges were also developing a group of remedies for people suing for injuries that had previously not been formally defined on the chart of wrongs catalogued by the common law. Beginning in the 1940s, a theory of "intentional infliction of emotional distress" came into being. In 1939, the torts scholar William Prosser had synthesized precedents from the earlier part of the twentieth century which appeared to recognize claims for "intentional or reckless" behavior that was "outrageous," at least when the distress was "severe."[16] Courts had imposed liability, without using that label, in cases ranging from "outrageous insults" by business owners to intolerably drastic methods used by bill collectors. This tort theory, formally articulated in a supplement to the first Restatement of Torts in 1948,[17] has swept in cases as diverse as the mishandling of dead bodies and a claim by a child who had to witness verbal abuse and physical assaults on his mother. A thread that ran through all these cases was abuse perpetrated on a vulnerable person by someone in a superior power relationship. An important 1952 precedent in the development of the tort—where Justice Traynor wrote for the California court to impose liability on that theory—involved vicious threats made by one business competitor against another.[18]

A power relationship that frequently has produced a legal pathology is the relation between insurer and insured. Although that relationship at base stems from contract, a large number of decisions have imposed a tort form

14. MacPherson v. Buick Motor Co., 111 N.E. 1050, 1051 (N.Y. 1916).
15. Greenman v. Yuba Power Prods. Co., 377 P.2d 897 (Cal. 1963).
16. See William L. Prosser, Intentional Infliction of Mental Suffering: A New Tort, 37 Mich. L. Rev. 874 (1939).
17. See Restatement of Torts, 1948 Supplement, §46, cmt. d.
18. State Rubbish Collectors Ass'n v. Siliznoff, 240 P.2d 282 (Cal. 1952).

of liability when insured persons—and even others—claim that insurance companies have wrongfully refused to settle or pay claims.

A landmark case establishing the right of an insured person to sue because of a refusal to settle was *Crisci v. Security Insurance Company*.[19] The plaintiff in this case was the landlord of an apartment building who faced suit by a tenant for injuries that resulted when a staircase gave way. Despite substantial psychiatric evidence relating the psychosis of the tenant to her fall, the landlord's insurer stood firm against a settlement demand which would have used up the $10,000 limit of its policy. The settlement having been refused, the case went to a jury, which awarded the tenant $100,000 against the landlord, a sum of which the insurer paid only the $10,000 for which it had contractually committed itself. As a result of the debt that the judgment imposed on the landlord, she became indigent, and she sued her insurer.

The California Supreme Court reviewed several possible tests for the liability of insurers in the circumstances, including a negligence test, a bad faith test, and a rule that any time an insurer rejected an offer to settle within the policy limits, it should be liable for the amount of any final judgment—even one *beyond* the policy limits. Although expressing some sympathy for the latter proposal, the court decided that the case easily met the requirements of a less demanding standard—whether the insurer had given its insured's interests as much consideration as it had given its own.

Many courts adopted a "bad faith" tort in the "classic fact situation" of "the refusal of an insurer to pay . . . policy benefits" and some went even further, "extend[ing] the duty of good faith and fair dealing to other situations," including those "where an insurer unduly delays payment."[20] The Sixth Circuit found it "contrary to public policy" to allow an insurer to cancel a dentist's malpractice insurance policy as punishment for his appearance as a witness against another insured of the same company.[21] In one prolonged litigation, both state and federal courts granted injunctive relief against insurers for their refusal to provide coverage to, or their raising of premium rates on, vessel owners who employed seamen who made claims against the insurers. Because of the disincentive this caused for vessel owners to hire these seamen, they found it very difficult to secure employment. In one decision holding that this conduct constituted tortious interference with contract, the First Circuit declared that there is "no privilege

19. 426 P.2d 173 (Cal. 1967).
20. See Roger C. Henderson, The Tort of Bad Faith in First-Party Insurance Transactions After Two Decades, 37 Ariz. L. Rev. 1153, 1159 (1995).
21. L'Orange v. Medical Protective Co., 394 F.2d 57 (6th Cir. 1968).

to deter people from exercising their legal rights by penalizing those who do."[22]

The growth of the law in this area reflects a judicial perception of the great power that insurance companies wield over individual citizens. Also evident is a corresponding judicial effort to strike a balance that recognizes those realities of power but preserves the principles of freedom of contract.

In a different territory of the battlefield of injury law, struggles arose over when courts should find officials and governments responsible for injuries they caused. A landmark in this body of law was the development of the "constitutional tort," a separate body of injury law that responded to claims against government officers for a variety of harmful activities.[23] In the case of local and state officials, courts imposed liability for behavior ranging from police misconduct and the maintenance of terrible conditions in prisons and other institutions to claims of suppression of voting rights and denials of various kinds of benefits, such as welfare benefits. The acts alleged on the part of individual officer defendants sometimes would fit comfortably into the categories of ordinary torts, for example batteries. Other acts by officials could not be classified so neatly. What tied all these claims together was the assertion by plaintiffs that defendants had violated their constitutional rights, which might or might not include rights historically protected by the common law. Although initially defendants in this type of case could only be individual officers, the Supreme Court later wrote a limited warrant for suits against governments, for example, in cases where officers carried out unconstitutional practices that in effect had been approved by local governments,[24] such as police enforcement tactics that effectively discriminated against minorities.[25]

A parallel set of actions arose for abuses of power by individual federal officials. There were limitations on this right; in a five to four decision in 1982, the Supreme Court refused to allow a suit against President Nixon by a former government official who claimed he had been fired for "whistle-blowing" on waste in defense procurement.[26] At the very same time, though, the Court established a limited ground for suing senior aides to the President

22. Pino v. Protection Maritime Ins. Co., 599 F.2d 10, 14 (1st Cir. 1979). See also Pino v. Transatlantic Marine, Inc., 358 Mass. 498, 265 N.E.2d 583 (1970) ("no lawful justification or cause for the defendant to decide unilaterally that plaintiff's claim was baseless and to attempt to punish or penalize him for prosecuting the claim").

23. See *infra*, chapter 7, text accompanying notes 9–29.

24. See *infra*, chapter 11, text accompanying notes 29–30.

25. See, e.g., Estate of Sinthasomphone v. City of Milwaukee, 878 F.Supp. 147 (E.D. Wis. 1995).

26. Nixon v. Fitzgerald, 457 U.S. 731 (1982).

who allegedly participated in a conspiracy against the same whistleblower.[27] And a federal appellate court refused to immunize—or at least to fully immunize—National Security Adviser Kissinger in a case that arose from the wiretapping of the home phone of a staff member of the National Security Council.[28]

Over a period of more than three decades, paralleling and bridging the development of these actions against officials, both Congress and the Supreme Court created a group of liabilities enforceable against the United States itself. As we have noted, in 1946 Congress passed the Federal Tort Claims Act, departing from the prior rule that immunized the government from liability for torts. This law made the basic rule one of government liability rather than immunity, although it included several exceptions, including a major loophole for "discretionary" acts of government officials, which still could not be the subject of suits against the United States. Then, in a one-two punch in the early 1970s, the Supreme Court and Congress engraved on the law a set of liabilities for a variety of acts by federal law enforcement officials. First, in 1971, the Court approved a damages action against federal narcotics agents for an allegedly brutal search and seizure of homeowners.[29] Three years later, Congress created a remedy against the government itself for such misconduct by amending the Federal Tort Claims Act.[30]

The essence of this history was that by 1982, suits could be brought against federal officials—from all the President's men to ordinary FBI agents—and against the government itself for abuses of power. At the same time, the Supreme Court was hedging in the liability of the government under the Tort Claims Act by a rather broad definition of "discretionary acts" by officials.[31]

A long, slow process beginning in the nineteenth century created a similar zone for liability suits in state courts against state and local officers.[32] That process also developed grounds for state court litigation against state governments themselves, bases for suit sometimes cemented into state tort claims acts that were similar to the Federal Tort Claims Act, and often with

27. Harlow v. Fitzgerald, 457 U.S. 800 (1982).
28. Halperin v. Kissinger, 807 F.2d 180 (D.C. Cir. 1986).
29. Bivens v. Six Unknown Named Agents of Federal Bureau of Narcotics, 403 U.S. 388 (1971).
30. Pub. L. No. 93–253 (1974).
31. Still the landmark case is Dalehite v. United States, 346 U.S. 15 (1953). An important later immunizing decision is United States v. S.A. Compresa de Viacao Aerea Rio Gradense (Varig Airlines), 467 U.S. 797 (1984).
32. See, e.g., Marshall S. Shapo, Municipal Liability for Police Torts: An Analysis of a Strand of American Legal History, 17 U. Miami L. Rev. 475 (1963).

limitations that continued to immunize those governments against discretionary acts.[33]

By the 1960s, the judicial development of tort law had inspired a Babel of commentary from diverse quarters of scholarship, with analysis that ranged from an unconcern with the elements of power and vulnerability to an emphasis on those aspects of injuries. Tort law proved a magnet for economists, who sounded a number of different notes as they sought to define the "efficient" level of injuries. One idea focused on determining which party to injury litigation was in the position to avoid injuries at the least cost. An interesting question in the area of economics was whether workers accepted relatively hazardous employment in exchange for higher wages. On one side of the argument were commentators who claimed that the amount of "compensating wage differentials" was "on the order of $100 billion a year."[34] Authors of a 2003 study took a quite different position, finding "little empirical support for the view that increases in occupational mortality rates are associated with higher wages."[35]

Similar questions arose about nontort compensation plans, in particular workers' compensation. The evidence did not all point in one direction. One study, for example, concluded that although increases in workers' compensation benefits tended to generate more investments in safety, there were some circumstances in which heightened benefits did not have that effect, or even reduced safety-oriented investments.[36]

Researchers also examined statistics on increased regulation. One scholar, Sam Peltzman, turned a skeptical eye on some major safety statutes of the 1960s. He concluded that building more safety into automobiles for the protection of passengers tended to make drivers more careless.[37] He also argued that the Drug Amendments of 1962, requiring drug manufacturers to show that their products were effective, had the perverse effect of diminishing consumer welfare because they reduced the introduction of new drugs.[38]

33. See, e.g., Minn. Stat. Ann. §3.736 subd. 3(b).
34. See 1 ALI, Enterprise Liability for Personal Injury 39 (1990).
35. William P. Jennings & Albert Kinderman, The Value of a Life: New Evidence of the Relationship Between Changes in Occupational Fatalities and Wages of Hourly Workers, 1992 to 1999, 70 J. Risk & Ins. 549, 558 (2003).
36. R. Victor, L. Cohen & C. Phelps, Workers' Compensation & Workplace Safety 50 (Rand R-2918-ICJ 1982).
37. See generally Sam Peltzman, The Effects of Automobile Safety Regulation, 83 J. Pol. Econ. 677 (1975).
38. See generally Sam Peltzman, Regulation of Pharmaceutical Innovation: The 1962 Amendments (1974): An Evaluation of Consumer Protection Legislation, 81 J. Pol. Econ. 1049 (1973).

By the 1990s, feminist scholarship had introduced a different modernism into the tort debates. Leslie Bender argued for a rejection of "the language of economics—costs, dollars, and efficiency—as the dominant discourse for tort law's understanding of injuries, remedies, and the requirements of justice."[39] She contended for an approach to tort law that would "recognize the human and social character of injured people rather than just their commodity or exchange value," and a change in "the meaning of responsibility in tort law to blend obligations to pay and obligations to give care."[40]

From another quarter came a volley from a self-declared advocate of a "socialist approach to the allocation of risk,"[41] Richard Abel. He issued a plague on more than one house, including both capitalists and "[c]apitalist tort law."[42] In part, Abel assailed those who committed torts for their averseness to "moral judgment," noting that "[m]ost cases are settled rather than adjudicated, and settlements often explicitly deny any acknowledgment of fault."[43] He also attacked the legal system itself for damages rules that "deliberately reproduce the existing distribution of wealth and income"[44]—for example, by awarding damages on the basis of lost wages and salaries—pointing out that those rules disadvantage those with low or even no earnings.

*** ***

The possession of power and the existence of power relationships help explain the results of many tort cases in varied settings, as well as the rules of many statutes that span the universe of injuries. Many factors feed into these cases and laws. Approaching the topic from the standpoint of economic theory, we find courts ruling in favor of claimants who are not in a position to make an efficient deal for goods and services because they lack sufficient information about either physical or legal risk, information that is readily available to the other party.

From a very different perspective, in some cases it may be argued that one party's possession of power makes it morally unjust to impose risks of injury on another. A related, difficult problem that straddles both economic and moral perspectives exists in situations where parties lack the education

39. Leslie Bender, Changing the Values in Tort Law, 25 Tulsa L. J. 759, 760 (1990).
40. Id. at 771.
41. See Richard Abel, A Socialist Approach to Risk, 41 Md. L. Rev. 695, 695 (1982).
42. See Richard Abel, A Critique of Torts, 37 U.C.L.A. L. Rev. 785, 789 (1990).
43. Id. at 793.
44. Id. at 799.

or informed intelligence to make rational decisions about risk, and in which sometimes the existence of risk itself is a surprise. Yet another lens on the subject also includes both social and economic components. It focuses on the way that vastly unequal power relationships may be crushing to the individuality of the weaker party, which is central to a society that values individual autonomy and the personal responsibility that flows from personal choice.

If one's point of departure is that everyone should have a decent, if not equal, chance at success in life as traditionally defined, then large imbalances in power make the game an unfair one from the beginning. Many judicial decisions and statutes in the field of injury law seek to create a playing field that has some elements of equality, and in the sense that we have spoken of an injury law constitution, may be said to have constitutional dimensions. The number of statutes with leveling tendencies is legion. In the injury law field, a very short list includes not only the Occupational Safety and Health Act, but the Americans with Disabilities Act and various sections of the Civil Rights Act of 1964.

CHAPTER 3

Rights

Whether we speak of injury law as a signal to guide conduct, or a check on power, or an enterprise to do justice in the narrow or broad sense, an important foundation is the concept of rights. Our definition of rights contains, to use a phrase of Holmes, the moral deposit of our society. Thus transcribing those foundations, it defines those harms we think of as legally compensable injuries, the subject of the next chapter.

Rights emerge from interests. We do not ordinarily walk around thinking about these interests, so internalized are our ideas about them. We have interests in our bodies including the interest in physical integrity. Closely related is an autonomy interest—Cardozo famously wrote, almost a century ago, about self-determination concerning one's own body.[1] We have interests in mental tranquillity, in reputation, in privacy. Property of various kinds—real estate, tangible personal property, intangibles like stocks and bonds—is another set of interests the law protects.

The recognition of all these things as interests presumably took place over millennia. They are now part of our evolved selves. Sometimes by the age of two, and certainly at three, the child aggressively shouts "mine" concerning an impingement of his or her interest in a toy or some other beloved object.

Gradually, recognized interests undergo a metamorphosis into a recognition of rights. Because we have come to internalize these ideas, often they are not at the surface of consciousness; they are part of our working assumptions about the way we should be able to live our lives in society.

As society evolves, it establishes various instruments through which these rights are announced and sometimes advertised. One of these, a constantly

---

1. Schloendorff v. Soc'y of N.Y. Hosp., 105 N.E. 92, 93 (N.Y. Ct. App. 1914).

developing repository of rights, is the common law. Over the years, courts have transformed various kinds of interests into rights. Early on, they transformed the interest in physical security into a right by creating the historic tort actions for assault, battery, and false imprisonment. They cemented the interest in reputation into a right that could be vindicated by suits for defamation. Later, they cast the interest in emotional tranquillity into a right enforceable against intentional acts, and sometimes negligent acts, that cause severe distress. They have protected some property interests by creating a group of tort actions for losses caused by misrepresentations, and others by defining torts like trespass and nuisance.

As judges have fashioned rights to protect these fundamental interests, they also have defined the kinds of behavior that violate those rights, ranging from intentional conduct to negligence to behavior that cannot be called "culpable" but that creates a high degree of danger or otherwise inflicts injuries for which a sense of justice demands compensation. Moreover, they have defined classes of persons who are proper targets to sue for violations of rights. In the common law, one such class consists of people who have not "done the deed" themselves, but who employ those who have committed torts. Thus, an employer may have to pay for the negligent act of its worker even though the employer was not careless in hiring or supervising the worker.

A special branch of injury law deals with harms caused by officials, and a principal source of this law is the Constitution. "Constitutional tort" rules cover activities by various kinds of government employees, from police on the beat to high-ranking political figures, activities in which those persons can engage only because they are representatives of the government. In language more poetic than that found in most legislation, a nineteenth century statute originally aimed at horrifying acts by members of the Ku Klux Klan provides injured persons a claim for acts committed "under color of law." It transforms what would be ordinary assaults and batteries into violations of constitutional rights if the perpetrator is a police officer and can be said, even in an artificial use of those words, to have "searched" a plaintiff's property or "seized" her. In some cases, it permits claims against school officials for acts that deprive students of their right to free expression. And it has allowed business people to sue local officials for denying licenses to them.

Many other kinds of legislation create rights. One very important type of statute, typified by workers' compensation, creates a right to money awards where none existed at common law. These laws provide monetary compensation for injuries without any inquiry into the culpability of either the injurer or the victim. They respond to harms to the same kinds of personal interests that are protected by the common law torts and by the tort-like action that provides remedies for violations of constitutional rights.

Beyond the money they transfer to injury victims, tort actions and statutes such as workers' compensation laws often generate more safety as a by-product. Other statutes more directly create greater rights to safety in particular areas, ranging from working conditions to foods and drugs and including such diverse subjects as drain cleaners, motorboats, radiation from cell phones, and cattle vaccines. This kind of legislation, often general in its rights-creating language, may or may not create specific rights in individuals to sue for violations, and sometimes the existence of the regulatory statute will establish a standard of conduct in tort suits. Whatever the mode of enforcement, these statutes effectively codify a right to physical integrity.

In a general way, all of these kinds of rights—protected or advanced both by courts and by legislatures—stem from interests in the preservation of people's personal conditions. Some might call those interests "natural rights." When courts give recoveries for torts, they are enforcing what many Americans would think of as a birthright, updated to the current state of their lives.

The concept of rights has a protective connotation, but the defensive character of rights shades into claims that may be enforced positively. The effect of the declaration of a right by an authoritative decision maker, court or legislature, is to entitle the holder of the right, regardless of his status in life, to have the interests secured by that right protected from invasion. A good example of the reach of rights regardless of status in life is the case of prisoners. Their status deprives them of certain political rights, like the right to vote, and of certain rights to physical integrity, for example a right that would otherwise be violated by search of body cavities. But they are theoretically, and in many cases in practice, protected from invasions of interests that free citizens enjoy, like the interest in being free of beatings. In some cases, they may have protections not available to free citizens, for example, the right to a minimum level of medical care. More generally, subject to such restrictions as statutes of limitations, rights come to be viewed as entitlements that can be "taken" only by a person's agreement with the one who takes the right—sometimes an agreement reached through a payment. One example is a payment for using a person's face in an advertisement.

This cluster of rights is part of a national injury law constitution in the process of development. That constitution traces the DNA of social mores, discovering as it goes a wedge of content that defines what it means to be an American—a definition that guides authoritative decision makers as well as ordinary people in their judgments of what is proper conduct. As is so with the United States Constitution, and many other modern constitutions, it is filled with ambiguities, subject to interpretation and indeed laden with a range of interpretations that vary with particular circumstances. It is a guide—no more, but no less.

SOME BASIC INGREDIENTS OF RIGHTS

What are the basis ingredients of the rights protected by injury law?

Differentiating or Disproportionate Effects of Injuries

By definition, the burden of injuries differentiates their victims from the rest of the population. At the moment of injury, the victim becomes distinguished from all those who do not suffer from that injury. When we learn about an accident that has hurt or killed someone, often our instinctive reaction is, "There but for the grace of God go I." This, I suggest, was one motivation, if a subconscious one, for the creation by Congress of the September 11th Victims Compensation Fund. As media repeatedly etched images of the World Trade Center Towers into our minds, we could picture ourselves in those buildings. We could imagine ourselves on a high floor as we saw a large plane heading right for our office; we could more than empathize with workers there as the building erupted in flame.

Aristotle captured a sense of disproportion in cases of injury caused by others in a famous passage about corrective justice:

> [T]he justice in transactions is a sort of equality indeed, and the injustice a sort of inequality; not according to [the kind of proportion at issue in cases of distributive justice as contrasted with corrective justice] . . . but according to arithmetical proportion.... [T]he law looks only to the distinctive character of the injury, and treats the parties as equals, if one is in the wrong and the other is being wronged, and if one inflicted injury and the other has received it. . . . [T]his kind of injustice being an inequality, the judge tries to equalize it. . . .[2]

In our own time, George Fletcher suggested in a frequently cited essay that one could figure out why courts rule as they do, in a diversity of cases decided under different doctrines, by looking to whether the injurer created a risk to the victim that was "nonreciprocal." He argued that "a victim has a right to recover for injuries caused by a risk greater in degree and different in order from those created by the victim and imposed on the

---

2. 2 Jonathan Barnes, The Complete Works of Aristotle 1786 (1984).

defendant." He gave as one illustration the risk imposed on persons on the ground by those who fly airplanes. An example of a reciprocal risk, perhaps not as convincing, was the case of a midair collision between planes.[3] The definition of rights, and of violations of rights, will depend on many circumstances. Courts will tend to impose liability on a party when some feature of that party's conduct, or product, is found to have exposed victims to an significant risk of harm, whether or not that party is technically culpable under tort doctrine. But often a foundational factor is the way that the injury differentiated the plaintiff from the rest of the population—putting her in a worse position than anyone else who was not injured in that way at that time.

Overwhelming Effects of Injuries

Part of the way the law defines rights is the nature of the injury. This aspect of harm often is directly chalked up under the heading of damages, rather than the label of a right. The seaman who screams in pain after being crushed between a truck on shipboard and a cargo container, even after injections of morphine, will get much more, even from a tightfisted court,[4] than the person who complains for months about a pain in the neck that followed a rear-end collision, when X-rays show no fracture or abnormality.

Yet sometimes the kind of injury has been argued to influence the definition of a right. An important declaration on this point came in an opinion by Justice Peters of the California Supreme Court in a judicial battle over the question of whether to apply a tort theory of strict liability for "defective" products to a truck that "galloped" in a way that made it impossible for the owner to use it in his business. Writing for a majority of the court, Justice Traynor said that liability for the "economic loss" suffered by the plaintiff could be imposed only under the law of contract. He opined that in tort—the traditional law of injuries—manufacturers could only be "held liable for physical injuries" attributable to defects, linking physical injuries to "overwhelming misfortune."[5] Disagreeing in a dissent on the type of injury required to apply the strict liability theory, Justice Peters said that although "'[o]verwhelming misfortunes' *might* occur more often in personal injury cases than in property damage or economic loss cases," that was "no reason to draw the line between these types of injuries when a more sensible line

3. See George Fletcher, Fairness and Utility in Tort Theory, 85 Harv. L. Rev. 537, 542 (1972).
4. Gretchen v. United States, 618 F.2d 177 (2d Cir. 1980).
5. Seely v. White Motor Co., 403 P.2d 145, 151 (Cal. 1963).

is available." An example of a "more sensible" line depended on power relationships—specifically on the plaintiff consumer's "bargaining power." This, in turn, involved the question of whether the consumer could "protect himself from insidious contractual provisions such as disclaimers, foisted upon him by commercial enterprises whose bargaining power he is seldom able to match."[6]

Expectations

This leads us to the ingredient of expectations, which is tied to the differentiating or disproportionate effects of injuries and to their sometimes overwhelming character. A typical account of the difference between contract law and the common law of injuries called tort is that contract law deals with "failed economic expectations"[7] whereas tort law requires a showing of a duty that "aris[es] independently of the contract," the breach of which injures persons or tangible property.[8]

Although the distinction between "economic loss" on the one hand, and physical injury and property damage on the other is a conventional one, it is not airtight. With respect to some basic types of damages, courts do not make this distinction. An obvious example of situations in which courts give recovery for harms that are essentially pocketbook losses is the case of personal injuries in which the principal items of damage are lost wages and medical bills. Although the initial harm is to the body, the damage award is for dollars paid out or foregone. To be sure, many courts do make the distinction, for example in cases of products liability. However, others define the category of "property damage" broadly to allow recovery under tort law even though there was no physical harm to property other than to the product alleged to be defective.[9]

The essential point is that injury law, as well as contract law, sometimes gives compensation for disappointed expectations. The laborer who cannot work any more because he lost a leg in an industrial accident, the patient who incurs heavy hospital expenses because of illness caused by a prescription drug, the executive who must pay doctors' bills because he was struck by a careless driver—all these victims have suffered disappointment of what

---

6. *Id.* at 155 (Peters, J., dissenting).
7. Nigrelli Sys., Inc. v. E.I. DuPont de Nemours & Co., 21 F.Supp.2d 1134, 1138 (E.D. Wis. 1999).
8. Flintkote Co. v. Dravo Corp., 678 F.2d 942, 948 (2d Cir. 1982).
9. See, e.g., Pratt & Whitney Canada, Inc. v. Sheehan, 852 P.2d 1173, 1177–81 (Alaska 1993).

ordinary people would think of as the normal expectations with which they began the day of their injury.

Representations

Allied to expectations are representations, declarations of value or intention that may directly create rights. Several kinds of misrepresentation have found homes in injury law as distinct from contract—certainly fraud, in some cases negligent misrepresentation, and occasionally even innocent representations that turn out to be wrong. Beyond liability directly based on misrepresentations lies a large group of decisions that take into account the background of images and portrayals that emerges from various kinds of representations. Just one example among hundreds,[10] from ninety years ago, is a case in which the plaintiff sued the packer of a can of pork and beans for ptomaine poisoning. The court found there was no case under the theory of express warranty, a contract theory. However, pointing out that "there was nothing in the appearance of the can to put plaintiff or his mother upon inquiry," the court concluded that the plaintiff could recover under theories of both negligence and implied warranty. It said with respect to the latter theory that the defendant's duty could be "treated as a representation or a warranty that, because of the sacredness of human life, food products so put out are wholesome."[11] Thus, appearances, rather than precise statements, play a part in the definition of rights.

Implied warranty is a theory primarily used in products liability cases, but implied representations of safety span a large spectrum of injury law. Not always invoked in the application of specific legal theories, they lurk below the surface when common carriers implicitly represent they will get passengers safely to their destinations, and when department stores in effect imply to their customers that their entrances are not slippery. Representations to a sexual partner that one is disease free, of one sort or another, provide a foundation for liability when the representation is in the nature of an intimation[12] as well as an explicit statement.[13]

10. See generally, Marshall S. Shapo, A Representational Theory of Consumer Protection: Doctrine, Function, and Legal Liability for Product Disappointment, 60 Va. L. Rev. 1109 (1974).

11. Davis v. Van Camp Packing Co., 176 N.W. 382, 392 (Iowa 1920).

12. Long v. Adams, 333 S.E.2d 852, 855 (Ga. Ct. App. 1985)(defendant's failure to tell partner she had herpes; negligence standard of "omission to do something which a reasonable person would do").

13. Kathleen K. v. Robert B., 198 Cal. Rptr. 273, 274 (Ct. App. 1984) (defendant, suffering from herpes, misrepresented to plaintiff that he was "free from venereal disease").

The concept of human dignity fuels a good part of the idea of rights in injury law. It cannot be quantified. Its topography is broad and difficult to map. Professor Dworkin captures the difficulty of definition in his reference to the "vague but powerful idea of human dignity." He summarizes "[t]his idea, associated with Kant, but defended by philosophers of different schools," as "[s]uppos[ing] that there are ways of treating a man that are inconsistent with recognizing him as a full member of the human community," and as "[h]olding that such treatment is profoundly unjust."[14] Lawyers and philosophers seek to dig below the surface of many concepts to discover what is underneath, but dignity is at bedrock. It is inherent in our status as human beings. A federal appeals judge once wrote of "a 'right of 'personhood.'""[15] Analyzing primitive law, the great scholar Roscoe Pound observed that the first interest protected was that of the group—the clan— but that after that, the law first recognized "an interest in one's honor, . . . rather than . . . an interest in the integrity of the physical person."[16]

In the common law of injuries, scholars speak loosely of a category of dignitary torts that includes "intentional torts" such as assault, battery, false imprisonment and intentional infliction of emotional distress, as well as defamation and invasion of privacy.[17] One writer has said that " . . . notions of personhood and dignity" can help provide a foundation for actions based on sexual harassment in the workplace,[18] and suggests that although tort law is not a judicial cure-all for sexual harassment, it "offers a way to fundamentally reconceptualize one's understanding of workplace harassment."[19] Anita Bernstein has suggested a standard based on the "respectful person" that employs those concepts.[20]

The idea of dignity is so broad that it extends across the range of physical and emotional injuries and includes torts in which intangible interests, like that in reputation, have some features of property interests. Whatever the breadth of application of the concept, a notable aspect of the commentary is how difficult it is to dig further beneath the concept of dignity. The Canadian commentator H. J. Glasbeek, discussing Canadian, American,

14. Ronald Dworkin, Taking Rights Seriously 198 (1977).
15. J. Braxton Craven, Personhood: The Right to be Let Alone, 1976 Duke L. J. 699, 701 & *passim* (1976).
16. Roscoe Pound, Interests of Personality, 28 Harv. L. Rev. 343, 357 (1915).
17. See, e.g., Rosa Ehrenreich, Dignity and Discrimination: Toward a Pluralistic Understanding of Workplace Harassment, 88 Geo. L.J. 1, 22–24 (1999).
18. See, e.g., *id.* at 63.
19. *Id.* at 44.
20. See Anita Bernstein, Treating Sexual Harassment with Respect, 111 Harv. L. Rev. 445, 482–92 (1997).

and English sources, said that in a case of the defendant's spittle being blown back to the plaintiff, the plaintiff was "more interested in having his dignity upheld than in having the discomfort caused by the wetting of his face redressed."[21] He quotes a judicial opinion on the idea that

> [e]very person has an inborn right to the tranquil enjoyment of his peace of mind, secure against aggression upon his person, against the impairment of that character for moral and social worth to which he may rightly lay claim and of that respect and esteem of his fellow-men of which he is deserving and against degrading and humiliating treatment.[22]

More recently, Jeffrey Berryman quotes Bruce Chapman on the idea that "'dignitary loss,' as commonly understood in the old adage," is "adding insult to injury.'"[23] He identifies a difference of opinion on the question of whether there are "gradations" of dignity. Chapman says no; Berryman says yes. Berryman's explanation of dignity divides it into two major categories: "'fundamental dignity,' which is held by all humanity," and "'prosaic dignity,' dignity attained as the result of individual talents, accomplishments, and social position."[24] His preferred view of dignity uses the concept of "referential loss," loss that can be calibrated by the reaction of third parties to the plight of the victim.[25] He draws a distinction involving the "loss in fundamental dignity of an individual" that "is not perceived through the eyes of others" but "rather, [] is shared by all others."[26] With an unavoidable "overlap" between conceptions of dignity, witnesses to loss of dignity will "feel differently depending on the gradation of humiliation and the period of its duration": "Our feelings act as a barometer of the victim's actual loss."[27]

The basic nature of dignitary interests has been traced to Roman law. The South African scholar Jonathan Burchell says that the Roman law "built the protection of human dignity, one of the foundation-stones of delictual liability"—a forerunner of tort law—"on the *actio injuriarum*, which safeguards person, dignity and reputation."[28] The foundational character of

---

21. See H.J. Glasbeek, Outraged Dignity—Do We Need a New Tort? 6 Alta. L. Rev. 77, 84–85 (1968).

22. *Id.* at 77, quoting Watermyer, A.J., in O'Keefe v. Angus Printing & Publishing Co., (1954), (3) S.A. 244 (C), at 247–48.

23. Jeffrey Berryman, Reconceptualizing Aggravated Damages: Recognizing the Dignitary Interest and Referential Loss, 41 San Diego L. Rev. 1521, 1533 (2004).

24. *Id.* at 1522.

25. See *id.* at 1537.

26. See *id.* at 1540–41.

27. See *id.* at 1542, 1546.

28. Jonathan Burchell, Beyond the Glass Bead Game: Human Dignity in the Law of Delict, 4 South Afr. J. Hum. Rts. 1, 1 (1988). One translation of that doctrine is that the claimant must

dignity is evident in Burchell's statement that it is "an inherent attribute of everyone."[29]

A reflection of the elusive character of dignity is an essay by Denise Reaume, who says that it is a "daunting task to say something meaningful about its place in legal thought." She speculates that "[a] philosopher might proceed by trying to provide a theoretical account of what dignity is, and why it is important that it be respected," but notes that "our philosophical intuitions about dignity seem no better developed than our legal ones."[30] Proceeding to a focused analysis of the tort of "intentional infliction of nervous shock," she seeks an explanation based in the law. One difficulty evident "in the American law," she notes, is that "the notion of dignity ... is overshadowed by the characterization of the interest deserving protection as that of freedom from emotional harm." This, she says, "mistakes a symptom of the violation of the relevant interest for the interest itself."[31] Reaume's focus on an intentional tort leads to a "starting point" that "to protect the inherent dignity of human beings requires that one person's suffering not be treated as a source of pleasure by others."[32] More generally, she refers to a concept of "social meaning," in which dignity "is a product of social practices and conventions," with "[h]arm to dignity" being "more a matter of the social meaning of particular behaviour than a matter of the specific emotional or physical impact on the victim."[33]

In an analogous conceptual channel, focusing on invasion of privacy, Robert Post drew on case law and commentary for the idea of a violation of "rules of decency" that could "damage a person by discrediting his identity and injuring his personality."[34] Post tied the idea of "social personality" to the linkage of the individual to the community, and, quoting Joseph Gusfield, to the "special claims which members [of a community] have on each other, as distinct from others."[35] He wrote of the concern of the common law for "maintaining the forms of respect deemed essential for social life,"[36] "forms of respect that are integral to both individual and

---

show that the other party "act[ed] in a willful manner ... with regard to someone else." Reinhard Zimmermann, The Law of Obligations 1050 (1992).

29. Burchell, *supra*, at 3.

30. Denise Reaume, Indignities: Making a Place for Dignity in Modern Legal Thought, 28 Queen's L.J. 61, 62 (2002).

31. *Id.* at 74–75.

32. *Id.* at 79.

33. *Id.* at 86–87.

34. Robert Post, The Social Foundation of Privacy: Community and Self in the Common Law Tort, 77 Calif. L. Rev. 957, 963 (1989).

35. *Id.* at 964 (quoting Joseph Gusfeld, Community: A Critical Response 29 (1975)).

36. *Id.* at 971.

social personality."[37] A graphic metaphor for the zone of privacy appears in Post's quotation of Erving Goffman's reference to a "territory," "a 'field of things' or a 'preserve' to which an individual can claim 'entitlement to possess, control, use or dispose of.'"[38] Another, also borrowed from Goffman, is the idea of "an 'information preserve,'" containing the "'set of facts about [an individual] to which [he] expects to control access.'"[39]

Thus, legal scholars have sketched a broad landscape in which dignity and allied concepts manifest themselves, with some of them viewing dignity as a function of the victim's relation to the wider community. The concept has magnetism: Berryman, for example, speaks of the "growing jurisprudence on the centrality of dignity—in labor and employment, human rights, and constitutional law."[40] I think it noteworthy that even as it may be becoming central in various areas of the law, dignity appears in the commentaries to be a first principle, articulated as bedrock without excavation.

Paralleling tort law, no-fault compensation statutes, though they tend to focus on income maintenance, implicitly accept the notion that a worker's ability to carry on her occupation is central to her self-conception, and thus her dignity. Moreover, these statutes arguably grant recovery for intangible fractions of identifiable physical losses—for example, when they give lump sums for the loss of limbs.

On another major track within the injury law constitution, legislative safety regulation assumes a holistic interest that is bound up in simply being a human being. A cosponsor of the Occupational Safety and Health Act captured some of this idea in a speech on the Senate floor. While speaking of the interest in physical integrity, Senator Ralph Yarborough declared, more broadly, "We are talking about people's lives, not the indifference of some cost accountants."[41]

Autonomy and Freedom

The idea of freedom announces itself in the law in many guises.[42] Injury law is illustrative, with decisions that employ freedom as a rationale to confirm

37. *Id.* at 985.
38. See *id.* at 971, (quoting Erving Goffman, The Territories of the Self, in Relations in Public: Microstudies of the Public Order 28–29 (1971)).
39. See *id.* at 984, (quoting Goffman, *supra*, at 38–39).
40. Berryman, *supra* note 23, at 1545.
41. 116 Cong. Rec. 37625 (1970), reprinted in Subcommittee on Labor of the Senate Committee on Labor and Welfare, Legislative History of the Occupational Safety and Health Act of 1970, 92d Cong., 1st Sess., at 511 (1970).
42. There is a substantial literature on rights as freedoms to speak and act, for example, freedom of expression and freedom of association. See, e.g., Ronald Dworkin, Taking Rights

or deny the existence of rights. One building block for freedom is autonomy. We have noted Cardozo's famous statement about one's rights in his or
her own body, a shield against unconsented impingements on personal
integrity. In the law of torts generally, the idea of autonomy receives confirmation in the concepts of consent and "assumption of the risk," employed
in many contexts.

Within certain boundaries established by principles of morality or public
policy, one may consent to contacts with the body that would otherwise be
held to be batteries or other torts. Clear examples, in the case of intentional
physical contact, are organized boxing or wrestling competitions. Another
obvious case is sexual intercourse where both partners manifest assent to
the act. However, both morality and public policy may vitiate consent, as in
cases mentioned earlier where a person knowingly and falsely represents to
his partner that he has no sexually transmissible disease.[43]

In the case of conduct by a defendant that otherwise would be found
negligent, or products that otherwise would be found defective, the doctrine of assumption of the risk may shield the defendant from liability.
In one extreme case, the court allowed that defense to a doctor who
employed "various mineral compounds" to treat a cancer victim, who he
told that his treatment regime did not have FDA approval and that
"he could offer no guarantees."[44] In quite another setting, a plaintiff who
literally signed on the dotted line of a release form could not impose liability on a parachute school for injuries suffered in his first jump.[45]

In other cases, the assumption of risk may be more subtle. A premier
jockey, whose experience in 22,000 races has taught him about the speed of
thoroughbreds and their tendency to bump into one another, cannot sue
another rider for a rather ordinary foul that cripples him.[46] In the amateur
category, weekend skiers cannot complain of injuries from obviously icy
slopes that theoretically could be found to be negligently maintained.[47]

The same patterns repeat themselves in decisions involving dangerous
products, in which some courts take a hard line against plaintiffs exposed to
the hazards of workplace machines. Just one example is a decision rejecting
an action against the maker of an earthmover, based on the claim that the

---

Seriously, chapter 12 (1977). The principal focus of this book is on rights defined more defen-
sively, as in rights not to be exposed to risk and not to be injured. However, I recognize—
sometimes explicitly and often implicitly—that our injury law arises in significant part from the
collision of one person's liberty with another's right to be free from injury.

43. See, e.g., Kathleen K. v. Robert B., *supra* note 13.
44. Boyle v. Revici, 961 F.2d 1060, 1062 (2d Cir. 1992).
45. Hulsey v. Elsinore Parachute Ctr., 214 Cal. Rptr. 194 (Ct. App. 1985).
46. Turcotte v. Fell, 502 N.E.2d 964 (N.Y. 1986), discussed *infra*, chapter 8.
47. Smith v. Seven Springs Farm, Inc., 716 F.2d 1002 (3d Cir. 1983).

machine lacked a parking brake. Finding the plaintiff "contributorially negligent as a matter of law," the court focused on the fact that he was "totally and completely familiar with the existence of the claimed defect" and "knew the tendency of the machine to roll."[48]

Courts have used several different concepts and phrases to capture a belief that plaintiffs should be allowed to chart a dangerous course in choosing risk. As in the case just mentioned, they may refer to "contributory negligence." They may indeed use the terminology of assumption of risk. They may employ the phrase "open and obvious" risk to describe both the plaintiff's ability to choose a risky course of conduct and the defendant's legal right to expose the plaintiff to that set of hazards. The idea of consumer autonomy reaches a high point in a case in which the court denied recovery to the buyer of a power mower: "in a free market, [the plaintiff] had the choice of buying a mower equipped with [safety devices], of buying the mower which he did, or of buying no mower at all."[49]

As in cases involving activities, this group of defenses exists in the dangerous products area for recreational plaintiffs as well as workers. One group of plaintiffs usually barred from recovery are people who suffer serious injuries when diving into the shallow end of above-ground swimming pools.[50] In an area of ordinary consumer vices that cause illness on a large scale, the Texas Supreme Court turned down a cigarette smoker's claim employing allegations of a "marketing defect" based on the dangers of smoking generally, saying that "the general health dangers attributable to cigarettes were commonly known as a matter of law by the community" when the plaintiff began smoking, although it allowed a "marketing defect" claim based on "the addictive qualities of cigarettes," which it found were not shown to be "commonly known" at that time.[51] In another area where risk assumption borders addiction, there is case law indicating that makers of liquor do not have to warn of the dangers of alcoholism.[52]

One should note, however, that there are decisions that favor product users against defenses based on their knowledge of risk, even defenses based on documents that purport to exculpate sellers. The New Jersey Supreme Court flatly rejected assumption of risk as a defense against claims

---

48. Waegli v. Caterpillar Tractor Co., 251 N.W.2d 370, 373 (Neb. 1977).

49. Myers v. Montgomery Ward & Co., 252 A.2d 855, 864 (Md. 1969).

50. Belling v. Haugh's Pools, Ltd., 511 N.Y.S. 2d 732 (N.Y. App. Div. 1987); Howard v. Poseidon Pools, Inc., 530 N.E.2d 1280 (N.Y. 1988); Sciangula v. Mancuso, 612 N.Y.S.2d 645 (N.Y. App. Div. 1994).

51. See American Tobacco Co. v. Grinnell, 951 S.W.2d 420, 427–31 (Tex. 1997). For a fuller discussion of liability law on cigarette-caused illness, see *infra*, chapter 6, text accompanying notes 47–56.

52. Joseph E. Seagram and Sons, Inc., v. McGuire, 814 S.W.2d 385 (Tex. 1991).

of workers injured by workplace machines, first under the doctrine of strict liability[53] and then as to suits based on negligence.[54] In a case involving a written disclaimer of liability for personal injuries, which involved a severe electric shock from a plumbing tool, the Rhode Island Supreme Court concluded that it would be "overly harsh and against public policy" to enforce the disclaimer.[55] Even in the area of recreational drinking, courts have not always favored beverage manufacturers. A federal appellate court gave some leeway to a plaintiff who claimed that her decedent should have been warned of the risk of illness from beer drinking.[56] And a Texas appellate court allowed a plaintiff to go to trial on allegations of a failure to warn a college freshman that drinking straight shots of tequila could kill her[57]— although eventually the court reversed a jury verdict in the plaintiff's favor.[58]

It is useful to distinguish the questions of how realistic a claimant's "choice" is, and how effectively the choice was communicated. As to realism, one court simply pointed out that a worker "who is required to use certain equipment in the course of his employment and who uses that equipment as directed by the employer has no choice in encountering a risk inherent in that equipment."[59] As to effectiveness of communication, there is a battery of cases in which courts refuse to exonerate product sellers who have not identified risks with enough particularity. One example is a case involving a meat mixer/blender in which the court pointed out that there was no evidence that the plaintiff "knew that the lock-out bar should be in place before cleaning" the machine.[60]

By contrast, where courts exonerate defendants, autonomy in the doctrinal cloaks of consent and assumption of risk operates both as a sword and a shield. As a sword, those doctrines allow people who otherwise would have viable tort claims to shoulder risks of injury that would otherwise be compensable, in order to obtain goods or services at reduced prices, sometimes to obtain them at all. As a shield, these doctrines protect risk-creating businesses. Conflicting results in cases in this area indicate the tensions in the

53. Suter v. San Angelo Foundry & Mach. Co., 406 A.2d 140, 148 (N.J. 1979).
54. Green v. Sterling Extruder Corp., 471 A.2d 15 (N.J. 1984).
55. Ruzzo v. LaRose Enters., 748 A.2d 261, 269 (R.I. 2000).
56. Hon v. Stroh Brewery Co., 833 F.2d 510 (3d Cir. 1987).
57. Brune v. Brown Forman Corp., 758 S.W.2d 827 (Tex. Ct. App. 1988).
58. Brown Forman Corp. v. Brune, 893 S.W.2d 640 (Tex. Ct. App. 1994).
59. Clark v. Bil-Jax, Inc., 763 A.2d 920, 925 (Pa. Super. Ct. 2000), appeal denied, 782 A.2d 541 (Pa. 2001)(table)(quoting Jara v. Rexworks Inc., 718 A.2d 788, 795 (Pa. Super. Ct. 1998), appeal denied, 737 A.2d 743 (Pa. 1999)).
60. Reed v. American Foods Equip. Co., Prod. Liab. Rep. (CCH) ¶13,759, at 43,486 (E.D. Pa. Oct. 14, 1993).

judicial mind, as well is in the public mind, about underwriting the freedom to choose risk.

Courts use freedom as a weapon for defendants in a variety of cases outside the products area, minimizing the legal risks for businesses whose operations necessarily involve some bumping of other people. Bill collectors, for example, need some leeway for unpleasantness. In a case in which the Tennessee Supreme Court adopted the plaintiff-friendly doctrine of intentional infliction of emotional distress, it ultimately concluded that a creditor's agent had not been shown to have acted "outrageous[ly]" when it persisted in abusive collection tactics that aggravated a debtor's "nervous condition."[61] In addition to facilitating the work of businesses whose very nature require aggression, courts provide people a fair amount of room to act out their personal stresses. In a Wisconsin case, the court noted that a contractor who had been nasty to a customer "carries with him his own feelings of hostility and his own set of emotional pressures."[62]

Lurking in the background of such exonerations of defendants who themselves occasionally require catharsis is a sense that people who claim victimization should have had tougher hides, or at least should understand that the law cannot compensate for every bump that life metes out. An opinion that combines rigor and compassion dealt with a suit against a teacher who told the classmates of a ten-year-old boy that he had a fatal disease, information that the boy's parents thought they had imparted "in strict confidence." When the classmates told the boy what they had heard, with predictable emotional consequences, the parents sued for the psychological toll taken by having to make false assurances to their son that he was not dying. But the court rejected their suit. It acknowledged that such events would "bring pain and sorrow to those affected," but it declared that "this pain and sorrow, part of the human condition, remain outside the sphere of injury for which courts provide relief through monetary compensation."[63]

An analogous emphasis on fortitude is evident in the very different setting of the law of defamation. In a landmark case that required public officials to prove a high degree of culpability against persons who allegedly libeled them, Justice Brennan spoke of "a profound national commitment to the principle that debate on public issues should be uninhibited, robust, and wide-open, and that it may well include vehement, caustic, and sometimes unpleasantly sharp attacks on government and public officials."[64]

61. Medlin v. Allied Inv. Co., 398 S.W.2d 270 (Tenn. 1966).
62. Alsteen v. Gehl, 124 N.W.2d 312, 319 (Wis. 1963).
63. Wynne v. Orcutt Union Sch. Dist., 95 Cal.Rptr. 458, 459–60 (Ct. App. 1971).
64. N.Y. Times Co. v. Sullivan, 376 U.S. 254, 270 (1964).

In another case, involving a professor who had been chosen to head a department of politics at a state university, Judge Bork pointedly stressed the need for tough hides in people who become involved in public affairs—not just public officials. Speaking of the "public and constitutional interest in free, and frequently rough discussion," he said that a person in the plaintiff's position "must accept the banging and jostling of political debate, in ways that a private person need not."[65] (Ironically, Judge Bork later penned some very bitter complaints about his treatment by various critics when he was nominated for the Supreme Court.)[66]

These varied conceptions of freedom and autonomy, with the different views they embody about human nature as it is—and to an extent about how people should behave—are bundled together in the definition of rights that can be vindicated by the law. In turn, they coexist within the framework of the injury law constitution, a constantly evolving social arbiter and template for justice.

Individualism: Battles Over Maneuvering Room

Closely related to notions of freedom and autonomy are concepts that pivot on the individual as an initiator of activities and a repository of rights. A politically popular version of individualism distinguishes it from collectivism. In this theology, the individual is the generator of creativity, whether it be as a family farmer, an inventor, or an architect of complex financial transactions. At the opposite pole in some of these tellings was the collectivized farm under Stalin, which crushed innovation and created disincentives to productive labor. More generally, collectivization deadened the human spirit. The exaltation of the individual, which speaks to spiritual intangibles and personhood, has been matched by individual rights in all kinds of property—real estate, tangible objects, and intangible financial instruments. The cluster of social goods that grow from the encouragement of individual effort and the protection of property interests provides a foundation for the kinds of rights that mark the protected territory of injury law.

---

65. Ollman v. Evans, 750 F.2d 970, 993, 1004 (D.C. Cir.) (Bork, J., concurring) cert. denied, 471 U.S. 1127 (1985).

66. See Robert Bork, The Tempting of America (Free Press 1990), e.g., at 336 (on charges against him "more vicious than those recounted here"), 337 ("major media" that "display[ed] blatant hostility and misrepresent[ed] facts"); 343 (portraying self as victim of "fury" of "groups of left-liberalism").

A special demarcation of that territory occurs when rights come into conflict. The maxim *sic utere tuo ut alienum non laedas*—use your own property so as not to injure that of another—is a general statement of the law on how to resolve those problems. One example with historic roots is the "law of ancient lights," which the English courts developed to decide suits by landowners against neighbors who built tall buildings that blocked the plaintiffs' properties. When Oliver Wendell Holmes wrote *The Common Law* in 1881, he referred to the decisions on this subject as an illustration of how the law moves toward more exactness—in this case, "a definite rule, that, in ordinary cases, the building complained of must not be higher than the distance of its base from the dominant windows."[67]

Conflict between landowners has indeed been a perennial in the effort to define rights in a way that balances individual freedom for various activities with the freedom to enjoy one's real estate. In a case that found its way to the Supreme Court, the plaintiff sued a railroad when sparks from a locomotive set off a fire in flax straw that the plaintiff stored near the tracks. The Court's majority effectively found for the plaintiff, holding that it was not contributorily negligent.[68] Holmes' crusty dissent declared that the question of whether the plaintiff had behaved prudently was for the jury.[69] This kind of issue was a centerpiece in much cited article by a Nobel Prize economist, who argued that from a purely efficiency point of view, it should make no difference on whom liability is placed when parties easily could bargain out such a conflict over the use of resources.[70]

A special variation on the problem has to do with the remedy, rather than the right. A leading case on this point arose from a suit by a developer against a company that maintained a large feedlot which, predictably, gave off stenches. The Arizona Supreme Court held that the plaintiff had a right, enforceable by the severe remedy of an injunction, but the court's remedy included a requirement that the developer "indemnify" the feedlot operator for "a reasonable amount of the cost of moving or shutting down" its operation.[71]

Thus, courts may check individualistic conduct in the pursuit of economic gain that impinges on others, but may provide re-checks on those who claim victim status.

---

67. See Oliver Wendell Holmes, The Common Law 128 (Little Brown 1881).
68. LeRoy Fibre Co. v. Chicago, Milwaukee & St. Paul Ry., 232 U.S. 340 (1914).
69. *Id.* at 352–54 (Holmes, J., dissenting).
70. See generally Ronald H. Coase, The Problem of Social Cost, 3 J. L. & Econ. 1 (1960).
71. Spur Indus., Inc. v. Del E. Webb Dev. Co., 494 P.2d 700, 708 (Ariz. 1972).

A natural consequence for a legal system with an individualistic tradition is a quest for individual responsibility—on the part of injury victims as well as injurers. This idea has considerable political resonance. In a national drama where assertions of culpability became routine, the financial crisis that dominated the news beginning in 2008, the term "accountability" became a mantra. Over a generation of wars over tort rules, the idea of individual responsibility became a mantra for advocates of limitations on tort law, who contended that some developments in the law diminished the care for themselves taken by persons who might be injured by risky activities and would view themselves as victims. At least implicitly, this was an arrow in the quiver of critics who thought it especially laughable that a jury should find McDonald's liable for burns suffered by a purchaser of coffee. As critics saw it, the court should have enforced on that badly burned plaintiff an awareness that "[o]ne of the properties of 'good' coffee is that it be 'hot.'"[72]

Courts tend to let cases involving alleged acts of both negligence and contributory negligence go to the jury. But sometimes they cannot stomach a plaintiff who has literally stepped beyond the bounds of prudence. A federal judge in the District of Columbia neatly buttoned up the facts of a case that supported her holding that a plaintiff struck by a car was "contributorily negligent as a matter of law." Reversing a jury verdict for the plaintiff, she summarized him as having seen "defendant's car approaching [an] intersection about one-third of a city block to his north" while he was "wearing dark clothing in a dark area," "but proceeded to cross anyway, in an unhurried, casual manner without looking to see if defendant had stopped."[73]

Holmes provided another crusty commentary in a case where the defendant's train killed a motorist whose car was on the tracks. His characteristically concise comment was that "When a man goes upon a railroad track he knows that he goes to a place where he will be killed if a train comes upon him before he is clear of the track."[74] Although Judge Cardozo challenged this all-or-nothing statement of the rule in a later case,[75] it stands as a symbol of the idea that injury victims as well as injurers have personal responsibility for the avoidance of accidents. A statement by the Indiana Supreme

72. This is one court's declaration in one of several "hot coffee" cases, Brown v. Tennessee Donut Corp., [1978–1979 Transfer Binder] Prod. Liab. Rep. (CCH) ¶ 8,148 at 16,848 (Tenn. Ct. App. 1978).
73. Garcia v. Bynum, 635 F.Supp. 745, 747–48 (D.D.C. 1986).
74. Baltimore & O.R. Co. v. Goodman, 275 U.S. 66, 69 (1927).
75. Pokora v. Wabash Ry. Co., 292 U.S. 98 (1934).

Court in a nineteenth century case typifies the moralism of responsibility judgments against injured parties. Denying recovery to a woman who sued a city for an ankle sprain, suffered when she walked off a sidewalk into a street under construction, the court said, "[a] person is bound to exercise the faculties with which he is endowed by nature, and if he fails to look, without excuse, when by so doing an injury could be avoided, if he is injured he cannot recover."[76]

Of course, individual responsibility is at the heart of decisions that impose tort liability rather than placing the burden on victims to avoid injury. In a landmark civil rights case involving egregious police misconduct, Justice Douglas broadly articulated the principle in a way that was relatively neutral yet contained the moral kernel of the idea. He wrote that the Ku Klux Act that he applied against the police defendant "should be read against the background of tort liability that makes a man responsible for the natural consequences of his actions."[77]

In ordinary holdings of negligence, courts do not frequently make this kind of pronouncement. They become rather more moralistic when they conclude that defendants' conduct is so culpable that it deserves punitive damages. Unusually strong language appears in a California decision, later vacated by the United States Supreme Court apparently because of the size of the $290 million punitive award, in which the state appellate court says that an auto maker's placing "on the market [of] a motor vehicle with a known propensity to roll over and, while giving the vehicle the appearance of sturdiness, consciously deciding not to provide adequate crush protection to properly belted passengers" "constitutes despicable conduct."[78]

Without quite reaching the linguistic depths of the term "despicable," the Supreme Court has firmly installed the word "reprehensible" as a limitation on the award of punitive damages.[79] And both state and federal courts have used morally flavored terms of various kinds to describe the kind of conduct that will merit a punitive award. Only illustrative is a Wisconsin case against the same auto maker in which the plaintiff claimed that the defendant had known that the fuel tank on its car was likely to burst into flames when there was a rear-end collision. The court decided that the plaintiff had alleged enough to support a finding that the defendant's conduct had been "intentional, reckless, willful, wanton, gross and

---

76. City of Plymouth v. Millner, 20 N.E. 235, 236 (Ind. 1889).

77. Monroe v. Pape, 365 U.S. 167, 187 (1961). For a fuller discussion of this opinion, see chapter 7, text accompanying notes 9–14.

78. Romo v. Ford Motor Co., 122 Cal.Rptr.2d 139, 158–59 (Ct. App. 2002), vacated and remanded, 538 U.S. 1028 (2003).

79. Pac. Mut. Life Ins. Co. v. Haslip, 499 U.S. 1 (1991).

fraudulent,"[80] adding for good measure that the law permitted punitive awards on a "showing of malice, vindictiveness, ill-will, or wanton, willful or reckless disregard of plaintiff's rights."[81]

Whatever the linguistic packaging, and whether or not the damages are only compensatory or include punitive awards, findings of negligence or morally culpable conduct are declarations of individual responsibility. And these declarations not only apply to individual human beings, but provide a face to otherwise faceless corporations, which theoretically are, after all, corporate "persons."

I note in this connection that it is possible to draw a distinction between personal responsibility and liability. Doing so, an English writer indicates that one can be liable without being personally responsible in the moral sense. He illustrates this idea with a famous nineteenth century case, *Vaughan v. Menlove*,[82] which involved the defendant's refusal to reduce the risk of fire from his hayrick that stood near the plaintiff's barn. In the usual recounting of this case, "[t]he defendant argued that, although an ordinary person would have recognized the risk of fire, he was too stupid to have done so."[83] This commentator says that "corrective justice does not require" a finding that the defendant "was personally responsible for what he did. Rather, . . . although he may not have been personally responsible, he was nevertheless rightly held liable, because fairness as between himself and the claimant demanded that result."[84]

Individualization

There is yet another facet of the American tradition of individualism that bears on decisions about whether rights exist. This is individualization, which is distinct from the fixing of individual responsibility although it overlaps with that process. There are at least three relevant aspects of this topic, discussed in this section and the next one: the individualization of justice, the question of how much to allow for individual aspects of injurers' ability and competence, and the question of how the law should deal with particular elements of the physical and mental makeup of injury victims.

80. Wangen v. Ford Motor Co., 294 N.W.2d 437, 462 (Wis. 1980).
81. *Id.*
82. (1837) 132 Eng.Rep. 490 (C.P.); 3 Bing. N.C. 468 (C.P.).
83. The summary is that of Allan Beever, Corrective Justice and Individual Responsibility in Tort Law, 28 Oxf. J. L. Stud. 475, 480 (2008).
84. *Id.* at 491.

Individualization of justice. The degree to which justice is or should be individualized has components that inhere in our court-based system of private litigation, but also has broad ramifications in policy choices made by legislatures. The standard litigation model is that of a lawsuit brought by one individual against another human being or corporation. An original premise of the system was the enforcement of individual responsibility, from both moral and economic points of view. This kind of dispute resolution produced individualized justice. But as life, particularly economic life, became more complicated, it began to wear away some of the assumptions behind this model. The facts that the majority of payments for injuries came from sources like health insurance and Social Security disability that are other than direct tort-based sources—and that an overwhelming percentages of tort payments came from insurance companies and not from injurers themselves—made some of those assumptions less real. As one scholar put it concerning automobile accidents, "the idea of a guilty driver paying an innocent injury victim" had the image of "Lassie averting a train wreck by awakening the railroad telegrapher"—"[i]t may happen, but not often enough to suggest that dog-raising is a good way to promote railroad safety."[85]

This blurring of the image of individualized justice contributed to the case for passage of no-fault legislation for automobile injuries. However, even the no-fault auto statutes enacted by approximately half of the state legislatures did not erase tort law completely; in fact, most of those statutes replaced only the first few thousand dollars of the tort action. One explanation for the failure of no-fault to command more widespread acceptance in the area of traffic injuries was political opposition from claimants' lawyers. Yet, even if the realities of how compensation was paid to many traffic victims blurred the image of the courtroom duel between two parties for justice in individual cases, one can assume that those realities did not entirely erase that image in the public mind.

Another impingement on the model of individualized justice came from situations involving injuries to many people. One solution to that problem, a problem which embodied tensions reflected in court decisions, court rules, and legislation, was the class action. Class actions permit attorneys to aggregate groups of people who claim the same type of injury. These groups of claimants sometimes sue groups of defendants, for example, several companies that made the same type of product. A straightforward example of a class action is a suit against an airline or an aircraft manufacturer, or both,

85. Alfred T. Conard, Macrojustice: A Systematic Approach to Conflict Resolution, S. Ga. L. Rev. 415, 422 (1971).

on behalf of scores or hundreds of people who died in a plane crash. Typically, there will be only the manufacturer and the carrier as defendants. Other cases present more subtle problems, which sometimes pose insuperable hurdles to the fashioning of a workable class. An illustration was a suit against a manufacturer of needles used in medical procedures. There was disagreement on some basic numbers—the manufacturer said there were "thousands" of types of needle devices, while the plaintiff said there were "perhaps ten." The court favored the defendant's argument that the plaintiffs had not shown enough "common" features in their cases to justify a class action. The court referred to evidence that "consistently describes a number of different products with substantially differing physical characteristics and intended uses, and consequently presenting a wide variation in risks and benefits from normal use." The plaintiffs argued that the defendant could have used a "feasible alternative design" for its products, but the court said that the question of whether there was such a design "would become an excessively individualized question varying from product to product" across the proposed class.[86]

The Supreme Court has wrestled with the question of whether a class has been properly constructed.[87] In an injury landscape involving hundreds of thousands of claims—both filed and prospective—Congress tried at length, but unsuccessfully, to fashion a scheme to consolidate disputes on illness allegedly caused by asbestos.[88] As the numbers of bankruptcies have mounted among companies involved in the mining of asbestos and the production and sale of asbestos products, the result has been that the system grinds along on the individualized model. The results for sufferers have been sad: One study showed that only about 39 cents on the dollar of available funds wound up in the pockets of claimants.[89] In one asbestos bankruptcy case, in which I served as an expert witness, because of the bankruptcy no payments were made to claimants for several years.

I note that the 39-cent figure in asbestos litigation is simply a particularly low point in a tort picture that features low percentages of compensation related to the pools of money theoretically available for that purpose. It has

86. Grant v. Becton Dickinson Co., 2003 WL 21267787 at *8, Prod. Liab. Rep. (CCH) ¶ 16,656, at 59,659 (Ohio Ct. App. June 3, 2003).

87. See, e.g., Amchem Prods., Inc. v. Windsor, 521 U.S. 591 (1997).

88. See, e.g., Patrick Hanlon & Anne Smetak, Asbestos Change, 62 N.Y.U. Am. Serv. Am. L. 525, 583 (2007)(bill "stymied" and "no prospect" that it would be passed soon).

89. See, e.g., Stephen J. Carroll et al., Asbestos Litigation Costs & Compensation: An Interim Report 63 (Rand Inst. for Civil Justice 2002) (of $54 billion spent on "asbestos personal injury claims, through 2000 . . . "[a]bout $33 billion, or 61 percent of the total, has been spent on defense and claimants' transaction costs," "while "[c]laimants' net recovery has been about $21 billion").

been a pretty regular statistic over the years that only 44 to 48 percent of liability insurance premiums in the area of vehicle accidents go to plaintiffs. In summary, the individualized justice model still prevails across a wide range of personal injuries, but it produces discounted quantities of justice, if justice is measured by full compensation for harms. This is a major area of stresses and strains under the injury law constitution.

I have observed that an individualization problem sometimes arises with respect to defendants as well as plaintiffs. I briefly summarize here the interesting body of law that has arisen around the issue of suits against several manufacturers of the same type of product when only one firm could have made the product that injured the plaintiffs. The most famous case is *Sindell v. Abbott Laboratories*,[90] in which the California Supreme Court devised a "market share" solution to a case involving a young woman who developed cancer as a result of her mother having taken the hormone product diethylstilbestrol (DES), designed to stave off miscarriage, during pregnancy. Some two hundred companies had made branded versions of DES, but only about a half dozen had made most of the DES marketed around the time the plaintiff's mother took the drug. Confronted with a suit against five of those companies, the court rejected several theories of liability that would have made the firms jointly liable, which would have enabled the plaintiff to collect her total damages from any one of them. However, the court decided that the plaintiff could recover from each of the defendants an amount that approximated each firm's market share of the product, at least where all the named defendants together represented a "substantial percentage" of the market.[91] A dissenting justice complained bitterly that this decision did away with the fundamental requirement that a tort plaintiff show that a defendant caused her injury, saying that a "[a] system priding itself on 'equal justice under the law' does not flower when the *liability* as well as the *damage* aspect of a tort action is determined by a defendant's wealth."[92] Variations of the market share theory have been applied to DES, and occasionally to a few other products,[93] but it has not commanded widespread acceptance.

Individual injurers. A second set of individualization questions concerns the capabilities and motives of injurers. Clearly, defendants who are professionals must meet an individualized standard in line with their degree of specialized knowledge. Courts have built the much-publicized area of

---

90. 607 P.2d 924 (Cal. 1980).
91. See *id.* at 937.
92. *Id.* at 940–41 (Richardson, J., dissenting).
93. See generally 1 Marshall S. Shapo, The Law of Products Liability ¶12.21 [3][c]-[d-1], ¶12.21[4][b](5th ed. 2010).

medical malpractice law on that foundation. At the other end of the competence curve, since the nineteenth century it has been a basic idea in English and American law that a defendant in an injury case may not plead that he wasn't smart enough to understand the risks he was imposing on the lives or property of others. Perhaps the most famous opinion on the point is the 1837 English case of *Vaughan v. Menlove*, mentioned above. The court there said that to depart from a standard of "ordinary prudence" would make liability "co-extensive with the judgment of each individual, which would be as variable as the length of the foot of each individual."[94]

The idea that the standard of care is an objective one, forbidding merciful variations for injurers who cannot measure up to the general population, has supported the imposition of liability on children who play with grownup toys. Examples are a thirteen-year-old boy driving a snowmobile[95] and a twelve-year-old operating a motorboat.[96] Giving especially poignant point to this principle is the well-established rule that persons with various kinds of mental deficiencies, even the insane, must pay for injuries caused by conduct that objectively would be viewed as culpable.[97]

There are, to be sure, some restrictions on the rights that injured persons can claim against injurers with mental limitations. A wrenching presentation of the problem is a case in which the defendant, an Alzheimer's patient, struck a nurse's aide several times in the jaw while that plaintiff was trying to get the patient into bed after she became "combative" with another aide. The majority of a California appellate court held for the defendant patient, using what essentially was a version of the idea that the plaintiff had assumed the risk. Acknowledging that general negligence law would impose liability for "failure to use due care," the court referred to an exception barring suits by "caretakers who are employed for financial compensation" against "[a] person institutionalized . . . with a mental disability . . . who does not have the capacity to control or appreciate his or her conduct." The court found it "untenable" to make patients "liable for 'conduct' part and parcel of the very disease which prompted the patient (or . . . the patient's family) to seek professional help in the first place." Quoting a prior decision, the majority referred to the plaintiff's "express knowledge of the potential danger inherent in dealing with Alzheimer's patients in general and [the defendant] in particular," and also pointed out that the plaintiff was covered

94. Vaughan v. Menlove, *supra* note 82, 3 Bing. N.C. 468, 475 (C.P. 1837).
95. Robinson v. Lindsay, 598 P.2d 392 (Wash. 1979).
96. Dellwo v. Pearson, 107 N.W.2d 859 (Minn. 1961).
97. See generally Note, Tort Liability of the Mentally Ill in Negligence Actions, 93 Yale L. J. 153, 154–55 (1983); see also Dan B. Dobbs, The Law of Torts 284 (2000) ("Insane adults and others suffering mental disability are liable both for their intentional and negligent torts").

by workers' compensation. It put the rhetorical question of whether imposing liability would produce the odd result that families checking elderly patients into nursing homes would have to get liability insurance for the patients' assaultive acts.[98]

A dissenter referred to a different concern about the probable effects of the majority's decision on the conduct of caregivers: "The next time [that those] caring for our elderly see an Alzheimer's patient attacking another patient, visitor or caregiver, they would be well-advised to use greater force on the patient to avoid injury to themselves," with the result being to minimize "the care provided to the ever increasing number of elderly patients."[99] The case is an excellent example of the intersecting dimensions of both individualization and individual responsibility. It departs from the general rule that prohibits defendants from relying on their individual incompetence to bar lawsuits; it places individual responsibility on the plaintiff because of her knowledge of the hazards of the job.

A little zone of legal defense for defendants focuses in part on the reasonableness of their perception of threats from others. A clear case is the privilege to use deadly force in self-defense against an assault that threatens death or serious bodily harm. The law generally requires that the self-defender have a reasonable belief about the seriousness of the threat.[100] Presumably that belief will depend on circumstances objectively viewed, but common sense suggests that juries would, at least in part, make an assessment of how the self-defender subjectively viewed the gravity of the attack. Again, we call on Holmes: "Detached reflection cannot be demanded in the presence of an uplifted knife."[101]

One other area where the law essentially individualizes is in the territory of punitive damages. When courts use formulas like "conscious or knowing disregard" of danger to others,[102] or even conduct that is "close to criminality,"[103] they are applying individualizing techniques with respect to discernable motivation in particular fact situations. Since a principal purpose of such awards is to punish, those awards are doing more than make cost-benefit judgments; they are venturing into the presumed inner life of actors.

98. Herrle v. Estate of Marshall, 53 Cal.Rptr.2d 713, 715–19, review denied (1996).
99. *Id.* at 725 (Wallin, A.J., dissenting).
100. 1 Restatement (Second) of Torts §65 (1965).
101. Brown v. United States, 256 U.S. 335, 343 (1921)(criminal case).
102. See, e.g., Shapo, *supra* note 93, at ¶ 29.03[3].
103. Roginsky v. Richardson-Merrell, Inc., 378 F.2d 832, 843 (2d Cir. 1967).

An important individualizing body of law focuses on plaintiffs in injury cases, asking if they possessed a subjective, specific knowledge of a hazard. In a case involving a "flash-over" from a copper tube that carried electricity, in which a power company lineman may have understood that flashovers might occur in his work, the Minnesota Supreme Court concluded that he could not be barred from recovery against the seller of work clothes that flared up when there was no tag warning that the garments were flammable.[104] And although another plaintiff was holding a fire extinguisher when a welder went to work near a pile of sponge-rubber carpet cushions, an Illinois appellate court found no indication that the plaintiff "subjectively knew or appreciated . . . the extreme flammability of the padding, the rapid spread of the resulting fire or the inextinguishability of the flames."[105] There are, of course, decisions concluding that the plaintiff had sufficiently particular knowledge of a hazard. A contrast to the flash-over case discussed above appears in a Pennsylvania case in which both the state appellate court and supreme court upheld a verdict for defendants in a suit by a veteran electrician for injuries that occurred when electricity arced from a capacitor to a screwdriver he apparently brought very close to the capacitor.[106] Decisions both ways simply underline the importance of individualized knowledge.

Beyond its concern with individual knowledge, tort law features several nuances with respect to the mental or physical makeup of individual plaintiffs. In the case of mental illness, at least of documented insanity, many courts have adopted a less rigorous standard for plaintiffs than defendants, holding that the doctrine of contributory negligence may not bar a mentally ill plaintiff.[107] There are strong arguments on both sides. On the one hand, those arguing that mentally ill people can be held contributorily negligent say that decisions to the contrary would undermine the case for "mainstreaming" the mentally ill into the community. Those who reject the defense will contend that it is simply unjust to require more intelligence or mental stability from a person than he or she possesses.

A fascinating question about how to define rights—as much a philosophical problem as a legal one—concerns the plaintiff with a special condition or sensitivity that renders him especially vulnerable to certain kinds

104. Bigham v. J.C. Penney Co., 268 N.W.2d 892 (Minn. 1978).

105. L.D. Brinkman & Co. v. National Sponge Cushion Co., 394 N.E.2d 1221, 1228 (1979).

106. Mackowick v. Westinghouse Elec. Corp., 541 A.2d 749 (Pa. Super Ct. 1988), aff'd, 575 A.2d 100 (Pa. 1990).

107. Note, *supra* note 97, 93 Yale L. J. at 157.

of injuries. The tort of assault imposes liability for an act intended to cause "an imminent apprehension" of a "harmful or offensive contact with the person" of another, which does put that person in apprehension.[108] It has been argued that the apprehension must be objectively reasonable,[109] but one suspects that in practice plaintiffs would have some room to argue that they should be compensated for a fright that they personally felt even though an "average" person would not react that way. An analogy appears in the "eggshell skull" idea, which imposes liability on the defendant who intentionally—or even negligently—injures a hemophiliac.

How far can people at the sensitive end of the bell curve press suits for injuries that would not occur in the great majority of people? There is some split in decisions concerning allergic reactions to products, where the battle lines have been drawn by a neat turn of phrase by a defense lawyer who argued that "an allergic response is not due to a defect in the product but rather to a defect in the person."[110] Judges will be least sympathetic to the victim whose adverse reaction to a product is the only one on record; citing a reference to "common sense" in a precedent, a federal appellate court denied recovery to such a plaintiff who claimed injury from a glue used to attach artificial fingernails.[111] Courts have employed a number of labels in dealing with such cases: besides "allergies," one finds references to "hypersensitivity," "abreactions," and "idiosyncrasies." But some decisions allow recovery when the percentage of affected users is "minuscule," requiring at least a warning if sellers could have foreseen that type of injury.[112] And where the percentages of adverse reactions go up, the chances of liability may also increase, even when an entire product line becomes vulnerable to suit. A striking example is that of skin reactions occurring to health care workers using latex gloves, when there was testimony that the product caused "allergic reactions in 5 to 17 percent of their consumers."[113] This problem triggered so much litigation that it required the creation of a national, multidistrict tribunal.[114]

108. Restatement (Second) of Torts §21 (1965).

109. Cynthia Bowman, Street Harassment and the Informal Ghettoization of Women, 106 Harv. L. Rev. 517, 572 (1993).

110. Warren Freedman, A Hatband and a Tube of Lipstick: The New Jersey Minority Rule on Allergic Responses, 43 U. Det. L. J. 355, 355 (1966).

111. Adelman-Tremblay v. Jewel Cos., 859 F.2d 517, 524 (7th Cir. 1988) (quoting Bennett v. Pilot Prods. Co., 235 P.2d 525, 527 (Utah 1951)).

112. Wright v. Carter Prods., Inc., 244 F.2d 53, 56–59 (2d Cir. 1957).

113. Green v. Smith & Nephew AHP, Inc., 629 N.W.2d 727, 754 (Wis. 2001).

114. For a historical summary, see In re Latex Gloves Prods. Liab. Litig., 2002 WL 32151775, at *1 (E.D. Pa. Aug. 28, 2002).

It should be noted that in the regulatory setting, the elaborate scheme of federal drug legislation does not try to achieve zero risk for all, including the hypersensitive. The standard of "safety" that governs the sale of drugs is a relative one. For example, with respect to an agency determination that "a risk evaluation and mitigation strategy is necessary" for "postapproval safety" of drugs, the statute specifies a test "to ensure that the benefits of [a] drug outweigh the risks of the drug." It names as some of the factors to be taken into account the "estimated size of the population likely to use the drug," the "seriousness of the disease or condition to be treated," and the "expected benefit of the drug."[115] Here, the question is not allergy or idiosyncrasy, but one of balancing potential benefits to many against bad results to a few.

Congress has delivered legislative verdicts on particular vulnerabilities that vary with different classes of people who have unusual physiologies or special needs. The Americans With Disabilities Act prohibits discrimination by employers "against a qualified individual on the basis of disability."[116] The legislation defines a disability as "a physical or mental impairment that substantially limits one or more major life activities," further defined by amendments passed in 2008 to "include" but not to be "limited to, caring for oneself, performing manual tasks, seeing, hearing, eating, sleeping, walking, standing, lifting, bending, speaking, breathing, learning, reading, concentrating, thinking, communicating, and working."[117] The amendments responded to a group of Supreme Court decisions that effectively constricted the coverage of the Act, but they still left room for argument. As one disability lawyer explained it, "we will still have to explain . . . why a particular limitation, even when broadly interpreted, is a 'substantial' one." Another lawyer pointed to a negative practical effect of the amendments— the reluctance of employers to provide accommodations for people claiming disabilities "until they have a lawsuit."[118]

Congress' choice to level the playing field for disabled persons was matched many years ago by a famous passage in a judicial decision that provided a margin of protection for those whose intellectual capacity or judgment falls below the average of what Will Rogers called the "Big Normal Majority." In a 1910 trademark case that predated the raft of direct consumer protection statutes now on the books, the Second Circuit said that the law was "not made for the protection of experts, but for the

---

115. 21 U.S.C.A. §355–1(a)(1)(2007).
116. 42 U.S.C. §12112(a)(2009).
117. Id. §12102(1)(A), (2)(A).
118. See Allison Torres Burtka, 42 U.S.C. §12102(2)(A), ADA Amendments take effect, broadening disability protections, Trial, Jan. 2009, at 14, 16–17.

public—that vast multitude which includes the ignorant, the unthinking and the credulous, who, in making purchases, do not stop to analyze, but are governed by appearances and general impressions."[119]

Critics of that view will argue that it poses serious questions for the operation of a democracy: how can people vote wisely if they can't buy detergents intelligently? The point is philosophically interesting, but one should recognize that it would require exclusion of significant parts of the population from legal protection. Consider some evidence at two poles of consumer attitudes about cancer cures, and cancer itself. In the 1970s, a government study found that 42 percent of those surveyed would reject "almost unanimous expert opinion" that a cancer cure was worthless.[120] A Georgia case captures another end of the spectrum of attitudes—in this case, concerning the disease. The court affirmed a punitive award against a seller of stainless steel cookware, who allegedly misrepresented to the plaintiff that the aluminum pots and pans she was then using "contained a cancer-producing substance which is consumed by persons who eat food prepared in such cookware." The credulous plaintiff ("Lord have mercy, I don't want my children to have cancer") bought the defendant's merchandise and gave her old cookware to him to throw away. In affirming the punitive award, the court spoke of the defendant "weav[ing] a web of fright" that "overreached" the plaintiff. Echoing the Second Circuit's liberal standard for those who "do not stop to analyze," the court quoted a precedent on the proposition that "[j]uries are the preachers" in such cases, said it was "not unmindful of those who prey upon the ignorant," and declared that "[t]he illiterate are entitled to the protection of the law as well as the educated."[121]

Social facts, including consumer credulity, sometimes influence the definition of rights by courts.

Humanitarian Considerations

Judges are supposed to detach themselves from feelings of sympathy for individuals. At least that is the theory, and in practice judges mostly tend to maintain that stance. Yet, now and then, judicial responses to tragic facts go beyond detachment. An example is a case in which the Eighth Circuit

---

119. Florence Mfg. Co. v. J.C. Dowd & Co., 178 F. 73, 75 (2d Cir. 1910).

120. HEW News Release No. 72–85 (Oct. 9, 1972), summarizing findings from report, "A Study of Health Practices and Opinions," quoted, Shapo, *supra* note 10, 60 Va. L. Rev. at 1306 n.977.

121. King v. Towns, 118 S.E.2d 121, 123–27 (Ga. Ct. App. 1960).

affirmed an award for the death of a twelve-year-old boy who fell from the top of a 72-foot grain silo that allegedly was inadequately protected from boys known to climb the structure to chase pigeons. Applying the child-friendly "child trespasser" doctrine, the court described precedents as "increasingly acknowledg[ing] the humanitarian viewpoint that the life of a child is to be balanced as a heavy interest when weighed against the utility of simple precautions to guard against danger."[122]

A similar humanitarian point of view is evident in a federal trial judge's rejection of the defense that an injured worker "misused" an industrial press. Noting that a foreman had ordered the plaintiff to work on the machine "in the dangerous manner that led to her injury," the judge noted that theoretically she might have quit her job, but said that this "option" was "effectively foreclosed, or at least quite circumscribed." Individualizing the case, he pointed out that "[t]he plaintiff lacked a trade or college degree and had to help support a family" and said that "[f]or a woman in her con-strained position, commanded to follow a questionable practice but need-ing her job, the facts strongly rebut voluntariness in the ordinary sense of the word."[123] Economists posit a fair degree of fluidity in labor markets, but this opinion implicitly is dubious of that premise. As economic times become tougher, courts will have to make more choices of this kind when they define rights. Those choices have an inescapably political content, and judicial manifestations of ideological preference are part of the continuing creation of an injury law constitution.

Decisions involving the amount of damages awarded for intangibles sometimes reflect a degree of personal sympathy. The very nature of catego-ries like "pain and suffering" allows judges some leeway to depart from detachment. Illustrative of compassion bound up with individualization is a case in which a woman died from burns suffered in a factory explosion. To the woman's husband, who had to view the death throes of his horribly disfigured wife, the court awarded $100,000. Besides that sum, which included the husband's "mental anguish," the court awarded $50,000 to the woman's mother, who it specified had "suffered more than normal grief in the loss of her daughter."[124]

A Seventh Circuit decision illustrates the nuances that may be involved in review of damage awards by appeals courts. This case focused on com-pensation for loss of a spouse. The court reflected on its "uncomfortable feeling" that a $414,000 award for intangibles like the loss to the plaintiff of

122. Cargill v. Zimmer, 374 F.2d 924, 930 (8th Cir. 1967).
123. Downs v. Gulf & W. Mfg. Co., 677 F.Supp. 661, 665 (D. Mass. 1987).
124. Lowe v. U.S., 662 F.Supp. 1089, 1098 (W.D. Ark. 1987).

her husband's "counseling and guidance and love and affection" was "too high." But despite its own belief about the size of the award, the court concluded that it would not substitute its judgment about the right dollar figure for that of the jury.[125] An interesting feature of this opinion is the way a federal appellate court refers, in effect, to its feeling about feelings. Another is how it symbolizes that while courts tend to adhere to a relatively detached perspective on whether the law supports liability, they are more inclined, at least implicitly, to take into account the role of emotion when they determine allowable amounts of intangible damages. Somewhat ironically, the determination of hard dollars sometimes allows a softening of the detached perspective, at least in the appellate review of such awards.

On another axis of the law, courts often give their blessings to altruistic acts, particularly when the plaintiff suffers injuries in an attempt to rescue a person in peril. One of the most famous phrases in all American case law is Judge Cardozo's declaration that "Danger invites rescue."[126] He said this in a case in which the plaintiff was hurt when he went to search for his cousin, who had fallen out of an overcrowded railroad car that was running on a trestle between Buffalo and Niagara Falls. In almost equally memorable phrases, Cardozo intoned that "[t]he cry of distress is the summons to relief" and that "[t]he emergency begets the man."[127] There is argument about the biological basis for acts that ordinary people would consider acts of altruism—for example, on the proposition that altruism is a function of efforts to perpetrate family genes.[128] Nevertheless, judicial perceptions of the high moral value of self-sacrificing behavior have contributed to the definition of tort rights for injured rescuers.

Yet, even judges with a consciously humanitarian orientation do not in tort cases provide relief for poverty, except in the indirect sense of approving dollar awards for people impoverished by injuries culpably caused by others. It should be stressed, indeed, that tort damages do not take account of need. A fairly universal view is that this form of "distributive justice" requires legislative action. Workers' compensation, which effectively provides income maintenance for workers deprived of their livelihood, is a kind of halfway house between tort law, which before workers' compensation became law often denied recovery to injured workers because of their own risky conduct, and full-dress social legislation. Social security disability payments represent a somewhat fuller blossoming of legislation that

---

125. Huff v. White Motor Corp., 609 F.2d 286, 297 (7th Cir. 1979).
126. Wagner v. Int'l R. Co., 133 N.E. 437, 437 (N.Y. 1921).
127. *Id.* at 437–38.
128. See, e.g., Richard Dawkins, God's Utility Function, 273 Sci. Am. No. 5, 80 at 85 (Nov. 1995).

relieves the financial burdens caused by injury—among other causes of disability. However, that program does not take need into account and indeed it requires claimants to have worked and paid into its fund for a certain number of quarters. Yet fuller blooms from the standpoint of need appear in the categorical assistance program of Aid to the Permanently and Totally Disabled, in which determinations of eligibility require consideration of "other income and resources" of claimants,[129] and the TANF program—Temporary Assistance for Needy Families—which uses a means test that includes income and household resources. Yet the TANF program requires able-bodied adults to work, unless they can qualify for an exemption like that for caring for young children in the home.[130]

Congress' creation of the September 11th Victim Compensation Fund, briefly mentioned above, is a most extraordinary legislative blending of common law concepts with distributive justice. That statute included a broad catalog of economic and noneconomic losses, defining the latter category to include "physical and emotional pain, suffering, inconvenience, physical impairment, mental anguish, disfigurement, loss of enjoyment of life, loss of society and companionship, loss of consortium (other than loss of domestic service), hedonic damages, injury to reputation, and all other nonpecuniary losses of any kind or nature."[131] Additionally, it permitted the Special Master to consider the "individual circumstances of the claimant,"[132] and the rules adopted for administration of the Fund specified that those "individual circumstances . . . may include the financial needs or financial resources of the claimant or the victim's dependents and beneficiaries."[133]

This blending of common law damages concepts and compassion for people impoverished by fortuitous events is a remarkable definition of rights by the national legislature. The rights created by the statute for this one event include not only a foundational definition of eligibility—basically, presence at the attack sites—but also a set of remedy categories that includes both types of harm and degrees of deprivation. I note, in this connection, that in practice courts deciding torts cases may sometimes blur a quite traditional distinction between "liability"—whether a defendant must pay at all for an injury—and "damages"—how much he has to pay. Even if judges do not announce what they are doing, on occasion the severity of an injury may influence them to decide that the defendant should be

129. 42 U.S.C. §1352(a)(8)(1997).
130. 42 U.S.C. §§601ff (2009) e.g., at §607(c)(2)(e)(2) (allowing exceptions for work requirement if suitable child care is unavailable or unaffordable).
131. 49 U.S.C.A. §40101 Note, §(402)(9).
132. *Id.* sec. (405)(b)(1)(A)(ii).
133. 28 C.F.R. §104.41 (2002).

held liable in the first place as well as to be relatively liberal in reviewing damage amounts.

The definition of rights by our law of injuries has many roots. An analysis of that body of law in the broadest sense, though, confirms that those who write it and interpret it respect and value the worth of every human being. This is a constitutive pillar of the law.

CHAPTER 4

Injuries

Our analysis of the factors that bear on the creation of rights by courts and legislatures provides a foundation for an examination of the idea of injury. Law, both case law and legislation, makes decisions about what we regard as injuries—decisions that sometimes exclude things that people perceive as harms to themselves. Our inquiry includes ways in which risks are created, the number of injuries that occur, and how our law calculates losses in money.

Sources of Risk

Risk confronts people in many guises, from the overt to the insidious, sometimes even the sinister. It arises from many different sources, which span the scope of human life and which sometimes overlap: activities, processes, and products.

Activities that produce risk break down further into acts of commission and omissions, and the boundaries of those categories sometimes are fuzzy. Take, as an example, a case in which a hotel hosts a banquet for a national sorority, which includes the setting up of long tables and chairs in a ballroom. That arrangement of furniture is an act. As the banquet progresses, it becomes evident that the seating is uncomfortably tight, so tight that waitresses have to pass food plates from guest to guest down the tables. Toward the end of the banquet, an elderly guest gets up to meet a family member. As she makes her way between tightly bunched chair backs, she is injured when she trips over a chair as she heads to the main aisle.[1] Arguably, the failure on the part of hotel management to keep watch on the narrowed

---

1. LaPlante v. Radisson Hotel Co., 292 F.Supp. 705 (D.Minn. 1968).

positioning of the tables and chairs is an omission, a failure to do something. Yet it emerges from the way the hotel set up the banquet in the first place—an act. The categories of act and omission overlap.

A myriad of other activities involve acts, which sometimes also occur in conjunction with omissions. A truck driver speeds, failing to respond to other vehicles weaving in and out of traffic. An obstetrician who has monitored a pregnancy for months makes the wrong call about when to deliver a baby that is overdue. A young man plays very aggressively in a pickup touch football game, injuring a woman on the other team. An airline attendant keeps plying a passenger with wine, although it appears to him and to fellow attendants that the passenger is becoming drunk.

Some activities merge into broader categories of endeavor: processes. The complaint of injury victims in these cases focuses on a cluster of decisions and choices on the part of the defendant, and on a sometimes complex, ongoing aggregation of events that merge into a unit of risk. Here we encounter the factory that employs asbestos in production of a consumer good, throwing off as a by-product a cloud of disease-causing particles that enter the lungs of factory workers. We find a chemical company or an oil refiner that mixes or distills substances in a tangle of pipes, vents, and stacks, producing poisons of various kinds that enter the atmosphere or streams. Oil gushing from a deepwater well that contaminates aquatic food reservoirs, waterfowl, and human playgrounds is the product of a process that arises from an activity. There are boundary questions about classification. Is it more descriptive to call running a business in a shopping mall, or governing a condominium, a process or an activity when criminals attack mall customers or condo owners?

A discrete source of risk is tangible products used by both consumers and workers. Goods that benefit many consumers sometimes pose risks that cause injuries to a few. A crack in a car's steering mechanism—for practical purposes not discoverable before it causes the vehicle to go off the road—may cause injuries to drivers, passengers and bystanders. The prescription drug that reduces pain or alleviates disease for millions may cause heart attacks in hundreds or thousands. The industrial press that turns out thousands of riskless products may become a downward battering ram that costs its operator her arm. A rather subtle legal problem arises when a manufacturer makes vehicles that it sells to the public and a defect in one of those vehicles injures one of its own employees who is using it to perform his job.

The manufacture of products sometimes becomes enveloped in processes that cause injury. The pressures associated with assembly lines may cause mental breakdowns. The worker who packages popcorn for microwaving may suffer from "popcorn lung," a disease associated with a flavoring agent. A potentially portentous set of problems, although at this writing its consequences are quite uncertain, may lurk in the exposure of employees in nanotechnology industries to tiny particles given off in their work.

The universe of injuries that contains these activities, processes, and products ranges from the most everyday incident to the regional catastrophe. A parallel set of issues relates to minimization of risk. There is a wide spectrum of possibilities for control of harm. The mundane injury, a slip on a raised sidewalk or a slippery floor, is often preventable by the builder or owner of premises. It has even been argued that there is a significant degree of human control over the raging of fires in great buildings which collapse when hit by airplanes. But presently there is no way to prevent the wiping out of entire communities, perhaps regions, by asteroids or enormous meteorites.[2]

The Statistical Dimensions of Injuries

The statistics of injury in the United States occupy a substantial wedge of death and pain. The child who scrapes her knee falling off her little scooter on the sidewalk may cry for a few minutes about her "boo boo," but she will not wind up in the doctor's office or the emergency room. However, forty-two million of her fellow citizens will each year; according to the National Center for Health Statistics, in 2008 that was the "[n]umber of emergency department visits for injuries," including "visits for adverse effects of medical treatment."[3] The number of deaths from all injuries, nationwide, was estimated at 173,753, with 117,809 deaths from "unintentional injury." The total number of deaths in traffic accidents, in a range that held fairly steady for many years, was 43,667 in 2006,[4] although it went down to 32,788 in 2010.[5]

The annual data on nonfatal injuries requiring visits to emergency departments over the period 2002–2004 included 3,443,000 visits for fractures, 5,756,000 for "open wounds," and 359,000 for injuries to internal organs.[6] The social and individual costs of these events are very large.

2. See, e.g., Death by Asteroid, Sci. Am., March 2011, at 80.

3. CDC FastStats homepage, http://www.cdc.gov/nchs/FASTATS/injury.htm, printed Sept. 10, 2011.

4. Id.

5. Traffic Fatalities in 2010 Drop to Lowest Level in Recorded History, NHTSA release PR/NHTSA-05-11, April 1, 2011, www.nhtsa.gov, printed from the Internet, June 29, 2011.

6. Nat'l Ctr. for Health Statistics. NCHS Data on Injuries, printed from the Internet, Jan. 16, 2009.

The medical costs of fatal injuries reckoned for 2000 were $1.1 billion, a figure dwarfed by "lifetime productivity costs" of $142 billion. The cost of hospitalizations for injuries was $33.7 billion with another $31.8 billion for injury visits to emergency departments and $13.6 billion for "other outpatient visits." The productivity costs were $58.7 billion for injury hospitalizations and $125.3 billion for nonhospitalized injuries.[7]

Fatal injuries in the workplace averaged 5,749 deaths in 2004–2005, with 14 percent of those deaths resulting from "assaults and other violent acts,"[8] and there were approximately "4 million nonfatal occupational injuries and illnesses in 2007."[9] A particularly troubling estimate, published by the Institute of Medicine in 2000, involved deaths arising from preventable errors in the process of medical care. That number, which presumably was not included in the fatality statistics summarized above, spanned a rather broad range—from 44,000 to 98,000.[10]

The Behavioral Causes of Injuries

Injuries do not just happen. Identifying a "cause" may be difficult from both scientific and legal perspectives, but usually there is an identifiable reason—or there are discernible reasons. It may be that someone meant to hurt someone else; the statistics on workplace homicides are a troubling column in this set of data. It may be because someone wasn't watching where she was going. It may even be because someone had a "death wish." This is literally the case more than 30,000 times a year: the National Institute of Mental Health recorded 32,349 deaths by suicide in 2004—the eleventh leading cause of death in the country.[11] One can speculate that at least an "injury wish" is at the bottom of many bumps, bruises, and fractures.

Sometimes it is difficult to label a particular person, individual or corporate, as an "injurer," although it is usually clear who the "victim" is. But on many occasions, choices made by decision makers properly target them as "injurers." The decision to drive beyond the speed limit is an obvious example. The doctor who prescribes a course of treatment without referring a patient to a specialist may be making a choice about which he or she should

7. Injury in the United States: 2007 Chartbook, at 13, printed from the Internet, Jan. 16, 2009.

8. Id. at 35.

9. http://www.bls.gov/iif/oshwc/osh/os/osnr0030.txt, printed Jan. 16, 2009.

10. See Linda Kohn et al., To Err is Human: Building a Safer Health System 26 (Inst. of Medicine Nat'l Acad. Press 2000).

11. http://www.nimh.nih.gov/health/publications/suicide-in-the-us-statistics-and-prevention.shtml, printed Jan. 16, 2009.

have known better. A famous 1981 decision imposed punitive damages on an auto manufacturer for placing a gas tank in a position more likely to cause explosions and fires in rear-end collisions than would have been the case with a different design,[12] and the same corporate choice has been the subject of closely fought litigation in this century.[13]

On many occasions, avoidable injuring behavior arises from a failure to provide information about risk to the victim. This problem poses a central question in many products liability cases—a topic we will discuss in detail later.[14] In many cases involving products, a practical analysis of situations involving alleged failures to warn—as well as the allegedly defective design of products—might judge injuries to have been "caused" by both the seller and the injured person. Two commentators identified the problem in a book chapter titled "The Inconvenient Public." They noted that some claimants in products liability cases allege that defendants could "have improved the design to prevent accidents," or that defendants had the opportunity to "provid[e] better warnings and instructions in how to use the product." But they also pointed out that it was "equally natural for producers and distributors to shift the blame back to the user," saying that it was "obvious" in "hindsight" "what the user should have done or seen in order to avoid an accident." Sellers, they said, would "remember all the care that was taken in the design process," and would "see no ambiguity at all in the instructions and accompanying warnings."[15]

Thus, the creation of risk may be a joint affair between alleged injurers and victims. We may sympathize with both. Producers using innovation to increase their market share—conscientiously, in their self-estimate—may find themselves labeled careless or worse. The consumer, wishing to order her life as efficiently as possible, may proceed to use a product hurriedly and in her hurry forego the reading of warnings. The marketer's search for sales and the desire of both seller and victim to save time and effort are just part of doing business, even of living. Except in the extreme cases where the law will mete out punishment, most risk-creating conduct that can be called a tort is of a kind that, while substandard, occurs within the range of the slips that all of us make some of the time.

12. Grimshaw v. Ford Motor Co., 174 Cal.Rptr. 348 (App. Ct. 1981).

13. See, e.g., Jablonski v. Ford Motor Co., 923 N.E.2d 347 (Ill. Ct. App. 2010) (affirming plaintiffs' judgment), reversed, 2011 Ill. Lexis 1136, Prod. Liab. Rep. (CCH) ¶ 18,702 (Sept. 22, 2011).

14. See *infra*, chapter 7, text accompanying notes 95–147.

15. Baruch Fischoff & Jon F. Merz, The Inconvenient Public: Behavioral Research Approaches to Reducing Product Liability Risks, in Janet Hunziker & Trevor Jones, Products Liability & Innovation 159, 159–60 (Nat'l Acad. Press 1994).

For judges applying the law in civil actions, the question is how to determine the creator of risk and how to allocate risk in individual cases. By contrast, legislatures that pass compensation statutes like workers' compensation laws make a more global judgment about risk creation. They examine the overall statistics of risk in the workplace and use the meat ax, rather than the scalpel, in their distribution of the costs of injuries. Worker carelessness may indeed contribute to many injuries, and the workers' compensation laws indirectly take that into account by restricting dollar awards to schedules typically below tort damage awards. Still, in workers' compensation the basic framework is one that allocates the cost of risky activity only to those who initially generate risk, the employers, rather than placing part of that cost on workers, often secondary risk creators.

Similarly, the many statutes that regulate safety—from the workplace to the marketing of drugs to the design of automobiles—do not make fine judgments after harm occurs about the responsibility of particular persons who may have contributed to injuries. Rather, before injuries occur they define categories of potential injurers by their participation in a particular business—running factories, or making medical devices or cigarettes or motorboats. Their focus is on the initial creation of risk. The agencies that fashion regulations to implement these laws may engage in balancing both risks that arise from business activities and risks that consumers create for themselves. But the basic legislative decision relegates to secondary status the facts that factory workers may choose risky shortcuts with machines, that drivers may take chances that involve them in crackups, and that some people smoke like chimneys. The statutes regulate the entrepreneur, who is effectively viewed as the injurer.

Harms Sometimes Not Recognized as Injuries

Lay people are sometimes dismayed to find that the law does not chalk up as injuries things that they clearly regard as harms.

An introduction to the subject comes from the sports-based aphorism, "No harm, no foul." If A bumps B carelessly or even intentionally, but leaves no mark even on soft tissue, that may technically give rise to a claim for negligence or battery in the law of torts, yielding at least nominal damages. But most lay people would probably apply the sports aphorism and say that if there is no evidence of physical harm, there should be no damages found at all—in fact, that there is no tort.

Beyond that, there are cases where there is definite evidence of harm of one kind or another, but the law—at least the law of injuries that includes torts—does not recognize the harm as compensable. A simple example is the insulting remark. Although it may in fact wound the person to whom it is directed, most American states do not recognize insult as grounds for a lawsuit. In chapter 3, we suggested two reasons applicable to insults: if you live in society, you have to expect some bumping, and you also are entitled to do some yourself as a matter of personal freedom. An additional, administrative, reason is that if courts allowed actions for insult, they might be swamped with litigation.

A similar kind of reasoning also supports the requirement that people who sue for the tort of intentional infliction of emotional distress must show that the defendant has acted in an "outrageous" way—"beyond all possible bounds of decency."[16] Similar rationales underlie the reluctance of many courts to impose liability at all for *negligent* infliction of emotional distress unaccompanied by physical consequences or even physical contact.

A graphic example of decisions that say that there may be harm but there is no foul is the case of the "Snowmen of Grand Central." That was a suit for an understandable fear of cancer on the part of pipefitters exposed to large quantities of asbestos dust—enough to make them look like snowmen—when they worked in tunnels under the terminal. They sued under the Federal Employers' Liability Act, a statute that was designed to liberalize negligence law in favor of railroad workers and one that historically has been interpreted rather liberally by the courts, including the Supreme Court. The Supreme Court, however, concluded that the suit of the "Snowmen" could not go forward. The Court refused to find that the contact the plaintiffs had with the asbestos dust was a sufficient "physical impact" to qualify them for damages. Referring to one of its own precedents, the Court rationalized its denial of liability on grounds of the difficulty of sorting out genuine claims from trivial ones, the potential of such claims to generate "'unlimited and unpredictable liability,'" and the "'potential for a flood'" of litigation.[17]

Some courts have disagreed with this reasoning and allowed recovery for negligently caused emotional distress without physical contact or demonstrable physical effects. An example of the kind of truly galling circumstances that may support liability is a case in which the defendants wrongly informed the plaintiff's wife that she had syphilis, which led to a breakup of the couple's marriage.[18] Yet judicial reluctance to recognize such claims still exists. A dissenter in that case argued that to impose liability would be "disproportionate to the degree of culpability." The loser,

16. Restatement (Second) of Torts §46, cmt. d (1965).
17. Metro-North Commuter R. Co. v. Buckley, 521 U.S. 424, 432–33 (1997), in part quoting Consolidated Rail Corp. v. Gottschall, 512 U.S. 532 (1994).
18. Molien v. Kaiser Foundation Hosps., 616 P.2d 813 (Cal. 1986).

he suggested, would be the public, "who must ultimately bear the cost—by sanctioning claims for hurt feelings."[19] The "hurt feelings" idea probably has kept many American courts from allowing recovery of this kind. At least when the other party does not intentionally cause emotional distress, these judges seem to be saying, generally you have to be able to take it.[20]

If ultimately judges vindicate the public interest, one may ask how the public is given voice in such cases. Those who argue for liability might be said to speak with a populist inflection, in favor of the weak and the vulnerable. But while judges who reject claims for negligently inflicted emotional distress could be viewed as a first line of defense against a tort law of tenderness, they may also sound a populist voice in favor of tougher hides. In this infighting under the constitution of injury law, they insist that even when there is intangible harm on which jurors could put a dollar sign, there is no *recognizable* injury.

There is a more technical area of legal doctrine where courts will not recognize harms that can be quantified in a relatively tangible sense—at least they will not chalk up those harms as injuries in the compartment of the law called torts. These are harms that are "purely economic," by contrast with injuries to the body or to tangible property. We introduced this refusal to call a harm a tort in chapter 3, with the case of the galloping truck. Many courts have restrictively applied against plaintiffs the view that any liability for "economic loss" can be imposed only under contract law and not the injury branch of private law called torts.

A leading case on this subject is the Supreme Court's decision in *East River S.S. Corp. v. Transamerica Delaval*.[21] The case is a leading one more because of its source, the Supreme Court, than the power of its reasoning; but many other courts, including state courts, have cited it. The *East River* case involved no physical injury to any person, and the only damage to property was to allegedly defective goods, components of turbines on supertankers. The defects were alleged to have contributed to malfunctions that harmed the turbines themselves. The Supreme Court entered this area of products liability, normally the preserve of state courts, because the case arose in the admiralty jurisdiction. Justice Blackmun wrote the Court's opinion favoring the defendant manufacturer of the turbines on a tort claim. He premised that tort liability for defective products rests on the policy basis that "people need more protection from dangerous products than is afforded by the law of warranty"—that is, contract law. He declared

19. *Id*. at 825 (Clark, J., dissenting).
20. For elaboration of the law on negligent infliction of emotional distress, see *infra*, chapter 8, text accompanying notes 105–111.
21. 476 U.S. 858 (1986).

that "[t]he tort concern with safety is reduced when an injury is only to the product itself," noting that when "by definition no person or other property is damaged, the resulting loss is purely economic." The law best suited for that kind of loss, he said, was "[c]ontract law, and the law of warranty in particular . . . because the parties may set the terms of their own agreement."[22]

This line of reasoning has proved persuasive to many courts, whether or not they cite *East River*. And some of the applications favoring defendants are rather severe, covering cases in which a defective product in fact created a serious physical risk to persons and other property, but caused injury only to the defective product itself. A group of decisions by lower federal courts and state courts has denied recovery to product owners when defects caused fires in the products they bought. Just one example is a case in which a fire allegedly was caused by a defect in a clamp that secured a hose in the hydraulic system of a utility truck that was damaged by the blaze. Rejecting a tort claim, Judge Haynsworth wrote for a federal court of appeals that the fact that the injury occurred in a "sudden calamity" rather than "more slowly or less dramatically" seemed of "no moment." The keys to the case for him were the facts that there was "only economic loss flowing from the destruction of the truck," that "[n]o person was hurt," and that there was "no claim for personal injury" in a situation where "[e]ach of the parties is a commercial entity with apparent equality in ability to provide for self-protection."[23] Beyond that, for the Wisconsin Supreme Court it did not make a difference that the purchaser of a vehicle that caught fire was an ordinary consumer. The Wisconsin court, typically relatively liberal to tort claimants, rejected a tort claim on those facts. It said that the idea that a buyer who could have paid more for "a certain level of protection against economic loss" applied "with equal force to consumer transactions" as to "commercial transactions."[24]

This reasoning appears to strain the reality that most consumers confront. Moreover, many people might find curious a distinction between damage to purchased property that catches fire and nearby property to which the fire spreads—which is, indeed, a distinction that rules out damage to the purchased property when it occurs from a risk that threatens people as well as other property. But the rigorous denial of liability in such cases shows the power of what has become sanctified as the "economic loss doctrine."

22. *Id.* at 866, 870, 872–73.
23. Laurens Elec. Corp., Inc. v. Altec Indus., Inc., 889 F.2d 1323, 1325–26 (4th Cir. 1989).
24. State Farm Mut. Ins. Co. v. Ford Motor Co., 592 N.W.2d 201, 211, 214 (Wis. 1999).

That doctrine parallels the case law that refuses recognition to some intangible harms, like emotional distress, if they are unaccompanied with physical contact or physical consequences. What is especially striking about the economic loss cases is that courts reject tort recovery even for losses that can be precisely documented, as contrasted, for example, with the intangible injury of emotional distress; they deny liability even when a purchased product literally burns itself up. Again, the lesson is that many harms, even palpable harms, are not considered injuries—at least under tort law.

I note that this legal issue may be thought of as involving the definition of rights as well as the definition of injury. Professor Dworkin takes a "rights" perspective on an English case in which the defendant's negligence in breaking an electrical cable resulted in a power outage that caused economic loss to the plaintiff. He views the choice facing the court as having to decide whether the plaintiff had a "right to a recovery, which is a matter of principle," or whether the question was one of loss distribution, "which is a matter of policy."[25] Dworkin's approach emphasizes the abstract theoretical process by which judges seek justification for their decisions.[26] By comparison, I tend to focus here on the practical outcome of decisions—viewing the issue in such cases as whether what is undoubtedly a loss to the plaintiff is characterized as an injury, a decision which reflects a set of policy choices.

Calculating Loss

Our discussion above of the concept of injury has ranged from sources of risk and the on-the-ground reality of harms to how people behave in fact, and it has included an analysis of how the law classifies certain kinds of harms as not involving legal injuries. But the most practical bottom line of the category of injuries lies in the calculation of loss. In tort law, the principal index to valuation is the damages that juries assess, under judicial control.

Tort damages, for intangibles as well as relatively precise items of loss, always receive an accounting in dollars. The most tangible classification is medical and hospital costs, which appear in black and white on the printouts of bills. Another cost of injuries, sometimes quite specifically calculable, but on other occasions not so, is income loss from deprivation of one's occupation. This can be done relatively easily for the first period of time after an injury. It becomes more difficult as time elapses, because of

25. See Ronald Dworkin, Taking Rights Seriously 83–84 (1977).
26. See e.g., *id.* at 120–21, 284.

uncertainty as to whether a person would have stayed in a particular job and whether his or her compensation would have stayed stable, increased, or even decreased.

There is a raft of intangible damages, which in current terminology are labeled "noneconomic losses." That category has proved controversial in tort law. It is not generally a separate item of damages in workers' compensation. However, it is somewhat ironic that, as we noted in chapter 3, the law that set up the September 11th Victim Compensation Fund—a legislative compensation plan—contains a diverse catalogue of noneconomic losses.[27]

Many thousands of judicial decisions have reviewed the amount of damages awarded in tort litigation for personal injuries. A fundamental question about pain and suffering damages, in particular, is whether they should be awarded at all, since they "cannot logically be monetized or commodified."[28] At this basic level, the question is whether that kind of harm—and most people will attest that it is a harm—should be regarded as a loss, and therefore an injury, at all. Thus, in a curious way, the argument that noneconomic harm that is a form of personal injury is not a legally recognizable loss parallels the refusal of courts to recognize certain kinds of economic loss as remediable in tort. Yet another parallel appears in the body of decisions denying recovery for negligent infliction of emotional distress.

The general view throughout the United States is that despite the difficulty of assigning dollar values to intangibles like pain and suffering, they are a proper measure of damages. The idea has deep historical roots. For example, writing in the thirteenth century, Maimonides listed pain and suffering as one of the major categories of damages for injuries.[29] Once one adopts the view that dollar values may be assigned to such intangibles, questions arise about the proper amount. It is not an easy task to achieve equality of damage amounts among injuries. However, in reviewing damages, courts may consult both case law and published services that report amounts awarded for presumably comparable injuries in past cases—sources also used by lawyers plotting strategies for litigation.[30]

27. This list is quoted supra, chapter 3, text accompanying note 131.
28. Joseph King Jr., Pain and Suffering, Non-Economic Damages, and the Goals of Tort Law, 57 S.M.U. Law Review 163, 185 (2004).
29. Code of Maimonides Book Eleven: Book of Torts (Hyman Klein transl. Yale University Press 1954).
30. See, e.g., D'Amato v. Long Island Railroad Co., 874 F.Supp. 57, 59–60 (E.D.N.Y. 1995).

We have noted that often judges will respect amounts awarded by juries even if they would themselves give fewer dollars as compensation.[31] There are, however, many cases in which courts conclude that awards are too high. A wrenching example is a case involving what the court itself labeled the "enormous suffering" "endured" by a man who died from the asbestos-caused tumor mesothelioma, in which the jury awarded twelve million dollars for pain and suffering. Judge Leval wrote for a Second Circuit panel that thought it could not justify an award above $3.5 million dollars. He made it clear that one could not consider the question as a matter of exchange transactions: "We take it as a given that reasonable people of his age, in good mental and physical health, would not have traded one-quarter of his suffering for a hundred million dollars, much less twelve."[32] A similarly tormenting set of problems arises in cases where juries put dollar values on the mental anguish experienced by airplane passengers who know their plane is about to crash; one decision allowed an award of $15,000 for four to six seconds of pre-impact fear.[33]

The varied spectrum of tort categories of noneconomic damages raises questions about exactly what the injury is for which awards provide compensation. In the case of wage loss and medical bills, there is a measurable deprivation, that of funds in the family exchequer. Noneconomic damages like those for pain and suffering might be said to represent compensation for a kind of deprivation, that is, the ability to lead a pain-free life. Indeed, some decisions deal with the category labeled the "loss of enjoyment of life," which presents especially difficult puzzles when the plaintiff is in a coma or semicomatose. A view favoring plaintiffs in that kind of situation is that "[p]roof of the loss of enjoyment of life relates not to what is perceived by the injured plaintiff but to the objective total or partial limitations on an individual's activities imposed by an injury."[34] Still, as with noneconomic damages generally, the argument recurs that such awards have no concrete reference point, by contrast with medical bills and wage loss.

From a social welfare point of view, it may be asked whether the law governing tort damages should take into account need, as contrasted with deprivation. As we have noted, the rules for the September 11th Fund, though not the legislation, told the Special Master that he could take into account "the financial needs or financial resources of the claimant," a category outside the boundaries of tort law. Diverse views on the question of

31. See chapter 3, text accompanying note 125.
32. Consorti v. Armstrong World Industries, Inc., 72 F.3d 1003, 1009 (2d Cir. 1995).
33. Haley v. Pan American World Airways, 746 F.2d 311, 317–18 (5th Cir. 1984).
34. McDougald v. Garber, 504 N.Y.S.2d 383, 386 (Sup.Ct. 1986), aff'd, 524 N.Y.S.2d 192 (App.Div. 1988), aff'd as modified, 536 N.E.2d 372 (N.Y. 1989).

whether need is a circumstance relevant to injury awards reflect a serious difference of opinion on what constitutes an injury for purposes of the law of injuries.

Workers' compensation provides another viewpoint on the way injuries are defined both qualitatively and quantitatively. A significant part of workers' compensation law operates on the basis of schedules. In each state, it pays a percentage of the wages that a worker earned when he or she became disabled. It also "schedules" particular kinds of injuries, for example, the loss of a limb or even particular fingers, or the loss of an eye or of hearing in one or both ears.[35] Except insofar as it takes into account the nature of particular injuries when it sets dollar awards for them—the loss of an arm at the shoulder is worth $315,597 in Illinois and $70,228 in Mississippi—workers' compensation makes no specific provision for the typical tort categories of intangible losses, like pain and suffering.

Thus workers' compensation, like tort, provides examples of the fact that injury is, for purposes of the legal system, a social construct. Some harms that most people would consider injuries in a real sense, like pain and suffering, do not get separate recognition in workers' compensation, being deindividualized into schedules. In its workers' compensation branch, the injury law constitution therefore supplies a substantial amount of ledger space for considerations of administrative efficiency and social justice on a large scale alongside the individual justice provided by tort law.

Further by contrast, the way that different regulatory agencies implement safety statutes exhibits a great range of views about the value of life. Various agencies make very different assumptions about the value of life, as revealed by estimates of the cost that regulations place on industry relative to the amount of lives saved. Illustratively, as Cass Sunstein has pointed out, for OSHA alone calculations of costs per statistical life ranged from $100,000 for a 1990 electrical safety regulation to $98,000,000 per life for a 1989 lockout/tagout regulation.[36] The variations in these numbers present a wide spectrum of social constructs in society's definition of the human costs of injuries, insofar as they can be translated into currency. They display the elasticity of the injury law constitution, including the breadth of discretion it gives to decision makers about the very nature of cognizable injury. At some point this discretion may strain the bounds of the rationality required by the main Constitution, its range of variations being justifiable principally on grounds of the administrative necessities required by

35. See, e.g., U.S. Chamber of Commerce, Analysis of Workers' Compensation Laws 2006, e.g., at 51 ff (income benefits for total disability); 62 (income benefits for scheduled injuries).
36. See Cass Sunstein, Is OSHA Unconstitutional?, 94 Va. L. Rev. 1440–43 (2008), which includes three pages of tables on cost estimates for several agencies.

the variety of decision makers and the diversity of product and process hazards that require response by the legal system.

*** ***

Injury law deals with both individuals and large groups of people. It must resolve fundamental questions: What kinds of harms should the law define as injuries? Once a harm is defined as an injury, how do we value it? An important set of data—with elements of economics, public policy, and emotion—involves the social losses that injuries cause. The statistics we mentioned early in the chapter only suggest the financial detriment to society when people are killed in vehicle accidents or injured in workplaces. Injuries have broad consequences in society, not only in direct social outlays for medical care and hospitalization, but also in the loss of productivity. Beyond that, and less measurably, the statute that set up the September 11th Fund embodies an unusual acknowledgment, on behalf of the nation as a whole, of the toll that injuries take on society. It recognizes that the September 11th attacks were events that "burden[ed] the national soul,"[37] including "elements of need, sacrifice and destroyed expectations."[38]

We now see that there is a reciprocal relationship between the rights that we analyzed in chapter 3 and injuries. To define an injury, one must first refer it to a right, but in practice the valuation of injuries may give definition to rights. The law of injuries focuses on consequences to individuals. But the injury law constitution recognizes, often implicitly—in safety regulation, compensation schemes, and tort law—the benefits that individuals bestow on society and the losses that society suffers when individuals are hurt. The definition of cognizable injuries therefore reflects the fact that society derives all of its benefits from individuals, as individuals derive many of their benefits from society.

37. Marshall S. Shapo, Compensation for Victims of Terror: A Specialized Jurisprudence of Injury, 30 Hofstra L. Rev. 1245, 1252 (2002).
38. Marshall S. Shapo, Compensation for Victims of Terror 234 (Oceana Publications 2005).

CHAPTER 5
Mechanisms of the Law

Many social mechanisms provide the background for our injury law. These range from legislation and its implementation by agencies to courts to private agreements.

The textbook basis for all of these mechanisms, even the private ones, is representative democracy within a federal structure. The governmental structure is relevant to even private agreements because the interpretation of those agreements is often done through the regular court system, although sometimes it is done by private resolvers of disputes, such as arbitrators and mediators.

The federal structure of government is important in injury law because state and federal authorities, both legislators and judges, make rules and announce decisions that govern private actions. One consequence of the existence of fifty states is that at the threshold of litigation, courts often must decide whether they have jurisdiction over a case with contacts in more than one state. For example, can a Texas court entertain a case involving a product manufactured in Wisconsin, when the manufacturer made only occasional sales to Texas, but Texas is where the injury occurred?

A very different set of issues arises when a state court renders a decision on a subject covered by a law passed by Congress. A raft of decisions, including several Supreme Court decisions, deals with questions of whether federal legislation "preempts" state lawsuits; these questions may be decided by both federal courts and state courts confronted with injury cases. We provide specific examples in some detail later.[1] Although most of the preemption decisions on individual suits for personal injuries pertain to

---

1. See, e.g., *infra*, chapter 7, text accompanying notes 184–206.

federal statutes, the issue also arises when states pass laws dealing with safety.[2]

Thus, at every turn, the nature of our government affects decisions on whether courts should impose liability for injuries, with judges having to interpret laws establishing the regulatory agencies that set safety standards. The competing sovereignties of nation and state harbor an irony: One mantra of American politics is that one should prefer decentralized decision making that puts choices closer to the people. And yet, when federal courts decide that federal laws preempt state judicial decisions or regulations promulgated under state statutes, they are turning over the decision on the proper level of risk exposure to a more distant governmental authority.

PRIVATE CONTRACT

It is useful in this hierarchical legal environment to begin with the simplest form of decision making, that embodied in ordinary contracts. The ideal is that private agreement is the most efficient way for individuals to obtain goods or services from others, a way of doing business that is mercifully free from the heavy hand of government. But even here there are potential complications because many contracts involve large entities—corporations—dealing with atomized individuals who may lack information about the subject of the contract, and may also lack the bargaining power possessed by the firm. Situations of this kind sometimes generate disputes that go to judges. They may even evoke a response from legislators, as in laws that prohibit deceptive practices, or force corporations to build more safety into workplaces or to design products more safely or attach to products more powerful warnings about hazards. Often rules devised by legislatures and courts to require more protection of consumers and workers have rationales based in ideas of fairness and justice; but from the perspective of corporate decision makers, sometimes such rules undermine the efficiency achieved by private markets.

2. See, e.g., Dowhal v. SmithKline Beecham Consumer Health Care, 88 P.3d 1 (Cal. 2004) (FDA-mandated warning on over-the-counter antismoking products containing nicotine is preemptive of state regulations under Proposition 65, an initiative measure requiring warnings about products "known . . . to cause reproductive toxicity").

The interaction between courts and legislatures in injury law goes beyond the question of whether legislation preempts lawsuits. For example, when statutes bar litigation or limit damages previously allowed at common law, claimants may argue that the legislation is unconstitutional as a violation of due process of law or equal protection of the laws. Judicial decisions that such a statute is invalid often set off a ping-pong match between judges and legislators. Legislators will try to repair legislation to make it constitutional, and another round of litigation will ensue. An example is statutes limiting the amount of damages that medical malpractice claimants may recover for pain and suffering. Some courts have ruled that such legislation denies equal protection on the ground that it treats medical malpractice plaintiffs unequally with plaintiffs in other injury cases. Courts employ various technical means of analysis to resolve such questions, but it seems plausible that their beliefs—even their feelings—about the nature of such injuries may sometimes incline them to the conclusion that the legislation is unconstitutional. They can "feel the pain" of a severely injured patient.

Like actors throughout the private economy as well as other parts of government, judges are inclined to be protective of their domains. Another judicial technique involves the use of what are known as "open courts" provisions in state constitutions. For example, the Ohio constitution provides that "[a]ll courts shall be open, and every person, for an injury done him . . . shall have remedy by due course of law, and shall have justice administered without denial or delay."[3] The Ohio Supreme Court used this provision in declaring unconstitutional a statute of repose that barred suits filed more than four years after the construction of an "improvement to real property," when the improvement at issue was constructed twenty-eight years before the litigated accident and the plaintiff sued within a year after the accident. As we previously noted, the legislation effectively put the plaintiffs in a catch-22 situation.[4]

The basis for the open courts provisions and the philosophy they embody goes all the way back to Magna Carta, which declared, "[t]o no one will we sell, deny or delay right or justice."[5] Originally designed as a check on the power of the king and other officials, in modern times the idea has been

---

3. Ohio Const. Art. I §16 (current through 2010).
4. Brennaman v. R.M.I. Co., 639 N.E.2d 425, 430 (Ohio 1994), quoted in chapter 1, text accompanying note 25.
5. Magna Carta, clause 40 (1215).

used to put an exclamation mark on decisions in various kinds of lawsuits. A famous statement that has been quoted in litigation against public officials is John Marshall's proclamation in the first major constitutional law case, *Marbury v. Madison*, that "[t]he very essence of civil liberty certainly consists in the right of every individual to claim the protection of the laws, whenever he receives an injury."[6] As this much-cited proclamation indicates, it is the idea of injury that supports the "open courts" concept, and pushes judges in the direction of opening the courthouse door.

Interpretation of Statutory Terms

An important zone of interaction concerning legislation has to do with rules adopted by safety agencies to further the purposes of statutes. Here the relationship among parts of government becomes triangular, with the court deciding whether agency rules fit within the purposes of laws passed by the legislature. The legislative history of a statute, including declarations by its sponsors about its purpose, will affect the court's view of an agency's regulation. A case that went all the way to the Supreme Court involved workers who refused to carry out a foreman's orders, which they believed exposed them to the "imminent" hazard of death or serious injury. The Court drew on a history that included a Congressional intent to reduce the level of individual injuries, as contrasted with a desire to make accident levels more efficient. As we noted in chapter 3, a senatorial sponsor of the legislation had said he believed that the safety of workers should not be subject to "the indifference of some cost accountants."[7]

Multiple Parties

An element of litigation increasingly pertinent to injury law is the presence of multiple parties. The traditional model is that of a suit by one plaintiff against one defendant. Today, though, there are many situations in which numerous claimants seek to sue several defendants for what the claimants allege are similar if not identical kinds of injuries. We noted above that suits for multiple deaths in a plane crash present a relatively simple problem from the standpoint of case management. The matter becomes more complicated, sometimes by orders of magnitude, when a large number of plaintiffs

---

6. Marbury v. Madison, 1 Cranch 137, 163 (1803).
7. Whirlpool Corp. v. Marshall, 445 U.S. 1, 12 n.16 (1980).

sue a maker of different types of products or a firm or firms engaged in an activity alleged to have caused hundreds of thousands of injuries. An extraordinary example that arose as I wrote this chapter was the metaphorical flood of litigation emanating from the literal flood of oil from the BP gusher. Here, thousands of claimants attributed business losses to not only BP but other firms involved in the construction or maintenance of the oil rig that exploded. Variations appear in suits against multiple defendants who have contributed to the pollution of a stream or farm, or who have made an undifferentiated group of toxic products used in the workplace.[8] When "mass tort" suits spread across the nation, one administrative solution is to create a special court for "multi-district litigation" to handle all cases involving a common subject matter, for example, breast implants. Another management technique is the class action, for which court systems have developed a complex set of rules. The application of some of those rules may sink class litigation before it starts.

Duty as a Limitation on Liability

A very different kind of limitation that courts place on injury litigation applies when there is a significant difference in time or distance between the careless conduct of a defendant and an injury to a plaintiff, or when the injury occurs in an unusual way. In cases of this kind, which we will discuss further below, courts rejecting liability will say that the plaintiff's injury was "unforeseeable," or that it was too "remote" from the defendant's conduct or was not "proximately caused" by it, or that generally the defendant did not owe a "duty" to the plaintiff with respect to that type of injury. The case becomes especially difficult for the plaintiff when the most obvious cause of an injury is the intentional act of a third person who is unavailable for suit— in the most exaggerated case, a crime—and the plaintiff sues a solvent and available defendant on grounds that it carelessly disregarded the possibility of that act occurring. An especially poignant example of this problem is the suits filed by survivors of September 11th victims against the airlines whose planes were commandeered by the hijackers, against the maker of the planes, and against the owner and operators of the World Trade Center. The defendants argued strongly that it was stretching their duty too far to hold

8. See, e.g., Bockrath v. Aldrich Chem. Co., 980 P.2d 398 (Cal. 1999) (55 defendants, remanded following dismissal by lower courts).

them responsible for the dastardly acts of the terrorists, although a preliminary decision favored the plaintiffs.[9]

Patterns and Particularities

Difficult problems in injury law, as in much of law generally, arise from the
particularity of fact situations. A perennial activity of those who define and
interpret legal principles is the search for similarities in cases that would
help to assure consistency of treatment. Complicating the quest for consistency are differences in the facts of cases, as well as differences in individuals. As we have explained, courts frequently reject class actions because of
such differences. These may lie in the varieties of injuries of which plaintiffs
complain. Or they may lie in the alleged causes of injury—as we have noted,
a dozen or even thousands of different kinds of needles used in medical
practice.[10]

In a great series of lectures in the nineteenth century, Holmes explained
the value of discerning patterns in types of injury-causing episodes. When
one found a pattern, then one could establish a rule that time after time
would cover specific cases that fit within that pattern. But when a case did
not fit within a pattern, it would have to be turned over to a jury for determination of how a general rule (for example, the rule that one should behave
reasonably in the circumstances) applied to the facts. Holmes preferred the
fashioning of standards that governed patterns, and indeed said that an
experienced judge would "acquire a fund of experience which enables him
to represent the common sense of the community in ordinary instances far
better than the average jury."[11] However, he acknowledged that "[t]he trouble with many cases of negligence is . . . that they are of a kind not frequently
recurring, so as to enable any given judge to profit by long experience with
juries to lay down rules"—cases in which "the elements are so complex
that courts are glad to leave the whole matter in a lump to the jury's
determination."[12]

A massive antidote to particularization of remedies for injuries appears
in the workers' compensation system. There, the law deindividualizes both
injury occurrences and the amount of compensation. Generally, it strips

9. In re Sept. 11th Litig., 780 F.Supp.2d 279 (S.D.N.Y. 2003).
10. See Grant v. Becton Dickinson & Co., 2003 WL 21267787, at 7–8, Prod. Liab. Rep.
¶16,656, at 59,659 (Ohio Ct. App. June 3, 2003), discussed in chapter 3, text accompanying
note 86.
11. O.W. Holmes Jr., The Common Law 124 (Little Brown 1881).
12. *Id.* at 129.

from particular cases the question of fault—of both employers and employees. And it also strips out specific sensitivities and life situations of injured employees when it determines the amount of awards. Instead, it leaves that amount to "schedules"—standardized amounts. Tied to charts with columns of predetermined numbers, the system awards so much for an arm and so much for a leg, with no specific recognition of individual pain, suffering, and inconvenience.

Even in the realm of tort litigation, there exists a desire to regularize legal rules as much as possible. We referred to this goal earlier with respect to damages amounts.[13]

A different question, concerning categories of plaintiffs, arises from an increasing diversity of population: whether product makers must give hazard warnings in languages other than English. A California case, involving severe effects of a dose of aspirin on a four-month-old child, drew very different responses from an appellate court and the state supreme court. The plaintiff's mother, who bought the aspirin and gave it to the child, knew only Spanish and she did not ask English-speaking household members to translate the label, which contained a warning about the danger of administering aspirin to young children. The appellate court favored the plaintiff, pointing out that the product had been "advertised in the Spanish media, both radio and television," and noting that the manufacturer "knew Hispanics were an important part of the market" for the product and that "Hispanics often maintain their first language rather than learn English."[14]

The supreme court, however, viewed the issue of whether there must be Spanish language warnings as being a question for the legislature, which had the ability to collect "empirical data" and to consider "the viewpoints of all interested parties." It illustrated the complexity of the subject with references to such elements of the problem as the costs of translation, "the feasibility of targeted distribution of products with bilingual or multilingual packaging," and "the number of persons likely to benefit from warning in a particular language"[15]—in that regard, the appellate court had acknowledged that "over 148 languages are spoken in the United States."[16]

Even a decision in a case arising in bilingual Puerto Rico took the same position. In that case, which involved a cleaning product ignited by sparks from a welding torch, the First Circuit noted that while regulations under the Federal Hazardous Substances Act required manufacturers to provide

13. See, e.g., chapter 4, text accompanying notes 29–30.
14. Ramirez v. Plough, Inc., 12 Cal.Rptr.2d 423, 430 (App.Ct. 1992).
15. Ramirez v. Plough, Inc., 863 P.2d 167, 176 (Cal. 1993).
16. Ramirez, 12 Cal.Rptr.2d at 430.

warnings in English, they said only that employers "may maintain copies in other languages as well."[17]

Different Roles of Courts and Legislatures

The allocation of lawmaking tasks between legislatures and courts is complex. Legislatures can do things that our legal traditions do not permit courts to do. A powerful illustration, as we have noted, is the creation of broad no-fault systems of compensation. The amount of money transferred to employees under workers' compensation laws, which are everywhere legislative, is significantly greater than that which changes hands under tort judgments. Those laws overrode the judge-made tort law requirement that employees prove employers were at fault and indeed the rules that allowed employers to use the careless conduct of workers to block tort claims. No-fault statutes for injuries caused by motoring accidents also accomplish compensation goals that are unavailable under tort law.

Moreover, there are differences between courts and legislatures in the standards for what constitutes reasoned judgment. Courts are relatively meticulous about stating the reasons for their decisions, anchoring those decisions where possible in precedent and sometimes constructing elaborate rationalizations where precedent is not available. By contrast, when courts review statutes for constitutionality, they often hold legislatures to a standard requiring only that a statute have some rational basis, emphasizing that they do not review statutes for their wisdom.

However, as we have noted, sometimes courts do find that statutes are not rationally related to their subject matter or that they treat some classes of people unequally. And even when a legislature enters the field, courts may remain to some extent in the grip of principles they have established in decisions under the common law. As I have suggested elsewhere concerning state statutes that effect changes in legal doctrines governing products injuries, one does not have to think that judge-made laws "represent Platonic forms" to believe that the "injury problems associated with products fall into broad, repetitious patterns" and to believe that, even when legislatures have passed products liability statutes, courts judging products cases will draw on lines of reasoning they adopted in their prior decisions at common law.[18]

17. Torres-Rios v. LPS Labs., Inc., 152 F.3d 11, 13 (1st Cir. 1998).
18. See, e.g., 1 Marshall S. Shapo, The Law of Products Liability §7.06 (5th ed. 2010), citing Harvey v. General Motors Corp., 739 P.2d 763 (Wyo. 1987), in which the court says that a prior decision should apply retrospectively as well as prospectively. Referring to its statement

A variety of institutions speak for society. Legislatures pass safety statutes and no-fault compensation laws, and sometimes legislation that cuts back on tort remedies—for example by imposing caps on damage amounts. Courts continue to decide tort cases with many individual factual variations, of the sort that legislatures flatten out when they pass compensation statutes. Despite the priority of legislation in the hierarchy of law, tort law continues to provide a means of achieving individualized justice.

In the development of tort law, judges sometimes articulate the moral basis for the precedents they set. At the same time, juries—a social mechanism that is unusually if not uniquely American in its function in injury cases—provide a special form of decision making in the definition of rights and the valuation of injuries. Often juries apply general legal principles on which judges have instructed them to facts developed in the evidence that the parties put before them, and thus play a role in the crevices of the law. Jurors decide, for example, whether on a trial record a physician has behaved below the appropriate standard of care or whether a product is unreasonably dangerous.

We should note, somewhat by contrast, a more technical aspect of judging which falls under the label of "judicial administration." As we have observed, judges—like any other public authorities not to mention officials of private companies—jealously guard their preserves. A threshold barrier lies in the question of whether a case is subject to judgment by courts at all. Illustratively, the issue arises in environmental litigation when an individual claimant sues to prevent pollution of a broad area rather than only to protect her own property. Sometimes courts will bar such persons from litigation, indicating that they lack the "standing to sue" that might be granted to others—for example, a public official or perhaps a well-established environmental group. The issue is basically whether it is the plaintiff's ox that is being gored—truly a question of whether that plaintiff in particular has been injured.

Preemption and Democracy

The preemption cases in injury law that we mentioned in the Introduction and will discuss in later chapters, particularly cases in the area of products liability,[19] present some interesting problems in the operation of a

---

of rationales for strict liability in the precedent, the court says that "[n]o justification exists why such reasoning is any less applicable when applied before" the date of the prior case.

19. See references mentioned in note 1 *supra*.

representative democracy. These problems involve as many as three, four, or even five levels of decision making on acceptable levels of risk. One may discern patterns like this:

- Congress passes a statute governing safety, for example, the Food, Drug and Cosmetic Act.
- The FDA promulgates a regulation governing the labelling of a prescription drug.
- When a consumer sues for injuries she attributes to the drug, a court must decide whether the Act preempts the suit on the ground that it fully occupies the field of drug safety.
- If the court holds against preemption, it defines for the jury the law governing the duty to warn of product hazards and the adequacy of warnings, taking into account the rule which says that drug makers may avoid liability if they give effective warnings about drug hazards to "learned intermediaries"—usually physicians—rather than to patients.
- The jury, with the judge's instructions as guides, renders a verdict on whether the drug maker had to warn the consumer directly and whether the warning was adequate—as well as whether the drug caused the consumer's injuries. If the verdict is for the plaintiff, the jury assigns a dollar value to her injuries.

Such cases involve American democracy across a range of applications. A statute passed by Congress, implemented by a regulatory agency, is a powerful articulation of the will of the people. The court, acting as a learned legal intermediary, makes a series of judgments that apply a translation of that collective will to a case involving scientific evidence and the effectiveness of communication. A jury verdict is a focused judgment on specific evidence by randomly selected representatives of the community.

Uncertainty or Ignorance about the Law

The actions of these varied social mechanisms thus articulate society's views about risk and the nature of injury, as well as about the worth of injuries in dollars. Entangled with this complex decision making process are problems involving knowledge of the law. The business that is planning to spend a lot of money on developing and marketing a new product is concerned about the imprecision of legal rules and the uncertainty of outcomes in potential litigation. A consumer who buys a product may have little or no understanding of the legal force of disclaimers or clauses limiting the liability of the seller; to borrow language from a century-old case quoted above, the consumer may be unthinking, ignorant, or gullible.

Scientific Uncertainty

A set of uncertainties outside the law that afflicts the administration of injury law are scientific uncertainties. A growing catalog of cases deals with the problem of scientific evidence under the general guidance of the Supreme Court's decision in *Daubert v. Merrell Dow Pharmaceuticals, Inc.,*[20] in which the key evidentiary question was whether an antinausea drug administered to the plaintiff's mother had caused birth defects. The Court in that case decided that a prior standard, which required parties to show that their scientific testimony had "general acceptance in the particular field in which it belongs," was too stringent. Instead, it set out a group of general guidelines, which it indicated were not mandatory or exhaustive, for the testing of scientific evidence. These included the question of whether the "theory or technique" offered by the party advancing the evidence "can be (and has been) tested" and whether it had "been subjected to peer review and publication." The Court did say that "'general acceptance' can yet have a bearing on the inquiry" and that "[w]idespread acceptance can be an important factor in ruling particular evidence admissible," while also quoting a precedent on the obverse point that "'a known technique which has been able to attract only minimal support within the community' . . . may properly be viewed with skepticism."[21]

Among the many cases involving the admissibility of scientific evidence, a pair of federal appellate decisions, both involving breast implants, provides illustrations of the difficulty of decision making in this area. In one case, although there was "no solid body of epidemiological evidence to review," the Ninth Circuit allowed testimony for the plaintiff by "a recognized expert on the immunological effects of silicone in the human body," based on the expert's "experience as a toxicologist, his review of medical records" and studies by the defendant, and his "general scientific knowledge of silicone's ability to cause immune disorders as established by animal studies and biophysical data." The court also allowed testimony by an expert "based on scientific studies he authored" and "his participation in a preliminary epidemiological study involving over 200 women." Undoubtedly

20. 509 U.S. 579 (1993).
21. 509 U.S. at 593–94.

persuasive on the admissibility of that witness's testimony was the fact that he had examined the plaintiff and found "evidence of silicone in her tissue and . . . symptoms consistent with exposure to silicone."[22]

A contrast appears in a Tenth Circuit decision involving the same type of product. Agreeing with the trial court that "epidemiology is the best evidence of general causation in a toxic tort case," the appellate court observed that "the body of epidemiology largely finds no association between silicone breast implants and immune system diseases." It declared that the plaintiff's experts had "completely ignored or discounted without explanation the many epidemiological studies which found no medically reliable link between silicone breast implants and systemic diseases." On the separate question of whether the defendant's implant specifically caused the plaintiff's disease, the court pointed out that the plaintiff's experts had agreed that "[a]t best, silicone-associated connective tissue disease is an untested hypothesis" and said it would not "allow the jury to speculate based on an expert's testimony which relies only on clinical experience in the absence of showing a consistent statistically significant association between breast implants and systemic disease." The court also noted that the opinions of the plaintiff's experts had not been "peer-reviewed," and it twice pointed out that those opinions were not "generally accepted by the relevant scientific community"—borrowing from the Supreme Court's statement that general acceptance could still play a part in such decisions.[23]

The lay reader may be forgiven a baffled belief that she is watching two different history plays when the historical subject seems to be the same. She is, but she isn't: she is observing two different courts responding to testimony by different sets of witnesses about the effects of similar products on the physiologies of two different women. Throughout the realm of chemical and biochemical products, divergent outcomes of this type can occur. This sort of apparent diversity in results is almost unavoidable in technically complicated areas of science to which the law must address itself.

The difficulty of pinning the admissibility of scientific evidence to just one or two factors is evident in another court's listing of no fewer than nine "indicia of reliability" for expert testimony—and this in a case involving a mechanical product, a forklift, rather than a chemical one. Those factors included whether an expert had "identified and discussed any relevant federal design or performance standards" and whether he had "supported his conclusions through discussion of the relevant literature, broadly defined." Among other factors the court mentioned were the "design history" of the

22. Hopkins v. Dow Corning Corp., 33 F.3d 1116, 1124–25 (9th Cir. 1994).
23. Harris v. Baxter Healthcare Corp., 397 F.3d 878, 882–87 (10th Cir. 2005).

product and its "accident history," as well as the "centrality of scientific test-ing" and "the court's scrutiny of the soundness of that testing."[24]

Quantitative Standards

Although courts cast most of their decisions on admissibility of scientific evidence in prose, they have on occasion referred to numerical standards for proof of causation with respect to the increase in the risk of diseases associated with particular substances. In a New Jersey case dealing with colon cancer allegedly caused by asbestos, the appellate court affirmed a dismissal, finding insufficient an expert's testimony on a relative risk of colon cancer of 1.55, a figure derived from a study of 17,800 asbestos insu-lators. The appellate court referred to case law that required at least a dou-bling of the risk "to be statistically significant."[25] The New Jersey Supreme Court, however, reversed. It said that "a relative risk of 2.0 is not so much a password to a finding of causation as one piece of evidence, among others, for the court to consider in determining whether the expert has employed a sound methodology in reaching his or her conclusion." As factors possibly relevant in this inquiry that required assessment by the trial court, the supreme court referred to the expert's "assumption that the decedent's asbestos exposure was like that of the members of the study population" and his "assumption concerning the absence of other risk factors."[26]

In another case that also involved alleged causation of colon cancer by asbestos, the Second Circuit rejected its trial court's blanket opposition to evidence of standardized mortality ratios of less than 1.5, levels that the trial court had said were "statistically insignificant." The appellate court found potentially persuasive evidence in conclusions by regulatory agencies—the Occupational Safety and Health Administration and the Environmental Protection Agency—that "a strong casual link does exist between asbestos exposure and gastrointestinal cancer, including colon cancer."[27]

Quite as much detail, and sometimes more, is evident in public regula-tion of product hazards. Sometimes statutes and regulations set standards on a very quantitative basis. One example is the definition of "highly toxic" substances under the Federal Hazardous Substances Act, under which one of three tests is so precise that it asks whether a chemical "[p]roduces death within fourteen days in half or more than half of a group of ten or more

24. Milanowicz v. Raymond Corp., 148 F.Supp.2d 525, 532–36 (D.N.J. 2001).
25. Landrigan v. Celotex Corp., 579 A.2d 1268, 1272 (N.J. App. Div. 1990).
26. Landrigan v. Celotex Corp., 605 A.2d 1079, 1087–88 (N.J. 1992).
27. In re Joint S. & E. Asbestos Litig., 52 F.3d 1124, 1135 (2d Cir. 1995).

white laboratory rats weighing between two hundred and three hundred grams, at a single dose of fifty milligrams or less per kilogram of body weight, when orally administered."[28] A behavioral way to put a safety standard into numbers appears in a regulation under the Poison Prevention Packaging Act, which focuses on the amount of time it takes children of specific young ages to open a container.[29]

Quantifying Lives

We referred in chapter 4 to another number-oriented angle on the injury problem, which appears in attempts to quantify the value of human life employed in safety standards put out by various agencies. These numbers have recently ranged from the $6.9 million value calculated by the EPA in 2008—down about $1 million from five years before—to $5 million per life estimated by the Consumer Product Safety Commission in a proposal concerning furniture fires, and "two separate values" of $3 million and $6 million used by the Customs and Border Patrol concerning a proposal on air travel security.[30]

A contrast to these very numerical standards appears in the FDA's proposal of criteria for when a patient can gain access to an experimental drug for which evidence about its effects "has not been entirely collected or has been collected but not yet analyzed and reviewed by the agency."[31] These criteria for patient access, which now appear in a regulation, included the existence of a "serious or life-threatening disease or condition" for which there is "no comparable or satisfactory alternative therapy," evidence of "potential patient benefit" that would justify the "potential risks of the treatment use," and a showing that the risks of the drug would not be "unreasonable in the context of the disease or condition." Another criterion was that an expanded access use would not "interfere with the initiation, conduct, or completion of clinical investigations that could support marketing approval of" that use or "otherwise compromise" its "potential development."[32]

This collection of standards—some precisely arithmetical, some involving numerical estimates, and others pitched in more abstract language and

---

28. 15 U.S.C.A., §1261(h)(1)(effective Aug. 14, 2008).

29. 16 C.F.R. §1700.20 (2011).

30. http://www.ombwatch.org/node/3205, printed Sept. 11, 2011. On costs per statistical life, see also chapter 4, text accompanying note 36.

31. Proposed Rule, Expanded Access to Investigational Drugs for Treatment Use, 71 Fed. Reg. 75155 (Dec. 14, 2006).

32. 21 C.F.R. §312.305 (effective Oct. 13, 2009).

requiring some interpretation—illustrates the range of judgments in public law about both the quantification of injuries and the definition of rights linked to those standards, sometimes implicitly and sometimes explicitly. They parallel the efforts of courts to establish evidentiary standards in tort cases, most often in prose but sometimes in numbers, for the admissibility of expert testimony on scientific issues. Operating under the umbrella of the injury law constitution, all of these standards are products of the vast mechanisms of injury law.

CHAPTER 6
Legal Doctrine

The way that our law defines rights and injuries within the context of power relationships, and under the umbrella of various social mechanisms, requires the application of many concepts that courts, legislatures, and safety agencies have developed over the years.

Tort law has employed a cluster of basic ideas as foundations for decision making about responsibility for injuries. The words that identify these legal doctrines and theories are familiar to every lawyer, more or less. However, it has been my experience that the familiarity of many lawyers with these doctrines, although they fall trippingly from the tongue, is often rather less than more. In this chapter I seek to define the meanings that have become attached to some words of legal doctrine that are often employed, words which are labels for basic ideas.

Risk. A principal basis for tort liability lies in the defendant's exposure of the plaintiff to risk—for these purposes, a probability of the kinds of losses the law calls injuries. Exposure of others to risk is fundamental to the liability doctrines based on culpability and also to theories of liability for behavior that is not culpable but exposes others to hazards to which people in general are not exposed.

Fault. A principal basis for tort liability is the fault of the defendant. The word fault, and its siblings culpability and blameworthiness, sound moral overtones. These terms include the idea of a breach of socially defined standards for the protection of others against harm. Whether those assessing acts at issue in litigation are philosophers, economists, or men and women in the street, to say someone's conduct was at fault means that she should, or ought to, have behaved otherwise. The idea of what a person should have done, or refrained from doing, often varies with the observer. Many economists, for example, will say that "should" takes its principal meaning from the result that would produce the most goods for society as a whole at the least cost. Others will stress that the test for culpability depends on such factors as reciprocity of risk, or decency, or morally based norms.

All of these words are slippery. You can get a sense of how difficult it is to define them by thinking about the images they raise in your mind. Some people thinking about blameworthiness may picture someone in stocks in Puritan New England. Others, asked what culpability means, may visualize a fire-and-brimstone preacher shaming a congregation member. Some will associate the word *fault* with a mental picture of an inadvertent careless act; others may visualize a deliberate, if noncriminal, act that imperils others. The images may be as varied as the number of people who are asked to define these terms.

Intentional torts. There is some loose agreement about the law governing the most culpable end of the spectrum of human behavior that causes injury. At one pole are acts that are deliberate in the extreme, sometimes involving malice in the ordinary lay meaning of the term. Here, it is understatement to speak of the creation of risk. The defendant means to hurt someone and does. An unprovoked punch on the jaw is a battery under tort law, as it is under criminal law. A battery is the classic intentional tort.

One step down the ladder of culpability is a definition of "intentional" that does not require the kind of mean behavior intended to do harm illustrated by the unprovoked punch. In wrestling with the definition of what constitutes "intent" for an "intentional tort," a succession of scholars has settled on a definition that requires a showing that the defendant "acts knowing that the consequence is substantially certain to result."[1] That simple definition, in the Third Restatement of Torts, is a variation of language in the first and second Restatements. The drafters of the first Restatement required at least "knowledge" on the part of the defendant that a harmful contact, or apprehension of a contact (such apprehension being technically an assault, rather than a battery) "is substantially certain to be produced."[2] The Second Restatement set as the minimum standard that the defendant "believes that the consequences are substantially certain to result" from his act,[3] adding that if the defendant "knows that the consequences are certain, or substantially certain, to result from his act, and still goes ahead, he is treated by the law as if he had in fact desired to produced the result."[4]

The First Restatement's version of the "substantially certain" formula provided a basis for a court to conclude that a five-year-old boy might be

---

1. Restatement (Third) of Torts: Liability for Physical and Emotional Harm §1(b)(2010).
2. Restatement of Torts §13 cmt. d (1934).
3. Restatement (Second) of Torts §8A (1965).
4. *Id.* cmt. b.

liable for a battery when he allegedly pulled a chair out from under an elderly neighbor[5]—a case still used to introduce this minimum standard for battery to law students. Recently, the formula has found a set of applications in workers' compensation law—specifically in exceptions that some states make for "intentional wrongs" as against the general rule that employees covered by workers' compensation cannot sue their employers for tort liability. One example is a New Jersey case in which an employer disabled a guard on an industrial machine and would temporarily restore the guard only when OSHA inspectors came to the plant. The plaintiff had had some "close calls" with the unguarded machine, but when he asked his supervisor to restore the guard, the supervisor said there was "not a problem" and walked away. With evidence that the employer had "deliberately and systematically deceive[d] OSHA into believing that the machine [was] guarded," the court said that the employee could sue his employer in tort for an "intentional wrong," overcoming the exclusive remedy provision of workers' compensation. It concluded that a jury could have decided that the employer "knew that it was substantially certain that the removal of the safety guard would result eventually in injury to one of its employees."[6] It is not likely that the supervisor's brush-off of the employee's complaint was born of viciousness—the sort of conduct that the term "intentional" would signify to many lay people. But the decision indicates that the conduct had a degree of culpability that fit into the broad definition the Restatements use for the concept of "intent" in tort.

Paralleling the definition of intent for the purposes of "intentional torts" is the body of case law that loosely defines the requirements for awarding punitive damages. As we have noted above,[7] courts use several adjectives for that purpose, including the term intentional. As with the definition of "intent" for intentional torts, they do not require malice in the common use of the term. Yet they try to capture a type of behavior that people generally would find particularly odious. As we pointed out, one of the Supreme Court's favorite words in the punitive damages context is "reprehensible." Another term courts employ in the discourse of punitive damages is "outrage," a word that does double duty as an element of the tort of intentional infliction of emotional distress. The type of behavior that justifies punitive awards must be egregious, conspicuously bad—something that sticks out in our culture like the proverbial sore thumb. The stoning of rape victims

---

5. Garratt v. Dailey, 279 P.2d 1091, 1093–95 (Wash. 1955).
6. Laidlaw v. Hariton Mach. Co., 790 A.2d 884, 897–98 (N.J. 2002).
7. See chapter 3, text accompanying notes 78–81.

may be countenanced by Shari'a, but it would occasion punitive damages (among other punishments) in American law.

In any event, intent and its cousins occupy the worst end of the culpability spectrum in tort law—although the concept of "substantial certainty" as a definition for intent in the intentional torts may be applied in a way that diminishes the moral flavor of intentionality. The spectrum of culpability that tort law paints moves down from intent to recklessness; sometimes courts use the adjectival triad of "wanton, willful and reckless conduct," a somewhat amorphous category that requires a plaintiff to show that a defendant acted without regard to the consequences of his act. The line that divides recklessness from substantial certainty is a blurry one, and for certain legal purposes, in some states a showing of reckless conduct will give a plaintiff a boost—for example rendering her eligible for punitive damages. The next step along the spectrum is "gross negligence." Dismissively described simply as a "vituperative epithet," it is the kind of bridge category distinction that lawyers love, although it has limited practical application between the categories of recklessness and negligence on either side of it.

Negligence. Negligence occupies the heartland of fault territory in tort and indeed occupies a central zone of tort doctrine in general. There are many different definitions of negligence, all pivoting in one way or another on the idea that a defendant has not behaved with reasonable care. They include the terminology of "ordinary care and skill,"[8] "ordinary prudence,"[9] acts that expose a person to "an unreasonable risk of harm,"[10] a failure to "exercise reasonable care under the circumstances,"[11] conduct the risk of which outweighs its utility,[12] acts the cost of which outweighs the cost of avoiding injury,[13] and acts whose risks exceed their benefits.[14] Also in the lexicon of the definition of negligence are the foreseeability of injuries[15] and its cousin, the question of whether the defendant "should have known" of the risk of injury.[16] The zoo of negligence standards is yet more complicated. Sometimes negligence may be a failure to measure up to the "state of the art," a phrase for which courts have used four or five different definitions.[17]

8. Heaven v. Pender, [1883] 11 Q.B.D. 503, 509.

9. Oliver Wendell Holmes Jr., The Common Law 106, 108 (Little Brown 1881).

10. Restatement (Second) of Torts §282 (1965).

11. Restatement (Third) of Torts §3 (2010).

12. Restatement (Second) of Torts §291.

13. See, e.g., U.S. v. Carroll Towing Co., 159 F.2d 169, 173 (2d Cir. 1947).

14. See, e.g., Barker v. Lull Eng'g Co., 573 P.2d 443, 456 (Cal. 1978) (alternative standard).

15. See, e.g., The Nitro-Glycerine Case, Parrot v. Wells, Fargo, & Co., 82 U.S. (15 Wall.) 524 (1872). (defendants "innocently ignorant" of explosiveness of contents of box).

16. See, e.g., McEwen v. Ortho Pharm. Corp., 528 P.2d 522, 530 (Or. 1974) ("knows, or has reason to know").

17. See, e.g., 1 Marshall S. Shapo, The Law of Products Liability chapter 10 (5th ed. 2010).

Some other, rather general concepts have been used to describe what negligence is: It can be said to be a breach of duty, with the question of whether a duty exists being a separable issue. And it can be labeled a violation of the relevant standard of care. So we can speak of a trio of synonyms to describe this fundamental question: the negligence issue, the standard of care issue, and the breach of duty issue.

This list of formulas for the negligence standard, both general and specific, is not exhaustive. And it does not exhaust the dimensions of negligence. The question of what is reasonable depends, as one of the definitions above makes explicit, on the circumstances—the particular context of the defendant's conduct. Thus, the idea of negligence takes its meaning from particular activities and processes: the maintenance of workplaces, the enforcement of discipline in schools, the setting up of places of recreation, the operation of motor vehicles and other means of transportation, and a wide range of professional practice including medicine, accounting, and the practice of law itself. The definition also becomes particularized to specific kinds of products alleged to be negligently made or sold: negligence takes on specific meanings with reference to the design of industrial machines, the labeling or promotion of medical products, and the precautions used in the preparation and sale of foods.

I have, for convenience, referred to negligent acts and activities, but even that does not give a complete picture of the strata of human behavior that present the question of what reasonable care is. As I indicated in chapter 3, negligence may be omissions as well as acts, and those definitions overlap. If a mechanic does not fully tighten a bolt on an automobile wheel, we could call that a negligent act or a careless omission. If he forgets to do it at all, that would be a negligent omission, and subject to suit just as if he had fallen below the ordinary standard in the way he tightened the same bolt. Even here there are definitional nuances. Lawyers often use terms like "failure to act" to describe situations like the one where someone does not come to the aid of another in peril. While linguistically, neglect to tighten a bolt at all might be classified as a failure to act, as a practical matter, lawyers would often lump that omission with the category of careless acts.

Legal theology posits that negligence is governed by an "objective" test, one that measures the conduct of all people by a minimum standard that, as we have noted, does not vary with the intellectual capacity of individuals or their state of alertness at the moment an injury occurs. Were that not the general standard, we would forever have to delve into people's minds to decide what their particular understandings of a situation were. This could result in a set of sympathetic decisions based on personal idiosyncrasies. So the basic standard is an objective one. But there are exceptions. One example at the low end of individual capacities is a forgiving standard for children. At the high end, rigorous standards exist for professionals; a neurologist doing a diagnosis must meet the ordinary standards for neurologists, however much out of the realm of possibility those standards are for laymen, or even for pediatric oncologists.

American courts faced with hard cases on negligence issues often resort to considerations of policy. On occasion, they make judgments about the social worth of activities.[18] They also may consider whether the ultimate purpose of a product or activity—for example, the alleviation of disease or the transportation of people and goods or the construction of a building—can be achieved in a less risky way than the defendant chose.[19]

*** ***

Inevitably, judges bring to decisions about injuries their own biases, conscious or semiconscious, about risk and fault. Some may be personally averse to risk, or believe that society is best served by a conservative approach to risk. Others may fervently believe in the benefits that may accrue to society from risk-taking, especially in the form of innovation. That view may coincide, to one degree or another, with a Darwinian view of human existence. In a parallel set of philosophical differences, some decision makers will base their views of blameworthiness on an economic conception of human life, while others will adhere to a more ethically oriented set of premises.

Liability without fault. The domain of fault bulks large in our injury law, and as we have suggested, often comes with emotive connotations. Yet some significant wedges of that body of law provide a basis for awarding compensation without a showing of fault on the part of those who cause injury, both under tort and statutory compensation systems. Quite separately, the law provides regulatory prohibitions or limitations on conduct which do not involve findings of fault, but rather involve policy choices about levels of acceptable risk.

Strict liability for activities. There is a substantial swath of territory in judge-made tort law in which courts impose what they call liability without fault, or strict liability. Some observers may believe that in most cases the label of strict liability in tort signifies nothing more than the imposition of an exceptionally high standard of care—a "super-care"—rather than a true liability without fault. There has been an academic argument about what

18. See Restatement (Second) of Torts §292(a)(1965) (referring to "the social value which the law attaches to the interest which is to be advanced or protected by the conduct").

19. See *id.* at §292(c) (referring to "the extent of the chance that such interest can be adequately advanced or protected by another and less dangerous course of conduct").

the theory of liability truly was in England as far back as the fourteenth century. One twentieth-century writer, later a federal judge, stood up for a strict liability interpretation. Analyzing pleadings in cases running back to pre-Renaissance times which today we would call tort cases, he observed that defendants did not plead a lack of negligence, pointing out that such pleas, if they had been made, would be "evidence that fault was thought of as part of the plaintiff's case."[20] Yet Holmes, in his great 1881 book *The Common Law*, had interpreted cases running from approximately the fourteenth through the seventeenth centuries as effectively containing a requirement of fault, "wherever the line of necessary precaution may be drawn."[21]

However one assesses these arguments about early English legal history, it is a fact that some more modern cases imposed what has generally been regarded as a strict form of liability. That liability began in the nineteenth century and continues up to today with cases involving spillovers, sometimes literally, from certain activities of landowners. The decision by the House of Lords in 1868 in *Rylands v. Fletcher*[22] set the pace. It involved the construction of a large reservoir from which water flowed into the plaintiff's mine. Lord Cairns declared that the defendants, in keeping water on their land that escaped onto the plaintiff's property, did so "at their own peril." He quoted at length "at his peril" language from an opinion of Justice Blackburn in the lower court, which used that terminology at least twice, emphasizing that the defendant would be liable unless the escape of the water "was owing to the Plaintiff's default" or to "the act of God." Justice Blackburn had said this rule would apply in a number of circumstances—the eating of a farmer's corn by the "escaping cattle of his neighbour," the escape of "filth of [a] neighbour's privy," and air pollution.[23] Embroidering this theme, Lord Cranworth declared that a party who "brings, or accumulates, on his land anything which, if it should escape, may cause damage to his neighbour" "does so at his peril." His famous legal explanation mark was that if the substance "does escape, and cause damage," the defendant would be "responsible . . . however careful he might have been, and whatever precautions he may taken to prevent the damage."[24] Over the course of many decades, many American courts bought into this rule, at least in small increments. They did not accept it for every episode of a spill of some liquid onto a neighbor's land, nor for every litigation on air pollution. But they did

20. Morris Arnold, Accident, Mistake, and Rules of Liability in the Fourteenth-Century Law of Torts, 128 U. Pa. L. Rev. 361, 368, 374–375, 377–378 (1979).
21. See Holmes, The Common Law, *supra* note 9, at 102–04 (1881).
22. L.R. 3 H.L. 330 (1868).
23. *Id.* at 337–40, quoting Blackburn, J., in Fletcher v. Rylands, L.R. 1 Ex. 265, 280 (1866).
24. Rylands, *supra* note 22, L.R. 3 H.L. at 340.

apply it in numerous cases that ranged from the use of explosives to fumigation activities to crop dusting,[25] setting the standard for non-negligent activity that would be considered a tort under the terms "ultrahazardous"[26] and "abnormally dangerous"[27] used by successive Restatements of Torts. Criticism of one of these efforts has included the argument that its listing of several factors as guidelines for decision gives courts too much leeway to apply those factors.[28] Yet the imposition of liability for certain kinds of activities without a showing of fault is the law in many states.

Strict liability for products. A vigorous strict liability sibling emerged in the 1960s. American courts then began openly to proclaim a form of strict liability for defective products, a tort liability that commentators suggested had been developing for some time under the surface of negligence and warranty law.[29] The first American court to use this doctrine in a majority opinion was the California Supreme Court, speaking through Justice Traynor, in 1963. He declared that a manufacturer's "responsibility for defective products" was not a liability "governed by the law of contract warranties but by the law of strict liability in tort."[30] Injury law in civil suits for products injuries was therefore tort law, as Justice Traynor read private law doctrine. This invention of a legal theory did not sweep the country immediately. For a while some other courts did not lightly give up their allegiance to the contract doctrine of warranty as the chosen theory for products claims.[31] Moreover, linguistic variations on strict liability in tort for products included Alabama's "extended manufacturer's liability doctrine."[32] Conceptual variations included the Pennsylvania Supreme Court's stretching of strict liability to make manufacturers "guarantors" of their products.[33]

Over time, courts applied the tort form of this liability, specifically baptized as strict, to a wide range of products—from a pearl in an oyster that

---

25. See Virginia Nolan & Edmund Ursin, The Revitalization of Hazardous Activity Strict Liability, 65 N.C. L. Rev. 257, 286–93 (1987).

26. Restatement of Torts §§519–20 (1934).

27. Restatement (Second) of Torts §§519–20 (1965), Restatement (Third) of Torts: Physical & Emotional Harm §20 (2010).

28. See, e.g., George Christie, An Essay on Discretion, 1986 Duke L.J. 747, 767–72 (1986).

29. See, e.g., William L. Prosser, The Assault Upon the Citadel (Strict Liability to the Consumer), 69 Yale L.J. 1099 (1960).

30. Greenman v. Yuba Power Prod., 377 P.2d 897, 901 (Cal. 1963).

31. See, e.g., Goldberg v. Kollsman Instrument Corp., 191 N.E.2d 81 (N.Y. 1963); Swartz v. Gen. Motors Corp., 378 N.E.2d 61, 62–64 (Mass. 1978).

32. See Casrell v. Altec Indus., 335 S.2d 128, 132–34 (Ala. 1976).

33. See Salvador v. Atlantic Steel Boiler Co., 319 A.2d 903, 907 (Pa. 1974).

cracked three teeth[34] to the design of a seat in a passenger vehicle[35] to a skip bridge, a set of steel rails that carried materials into a blast furnace at a steel plant.[36]

There were quarrels along the road—sometimes literally along the road—as to whether something was a "product" for purposes of strict liability for products. The Illinois Supreme Court seemed to accept implicitly that an exit sign on a highway could be a product[37] while its appellate court said that a guardrail wasn't.[38] In a reverse image of this pair of Illinois decisions, the Florida intermediate appellate court concluded that a company that manufactured and laid down materials used in the repaving of a county road was strictly liable for defects in the road,[39] but the Florida Supreme Court disagreed.[40]

Woven into these direct and slant-wise disagreements were arguments about the policies applied in balancing the scales between incentives to make useful products and the prevention of injuries. An important font of rationales for strict liability, published in the 1960s, was the comments to section 402A of the Second Restatement of Torts. The drafters of that section spoke of the "special responsibility" of product sellers to members of the "consuming public,"[41] and one court went so far as to declare that "[t]he public interest in human life and health demands all the protection the law can give."[42] One rationale in the Restatement comments posited that "the public has the right to and does expect, in the case of products which it needs and for which it is forced to rely on the seller, that reputable sellers will stand behind their goods."[43] This idea, in which some might have found a contractual flavor, has been translated in many decisions into the language of "consumer expectations."

It is pretty much agreed that strict liability for products applies to cases involving what commonly would be considered a flaw in a product—an

34. See O'Dell v. DeJean's Packing Co., Inc., 585 P.2d 399, 403 (Okla. Ct. App. 1978).

35. See Carillo v. Ford Motor Co., 759 N.E.2d 99, 105–07 (Ill. Ct. App. 2001).

36. See Abdul-Warith v. Arthur G. McKee & Co., 488 F.Supp. 306, 312 (E.D. Pa. 1980), aff'd without opinion, 642 F.2d 440 (3d Cir. 1981).

37. See Hunt v. Blasius, 384 N.E.2d 368 (Ill. 1978)(denying recovery on grounds that there was no proof of defect).

38. See Maddan v. R.A. Cullinan & Son, Inc., 411 N.E.2d 139, 141 (Ill. Ct. App. 1980).

39. See Vaughn v. Edward M. Chadbourne, Inc., 462 So.2d 512 (Fla. Dist. Ct. App. 1985).

40. Edward M. Chadbourne, Inc. v. Vaughn, 491 So.2d 551, 553 (Fla. 1986), rev'g Vaughn v. Edward M. Chadbourne, Inc., 462 So.2d 512 (Fla. Dist. Ct. App. 1985).

41. Restatement (Second) of Torts §402A cmt. c (1965).

42. Suvada v. White Motor Co., 210 N.E.2d 182, 186 (Ill. 1965) (referring to Wiedeman v. Keller, 49 N.E. 210, 211 (Ill. 1897), a case involving illness caused by meat, in which the court says that "public safety demands that there should be an implied warranty on the part of the vendor that the article sold is sound, and fit for the use for which it was purchased").

43. Restatement (Second) of Torts, supra, §402A cmt. c.

imperfection that departs from the intended design of the product. By contrast, there is considerable dispute about the application of strict liability to design defects. One stoutly defended position would require plaintiffs to show that there is a reasonable alternative to the design chosen for the product at issue[44] and that the product's risks outweigh its utility.[45] A very different view is that courts should be able to employ a number of considerations, including consumer expectations as well as a comparison of risk and utility, to determine whether a product is unreasonably dangerous.[46]

One of the most controversial product areas with respect to the definition of defect centers on cigarette-caused illness. The decisions in cigarette cases occupy a spectrum of positions, their diversity symbolic of the disagreements that occur in the development of the injury law constitution. One set of decisions borrows from a comment to the Second Restatement that insisted there could be no liability for "good tobacco"[47]; unless tobacco was contaminated, it was by definition not defective. A frontal attack on this idea came from a federal court that noted that cigarettes were "subject to design, packaging, and manufacturing variations which may render them defective even if the tobacco used in their manufacture was initially unadulterated."[48]

Arguments arose across the country on the facts about the public's knowledge of the hazards of smoking. The Texas Supreme Court said that as far back as the early 1950s, "the general health dangers attributable to cigarettes were commonly known as a matter of law by the community."[49] One court even cited a 1947 song that included the words,

> Smoke, smoke, smoke that cigarette
> Puff, puff, puff, and if you smoke yourself to death,
> Tell Saint Peter at the Golden Gate,
> That you hate to make him wait.[50]

By contrast, a Missouri appellate court said that evidence of general knowledge was not enough to bar a lawsuit, citing statistics indicating that as late as the 1980s, significant percentages of the population were "not at

44. See Restatement (Third) of Torts: Products Liability §2(b) (1998).

45. See id., cmt. d.

46. See, e.g., Marshall S. Shapo, In Search of the Law of Products Liability: The ALI Restatement Project, 48 Vand. L. Rev. 631, e.g., at 668, 693–96 (1995).

47. Restatement (Second), supra, §402A cmt i.

48. See Burton v. R.J. Reynolds Tobacco Co., 884 F.Supp. 1515, 1522 (D. Kan. 1995).

49. See American Tobacco Co. v. Grinnell, 951 S.W.2d 420, 429 (Tex. 1997).

50. Estate of White ex rel. v. R.J. Reynolds Tobacco Co., 109 F.Supp.2d 424, 433 (D. Md. 2000).

all concerned about the health effects of smoking" and that "as far back as 1967 . . . 90% of people diagnosed with laryngeal cancer were cigarette smokers, but that the general public was generally less familiar with the fact that smoking causes laryngeal cancer than with knowledge that smoking causes lung cancer."[51] The addictive properties of cigarettes also came under judicial fire. In one Indiana case, the state's appellate court found a factual question on "whether a consumer who chooses to use cigarettes without knowledge of the risk of addiction . . . does so unreasonably."[52]

The vector of law swayed back and forth among courts and legislatures on the question of whether cigarette companies could be sued for the deadly consequences of smoking. The Texas legislature prohibited suits for products that are "inherently unsafe and . . . known to be unsafe by the ordinary consumer who consumes the product with the ordinary knowledge common to the community." Drawing on the Restatement comment mentioned above, it placed cigarettes in that category, along with sugar, castor oil, alcoholic beverages, and butter.[53] The California legislature passed a similar statute, naming the same products.[54] Ten years later, it turned around and erased the immunity it had given to tobacco companies.[55] Completing a legal curlicue was a series of cases dealing with the question of which time periods the immunizing statute covered.[56]

The conflicting views of various courts and legislatures on cigarette-caused illness represent, in the raw, arguments similar to those that play out in the interpretation of the federal Constitution. Those arguments typically deal with the application of abstract Constitutional clauses to particular fact situations; the constitutive injury law is an ongoing dialectic flowing from case law and legislation pertinent to specific cases.

The arguments over the desirability of imposing strict liability on those who create certain kinds of risks are a vibrant part of that dialectic. Certainly in *Rylands*-type cases and at least some products cases, courts mean what they say when they speak of strict liability. To contend that they really are imposing liability because the defendant fell below some stretched standard of reasonable care is to fly in the face not only of the judicial language but of the possibilities for accident avoidance available to mortals.

---

51. Thompson v. Brown & Williamson Tobacco Corp., 207 S.W.3d 76, 105 (Mo. Ct. App. 2006).

52. Rogers v. R.J. Reynolds Tobacco Co., 557 N.E.2d 1045, 1054–55 (Ind. Ct. App. 1990).

53. Tex. Civ. Prac. and Rem. Code. §82.004(a)(2) (V.T.C.A. 2007).

54. Cal. Civ. Code §1714.45 (1987 Cal. Legis Serv. 1498 (West)).

55. Cal. Civ. Code §1714.45 (1997 Cal. Legis. Serv. ch. 570 (S.B. 67)(West)).

56. See, e.g., Myers v. Philip Morris Cos., 50 P.3d 751, 763 (Cal. 2002)(saying that the statute repealing immunity did not remove immunity with respect to conduct during the "10-year period when the Immunity Statute was in effect").

Exculpations and limitations on liability. We have noted that one of the social mechanisms involved in injury law is private contract. In a smoothly working market where buyers and sellers are all reasonably well informed, society gains from the efficiencies achieved by people making deals for themselves. In that happy universe, government intervention, by courts or by legislatures, is simply sand in a machinery which, ideally, works without friction. Moreover, reliance on private contract preserves freedom for all. Indeed, it enhances personal dignity when people can act on their own account while understanding any risks they are taking.

We have referred to various rules of law that bar plaintiffs from suit because of their risk-taking conduct.[57] Even more direct is the bar against plaintiffs who must repent later for literally signing on the dotted line, although there also are decisions that for one reason or another prohibit the enforcement of exculpatory clauses.

The simplest case for defendants employing such clauses is one in which the plaintiff's signature is as much a product of free will as is possible in a world in which all our choices are constrained in some way. The amateur stock car racer who signs an agreement that he will not sue the owner of the race track for injuries must abide by his bargain.[58] It's the same for the patron of a fitness club who tries to avoid an exculpatory clause when he suffers injuries on an exercise machine, especially when there is plenty of competition among fitness clubs in his area.[59] And people who do parachute diving for fun must shoulder the burden of injuries in that activity, even if they allege that the parachute center was negligent.[60]

But courts incline the other way when they view the good or service at issue as a necessity. Still a classic is the California decision that refused to enforce a exculpatory clause with broad language that barred suits for "negligence or wrongful acts" against a hospital. The state supreme court referred to six factors relevant to the enforceability of such agreements, including the case where the defendant "is engaged in performing a service of great importance to the public, which is often a matter of practical necessity for some members of the public." Among other factors, it listed the case where the defendant has "a decisive advantage in bargaining power," especially when the plaintiff has to sign a "standardized adhesion contract" and cannot even buy protection against injuries caused by negligent acts.[61]

---

57. See, e.g., chapter 3, text accompanying notes 73–76, 98–99.
58. See Schlessman v. Henson, 83 Ill.2d 82, 413 N.E.2d 1252 (Ill. 1980).
59. See Seigneur v. National Fitness Inst., Inc., 752 A.2d 631, e.g., at 639 (Md. Ct. App. 2000).
60. See Hulsey v. Elsinore Parachute Ctr., 214 Cal.Rptr. 194 (Ct. App. 1985).
61. Tunkl v. Regents of the University of California, 383 P.2d 441, 444–46 (Cal. 1963).

In products liability suits, courts have often opposed the use of exculpatory clauses or disclaimers of liability. Technical doctrine can be significant here; courts may be particularly hostile to disclaimers or limitations of liability in suits for personal injuries under the theory of strict liability. In a case involving injuries from the overturning of a golf cart—in which a country club was a defendant in addition to the manufacturer of the cart—an Illinois appellate court stressed that such liability "is imposed independent of contractual considerations." It declared that "the one liable cannot contract away his own responsibility for having placed a defective product into the mainstream of public use."[62]

There is also case law opposing the use of disclaimers against personal injury claims for negligence, presenting a contrast with commercial law doctrine under the Uniform Commercial Code.[63] However, there are plenty of decisions that enforce disclaimers in suits for economic harm caused by defective products when the plaintiff is a commercial party—for example, a utility suing the maker of complex equipment used in generating power.[64]

It may seem to complicate the picture when one learns that a rural electric co-op overcame a disclaimer clause of an equipment manufacturer when a fire attributed to a defect in the equipment caused damage to the co-op's substation.[65] But one can house all these stories under the roof of the injury law constitution. We believe in freedom to agree explicitly to subject oneself to risk. It saves the cost of official decision making and it promotes individual autonomy. But when it is the person who offers the exculpatory or liability-limiting document who basically creates the subjection to risk, we may object. We may object particularly when the risk at issue threatens personal safety, even if the only damage that occurs is to physical property. And when the fundamental legal doctrine that applies to the case has a special focus on protecting life and limb, we won't permit absolution for personal injury. Thus, the applicable legal doctrine ties in with considerations of morality—often summed up in the admittedly elastic term "public policy"—to set a social standard. In part, that standard

---

62. Sipari v. Villa Olivia Country Club, 380 N.E.2d 819, 823 (Ill. App. Ct. 1978).

63. See, e.g., Kueppers v. Chrysler Corp., 310 N.W.2d 327, 334–35 (Mich. App. Ct. 1981), quoting Blanchard v. Monical Mach. Co., 269 N.W.2d 564, 567 (Mich. App. Ct. 1978), on the proposition that "[c]ommon law tort liability in Michigan is distinct from the warranty liabilities imposed by the Uniform Commercial Code, and may not be abrogated by the disclaimers permitted under the code."

64. See, e.g., Public Serv. Co. of N.H. v. Westinghouse Elec. Corp., 685 F.Supp. 1281, 1288 (D. N.H. 1988) (saying that "[t]he doctrine of unconscionability is of questionable applicability" where "the buyer retains 'impressive negotiation power'").

65. McGraw-Edison Co. v. Northeastern Rural Elec. Membership Corp., 678 N.E.2d 1120 (Ind. 1997).

defines the zone in which we believe the exercise of personal freedom is, or is not, meaningful. Illustrative are cases involved purported "informed consent" documents in the medical setting. The Virginia Supreme Court, for example, refused to enforce a general consent form signed by a woman about to give birth when she was awake enough that her obstetrician could have asked her whether he could use forceps to deliver her baby.[66]

No-fault compensation systems: Workers' compensation. The richest lode of compensation for personal injuries, in overall monetary terms, is not tort law. It is workers' compensation. And while negligence is still the central legal doctrine for tort, workers' compensation is principally a no-fault system. To secure an award, a worker must show that an injury occurred in the course of her employment, but need not show that the employer was negligent.

Underlying workers' compensation is a mixed foundation of rationales that enrich the constitution of injury law. Obviously motivating the passage of workers' compensation statutes by every state legislature and by Congress—including a system for federal employees and in a separate statute a system for people who toil on the docks—was a sense of compassion for injured people who otherwise would face insuperable obstacles to compensation thrown up by defensive doctrines of tort law. Also undergirding those laws are the idea that as a matter of social justice the employer is the most appropriate party to shoulder the responsibility for workplace injuries and the quite separate belief that the employer is the most efficient distributor of the costs of workplace injuries. Moreover, although workers' compensation awards often are smaller than those received by successful tort plaintiffs, the system eliminates a lot of the administrative costs required for individual determinations of fault.

Workers' compensation has a variety of relationships with tort law, not all of them friendly. The legislatures that originally cemented workers' compensation into injury law wanted to make it an exclusive remedy—as we have noted, if you're in the system, generally you can't sue your employer in tort. But as we also noted above, some states allow workers to bring tort actions if an employer has behaved very badly, with courts using tort definitions to interpret language like "intentional wrongs" in workers' compensation statutes that allow tort suits.

The general exclusivity rule tempers social justice with cost control. It probably also embodies some skepticism about whether we should monetize intangible losses like pain and suffering: Unlike tort law, workers' compensation does not allow recovery for such harms as separate items.

66. Rizzo v. Schiller, 445 S.E.2d 153, 155–56 (Va. 1994).

At the same time, the exceptions some states have crafted for highly cul-pable conduct manifest a moral condemnation of conduct that impinges on the dignity of persons, here employees, who are on the disadvantaged side of a power relationship. Those exceptions do not necessarily require a show-ing of direct infliction of injury, as by a physical assault, and on occasion courts may even effectively construct an exception to the exclusivity rule. Illustrative is a case in which an employer concealed from a worker its knowledge that the worker had an asbestos-related illness, the result of which was that he continued to work in an asbestos-filled environment and, of course, did not seek treatment. The California Supreme Court said that "the policy of exclusivity of workers' compensation as a remedy for injuries in the employment would not be seriously undermined by holding defen-dant liable for the aggravation of this plaintiff's injuries." The court declared that it could not "believe that many employers will aggravate the effects of an industrial injury by not only deliberately concealing its existence but also its connection with the employment," or "that the Legislature in enact-ing the workers' compensation law intended to insulate such flagrant con-duct from tort liability."[67] The court thus loads its own moral judgment upon the moral foundations embedded in the workers' compensation stat-ute itself.

The relations between tort and workers' compensation prove markedly uneasy when the issue is whether a third party, successfully sued by a worker for a tort based on a workplace injury, can recover from a negligent employer all or part of the tort damages it has had to pay the worker. A recurring example is the case where a worker wins a tort award against the manufac-turer of a workplace machine on the basis that the machine had a defect, and the maker of the machine argues that the employer should pay the manufacturer because the employer's negligence in using the machine was primarily responsible for the injury. A majority of courts hold that the machine manufacturer cannot win some or all of the tort damages from the employer. They say that the exclusivity clauses of the workers' compensa-tion laws, which bar employees from getting tort damages against an employer, have a broader reach. Given that the exclusivity clause was part of a historical "bargain" in which the employer agreed that it would pay for practically all workplace injuries without being able to defend on the basis of the employee's conduct, these courts have said that the reciprocal grant of immunity to employers from having to pay the amounts represented by tort damages should extend to third parties like the manufacturer.

---

67. Johns-Manville Prods. Corp. v. Super. Ct., 612 P.2d 948, 956 (Cal. 1980).

This rule, although it represents the preponderant view, has not won adherents universally. In the historic setting of the United States' exit from Vietnam, the Supreme Court held in favor of a third party suing the Government itself in its capacity as a workers' compensation employer. The case arose from the crash of a big Air Force plane being used to fly 250 orphans out of the country just before the Saigon government collapsed. One of the 150 people who died was a civilian employee of the Navy who was covered by the Government's version of workers' compensation, the Federal Employees' Compensation Act (FECA). Her administrator sued Lockheed, the maker of the plane, which settled. Lockheed then sued the United States—which "did not dispute that it was primarily responsible" for the crash, seeking full indemnification for the settlement it had paid. Justice Powell's opinion for the majority, which held that the exclusivity provision of the FECA did not "directly bar" Lockheed's indemnity action against the Government, drew on a remark in an admiralty precedent involving another FECA claim that there was "'no evidence whatever that Congress [in enacting the FECA] was concerned with the rights of unrelated third parties . . .'"[68]

In this area of controversy about the reach of the exclusivity provisions of the workers' compensation laws, courts are left to find justice in a mélange of history with mixed considerations of fairness and efficient loss distribution. The injury law constitution is supple in the joints, especially where it is not clear which rule is more fair or allocates losses most efficiently. When a decision either way will draw accolades and brickbats from different interest groups, that constitution exhibits an ongoing dialectic about the meaning of justice in workplace injuries.

Safety regulation. Government steps part of the way into injury law when it sets up workers' compensation laws, pushing tort to one side. It occupies even more injury territory—although there are many questions about how much space it occupies—when it passes laws that directly set safety standards. Provisions for criminal and civil penalties in regulatory statutes include culpability language reminiscent of tort, and there is a flavor of that in other provisions. However, the legislative history often seems principally to embody a social judgment that injury rates in a particular area of the economy are unacceptably high, rather than that businesses that cause injury are blameworthy. Although these laws often have moral overtones, they present a picture of technocratic execution of social judgments.

---

68. Lockheed Aircraft Corp. v. U.S., 460 U.S. 190, 195–99 (1983), quoting Weyerhaeuser S.S. Co. v. U.S., 372 U.S. 597, 601 (1963).

A good example of the mixture of such technocratic judgments and some culpability language in safety standards appears in the 1972 amendments to the Federal Insecticide, Fungicide and Rodenticide Act (FIFRA). Those amendments were designed to transform the original 1947 legislation, which was classified as "primarily a labeling law,"[69] into a "comprehensive regulatory statute."[70] The amended law, which focuses on minimizing the dangers of agricultural pesticides, requires sellers of those products to register them with the EPA. The agency must approve the labels of the products, including instructions for safe use, or show that they are eligible for specific exemptions. In the development of the bill, a significant battle over language took place over the question of whether the standard for regulation should be "substantial adverse effects" or "unreasonable adverse effects"—a stronger regulatory test. The legislation settled on the term "unreasonable."[71] This is a somewhat technocratic usage of the term, although it has some overtones of what in the tort law context has a moral harmonic.

In the infighting on the bill, the Senate Commerce Committee rejected the Agriculture and Forestry Committee's omission of a specific reference to the protection of farmers and farmworkers.[72] A balance weight on the side of pesticide manufacturers was a conference report of the House and Senate that eliminated from the bill a provision that would have limited pesticides to "essential use."[73] An interesting sidelight in the debates on the bill appears in a comment by Congressman John Henry Kyl of Iowa, who opposed relatively strict regulation like an "essentiality" provision.[74] Kyl— the father of Jon Kyl of Arizona, a conservative who has served in both the House and the Senate—said, "we do not bring this legislation here permitting some regulated use of pesticides because we hate worms. We bring it to you because the people of the United States like to eat apples without worms. They want good products and they want them at a price they can pay."[75]

69. Congressional Quarterly, 1972 CQ Almanac 934. I am grateful to Leighton Leib for research on the history of FIFRA.

70. H.R. Rep. No. 92–511 at 1 (1972).

71. 7 USC §136(x). For an illustration of the infighting, see S. Rep. 92–838, 1972 U.S. Code Cong. & Admin. News 3993, 4030–33.

72. See 1972 USCCAN at 4111.

73. See id. at 4132, P.L. 92–516, §3(c)(5)(C).

74. See 117 Cong. Rec. 40062 ("[i]f we apply this doctrine economywide, the Federal Government would say, 'we have a Ford automobile; therefore we do not need a Chevrolet, a Plymouth, a Dodge, or a Chrysler'").

75. Id. at 39979.

Losing on this point was Congresswoman Bella Abzug of New York, who advocated the "essentiality" standard with a reference that linked litigation brought by private parties to regulatory legislation. Declaring that "[t]he essentiality standard has been one of the major victories won by environmentalists' lawsuits," she said that "[w]ithout the essentiality doctrine, the sole criterion will be the persuasiveness of the pesticide manufacturer in marketing it to the farmer."[76] The philosophical competition between these quotations is part of a larger competition within the constitution of injury law, which includes differing views on consumer choice. Although that competition is ideological in character, here it is focused on the relatively technocratic concept of essential use rather than on questions of whether the marketers of products are acting culpably. Foot by foot and yard by yard, small decisions like this choice of legislative language define the vector of that constitution.

The Consumer Product Safety Act (CPSA), enacted two years before the FIFRA amendments, is notable in many respects. It covers a very wide spectrum of products and it includes a remarkably broad range of consumer-friendly provisions, including a provision allowing direct suit by consumers for "any knowing (including willful) violation of a consumer product safety rule" issued by the Consumer Product Safety Commission.[77] The main substantive provisions feature the language of reasonableness. For example, the section on consumer product safety standards requires that standards "shall be reasonably necessary to prevent or reduce an unreasonable risk of injury."[78] The statute repeats the "unreasonable risk of injury" language in a section that allows the Commission to ban hazardous products when "no feasible consumer product safety standard . . . would adequately protect the public from" that risk.[79]

Again, though, the tone of this language is rather more technocratic than moralistic. More morally oriented language appears in the comments of various legislators on the law. Democratic Senator Abraham Ribicoff, who had spearheaded the legislation that created an agency to regulate motor vehicle safety, said with respect to the CPSA that "[c]onsumers will no longer accept the morals of the marketplace." Strikingly, he declared that consumers "expect their Government to act as guardian of the market to assure that the goods they purchase are safe, effective, and meet the claims

76. *Id.* at 40036.
77. 15 U.S.C. §2072(a)(2006).
78. *Id.* §2056(a)(2)(2006).
79. *Id.* §2057.

made for them."[80] Republican Senator Charles Percy of Illinois employed equally strong language with a rights-based flavor: "The American consumer has a right to safe products for use in his home . . . [t]oday we are faced with a number of unreasonable hazards in and around the home."[81] Evidencing the highly political content of the definition of desirable levels of consumer safety was a remark of Senator Montoya of New Mexico that "[c]orporate enterprise can afford to maintain full-time, highly-paid lobbyists year round in Washington" where "[t]he consumer cannot."[82]

Moralistic language flying around the Senate chamber reflected legislators' concerns about an environment very different from the daily shopping trip to the greengrocer or dealings with a shoemaker. Republican Senator Edward Gurney of Florida said that "something important has been lost— the personal relationship between producer and consumer that helped promote a mutually beneficial exchange of quality goods at a fair price."[83] A significant part of the problem, as a report of the Senate Commerce Committee emphasized, lay in the "technological revolution" that had brought "a variety of new products"—and simply many more new ones— "employing new energy sources with potential for injury which is both greater and less easily comprehended." The increase in the number of products proportionally increased "the consumer's exposure to risk of injury."[84] Additionally, the character of advertising had changed the social setting of product sales and purchases. Advertising had for centuries been part of the background of consumer life, but senators perceived a significant change in its nature. Heatedly, Senator Montoya not only spoke of "a bewildering variety of concoctions, attractively packaged and promoted," with promotions that "flash across our bewildered consciousness like a motion picture projector gone wild," but went so far as to describe manufacturers as "engaged in a violent, vicious daily grapple."[85]

We can only wonder how Senator Montoya would have described TV advertising in the twenty-first century. The questions we now address are how Congress decides what areas of risky activity to regulate and how it frames its regulatory laws in words that both respond to public sentiment and attempt to guide safety agencies.

---

80. 118 Cong. Rec. 21848–49. I am grateful to Leighton Leib for research on the legislative history of the Consumer Product Safety Act.
81. *Id.* at 21850–51.
82. *Id.* at 21891.
83. *Id.* at 21880–81.
84. S. Rep. No. 92-749, at 2 (1972).
85. 118 Cong. Rec. at 21891.

There are different motivations for selection of areas to regulate. In some cases, over time the statistics of injury become so worrisome that legislators believe they must act to control the impact of costs on individuals and society. Various kinds of events get members of Congress stirred up enough to pass laws related to injuries. Sometimes a single occasion, or cluster of incidents, may trigger the creation of a regulatory system to solve a range of related problems. That was the case with the more than 100 deaths caused by the drug elixir sulfanilamide in 1937, which led to the passage of the 1938 Food and Drug Act. Now and then a single death may be the trigger for legislation: in an area related to safety we find the Ryan White Comprehensive AIDS Resources Emergency Act. Named after a boy who contracted AIDS from blood products used to combat his hemophilia, this statute appropriates funds for the relief of families whose members have HIV/AIDS.[86]

Safety regulation contributes to injury law the creation of standards that cannot be set by private action or private law, either by prices that arise from marketplace transactions or indirectly by tort suits. Even when there are no significant imbalances in bargaining power between those exposed to risk and product sellers or those who conduct risky activities, and even when there are reasonable levels of competition, it may be practically impossible for those exposed to risk to have a say in setting the level of safety. They often have no way to discover the data on hazards that a well-informed purchaser would want, and no way to monitor safety levels over time.

There surely is a moral component to safety statutes—in effect, legislators say we've seen enough blood on the floor and it's time to stop it, or at least reduce it significantly. But the social decision that safety laws enact is a compromise between the anguish and rage of victims and those who empathize with them, and the anger of business persons who claim excessive government interference.

So legislatures—state legislatures as well as Congress—strike several balances in creating regulatory statutes: among the angers of various groups, conflicting desires for better things in life, cultural definitions of progress. In brokering the angers, legislators do make moral judgments. But even the morally tinted language in some statutes has more to do with defining a socially acceptable level of risk than with wrath. Born of problems that arise from passions, the solutions often are technical compromises that attempt

---

86. Originally passed as Pub. L. No. 101–381, 104 Stat. 576 (1990) (reauthorized and amended several times, e.g., by Pub. L. No. 106–345, 114 Stat. 1319 (2000), and codified at various sections of 42 U.S.C.A. §300 ff).

to wash the passions out. A parallel appears in the dollar schedules for workers' compensation awards. They represent a social judgment about acceptable levels of compensation, reducing some individuality in the service of more justice, if a more homogenized justice, for more people.

Safety laws thus tie in, not always easily, with tort and with compensation statutes as the components of a working constitution of injury law. The abstract guides of that constitution include conceptions of right; ideas about necessary controls on various types of power; legal definitions of injury; cost control—of the frequency and severity of injuries and the private and social expense they cause, but also of the costs of regulation; compensation for as many injured persons as possible, with the boundaries for amounts being left to a choice among social mechanisms; corresponding acknowledgments of the need for balance between individualization and social efficiency; a standard of basic decency, not always articulated; and, very seldom articulated, some small measure of compassion.

CHAPTER 7
Functional Elements of the Law

The words of the law are surrogates for what the law does: for its function, how it operates. We begin with the words, and then turn to function. Crucial words in tort law include the terms used to describe the categories that lawyers work with: doctrines and theories like intentionality, negligence, and duty. The practical operation of compensation statutes like workers' compensation depends on the language of categories created by the legislature—categories that often appear under the judicial microscope in litigation. They include terms like "out of and in the course of employment" and "accidental injury." When we focus on safety statutes, the operative terms occupy a wide range of language. Under the Occupational Safety and Health Act, they include phrases like "imminent danger" and "serious physical harm."[1] Sometimes this language parallels that of tort law. The National Traffic and Motor Vehicle Safety Act defines the crucial term "motor vehicle safety" to mean protection of the public "against unreasonable risk of accidents" and "against unreasonable risk of death or injury in an accident"[2]—language that draws a distinction between occurrences of events and their consequences.

Regulatory statutes do construct their classifications in terms of risk, but also, necessarily, in terms of the areas of activity and products that they regulate. Thus, the Food, Drug and Cosmetic Act has separate sections for foods and drugs, to which the Medical Device Amendments were added.[3] The provision on "adulterated food," a basis for regulation in cases like the problem of salmonella in peanut products in 2009, condemns a food if

---

1. 29 U.S.C. §662(a)(2006).
2. 49 U.S.C.A. §30102(a)(8)(2006).
3. See 21 U.S.C. 360c.

"it bears or contains any poisonous or deleterious substance which may render it injurious to health"[4]—adding, for disgusting good measure, a food that "consists in whole or in part of any filthy, putrid, or decomposed substances," or that "is otherwise unfit for food."[5] A more technical definition appears in the definition of a "food additive"—a category that could result in a product being banned from the market unless it falls within tolerances prescribed by the government—as a substance that "is not generally recognized, among experts qualified by scientific training and experience . . . as having been adequately shown through scientific procedures . . . to be safe under the conditions of its intended use."[6]

The quite separate category of drugs includes definitions for safety and effectiveness. The standard of safety for "new drugs"—a category unto itself—keeps drugs from the market if the "results of . . . tests" that the seller must conduct "show that such drug is unsafe for use" under the "conditions prescribed, recommended, or suggested" in proposed labeling "or do not show that such drug is safe for use under such conditions."[7] The language on effectiveness of new drugs is more technical. It keeps drugs off the market unless sellers can show "substantial evidence" of their effectiveness, which is defined to mean "evidence consisting of adequate and well-controlled investigations, including clinical investigations, by experts qualified . . . to evaluate the effectiveness of the drug involved, on the basis of which it could fairly and responsibly be concluded by such experts" that the drug "will have the effect it purports or is represented to have under the conditions of use," specified in the labeling.[8]

Thus, the language of both tort law and public regulatory law provide a set of relatively abstract standards for measurement of both benefits and hazards of products and activities, with compensation statutes and regulatory laws defining specific activities. These definitions are functional in the sense that they grow out of particular products and activities. But if we slice the law at a different angle, we find other functional elements that explain why courts decide the way they do in particular cases, and why legislators have picked out certain products and activities for regulation—even, sometimes, prohibition.

4. 21 USCA §342(a)(1) (2006).
5. Id. §342(a)(3).
6. See id. §321(s).
7. 21 U.S.C. §355(d)(e)(2006)(grounds for refusing new drug application with overlapping language on withdrawal of approval).
8. Id. §355(d).

We indicated in chapter 2 some of the ways in which the uses and misuses of power affect our injury law. Here we elaborate on some particular areas of activity in which the possession of power, and imbalances in power, appear to be central to the development of our law of injuries.

Police Behavior

Police activity is an important territory where the law responds to collections of power. When police brutalize citizens or otherwise use their power to interfere with them unlawfully, there has been a historic basis in the common law for checking that power. The torts of battery, false arrest and false imprisonment have long provided citizen remedies in extreme cases. The Supreme Court added a large new remedy to that roster of doctrines in the great 1961 case of *Monroe v. Pape,*[9] which arose from allegations of a shocking misuse of the badge. According to the powerful summary of those allegations by Justice Frankfurter, who in the end dissented from a decision in favor of the plaintiffs, Deputy Chief of Detectives Frank Pape of Chicago, along with a dozen other officers, broke through two doors of the apartment of James and Flossie Monroe at 5:45 a.m. They woke the couple "with flashlights, and forced them at gunpoint to leave their bed and stand naked in the center of the living room" and roused their six children "and herded them into the living room." Pape allegedly struck James Monroe "with his flashlight, calling him 'nigger' and 'black boy.'" "[A]nother officer pushed Mrs. Monroe" and others "hit and kicked several of the children and pushed them to the floor." The police ransacked the apartment. They then took James Monroe to the police station, where they detained him "on 'open' charges for ten hours," interrogating him about a murder and exhibiting him in lineups. They did not take him before a magistrate, although magistrates were available, they did not let him call his family or a lawyer—and, after all that, they let him go without filing any charges.[10]

In an opinion for the Court that was relatively brief with respect to the mighty principle it laid down, Justice Douglas concluded that the Monroes had stated a claim against Pape under 42 U.S. Code section 1983, a law that became known as the Ku Klux Act which originally was passed in 1871.[11]

9. 365 U.S. 167 (1961).
10. *Id.* at 203 (Frankfurter, J., dissenting).
11. See *id.* at 171–73.

That law made available a basis for damages actions, and indeed for injunctive relief, against persons who "under color of any" law deprived others of "any rights, privileges, or immunities secured by the Constitution and laws."

The parallels between the invasion of the Monroe apartment and some of the incidents mentioned in the debates of the 42nd Congress that passed the Ku Klux Act are striking: the viciousness of the attackers, the vulnerability of the abused citizens, the trampling of the most basic rights. An obvious feature of the post-Civil War incidents that originally generated the statute was their racial content: whites (acting in that environment without licensed police authority) were brutalizing blacks. But Justice Douglas' broad, brief opinion went far beyond the race-based foundation of the Ku Klux Act. First, he vaulted a technical hurdle of language, the phrase in section 1983 that required plaintiffs to show that defendants had acted "under color of" law. Defendants like Pape would argue that "under color of" meant that they were acting "pursuant to state law." However, quoting a prior opinion of the Court concerning a criminal statute that contained the same language, Justice Douglas stressed that "under color of" included "[m]isuse of power, possessed by virtue of state law and made possible only because the wrongdoer is clothed with the authority of state law."[12] This reading provided a platform for an opinion that reached not only to the kinds of wrongs commonly associated with police abuses, like physical beatings, arrests and imprisonment, but to violations of any rights that people possess under the Constitution, and other laws of the United States to boot. The fact that a state might provide grounds for suit in such circumstances did not block the assertion of a federal right: "[t]he federal remedy is supplementary to the state remedy."[13] Yet Douglas did not put aside the ordinary state law remedies; in fact, he incorporated the spirit of them: section 1983 "should be read against the background of tort liability that makes a man responsible for the natural consequences of his actions."[14]

A central feature of this great decision was its emphasis on "misuse of power," which courts over almost half a century have applied in cases ranging over a broad range of activities and fact situations. Many of these cases have involved police behavior of a sort familiar to headline readers. One Supreme Court case, which involved what to lay people might be considered hairsplitting of legal doctrines, involved an incident in which police took into custody a diabetic man whose only offense was that he went into

12. *Id.* at 184 (quoting United States v. Classic, 313 U.S. 299, 326 (1941)).
13. *Id.* at 183.
14. *Id.* at 187.

a convenience store to get some orange juice to counteract an insulin reaction. An officer, suspicious of the plaintiff's behavior, called for backup, which brought several other officers. In the events that ensued, the plaintiffs rolled the helpless plaintiff over on the sidewalk and handcuffed him, slammed him face down on the hood of a police car, and threw him head first into the vehicle. The police defendants argued, using a precedent from a federal court of appeals, that the plaintiff must show that they had acted "maliciously and sadistically." However, Chief Justice Rehnquist—no liberal bleeding heart—rejected that argument. He said that the appropriate test for a case involving a claim of "excessive force" "in the context of an arrest or investigatory stop of a free citizen"—as a practical matter, someone not in prison—was whether the police had acted "reasonabl[y]," language that tracked the Fourth Amendment's prohibition of "unreasonable . . . seizures" of the person.[15] Noting that reasonableness in such situations must take into account circumstances that might be "tense, uncertain, and rapidly evolving," he stressed that the standard was an "objective" one, measured "from the perspective of a reasonable officer on the scene."[16] This test did not take into account either the "good" or "evil" intentions of the officer and, the Chief Justice said, "subjective concepts like 'malice' and 'sadism'" had "no proper place" in applying this "objective reasonableness" concept.[17]

Other applications of section 1983 to police behavior by the Supreme Court have included a suit for failure to protect a prisoner against foreseeable assaults by other prisoners—a case in which the Court affirmed an award for punitive damages[18]—and a case in which officers took an axe to a door of a medical clinic in a fraud investigation.[19] Strikingly, the Court applied the statute to the actions of high state officials, including a governor, in efforts to contain campus unrest in a time of national political upheaval that resulted in fatal shootings by National Guardsmen.[20]

The courts have extended the reach of the statute beyond beatings, the use of axes and ransackings to include many other kinds of acts by officials. The Supreme Court applied section 1983, with a special twist, when female employees sued a city for a policy that required them to take unpaid pregnancy leaves before it was medically necessary. The special twist lay in the Court's statement that in certain cases—involving governmental policies

15. Graham v. Connor, 490 U.S. 386, 394 (1989).
16. *Id.* at 396–97.
17. *Id.* at 399.
18. Smith v. Wade, 461 U.S. 30 (1983).
19. See Pembaur v. City of Cincinnati, 475 U.S. 469 (1986).
20. See Scheuer v. Rhodes, 416 U.S. 232 (1974).

rather than only specific acts—plaintiffs could sue governments and not just individual officials.[21] Other examples of the application of section 1983 against conduct far removed from the blood and guts of mean streets have involved denials of welfare benefits[22] and the desegregation of public schools.[23]

The Court has also defined boundaries for this "constitutional tort." For example, it has made it clear that what amounts to a traditional suit for defamation does not fit the requirements of section 1983, so a man could not sue a police department for the "stigma" caused by the circulation of his mug shot as an "active shoplifter."[24] To qualify for section 1983 treatment, the plaintiff must demonstrate "stigma plus."[25]

And in situations much more poignant, the Court has refused to impose section 1983 liability for the failure of state officials to prevent the most brutal child abuse[26] and even murder.[27] The Court has also employed technical interpretations of Constitutional provisions to deny recovery under section 1983 in other cases involving physical injury. Illustrative is a case in which a convict claimed a violation of the Eighth Amendment's prohibition on "cruel and unusual punishment" when a prison guard shot him as he was trying to move elderly prisoners out of a potential tear gas zone during a prison riot. Justice O'Connor, acknowledging that the guard's conduct might have been "unfortunate," said that the case did not measure up to an Eighth Amendment standard that required "a wanton willingness to inflict unjustified suffering."[28]

This set of interpretations of specific provisions of the Constitution, which are the main foundations for actions under section 1983, are part of the broad injury law constitution this book explores. The federal decisions on the "constitutional tort" comprise a compartment of the injury law constitution that includes the "background of tort liability"—that is, ordinary tort liability—of which Justice Douglas spoke in *Monroe*.

A motif common to both common law tort and "constitutional tort" is the misuse of power. The decisions on the constitutional tort provide

21. Monell v. Dep't. of Soc. Servs., 436 U.S. 658 (1978), discussed further in chapter 11, text accompanying notes 29–30.
22. See, e.g., Maine v. Thiboutot, 448 U.S. 1 (1980).
23. See, e.g., Bradley v. School Board of City of Richmond, 416 U.S. 696 (1974).
24. Paul v. Davis, 424 U.S. 693 (1976). For discussion of other decisions of the Court in this area, see chapter 11, text accompanying notes 31–36.
25. See, e.g., Colaizzi v. Walker, 542 F.2d 969, 973–74 (7th Cir. 1976).
26. DeShaney v. Winnebago County Dep't. of Soc. Servs., 489 U.S. 189 (1989), discussed in some detail, chapter 11, text accompanying notes 37–41.
27. Town of Castle Rock v. Gonzales, 545 U.S. 748 (2005), discussed in some detail, chapter 11, text accompanying notes 42–48.
28. Whitley v. Albers, 475 U.S. 312, 325 (1986).

an especially complex reading of the relationship of injury law to power: they condemn the misuse of power, but they recognize that with the responsibility to exercise official power goes a right to employ it in exigent circumstances. And, as in the case that produced the "stigma plus" idea, these decisions find in the Constitution a layer of legal protection for officials that does not exist under the common law. A substantial part of that layer appears in the defense of "qualified immunity."[29]

Sex

An important functional category of the misuse of power involves sexual imposition. Theories on which plaintiffs might seek recovery are several, ranging from various common law torts to actions under federal statutes for sex discrimination. One set of cases deals with alleged misrepresentations that defendants are free from sexually transmitted disease or failure to disclose that defendants had such a disease. A California case arose from the defendant's misrepresentation that he was free from disease when he at least should have known that he had genital herpes, which the plaintiff allegedly contracted after intercourse. The plaintiff appealed from a dismissal of her suit that alleged a variety of torts, including battery, intentional infliction of emotional distress, fraud, and negligence. Without nicely distinguishing among those theories, the court reversed in favor of the plaintiff. The power inherent in information was clearly a factor in the court's consideration. In rejecting the defendant's argument that an unmarried plaintiff did not stand on the same ground as a married one, the court said that "a certain amount of trust and confidence exists in any intimate relationship, at least" in cases involving misrepresentations of freedom from sexually transmitted disease.[30]

A Michigan court eventually reached the same result after some hair-splitting in a case in which the unmarried plaintiff contracted human papillomavirus (HPV) from the defendant, a married man who withheld his knowledge that he had the disease. The court refused to credit the plaintiff's argument that a statute that made adultery a felony was "never enforced" and "regularly ignored." However, again without making fine distinctions based on particular theories, the court used a "culpability exception" in reversing a dismissal, saying that "the blame for plaintiff's contracting HPV rests largely with [the defendant] because he is almost entirely responsible

29. See, e.g., Scheuer v. Rhodes, 416 U.S. 232, 247–48 (1974).
30. Kathleen K. v. Robert B., 198 Cal.Rptr. 273, 276–77 (App. Ct. 1984).

for [the] injury." The court made clear that the culpable imposition came from the power that lay in the defendant's knowledge: "it is one thing to engage in illegal adultery, as both plaintiff and defendant did, but quite another to do so knowing that a likely result will be infecting a sexual partner with a serious disease while not making that fact known, an offense of which only defendant is allegedly guilty."[31]

Although the transmission of undisclosed disease lowers the bar for plaintiffs claiming sexual imposition, the case becomes more difficult when the claim is that the defendant withheld another kind of information. An interesting problem of this type arose in a Massachusetts case in which the plaintiff, in her early forties, had a sexual relationship with a man who she believed wanted children although he did not disclose to her that he had had a vasectomy. The court held for the defendant on several theories of liability. Illustrative of its point of view was its statement, with reference to the tort of intentional infliction of emotional distress, that "even if the defendant had created false expectations about his future relationship with the plaintiff, nothing in his conduct throughout the relationship can be said to rise to the 'high order of reckless ruthlessness or deliberate malevolence' required for a showing of conduct that is 'intolerable.'"[32]

It follows that most courts are not inclined to allow a claim against a particularly aggressive suitor who does not literally thrust himself upon the plaintiff. The idea that there is "no harm in asking"[33] has been pretty well cemented into the common law. It has even been applied in cases involving an employment relationship, as a state employee named Paula Jones learned in her suit against the governor of her state, who not only importuned her for a sex act but put his hands on her body. In that case, a female federal judge in Arkansas, acknowledging that Bill Clinton's advances were "odious," said she could not find "any authority holding that such a sexual encounter or proposition . . . gives rise to a claim of outrage"—the Arkansas term for the tort of intentional infliction of emotional distress.[34]

Backing up the case law that restricts actions for torts with sexual content are the so-called anti-heartbalm statutes, which bar litigation for seduction and a group of other torts including breach of promise to marry and alienation of affections. The political coalitions that originally supported

31. Stopera v. DiMarco, 554 N.W.2d 379, 381 (Mich. Ct. App. 1996).

32. Conley v. Romeri, 806 N.E.2d 933, 938 (Mass. App. Ct. 2004).

33. Calvert Magruder, Mental and Emotional Disturbance in the Law of Torts, 49 Harv. L. Rev. 1033, 1055 (1936). In the older case law, see, e.g., Reed v. Maley, 74 S.W. 1079 (Ky. 1903)(rejecting claim by "a woman against a man who solicits her to sexual intercourse with him[]").

34. Jones v. Clinton, 990 F.Supp. 657, 677 (E.D. Ark. 1998).

this legislation could be complex; men vexed by seduction suits brought by "gold-digging" women sometimes became allied with women offended by the idea that women needed the kind of protection that "heartbalm" torts afforded.[35]

The totality of the law in this area—tort cases and statutes—forms a loose constitutive fabric. A basic rule is, don't lie to a sex partner, especially about not having a transmissible disease, but beyond that there is a lot of room for the attitude that all's fair in sexual pursuit. In a world of changing mores, the injury law constitution leaves a lot of space for social experimentation.[36]

Sex in the workplace. In less than a generation, the workplace has generated volumes of law related to sexual imposition. With changes occurring in parallel sets of mores, and despite the result in Paula Jones' case, courts began to indicate that there indeed could be "harm in asking" if the asker was an employer and the person asked was an employee. The basis in tort doctrine for such actions has evolved. Under traditional doctrine, a principal theory of recovery has been intentional infliction of emotional distress, but some courts have referred to a separate "tort of sexual harassment."[37] A representative early decision on the common law side, using the intentional infliction tort, identified a pattern of behavior with three elements that would support a claim: "a continued course of sexual advances, followed by refusals and ultimately, retaliation."[38]

A powerful addition to this claimants' arsenal is Title VII of the Civil Rights Act of 1964.[39] The courts have planted two standards on that foundation. One, which responded to the kind of pattern just described, required the plaintiff to show that the defendant sought a "quid pro quo"—sexual favors for employment advantages.[40] On a different track, the Supreme Court articulated a test of "severe or pervasive" harassment that created a "hostile environment." In the first case in which the Court employed the "hostile environment" test, the plaintiff testified that she had had intercourse with the defendant forty or fifty times over a period of years, that he

35. See, e.g., Jane E. Larson, "Women Understand So Little, They Call My Good Nature Deceit": A Feminist Rethinking of Seduction, 93 Colum. L. Rev. 374, 393–99 (1993).

36. An argument for an expanded view of "sexual autonomy misappropriation" that would "more fairly reflect American sexual norms" appears in Deana Pollard Sacks, Intentional Sex Torts, 77 Fordham L. Rev. 1051, 1086–95 (2008), advocating an "[i]nformed consent analysis" in intentional tort sex cases.

37. See, e.g., Jin v. Metropolitan Life Ins. Co., 295 F.2d 335, 343 (2d Cir. 2002).

38. Shaffer v. Nat'l Can Corp., 565 F.Supp. 909, 915 (E.D. Pa. 1983).

39. A principal provision is 42 U.S.C. §2000e, sec. 202(a).

40. See, e.g., Faragher v. City of Boca Raton, 524 U.S. 775, 790–91 (1998)(referring to precedent).

"fondled her in front of other employees," and that he "even forcibly raped her on several occasions."[41] She submitted to all this, she said, because of fear of losing her job.

Later the Court elaborated on the "hostile environment test" in a case in which the defendant's president "often insulted" the plaintiff because of her gender, once telling her that she was "a dumb ass woman," and "occasionally asked [the plaintiff] and other female employees to get coins from his front pants pocket." He also once suggested that he and the plaintiff "go to the Holiday Inn to negotiate [the plaintiff's] raise." This collection of statements and behaviors led the Court to reverse a judgment for the defendant. Justice O'Connor rejected the trial court's focus on "whether the conduct 'seriously affect[ed] plaintiff's psychological well-being' or led her to 'suffe[r] injury.'" She said that although "[c]ertainly Title VII bars conduct that would seriously affect a reasonable person's psychological well-being," it "is not limited to such conduct." For her, the test was whether "the environment would reasonably be perceived, and is perceived, as hostile or abusive."[42]

We have shown that the injury law constitution has broad room for interpretation about the definition of sexual imposition. But in the particular context of the workplace, the imbalance of power in many employment relationships significantly weighs in favor of remedies for persons who claim they have been overborne.

The Workplace, Generally

OSHA. A central document in injury law, which exhibits in many ways an understanding of the power that employers have over employees, is the Occupational Safety and Health Act. Congress' professed goals in the statute, while not specifically downplaying cost-benefit analysis, tilt toward safety. The second clause of the entire legislation identifies a purpose "to assure so far as possible every working man and woman in the Nation safe and healthful working conditions."[43] The statute then speaks of "encouraging" both "employers and employees in their effort to reduce the number of occupational safety and health hazards at their places of employment" and to "stimulate" them "to institute new and to perfect existing programs for providing safe and healthful working conditions."[44] While the statute does

---

41. Meritor Sav. Bank, FSB v. Vinson, 477 U.S. 57, 60 (1986).
42. Harris v. Forklift Sys., Inc., 510 U.S. 17, 22 (1993).
43. 29 U.S.C.A. §651(b).
44. *Id.* §651(b)(1).

not make employers "insurer[s]" of the safety of employees,[45] it is rich in unqualified declarations favoring employee protection. Its "general duty" clause uses mandatory language on employer responsibilities: "Each employer ... *shall* furnish ... employment and a place of employment which are free from recognized hazards that are causing or likely to cause death or serious physical harm to his employees."[46]

The statute includes enforcement teeth,[47] implicitly subject, however, to the availability of personnel. These mechanisms include the issuance of injunctions against workplace "conditions or practices" that present dangers "which could reasonably be expected to cause death or serious physical harm immediately or before the imminence of such danger can be eliminated" by less drastic enforcement procedures.[48] The legislation also provides civil penalties for "serious violation[s]" of the general duty clause or of "any standard, rule, or order" under the statute.[49] In a case involving an explosion in a dust collection system in a tire factory, the Fifth Circuit rejected an employer's argument that the "likely to cause death" language of the general duty provision should be interpreted to include a requirement of a significant likelihood of injury. Quoting the statutory declaration of purpose as assuring "so far as possible ... safe and healthful working conditions," the court summarized case law as establishing "beyond dispute" "that a violation may be deemed serious 'where, although the accident itself is merely possible (i.e., in statutory terms 'could result from a condition'), there is a substantial probability of serious injury if it does occur.'"[50]

The power of a general legislative commitment to worker safety is evident in a case involving the lack of safety nets to protect employees from falling as they erected the steel frame of a building at a nuclear power plant. The court rejected an argument by the steel erector that a general safety standard issued by the Occupational Safety and Health Administration had been preempted by "more specific steel erection standards," contained in occupational safety and health regulations for construction, which however did not include a specific requirement for perimeter safety nets. The court quoted a precedent on the proposition that "[l]acking the omniscience to perceive the myriad conditions to which specific standards may be addressed, ... the Secretary, in an effort to insure the safety of employees as required by the Act must at times necessarily resort to the general

---

45. Ocean Elec. Corp. v. Sec'y of Labor, 594 F.2d 396, 399 (4th Cir. 1979).
46. 29 U.S.C. §654 (emphasis added).
47. See, e.g,. *id.* §659.
48. See *id.* §662.
49. *Id.* §666(b).
50. Kelly Springfield Tire Co. v. Donovan, 729 F.2d 317, 325 n.12 (5th Cir. 1984), quoting Shaw Const., Inc. v. OSHRC, 534 F.2d 1183, 1885 (5th Cir. 1976).

safety standards."[51] The court also rejected the steel erector's argument that even if the general safety standard—which required safety nets "when workplaces are more than 25 feet above the ground or water surface"—were applicable, the secretary would have to "show that a reasonable prudent employer, familiar with the requirements of fall protection and the steel erection industry, would have protected against the hazards" at issue. Here the court placed the steel erector in a legal pincer, pointing out that while the general standard was "'general' in the sense that it applies throughout the construction industry," it was quite specific on the requirement of safety nets where there was a drop of more than 25 feet. The court declared, simply, that "[t]here is no necessity to refer to industry practice to ascertain what is required."[52] The thrust of these decisions, whether they rest on rather broad philosophical declarations or relatively technical judgments on legal arguments, is a recognition of the ability of employers to control the level of safety of their employees.

Workers' compensation. The level of control also links up to an issue that recurs in litigation over eligibility for workers compensation, the issue of whether an employee's injury arose out of his or her employment. A pair of cases on back injuries, decided by the Virginia Supreme Court on the same day, presents an interesting contrast. In one case, the claimant was a customer representative whose regular office garb included high-heeled shoes, which she was wearing on the day that her employer moved offices. She was directed to help out in moving and unpacking boxes. Her supervisor testified that she "had high heels on and she bent over ... and picked up the side of [a] box and got it off the floor" and that as she "was beginning to pull it up ... she screamed with pain ... broke out in a sweat ... and she dropped the box." She had suffered a severe lumbar sprain. The court concluded that her accident arose out of her employment, noting that the work she was doing "was ... specially assigned by the employer" and "occurred while she was engaged in a new work assignment involving physical exertion to which she was unaccustomed."[53]

In the other Virginia case, the claimant was a UPS driver who suffered a lumbosacral strain while he bent over to tie his shoe as he was unloading packages from his truck. Disagreeing with a decision by the workers' compensation commission that he should get compensation, the court noted that "[e]very person who wears laced shoes must occasionally perform the act of retying the laces" and concluded that "[t]he situation of a loose

<hr>

51. Donovan v. Daniel Marr & Son Co., 763 F.2d 477, 482 (1st Cir. 1985), quoting Bristol Steel & Iron Works, Inc. v. OSHRC, 601 F.2d 717, 721 n.11 (4th Cir. 1979).
52. *Id.* at 484.
53. Olsten of Richmond v. Leftwich, 336 S.E.2d 893, 894 (Va. 1985).

shoelace confronting the claimant was wholly independent of the master-servant relationship."[54] Such judicial responses to the question of whether injuries arise out of the scope of employment indicate that the element of the injury law constitution involving power to control others applies to employer power to control the conditions of employment as contrasted with occasions when injuries occur from what most people would consider everyday activities unrelated to the following of orders.

Sometimes the boundary line can be blurry as to what an employer can expect of employees. A serious difference of opinion erupted in the Oklahoma Supreme Court in a unique case involving two truck drivers who had been "living in an intimate relationship." There was evidence, unsurprisingly disputed, that the two were having sexual intercourse while the male partner was driving across railroad tracks, on which the truck was hit by a train. The female codriver died and the male driver, who was injured, sought workers' compensation. The majority of a divided court found "ample evidence reasonably supporting the notion that claimant's injury was work-related, i.e., occurred while he was en route to his assigned destination."[55] It noted that it was "uncontroverted" that the claimant "occupied his assigned work station" at the time the train hit the truck and concluded that "[b]ecause the perils of this servant's travel for his master are co-extensive with the risks of employment, [the claimant's] injuries undeniably arose out of his work." A somewhat astonished dissenter declared that "[s]ustaining an injury while engaged in sexual intercourse is not the type of risk reasonably incident to driving a semi tractor-trailer rig," and observed that "[c]laimant's employer neither condoned such acts nor could it have derived any benefit therefrom." The dissenter's legal conclusion that the claimant's injuries "did not 'arise out of his employment'" followed from the premise that his "willing participation in such non-work-related activities were independent of and completely disconnected from the performance of any duties of his job as a truck driver."[56]

A variety of other skirmishes occur in the workers' compensation arena. A challenging set of problems has to do with whether injuries to the psyche—which can be as severe as total breakdowns—could be found to arise out of employment. There are disagreements aplenty, both between courts and within courts.[57] This group of cases in the workers'

---

54. United Parcel Service of America v. Fetterman, 336 S.E.2d 892, 893 (Va. 1985).
55. Darco Transp. v. Dulen, 922 P.2d 591, 596 (Okla. 1996).
56. Id. at 599–600 (Watt, J., dissenting).
57. For a strong disagreement in one court in an early case, see the opposed opinions in Carter v. General Motors Corp., 106 N.W.2d 105 (Mich. 1960) (approving compensation for schizophrenic breakdown of worker who could not keep up with assembly line job).

compensation area simply reflects a set of disputes, partly factual and partly ideological, about the degree of control that employers exercise over employees' lives—and about the propriety of that amount of control.

Tort. A strong ideological clash on the nature of power appears in ordinary tort cases involving employment. However judges may strive for political neutrality, in some cases where the employer argues that an employee "assumed the risk" of injuries, it is hard to escape the ideological aspects of the issue. A representative case, eerily reminiscent of some features of the explosion on the Deepwater Horizon that caused the great oil gusher of 2010, arose on a drilling platform off the Louisiana coast. The plaintiff in this case was assigned to a job he had never done before. This was a "gas lift operation," in which workers used natural gas under pressure, brought in from a well by hose, to force liquid out of a clogged well. Although the plaintiff expressed concern to a production supervisor that bubbles forming on a hose indicated that it might rupture, the supervisor said that this was a normal event, "that he saw no need to change the hose, and that the bubbles did not affect the integrity of the hose." He told the plaintiff and his coworker to go ahead with the operation using the same hose. They obeyed. Not long after they turned on the pressure again, and the supervisor had left the platform, the hose burst and there was an explosion and fire.

The Fifth Circuit reversed a judgment for the defendant, noting that the supervisor "was in a position of authority," that he "purported to exercise that authority by giving instruction with the respect to the gas lift" and that the plaintiff and his co-worker had obeyed those instructions. To the argument that the plaintiff "should have refused to work and shut down the job," the court said that under state law this was "not a reasonable alternative for him" and that "[w]hether phrased in terms of surrender to superior authority, or lack of an available alternative, [the plaintiff's] actions were not voluntary, and therefore as a matter of law, not assumption of risk."[58]

Cases like this are at a vortex of argument about the constitution of injury law. In these cases there come together issues of freedom and theoretically free markets, the meaningfulness of choice, and justice. A key component of justice is an individualized one in situations where one party possesses all the significant elements of control, but in these cases there also is an element of social justice: employers, as a group, typically possess most of the control over the conditions of workplace life for their workers. Judges unavoidably make decisions tinged with political elements in such cases. Here we encounter multiple layers of the injury law constitution. With respect to compensation, it was to eliminate the injustice of the

58. Arnold v. Union Oil Co., 608 F.2d 575, 576 (5th Cir. 1979).

application of assumption of risk-type defenses that legislatures passed the workers' compensation laws. Now, many modern tort decisions on employee injuries take into account the degree of control that employers exercise over workers. And on the prevention side, the Occupational Safety and Health Act powerfully recognizes the realities of power in the workplace.

Products

In cases involving products injuries, the power of the parties to assess and minimize the risk of injury is often at the root of the dispute. That kind of power frequently resides in the possession of information about risk and the way it is communicated, subjects we will separately discuss below. A different aspect of power, although one that overlaps with information and communication, has to do with control of product design and product quality.

In the beginning, it is the manufacturer that blueprints the product, making choices among various aspects of the product that include safety, cost, and consumer appeal. Responding to its perceptions of consumer demand, it defines the function of the product, and this may include the circumstances of its use. To employ a chess analogy, these choices may involve some judgments that anticipate moves by the consumer that go beyond the openings. They may even involve other products, used in combination with the manufacturer's goods, which statistically have flaws. An example of the need for prevision on the part of manufacturers is a case involving a suit against the maker of a pistol the plaintiff was using for target practice with reloaded or remanufactured ammunition. The plaintiff suffered injuries when a "highly overpressured cartridge" exploded in the weapon. The trial court found that "the round that ruptured was overloaded with powder," which might have seemed to exonerate the maker of the pistol, but it also noted that "overloads are a common occurrence and well known in the industry as is the use of reloaded or remanufactured ammunition." An expert for the plaintiff, opining that there was a design flaw in the weapon— "an insufficiently supported chamber at the bottom of the cartridge in the chamber"—also said that "reloaded ammunition is more likely subject to overloading than brand new ammunition." This combination of hazards was enough for the North Dakota Supreme Court to find that the trial court did not err in deciding that the injury "was proximately caused by the combination of an overloaded cartridge and a defectively designed handgun," justifying a judgment against the maker of the pistol.[59] This decision places a

59. Endresen v. Scheels Hardware & Sports Shop, 560 N.W.2d 225, 228, 231–32 (N.D. 1997).

substantial burden on the manufacturer, but the justification for the result lies in the defendant's choice of a design in the context of its presumed knowledge about the statistical risks of reloaded ammunition: in short, its control of risk at the outset.

A New York case involving a table saw adds another layer of complexity, with a split of results under different doctrines demonstrating that control is sometimes divided between seller and buyer according to specific features of a product. The plaintiff was injured when his hand brushed up against the blade of the saw. Although he had not attached an available blade guard, he argued that the saw was defective because the defendant, maker of the device, had not used a permanently affixed guard. The court rejected this argument, pointing out that the removability of the guard on this particular saw allowed users to perform certain special types of sawing tasks. However, the court did allow a claim for negligent design on the basis that the saw had no brake, saying that the plaintiff should have a chance to show it would be feasible to include a brake that "would have automatically stopped the blade as soon as the saw was turned off."[60] The power to choose a particular set of risks and benefits thus varied between the buyer, who would benefit from the extra versatility afforded by a removable guard, and the manufacturer, which was aware of hazards that could be avoided by the inclusion of a brake.

The need for product designers to visualize their goods in the context of the way they actually will be used, rather than in a theoretical frame of reference, is evident in a Maryland case dealing with a conveyor that moved chicken feathers to cookers where they would be processed into feed. The nip points on the conveyor were unguarded, and there were no warning signs concerning the hazards of a decision the plaintiff made to use a stick to keep feathers from building up on the conveyor, which the evidence showed was common practice even if the machine was running. The court held that the plaintiff made a case that the conveyor was defective, referring to testimony by a mechanical engineer that "'common sense' is not relied upon in the industry because 'people don't follow it.'"[61] This decision indicates that the power to choose levels of safety may tag a design as "defective" even when the act that immediately causes the injury is a risky one by the claimant.

The fact that a product has multiple uses may not protect a manufacturer from liability when injury occurs from one of those uses that foreseeably exposes a user to a danger which could be avoided. One example is a case

---

60. David v. Makita U.S.A., Inc., 649 N.Y.S.2d 149, 151 (App. Div. 1996).
61. C&K Lord, Inc. v. Carter, 536 A.2d 699, 708–10 (Md. Ct. Spec. App. 1988).

involving a multipurpose crane that was being used near power lines. The plaintiff suffered severe injuries when the crane boom either touched a line or came so close to it that electricity surged into a steel pipe he was guiding that was being lifted by the crane. An Illinois court decided that despite the "multifunctional nature of the crane," the manufacturer could be held strictly liable for not equipping the machine with safety devices or at least informing purchasers about the dangers of not using them.[62]

The meshing of choice with knowledge about the realities of working environments may deal literally with climate. An example is what a court called a "gruesome" accident attributed to the failure of a valve to close on a piece of pipe spinning machinery on an oil platform in the Gulf of Mexico.[63] When the valve failed, the machine unexpectedly became activated, squeezing the plaintiff's decedent in steel cables. In affirming a judgment for the plaintiff, the court pointed out that the valve had been manufactured "for use in the irregular and corrosion causing climes of the Gulf of Mexico." It said the corrosion of the valve "[w]ell within its useful commercial life" created a condition that was "contrary to the normal and reasonable expectations of the users." Thus, power may be exercised in ways far removed from making a worker do something very risky on the spot or importuning for sexual favors; it may involve something like the selection of materials for use in a particular environment, for that is a choice entirely within the purview of a product designer. Such a choice, although made without the overbearing imposition that managers sometime employ against vulnerable subordinates, can eventuate in a result truly brutal to the product user.

Even when the design of a product is legally a solid one from a blueprint standpoint, a manufacturer may be exposed to suit for flaws it might have detected by closer scrutiny of mass-produced products. Products liability law includes a broad rule of strict liability for so-called manufacturing defects—flaws in the layperson's sense of the term. Such departures from the designer's norm may seem entirely fortuitous, but the defect may well arise from a failure of quality control. A commentator observed more than a generation ago that quality control literature speaks in terms of the level of risk that is assigned to consumers ("consumer's risk") by the sampling procedures manufacturers choose to check batches of products.[64]

To be sure, manufacturers are not "insurers" of the cost choices they make. This is evident when those choices attempt to rationally balance a variety of risks in useful products, in an effort to weigh the interests of

---

62. Burke v. Illinois Power Co., 373 N.E.2d 1354, 1367 (Ill. Ct. App. 1978).
63. Myers v. Pennzoil Co., 889 F.2d 1457, 1460 (5th Cir. 1989).
64. See Thomas A. Cowan, Some Policy Bases of Product Liability, 17 Stanford L. Rev. 1077, 1090–93 (1965).

consumers as well as sellers. An example is a case in which a car hit a motor-cycle ridden by the plaintiff, causing injury to his lower leg. He argued that he would have avoided the injury if the cycle had had robust crash bars. However, the court disagreed on the basis that making that one choice among many in favor of safety might adversely affect the overall safety of the cycle. It said that "[o]ne cannot eliminate the risk of injury to the leg at the expense of a significantly increasing risk of injury to other parts of the body."[65]

Beyond that, the law recognizes that sometimes it is the consumer who has control at crucial junctures. True, sometimes a manufacturer may lose because its own definition of how a product will be used is the type of use in which injury occurs. But the manufacturer's conception of how the prod-uct will be used—as the manufacturer may phrase it, how the product "should be used"—may cut both ways. On occasion, the consumer's use of the product may be at odds with the manufacturer's original definition of its function.

A decision involving tractor-scraper machines shows how lawyers can shape such a case with words and concepts. A buyer of these machines, an independent dealer of the manufacturer, sued the manufacturer because of damage to them while they were unloaded from a vessel on which they had been shipped in a "breakbulk shipment." Such shipments required a par-ticular kind of preparation when no vessel was available with what are known as Ro-Ro capabilities—that is, a vessel on which cargo could be driven on and off the ship. In rejecting the suit, the court said that the plain-tiff could not argue that lifting and unloading of a breakbulk shipment was "within the ordinary or intended use of these machines." The court said there were "really two intended functions" of the machines—that is, "scrap-ing roads and shipment on a Ro-Ro vessel." Important to the court's deci-sion was the fact that when the manufacturer shipped by breakbulk it would "charge[] the shipper for blocking and unloading instructions." In that con-text, the court said, the product that the manufacturer provided "for ship-ment via breakbulk carrier is . . . very different from the product [the plaintiff] requested and received." The court said that in this case, the pur-chaser had "on its own initiative sought responsibility for shipping these machines in an effort to save money" and had informed the manufacturer "that the machines would be shipped on a Ro-Ro vessel." "Under these cir-cumstances," the court said, the plaintiff "either knew or should have known that [the defendant's] tractor-scrapers had to be prepared in a special manner for breakbulk shipment." Thus, the court concluded, the plaintiff

65. Ziegler v. Kawasaki Heavy Indus., Ltd., 539 A.2d 701, 708 (Md. Ct. Spec. App. 1988).

could not "complain that the lifting and unloading involved in breakbulk shipment fell within the intended or ordinary use of these machines."[66]

Another decision involving a different kind of tractor focuses on the user's choice of a particular level of safety. In this Missouri case, which involved a fatal rollover of a utility tractor, the plaintiff claimed that the vehicle should have had a rollover protective structure (ROPS), but the court was unsympathetic. It said the manufacturer had done enough when it made clear in a manual that a ROPS was "recommended . . . for most" uses of the tractor. The court quoted precedent on the proposition that the buyer of a product with optional safety features is "in the best position to exercise an intelligent judgment to make the trade-off between cost and function."[67] Infighting on this issue shows how fiercely contested the arguments can be about both manufacturer and consumer choice of particular product designs. In an Alabama case, the court concluded that the plaintiff could make a claim for failure to provide a ROPS as standard equipment on a tractor, although the defendant provided evidence that "customers were hesitant to buy tractors that were ROPS-equipped," that ROPSs "got in the way" of farmers plowing orchards, and that it was "harder to change implements" on machines with ROPSs. The court said this evidence would "not support a holding that as a matter of law the installation of ROPS was so impractical that the tractor cannot be considered defective."[68] Both of these cases, with their seemingly contradictory outcomes, show that the functional question is where the locus of power lies. The overarching question under the injury law constitution arises from how the law responds to the crucial element of power.

An interesting comparison with these two cases in which ROPS were not standard equipment appears in a decision involving a type of product used in hospitals, a connector for intravenous tubing, for which there were two different designs. The design used in the case at issue was a luer slip connector, a device which had been in use for forty years, and which required five and one half pounds of separation force before it would disconnect. Another product, which had been used for about twenty years, was a luer lock connector, which used threaded collars and flanges that screwed together for "a more secure connection" and which "must withstand eight pounds of force." The appellate court found evidence for the

66. Ulrich Amman Building Equip. Ltd. v. M.V. Monsun, 1985 WL 3822, at 3–4, Prod. Liab. Rep. (CCH) ¶10,869, at 29,531 (S.D.N.Y. Nov. 20, 1985).

67. Morrison v. Kubota Tractor Corp., 891 S.W.2d 422, 427–28 (Mo. Ct. App. 1994), application to transfer denied (1995), quoting Biss v. Tenneco, Inc., 409 N.Y.S.2d 874, 876–77 (App.Div. 1978).

68. Deere & Co. v. Gross, 586 So.2d 196, 199–200 (Ala. 1991).

jury that the manufacturer should have known that "nurses at times would, for convenience, loosely connect the luer slip," and that it had "made and sold a luer lock line that did not come apart inadvertently" which "cost only a few pennies more than the luer slip."[69] A product manager for the defendant acknowledged that luer lock connectors "could potentially be more secure," but pointed out that there were "obviously customers that wanted" the slip connector, saying that "[i]t was selling in the marketplace." He said, "you have customer preference . . . it's just like anything else. You offer a variety of products to fit the customer's requirement."[70] Despite that hymn to consumer preference as summarized by the appellate court, the Illinois Supreme Court affirmed a large judgment for the plaintiff, whose decedent died after a disconnection of IV tubing. The supreme court affirmed the judgment on a design defect theory under both the risk-utility test and the consumer expectations test. With reference to the latter, it said that the plaintiff's decedent "could have reasonably expected that her IV catheter connection, if properly designed and manufactured, would be safe to use for its intended purpose."[71] Although there were choices to be made by hospitals that chose luer slip connectors instead of luer lock connectors, this decision effectively locates the crucial use of power in the manufacturer's design choice.

A poignant example of how the locus of choice may yield results that favor product makers involves a choice made by an employer. In this case, a state trooper died when bullets shot by a man he stopped for questioning hit him in places not covered by his protective vest, which was purchased by the state highway patrol. In overturning a jury verdict of more than a million dollars against the maker of the vest, the court noted that the vest the plaintiff's decedent was wearing was "one of several different styles then on the market" which varied in the degree of comfort and mobility they provided to wearers, as well as the amount of coverage of the body they afforded.[72] Analogous results appear in other cases involving a variety of products. Just one example is a case that focused on a life vest "designed for use by experienced, skilled wakeboarders, and often worn in competitions," which was "not an ordinary life jacket." An advanced wakeboarder apparently was knocked unconscious as he was trying a difficult aerial trick and sank within seconds of the accident. Rejecting a suit against the distributor and sellers of the vest, the court observed that the advanced wakeboarders who were "the ordinary consumers of this vest" were "willing

69. Hansen v. Baxter Healthcare Corp., 723 N.E.2d 302, 305, 313 (Ill. Ct. App. 1999).
70. Id. at 308.
71. Hansen v. Baxter Healthcare Corp., 764 N.E.2d 35, 45 (Ill. 2002).
72. Linegar v. Armour of America, Inc., 909 F.2d 1150, 1151 (8th Cir. 1990).

to forgo some degree of floatation for the sake of enhanced mobility."[73] In this case, the consumer must take responsibility for what turns out to be a very risky choice. Under the injury law constitution, the exercise of the power to choose is dispositive.

INFORMATION

A set of functional elements, overlapping with power, resides in information. These elements range across the wide landscape of injury law, including safety legislation and several doctrines of tort law. Many levels of science and philosophy underlie this subject, including topics that concern the nature of knowledge. When we say that we "know" something, what do we mean? When we say that some things have been proved, what are we saying? In the crucible of law, it is frequently difficult to define these terms.

Communication

A threshold element of the informational background of injuries lies in the form of communication. The media of communication may affect decisions about where the law places burdens.

Jurisdiction. At the very threshold of liability judgments is the question of whether a defendant has penetrated the market of a particular state to the point that it can be subject to the jurisdiction of that state. An example of the legal issues that arise with respect to jurisdiction is a case involving peripheral equipment for a parachute, which failed on a jump that occurred in Alabama, killing the chutist.[74] The defendant had originally sold the peripheral to a dealer in Michigan but it "ended up in Alabama"—how, it was not clear. An Alabama company that ran a parachute jumping operation had sent the peripheral to the defendant for repair, and the defendant had sent it back to the Alabama company. Operating under the guidance of a Supreme Court decision[75] in which several justices wrote opinions, the Eleventh Circuit decided that the defendant had "sufficient contacts with Alabama to satisfy the 'minimum contacts'" criterion that the Supreme Court had employed. One factor the court of appeals mentioned was that the defendant had "advertised in national trade magazines during the year

---

73. Wheeler v. H.O. Sports, Inc., 232 F.3d 754, 758 (10th Cir. 2000).
74. Morris v. SSE, Inc., 843 F.2d 489 (11th Cir. 1988).
75. Asahi Metal Indus. Co. v. Superior Ct., 480 U.S. 102 (1987).

prior to the parachuting accident and that such advertisements were a major source of business" for the defendant. The court of appeals said this led to "a reasonable inference" that the defendant had "advertised in Alabama." It declared that it was "clear that the defendant was aware that is was sending a hazardous product to [the parachute jumping firm] in Alabama and that the hazardous product would be used in Alabama."[76] Similarly, a firm may subject itself to the jurisdiction of a state in which that firm's product causes injury when it uses large-scale mail advertising, including the sending out of "thousands of brochures and catalogues . . . throughout the United States, including" that state.[77]

The Internet. Jurisdiction may also arise on the basis of electronic communication—in one case, for example, an infomercial broadcast to a state in which the plaintiff had a heart attack that he attributed to a diet drug made by the defendant.[78] The rise of the Internet has added to the catalogue of jurisdictional issues related to the method of communication, with courts basing decisions both ways on the use or non-use of websites. In one case, involving an allegedly defective tire, a Texas appellate court referred to Internet communication as a basis for jurisdiction over Bridgestone, the Japanese corporation that wholly owned Bridgestone/Firestone North American Tire. The court referred, among other elements of the case, to "information on Bridgestone's website such as representations that Bridgestone's eight proving grounds included those in Texas," saying that this information "blurred the distinction between Bridgestone and Firestone." In that sales environment, the court said that it did "not offend traditional motions of fair play and substantial justice" for a Texas court to take jurisdiction over Bridgestone.[79] One may compare a decision, also from the Texas appellate court, in a case involving a fire in a clock radio in which an electrical plug allegedly was made by Hitcachi Shin Din Cable (HSD), a Chinese corporation, in which Hitachi Cable (HC) owned a substantial amount of stock. The HC website allowed "Internet users to e-mail questions or submit comments to HC," but there was no proof that "those same users may e-mail questions or comments to HSD through HC's website." Moreover, there was no evidence "that someone in Texas would be able to complete a purchase order for HSD products over the Internet." On those facts, the court decided that "HSD's website has such an extremely

76. 843 F.2d at 494.
77. Welkener v. Curtwood Drugstore Co., 734 S.W.2d 233, 239–40 (Mo. Ct. App. 1987) (defective crutch).
78. Spicer v. New Image Int'l, Inc., 447 F.Supp.2d 1226 (D. Kan. 2006).
79. Bridgestone Corp. v. Lopez, 131 S.W.3d 670, 686–87 (Tex. Ct. App. 2004).

low level of interactivity that HSD may not fairly be subjected to general personal jurisdiction in Texas."[80]

Issues that may test courts in the future may include the question of whether words of warranty communicated over the Internet should have the same effect as those in conventional print. It seems that they should,[81] but a somewhat more difficult question is whether a consumer has to show specific reliance on "affirmations or promises" made on the Internet. Venting some potential issues is a disagreement on this point between a federal district judge and the Third Circuit in a cigarette case that involved magazine and TV advertisements. The district judge said that the question on an express warranty claim was one of "whether the agreement or bargain . . . objectively viewed, contains the affirmations or promises—not on whether a buyer's purchasing decision, subjectively viewed, depends on the statements." He said that "a statement in an advertisement becomes part of the basis of a bargain, if, objectively viewed, the statement would tend to induce the purchase of the advertised product."[82] The court of appeals, however, said that the district judge's "purely objective theory" "fails to explain how an advertisement that a buyer never even saw becomes part of the 'basis of the bargain.'" By contrast, the court of appeals said that a plaintiff would fulfill the "basis of the bargain" requirement of express warranty doctrine "by proving that she read, heard, saw or knew of the advertisement containing the affirmation of fact or promise."[83]

Courts will have to confront the question of whether the Web environment will affect attempts of sellers to disclaim or limit liability. The existence of disclaimers is vital information to consumers, and disclaimers are supposed to be conspicuous, but the presentation of a complex contractual document on a screen may not be as communicative as it would be in hard copy. Thus Web sellers may have to figure out ways to make their efforts to disclaim or limit liability stand out.[84] A similar problem may arise with respect to the conspicuousness of warnings. More generally, as a colleague and I have suggested, it is possible that courts may take into account the catchiness of promotions on the Web when plaintiffs argue that an Internet presentation implies that a product "is particularly advanced in its technology."[85] We raise the question of whether the Web carries

---

80. Hitachi Shin Din Cable, Ltd. v. Cain, 106 S.W.3d 776, 786–87 (Tex. Ct. App. 2003).

81. See, e.g., Marshall S. Shapo & Kurtis B. Reeg, E-Commerce and Products Liability: A Primer on Exposure at the Speed of Light, 51 FICC Q. 73, 76 (2001).

82. Cipollone v. Liggett Group, Inc., 693 F.Supp.2d 208, 214 (D. N.J. 1988).

83. Cipollone v. Liggett Group, Inc., 893 F.2d 541, 567 (3d Cir. 1990).

84. See Shapo and Reeg, *supra* note 81, at 94, 90.

85. *Id.* at 88–89.

"an amorphous indefinable 'fast track' or 'new age' penumbra that suggests superior technological advancement."[86]

Defamation. An area of the law that features cases fascinating because of their language includes statements that portray individuals falsely—or in an embarrassingly truthful way. The injury law constitution oversees the balancing of various interests in this area as it does with respect to other injury-causing behavior. Defamation suits, which involve false statements that damage reputation, have a negative informational element. A defamation plaintiff claims that the defendant falsified the facts and that thus the consumers of communications—readers and viewers—lacked accurate information because of the falsehood. In defamation cases, the medium may become entwined with the message. There are different rules, sometimes rather complicated ones, for libel—historically, written communication—and slander, which historically is spoken defamation. It has now been settled that radio and television—communications entirely spoken in one and in large part spoken in the other—fall into the libel category. It seems to follow that communication on the Web is also libel, given that it has the appearance of print and is electronically conveyed, thus reaching potentially larger audiences than traditional oral messages like face-to-face statements. One interesting wrinkle that has arisen from the Internet involves the question of who shall be deemed to be a "publisher" of defamatory information on the Web. A federal statute now says that "[n]o provider or user of an interactive computer service shall be treated as the publisher or speaker of any information provided by another information content provider."[87] This means that a so-called Internet service provider is not liable for a nasty posting by someone who simply uses its service.

As with beatings and bludgeonings, false words can damage all kinds of individuals. However, the courts have developed classifications that categorize defamation plaintiffs according to their involvement in public affairs. The Supreme Court weighed in in 1964, when it said that the only way a public official could sue for defamation concerning his or her official duties was to show that the defendant had published a statement with "reckless disregard of whether it was false or not."[88] Later, in two headline-making cases, the Court concluded that people who were "public figures" claiming defamation would have to measure up to that same demanding "reckless disregard" standard.[89] The courts later elaborated on the kind of plaintiff who would be regarded as a "public figure" for the application of that test.

---

86. See *id.* at 89.
87. Communications Decency Act, 47 U.S.C. §230(c)(1)(2006).
88. New York Times v. Sullivan, 376 U.S. 254, 280 (1964).
89. See Curtis Publ'g Co. v. Butts, 388 U.S. 130 (1967).

They developed the category of the "limited purpose public figure," borrowing from the Supreme Court's reference to one who "voluntarily injects himself or is drawn into a particular controversy and thereby becomes a public figure for a limited range of issues."[90] By contrast, those defined as "private individuals" get somewhat more liberal treatment. Generally speaking, they do not have to show "reckless disregard" of the truth on the part of a publisher of defamation, although they do have to prove that the publisher was in some way at fault—at least negligent—and they must show "actual injury" rather than the "presumed" damages that defamation plaintiffs historically were able to demonstrate.

"Fact" and "opinion." An important example of the tensions in this area is the distinction that courts in defamation cases draw between "fact" and "opinion." The importance of the distinction is that one can sue for a false statement of fact but not for a statement of opinion. The basic idea is that if you can't verify the "truth" of a statement, it cannot be said to be false.[91] In a leading case, the writers of an op-ed column said that a political science professor who had been nominated to head a department at a state university "[had] no status within the profession, but is a pure and simple activist." Judge Kenneth Starr's plurality opinion for the D.C. Circuit found this statement to be "rhetorical hyperbole," which at least in an op-ed column would be taken by "the average reader" to be a statement "of opinion." Judge Starr said for the plurality that to call this defamation would reduce "'breathing space,'" inhibiting "the scope of public discussion on matters of general interest and concern."[92] A particularly interesting contrast appeared in the argument, made in partial dissent by then Judge Scalia of that court, that the defendants had not said that the plaintiff was incompetent but rather "that his professional peers regarded him as incompetent"—which would be a factual statement.[93]

Truth: acquisition of information and publication. Sometimes the truth hurts, and the courts have taken into account not only the hurt but the method of getting the information. One tort action that has developed concerning the method is the action for "intrusion." It is clear that the obtaining of information by wiretapping and electronic eavesdropping may provide grounds for a lawsuit. Stalking—now defined as a crime in many states—may also support a tort action for the way someone gets information.

90. Gertz v. Robert Welch, 418 U.S. 323, 351 (1974).

91. Ollman v. Evans, 750 F.2d 970 (D.C. Cir. 1984). Judge Starr identified one criterion for deciding whether a statement was fact or opinion as its "verifiability"—whether it was "capable of being objectively characterized as true or false[]," *id.* at 979.

92. *Id.* at 991.

93. *Id.* at 1037 (Scalia, J., dissenting in part).

One colorful case yielded the unusual remedy of an injunction against a photographer who made himself extremely bothersome to Jacqueline Kennedy Onassis and her children, for example by "jump[ing] and postur[ing] around while taking pictures" of a party she gave at a theater opening. The Second Circuit, building on a finding by the trial judge that the defendant had "insinuated himself into the very fabric of Ms. Onassis' life," decided that it was appropriate to grant an injunction "under New York's proscription of harassment."[94]

There exists a separate tort action that courts have distinguished from defamation under the label of "false light"—for example, a true photograph of someone which presents that person in a compromised position. In another category of tort doctrine, there has been argument over whether the publication of accurate material, including photographs and moving pictures, can be held to be a misappropriation of the plaintiff's personality—an economic gain to the defendant derived from a "property right" that belongs to the plaintiff.

Perhaps the most difficult case involving the publication of information is the one in which the plaintiff claims that truthful revelations about him or her are a compensable injury—a tort sometimes called "public disclosure of private facts." The courts have largely, although not unanimously, held for defendants in cases of this kind. In some cases they have suggested that bringing to public attention long-buried facts in someone's life, for example a criminal conviction, is no more than the writing of history, which may, overall, redound to the good of the public.

A functional analysis of the law of injuries exhibits many tugs of war in which the decisions of courts have a tendency to encourage or discourage particular forms of communication. As judges decide how to set those incentives, they consider that the dissemination of information informs people of the availability of useful products, and if done properly, of their risks as well as their benefits. They also weigh the way communication enables the public to understand more about public affairs. By contrast, they may also take into account that communications like certain advertisements may get people to buy things that may harm them or that promotional messages may stimulate people to purchase things they don't really "want"—although that is a judgment that, on the whole, we are loath to have government make for us. Moreover, certain kinds of communication may result in damage to reputations or the creation of embarrassment to people who do not want others to know certain facts about them that many people would consider to be private.

94. Galella v. Onassis, 487 F.2d 986, 994–95 (2d Cir. 1973).

Generally speaking, we regard communication as a public good. But the communication of information, or what is presented as information, requires courts to strike many balances. As they do that, we see in the nuances of their decisions some elements of a constitution of injury law. That constitution challenges us to think more deeply about the kind of society we are building and provides a check on the misfeasance of public officials as well as the misadventures of people, often powerful people, who may have an influence on events important to the public. It also increases our ability to make thoughtful consumption judgments: what to buy in the way of material goods, in the process comparing the many items that are marketed for consumption. This evolving constitution then pits the public benefits of many forms of communication—including the benefits of individual autonomy in speaking one's mind and of freedom in advertising one's wares—against another set of goods. These include fundamental dignitary elements—to keep one's private life to oneself, not to be overborne commercially, not to be injured by risks one did not freely choose. And those private, individual goods blend into the advantages they bring to society: of reasonable expectations protected, of civility preserved, and of stability maintained.

*** ***

Duties to Provide Information

A foundational set of issues about information asks when people who possess it have an obligation to communicate it. These issues abound in both tort law and regulatory law, and the way they are resolved by courts and regulators reflect elements that are constitutive of society's view of injuries.

Products Liability and Warnings. The power resident in information is manifest in several aspects of the law of products liability, in particular those that deal with sellers' duties to warn consumers of product hazards. We encounter here the question of who is in the best position to acquire and assess information—a question that pertains both to various layers of product sellers and distributors and to consumers. We analyze a variety of cases that deal with issues of how much different parties know about hazards, the ability of parties to convey information and to absorb it, and the assumptions courts make about the effects of warnings.

As with the topics we examined above, a question that threads its way through the cases on duty to warn is where the locus of control sits with reference to the acquisition and use of information. Since the marketing of products is a dynamic process, which includes information about injury risks that pops up from time to time after a product has been on the market, an important set of issues concerns the duty of manufacturers with respect to risks that develop after sale.

Manufacturers' duties may extend to information concerning well-known, relatively simple technologies. One case involved a suit against a motorcycle helmet manufacturer because it did not warn cyclists that it was dangerous to use a Velcro strip to fasten the defendant's helmets without properly securing the chin strap. A federal court in Minnesota said that if the defendant had had adequate notice that "that the velcro strip could induce users to misuse the helmet and render it ineffective" for the purpose of preventing head injuries, the defendant would have "a duty to take reasonable steps to alert the public of the risks associated with the misuse of the velcro strip."[95]

The fact that a seller does not think much of allegations of risk about a product may not save it from liability. As the Kansas Supreme Court said in a case involving birth control pills, "where scientific or medical evidence exists tending to show that a certain danger is associated with use of a drug, the manufacturer may not ignore or discount that information in drafting its warning solely because it finds it to be unconvincing."[96] The Maryland Court of Appeals has even said that the discontinuance of a product line—in this case asbestos products—would not necessarily give a manufacturer "automatic relief from its continuing duty to warn merely because it no longer manufactures a defective product."[97] The duty to give post-sale warnings is well enough established that it has found a home in the Restatement of Products Liability, which requires such warnings "if a reasonable person in a seller's position would provide such a warning."[98]

The possession of information about multiple dangers may impose obligations to warn about more than one risk. In another Maryland asbestos case, the court said that even if the defendant could not have foreseen that the "ultimate harm" suffered by the plaintiff "would take the form of mesothelioma rather than asbestosis," that would not save the defendant from liability. The court said that "the jury could find that [the defendant] knew or should have known of the hazard of lung disease produced by inhaling asbestos fibers" and that "[m]esothelioma is a form of lung disease caused

95. McDaniel v. Bieffe USA, Inc., 35 F.Supp.2d 735, 742–43 (D. Minn. 1999).
96. Wooderson v. Ortho Pharm. Corp., 681 P.2d 1038, 1042 (Kan. 1984)(syllabus by the court).
97. Owens-Illinois, Inc. v. Zenobia, 601 A.2d 633, 647 (Md. 1992).
98. Restatement (3d) of Torts: Products Liability §10(a) (1998).

by inhaling asbestos fibers." It concluded that there was "sufficient evidence to support a finding that [the defendant] had a duty to warn."[99]

A particularly interesting battleground under the injury law constitution features arguments about "sophisticated users" of products. Often, the "sophisticated user" is the employer of a worker injured by a chemical used on the job. An illustrative case involved employees of Gore, the company that makes Gore-Tex, which considered its coating operation for the fabric "a trade secret"—so secret that the company would "not invite other chemical companies into its plants" and would not tell them "how the substances they supplied would be used or with what they might be mixed." The Gore employees sued DuPont for injuries they attributed to DuPont chemicals used in making Gore-Tex, but the court rejected the suit, saying that "DuPont reasonably relied on Gore to protect its employees from the various hazards of the product."[100]

Yet, the more a manufacturer pushes itself into the marketing process, the more it may expose itself to liability. In another case involving DuPont as a defendant, a Georgia court denied summary judgment to the company, which made a patented material, Tyvek, that was used in the manufacture of coveralls that flared up when oxygen ignited in a tank car. The court noted that DuPont had actively promoted the product "as a material that may be used to make 'protective apparel' for the workplace" and that DuPont had even paid makers of garments to put a Tyvek label on the collars of clothes containing the material. Since DuPont had "ordered its assemblers 'as a condition of sale' to adhere" to standards for the labeling of garments, the court said this suggested that "DuPont would have little difficulty in requiring garment manufacturers to place warning labels" about the flammability of products containing its chemical "as a condition of sale."[101]

If knowledge is power, communication of general knowledge about risk may not save product sellers with respect to specific elements of risk. The level of particularity that may be required of sellers is evident in a Minnesota case in which the defendant was a supplier of silica. Although this defendant had provided the plaintiff's employer "with a general warning of the dangers of silicosis," the state supreme court noted that the defendant had not warned the employer "about the ineffectiveness of disposable respirators or instruct[ed] that only high efficiency respirators be used." Although there was evidence about the employer's "general knowledge" concerning the risk of silicosis and concerning information available to it

99. Eagle-Picher Indus. v. Balbos, 604 A.2d 445, 453 (Md. 1992).
100. Kennedy v. Mobay Corp., 579 A.2d 1191, 1203 (Md. Ct. App. 1991), aff'd per curiam, 601 A.2d 123 (Md. 1992).
101. Carter v. E.I. Dupont de Nemours & Co., 456 S.E.2d 661, 664 (Ga. Ct. App. 1995).

"from government and industry publications, other sand suppliers and . . . suppliers of respirators," the court said that information could not "be said to conclusively establish that [the employer's] knowledge was equal to that of" the defendant.[102]

Another silicosis case illustrates how tightly bunched may be the opposing arguments about hazard information. The defendant in this case "sold flint both in bulk and in 100-pound bags, and only to industrial customers." The Texas Supreme Court said that the defendant did not have a duty to warn industrial customers who conducted abrasive blasting operations "that inhaling silica dust can be disabling and fatal and that workers must wear air-fed hoods, because that information had long been commonly known throughout the industry." However, the court also concluded that there might be a fact question about whether a warning proposed by the plaintiff would have been effectual, and that the defendant would have to show that the warning "would not have been effectual."[103]

The obligations of sellers can extend to their knowledge that users will be careless, or even deliberately incur risks, in the use of a product. An example is a case involving a plastic injection molding machine on which the defendant had put several warnings, including a warning against operating the screw when the hopper was removed from the machine. Ruling for a worker injured when hot plastic erupted from the machine, the court said that the defendant should have realized that if a blockage occurred, users would try to deal with it by removing the hopper cover and head, and pointed out that the dangers in doing this were not explained by the warnings.[104]

A manufacturer's duty may even embrace illegal conduct by distributors. A sad example is the case of an infant who died after drinking mineral spirits that a retailer had packaged illegally in a half-gallon milk container. The court said that the defendants, manufacturers and bulk distributors of mineral spirits, had done "nothing in the face of their knowledge" that their products were "commonly sold illegally in retail stores" which "used milk containers that bear no warnings of their dangerous propensities."[105]

A large set of cases in which the courts firmly locate the crucial site of information lies in the area of medical products. There, courts have developed a doctrine which bars suits against manufacturers on the grounds that they only have to communicate warnings about product risks to

102. Gray v. Badger Mining Corp., 676 N.W.2d 268, 279 (Minn. 2004).
103. Humble Sand & Gravel, Inc. v. Gomez, 146 S.W.3d 170, 184, 195 (Tex. 2004).
104. See Nelson v. Hydraulic Press Mfg. Co., 404 N.E.2d 1013, 1018–19 (Ill. Ct. App. 1980).
105. Hunnings v. Texaco, 29 F.3d 1480, 1486 (11th Cir. 1994).

physicians—so-called learned intermediaries. That rule has particular force where the doctor is "fully aware" of the risks associated with a product.[106] Indeed, in a case focusing on interactions of the defendant's anticonvulsant drug with acetaminophen, a doctor's testimony that she "still would have prescribed" a drug even if she had known about a risk strengthened the argument that the knowledge of the "learned intermediary" supersedes that of the manufacturer.[107] Another case involved the drug Prozac, which allegedly caused a suicide. The plaintiff argued that the defendant should have provided to American doctors a warning about the monitoring of patients that it had provided with the German version of the drug. However, when the prescribing doctor said he would have prescribed the drug even if the American package insert for it had "contained the precise language" in the German warning, the court held for the drug maker.[108]

Even where prescription drugs are involved, though, manufacturers may open a gap in the wall of the learned intermediary doctrine by advertising their products to the public. There is at least one case on this point, in which the New Jersey Supreme Court said that a plaintiff could make a claim for injuries allegedly caused by Norplant, an implanted contraceptive for which the manufacturer had put on a "massive advertising campaign," "which it directed at women rather than at their doctors." Noting that "[p]atient choice is an increasingly important part of our medical-legal jurisprudence," the court said that "[w]hen a patient is the target of direct marketing, one would think, at a minimum, that the law would require that the patient be not misinformed about the product."[109] The court did create a rebuttable presumption that a drug manufacturer would satisfy its duty to warn physicians if it "complies with FDA advertising, labeling and warning requirements."[110] However, the decision indicates that the promotion of products, rather than just their labeling, is an important ingredient in the soup of knowledge about drugs, in a day when even prescription products are the subject of mass advertising.

A manufacturer of medical products may also be held to knowledge about what happens on the ground of their use, for example in a hospital setting. In a case mentioned earlier, involving connectors for intravenous tubes, the defendant made two products, one of which had a more secure kind of connection. In that case, which involved the less secure connector, the court noted that "[t]he nurse responsible for the actual purchase and

---

106. See, e.g., Hunt v. Hoffman-La Roche, Inc., 785 F.Supp. 547, 550 (D. Md. 1992).
107. Eck v. Parke, Davis & Co., 256 F.3d 1013, 1022–23 (10th Cir. 2001).
108. Woulfe v. Eli Lilly & Co., 965 F.Supp. 1478, 1481 (E.D. Okla. 1997).
109. Perez v. Wyeth Labs., Inc., 734 A.2d 1245, 1257 (N.J. 1999).
110. Id. at 1259.

distribution of medical supplies" at the hospital where the plaintiff's decedent was treated said that "she did not know the difference" between the types of connector. Indeed, the doctor who had placed a catheter in the jugular vein of the plaintiff's decedent said he was "unfamiliar" with the more secure connectors and "did not learn about them until after the incident."[111]

An important element in the availability and the transmission of information is the cost of providing it. Judge Williams of the Court of Appeals for the District of Columbia Circuit spoke to this point in a case where the plaintiff contended that the defendant should have warned about the "explosive, as well as flammable" nature of propane cylinders. Responding to the argument that it is very cheap to put extra information in a warning, Judge Williams said that "[t]he primary cost is, in fact, the increase in time and effort required for the user to grasp the message." He said that the addition of more bits of information "dilutes the punch of every other item" and results in pieces of information "get[ting] lost in fine print."[112] A variation on this position appears in a case of the much-discussed problem of burns caused by hot coffee. Judge Easterbrook of the Seventh Circuit rejected what he viewed as a line of argument that could require warnings about such details as "the risk of burns in real life, starting with the number of cups of coffee sold annually, the number of these that spill (broken down by location, such as home, restaurant, and car), and the probability that any given spill will produce a severe (as opposed to a mild or average) burn." He appended to this rather exaggerated catalog the common sense observation that state law "expects consumers to educate themselves about the hazards of daily life . . . by general reading and experience, knowledge they can acquire before they enter a mini mart to buy coffee for a journey."[113]

The information problem often comes down to a question of what consumers know and what they don't know. In another hot coffee case, the court noted that the plaintiff in her complaint said she had put coffee on a folding shelf in front of her airline seat "to allow the coffee to cool before she drank it." The court simply observed that "[o]ne needs no warning if he or she is aware of the danger as to which a warning would apply."[114] Striking the balance in a different way—as to what consumers don't know—is a case in which an explosion occurred when a gasoline can used for a lawnmower was placed near a gas water heater. In reversing a partial summary judgment for the heater manufacturer, the court adduced testimony of a firefighter

111. Hansen v. Baxter Healthcare Corp., 764 N.E.2d 35, 40, 43 (Ill. 2002).
112. Cotton v. Buckeye Gas Prods. Co., 840 F.2d 935, 938 (D.C. Cir. 1988).
113. McMahon v. Bunn-O-Matic Corp., 150 F.3d 651, 656–57 (7th Cir. 1988).
114. Lamkin v. Braniff Airlines, 853 F.Supp. 30, 32 (D. Mass. 1994).

that people should be warned not to put anything combustible next to a hot water heater. It also referred to a professor's testimony that if there "had been previous knowledge of explosions of gas-fired hot water heaters being the primary ignition source that would have made it proper and dutiful to have warned unsuspecting users and operators . . . of the potential hazard."[115]

An illustration of the issue of what consumers know in fact in the area of over-the-counter drugs is a case in which the plaintiff took six to eight tablets of Anacin a day for more than a year and sued for gastrointestinal hemorrhaging. The trial judge rejected the suit on the grounds that the risks of prolonged use of aspirin, a component of Anacin, were "commonly appreciated by laymen." However, a New Jersey appellate court reversed, pointing to the "basic marketing predicate" that "nonprescription drugs" were used for self-medication without the intervention of doctors, and concluding that there was a duty to warn consumers of over-the-counter drugs "of all known specific and appreciable inherent product dangers."[116]

A linguistic device that courts use to shift the burden of knowledge to the consumer is to refer to a danger as "obvious." Several courts have used terminology like that in cases where plaintiffs suffer crippling injuries from diving into the shallow end of aboveground swimming pools.[117] It should be noted, however, that there is disagreement even on this point. In one case, a dissenter against a denial of liability said that if there were "a specific latent risk" like quadriplegia, "there is an obligation to warn, even if there is a more general obvious risk."[118] In another case, the plaintiff said that she would not have dived into the shallow end of a pool if she had known that it might lead to permanently paralyzing injuries. A Connecticut court said that the facts did "not conclusively establish that the plaintiff would have dived into the pool if warnings and depth markings . . . were posted" and concluded that "whether the lack of warnings and depth markings was the proximate cause of the plaintiff's injuries was a disputed issue of material fact."[119]

The question of what's obvious and what isn't presents disputes across a spectrum of hazards. It is certainly established that people walk on ice at their own risk.[120] Moreover, a court used "open and obvious" language in

---

115. Hohlenkamp v. Rheem Mfg. Co., 601 P.2d 298, 300 (Ariz. Ct. App. 1979).
116. Torsiello v. Whitehall Labs., 398 A.2d 132, 137, 139 (N.J. Super. Ct. App. Div. 1979).
117. See, e.g., Glittenberg v. Doughboy Recreational Indus., Inc., 462 N.W.2d 348 (Mich. 1990); see also Glittenberg v. Doughboy Recreational Indus., Inc., 491 N.W.2d 208 (Mich. 1992).
118. Glittenberg, 491 N.W.2d at 227 (Levin, J., dissenting).
119. Battistoni v. Weatherking Prods., 676 A.2d 890, 895 (Conn. Ct. App. 1996).
120. Kokoyachuk v. Aeroquip Corp., 526 N.E.2d 607 (Ill. App. Ct. 1988).

denying recovery to the survivors of a company lawyer who was killed by the spinning rotor blade on a helicopter.[121] And the "dangers of riding unrestrained in the open cargo bed of a moving pickup truck" are also "obvious."[122]

Even when dangers are seemingly apparent, though, factual questions may arise about the precise level of information that will bar a lawsuit based on failure to warn. A federal court of appeals, dealing with eyeglasses that shattered during a volleyball game, criticized the trial court for taking "it upon itself to decide that it was not a requirement for a manufacturer or seller of eyeglasses to tell a teenager or anybody 'if you wear glasses and get hit while you've got them on, they might break.'" Instead, the court said, the question was one for the jury.[123] A similarly rigorous requirement on communicating a specific risk appears in a decision involving a 400-pound desktop copier that appeared to be "tipping and wobbly" when the plaintiff, a field service technician, was demonstrating the device to a customer. Where two legs of the copier came off and the device collapsed on the plaintiff's hand, the court said that "[t]he danger of a photocopier toppling over when enough force is applied may be obvious, but the danger of the legs of the device detaching from it so as to fully remove any support holding up the copier above a desktop is not so apparent."[124] Judicial sympathy for plaintiffs can even extend to the flammability of clothing. In one case the Sixth Circuit said that even though "[a] consumer might reasonably be expected to know that a rayon shirt that will catch fire more easily and burn more quickly than a shirt made of heavy flannel," yet "[a]n ordinary consumer would have no way of knowing . . . that a particular rayon shirt was substantially more combustible than another rayon shirt."[125]

The importance of information in torts cases sometimes links inseparably to the disadvantaged position of workers. The New Jersey Supreme Court directly confronted both factors in a pair of cases involving what is known as the "heeding presumption"—the idea that if a defendant had provided a warning of a hazard, the plaintiff "would have heeded" it.[126] In one asbestos case, the New Jersey court premised that "[j]ust as it is fair and reasonable to assume that such a warning will serve to render the product safe because it is calculated to alert the foreseeable user of the product of its dangers, so should one assume that such a warning if provided will

121. In re Inlow Accident Litig., 2002 WL 970403, at 13–15 (S.D. Ind. 2002).
122. Maneely v. General Motors Corp., 108 F.3d 1176 (9th Cir. 1997).
123. Boudreaux v. Jack Eckerd Corp., 854 F.2d 85, 87–88 (5th Cir. 1988).
124. Landberg v. Ricoh Int'l, 892 F.Supp. 938, 942 (E.D. Mich. 1995).
125. Hollister v. Dayton Hudson Corp., 201 F.3d 731, 741 (6th Cir. 2000).
126. Coffman v. Keene Corp., 628 A.2d 710, 714 (N.J. 1993).

be followed." The court said that a manufacturer seeking to overcome the heeding presumption in a workplace case would have to show that "had an adequate warning been provided, the plaintiff-employee with meaningful choice would not have heeded the warning" or that the plaintiff's employer "would not have heeded the warning by taking reasonable precautions for the safety of its employees."[127] In another case decided the same day, the court said that in a workplace environment laden with asbestos dust, a maker of asbestos products would have to "adduce evidence that decedent would have had a meaningful choice to take effective precautions against hazards had he so chosen" and that "[i]n the employment context," defendants would have to "produce evidence to overcome the heeding presumption with respect to the employer's conduct."[128]

This section on warnings in products liability law presents a varied set of environments in which the possession of relevant information is crucial—from the workplace choked with asbestos dust to the doctor's office as the physician writes prescriptions to the backyard swimming pool. As courts across the country have developed this common law zone of injury law, they often have focused on the facts available to consumers and workers. But as they contribute to the development of a practical constitution representing the most fundamental attitudes of the American people about risk and injury, they also draw preferences about justice into their decisions. Some of the decisions involving workplace injury, in particular, reveal those preferences. And such decisions manifest judicial choices in the continuous competition of ideologies within the broad framework of the injury law constitution.

The Quality of Information. We have focused so far on the primary question of when people possessing information have an obligation to disclose it at all. A set of issues that arise within that problem concerns the quality of information that is disclosed, and judicial responses to those issues also add elements to the injury law constitution. Claimants may challenge the quality of information—while sometimes also establishing that there is a duty to provide information in the first place—under various doctrines. They may sue for misrepresentation, under theories including fraud, negligent misrepresentation, and in some states a tort doctrine of innocent misrepresentation. They may also allege that an express warranty was deficient in the information it communicated. An example is a case in which a patient pamphlet for an antibiotic, which said that it contained "everything you need to know about your prescription" and included the words "take with food or

127. *Id.* at 723–24.
128. Theer v. Philip Carey Co., 628 A.2d 724, 730 (N.J. 1993).

milk if upset stomach occurs." The plaintiff, who consumed a lot of dairy products when she took the drug, sued on the occurrence of an autoimmune response to the product that mimicked the illness—Lyme disease—for which she was taking the drug. The court interpreted the pamphlet as constituting an express warranty that the antibiotic was "compatible with dairy such that it became part of the basis of the bargain."[129]

In addition to theories based directly on specific representations, plaintiffs may use the theory of strict liability to take advantage of failures to provide information. In a case in which the plaintiff alleged that raw asbestos fiber was defectively packaged, the Sixth Circuit acknowledged that the defendant "could not be held strictly liable based upon the failure to warn." However, the court said that "the failure to warn, as well as the defective packaging, were part of 'the totality of circumstances' which make [the] product defective" under a design defect theory. Opining that "[t]he packaging of a product is also an element to consider when determining whether the consumer would reasonably expect the content of the package to pose the danger that it did," the appellate court said that the trial court "was correct in considering these factors in evaluating the totality of the circumstances from which the consumers' expectation"—one of the tests for strict liability—"would have been formed."[130]

Specificity of Information. The specific type of hazard information conveyed with a product may affect the outcome in a variety of cases. One example is a case in which the Material Safety Data Sheets (MSDS) for a solvent said that if it was used without protective clothing, dermatitis could occur. The sheets also warned of the risk of "respiratory tract irritation" and "central nervous system effects" which could include asphyxiation if the product were used without ventilation and protective respiratory equipment. However, the MSDS did not specifically mention the risk of damage to vital organs, and where a mechanic claimed that the solvent had caused liver failure, the court denied summary judgment to the defendants, saying that "liver damage is far more apt to have a devastating effect . . . than is dermatitis."[131]

The medical products area has yielded a number of cases on the specificity of warnings. Specific facts will turn cases involving both drugs and devices in favor of both plaintiffs and defendants. Illustrative of decisions favoring plaintiffs is a Fifth Circuit case in which a drug manufacturer

129. Rite Aid Corp. v. Levy-Gray, 894 A.2d 563, 579 (Md. 2006).
130. Adkins v. GAF Corp. 923 F.2d 1225, 1228–29 (6th Cir. 1991).
131. Schwoerer v. Union Oil Co., 17 Cal. Rptr. 2d 227, 231–32 (Cal. Ct. App. 1993). On specificity of risk information, see also *supra*, text accompanying note 102.

argued that it did not have to warn about risks of using its product for more than twelve weeks because the label of the drug clearly said that it was "indicated for treatment of no more than that duration." Where the defendant at least should have known that the drug "was prescribed routinely for long-term use" and possessed statistics showing that 84 percent of users were using the product on a long-term basis, the court said that "a jury could infer that [the] warning was ineffective and thus inadequate."[132]

By contrast, a Viagra case is an example of the situation where a physician's knowledge of his patient and of some information about a drug will bar a lawsuit against a drug maker. In this case, the plaintiff's decedent had sexual intercourse after his first dose of the drug and died two hours later. Before he took the drug, he had had a coronary artery bypass and his doctor had prescribed nitroglycerin tablets. At that time, the package insert for Viagra "clearly indicate[d] that patients taking nitrates should not take Viagra."[133] The plaintiff's doctor said that if he had known about information in a later package insert concerning risks to "patients with preexisting cardiovascular disease," "he would have ruled out a Viagra prescription" for the patient. However, invoking the learned intermediary doctrine discussed earlier, the court said that "[a] physician who is aware of his patient's heart disease is cognizant that the patient is at risk both during sexual intercourse and during any other strenuous exercise," and that "neither version" of the package insert used "any language that would delude a physician into thinking that Viagra would lessen this risk." The court concluded that both of the warnings "merely alert physicians to a risk of which they already should be aware—the danger that strenuous physical activity poses to patients with heart disease."[134]

Parallel results on the specificity of warnings, differing with specific facts, appear in the area of medical devices. In a case involving silicone gel-filled breast implants that ruptured, the plaintiff's surgeon tried to loosen scar tissue that formed around the implants by using a closed capsulotomy, which the court described as "applying force and squeezing the breasts." The manufacturer argued that it had warned sufficiently by a statement that it "cannot guarantee the structural integrity of its implant should the surgeon elect to treat capsule firmness by forceful external stress," but a former official of the defendant testified that he would "never recommend a closed capsulotomy" for the product at issue because it was "too fragile and too likely to rupture." The court decided that a jury could have found

---

132. McNeil v. Wyeth, 462 F.3d 364, 369 (5th Cir. 2006).
133. Brumley v. Pfizer, Inc., 200 F.R.D. 596, 600 (S.D. Tex. 2001).
134. Brumley v. Pfizer, Inc., 149 F.Supp.2d 305, 310, 311–12 (S.D. Tex. 2001).

that the manufacturer's warning "did not properly convey the risks of the closed capsulotomy."[135]

One may compare a case in which the plaintiff contended that the maker of a surgical nail should have given "more precise information" about the comparative weakness of the product with reference to another nail, and that it should have said the product ought not to be used for fractures like those of the plaintiff, whose bones had been weakened by radiation therapy. The court said that a warning does not have to "warn against every conceivable risk under every conceivable circumstance," pointing out that the defendant's warnings had said that the nail was not as durable as another products and advised precautions about using the nail "in patients with poor bone quality."[136]

Important considerations with respect to the content of risk information are the severity of potential risk and the frequency with which injury may occur. In a case involving a gold salt product used to treat rheumatoid arthritis, the court said that although a doctor knew that the drug could cause death, this would not keep a fact-finder from "concluding that had [the doctor] known the actual degree or extent of risk of death or other serious adverse effect, he would not have prescribed the drug for [the plaintiff] in particular, or for other patients in general having the same state of severity of diagnosis or prognosis" as the plaintiff.[137]

The issue of specificity of warning sometimes carries over into the issue of materiality: in the products liability cases, the question of whether an allegedly better warning would have changed the plaintiff's decision to use or encounter a product. An opinion in a landmark cigarette case indicates that a seller may have to include warnings about dangers other than the one at issue in a particular litigation. In this case, the plaintiff contended that the manufacturer knew or should have known of smoking hazards other than lung cancer, the disease that killed the plaintiff's decedent. The manufacturer argued that failure to warn about diseases other than cancer "could not have been the proximate cause of [the decedent's] injury" because the decedent only had cancer. In an early opinion in this lengthy litigation, Judge Sarokin was unpersuaded, saying that "[i]f there are numerous risks from cigarette smoking, the mere fact that plaintiffs suffered from only one does not limit defendants' duty to warn to that risk alone." He declared that "[t]he adequacy of warning depends upon all of the risks encountered by the average consumer" and said that a plaintiff could "well argue that had

---

135. Toole v. McClintock, 778 F.Supp. 1543, 1546–47 (M.D. Ala. 1991).
136. Ralston v. Smith & Nephew Richards, Inc., 275 F.3d 965, 976 (10th Cir. 2001).
137. Tatum v. Schering Corp., 795 F.2d 925, 927 (11th Cir. 1986).

she or he been warned of all the risks, cigarettes would have been avoided."[138]

However, in some cases a court will not split the hairs the plaintiff wants it to split if a warning may be said to cover the relevant ground, even if another warning arguably would be more precise. In a case involving a pneumatic tourniquet, a warning statement in the owner's manual said, "IMPORTANT! MONITOR CUFF PRESSURE CONTINUOUSLY DURING USE," and also contained the language, "IMPORTANT! IMPROPER USE COULD CAUSE PARALYSIS AND NERVE DAMAGE . . . CUFF PRESSURE MUST ALSO BE MONITORED CONTINUOUSLY DURING USE." The plaintiff's expert asserted there should have been a warning that the tourniquet could malfunction "at any time because of the way the pressure regulator was designed." However, the trial court said there was no "substantial difference" between the warning the defendant gave and "a warning that says 'Important! Monitor Cuff Pressure Continuously during Use Because the Tourniquet May Malfunction Unexpectedly.'"[139] The appellate court affirmed in favor of the defendant, asking rhetorically, "what is clearer than the fact that improper pressure could cause nerve damage and that this might occur in so short a time that continuous monitoring . . . is 'IMPORTANT!'?" Scorning the interpretation that the word "'continuously' permitted totally undefined interruptions for the anesthesiologist's medical observations," duties that "clearly would require several minutes," the appellate court commented that "[t]he very thought that this would be continuous monitoring is absurd." The court declared that "[t]he user was warned 100%."[140]

Sometimes the vice of a warning is that it is simply not communicative. This may have to do with whether it is comprehensible generally, or it may concern the sophistication of the intended audience. A nice example of language bordering on euphemism when bluntness is required is a case in which the maker of stereo receiver said that it should not be put on a soft or yielding surface because that could "impede ventilation through the underside of the chassis." The court said that the manufacturer might be held for a failure to warn because it had not specifically said that putting the unit on such a surface might cause a fire.[141] An illustration of inadequate communication to a specific audience is a case involving a manila rope that broke,

138. Cipollone v. Liggett Group, 1987 WL 14666, at 3–4, Prod. Liab. Rep. (CCH) §11,637, at 33,086–33,087 (D. N.J. Oct. 27, 1987).
139. Jones v. Walter Kidde Portable Equip., 16 F.Supp.2d 123, 126–27 (D.Mass. 1998).
140. Jones v. Walter Kidde Portable Equip., 183 F.3d 67, 70 (1st Cir. 1999).
141. American Guar. & Liab. Ins. Co. v. Little, 328 So.2d 706, 711 (La. Ct. App. 1976).

causing injuries to a tree worker. Pointing out that the maker of the rope knew "that tree-workers commonly knot their ropes," the court said, acidly, that the defendant "chose to communicate the effect of knots in obscure charts." The court also pointed to evidence that the defendant "had no reason to believe [the plaintiff] and his employer would be aware of the rope's limitations without . . . clear warnings of the limitations of rope marketed as 'tree' rope."[142]

The problem of the unsophisticated consumer presents some philosophical difficulties. Here, the issue arises not from the quality of information but from the ability of consumers to absorb it and act on it. We have mentioned the century-old opinion in an unfair competition case in which a federal court referred to the "ignorant, the unthinking and the credulous, who, in making purchases, do not stop to analyze, but are governed by appearance and general impressions."[143] If a court must decide whether to favor persons in that position, it cannot avoid making a policy choice.

In the products liability area, courts have shown some sympathy to plaintiffs who lack the capacity to understand a risk. An example is a case in which an employee slipped or misstepped into the furnace of a salt bath, suffering burns that required an amputation of his leg. In reversing a summary judgment for the defendant, the court referred to testimony by an official of the plaintiff's employer to the effect that his intelligence level "inhibited his full understanding of the relative danger"; the official said that the plaintiff was "a great person but it's hard to guard against ignorance."[144] Courts may even provide some slack for inexperience as well as lack of intelligence. In a case involving a trampoline, the maker had put a warning in capital letters in the user manual that "USE OF A TRAMPOLINE SHOULD ALWAYS BE UNDER THE DIRECT SUPERVISION OF A QUALIFIED INSTRUCTOR." Although this statement appeared to advantage the manufacturer, the court said it was "reasonable to infer that ordinary consumers purchased [the defendant's] trampolines as recreational toys for informal use at home and that they were not aware that the product was only to be used under the direct supervision of a certified instructor and that the lack of proper instruction in basic skills . . . was the single greatest cause of injury." Despite the fact that the owner of the trampoline had put warning stickers that came along with the materials for the device on its mat and frame, the court rejected an "open and obvious" defense, saying that "[t]he instructions and warnings demonstrate that the

---

142. Columbian Rope Co. v. Todd, 631 N.E.2d 941, 946–47 (Ind. Ct. App. 1994).

143. Florence Mfg. Co. v. J.C. Dowd & Co., 178 Fed. 73, 75 (2d Cir. 1910), discussed *supra*, chapter 3, text accompanying note 119.

144. Pargo v. Elec. Furnace Co., 498 So.2d 833, 834 (Miss. 1986).

consequences of encountering these hazards are not obvious and are not appreciated or understood by foreseeable purchasers and users."[145]

An interesting parallel to the problem of lack of sophistication, which may produce the same outcome in terms of consumer ignorance, arises from the hurried conditions of modern life. In even the less stressed days of 1960, in an FTC deceptive sales practices case focusing on the sale of abridged paperback books with insufficient notice of their abridgment, one judge scornfully referred to a "standard of clarity" based on the idea that "he who runs may read."[146]

Although courts have provided some cushion for a lack of sophistication or knowledge, in some cases that factor may cut against consumers, especially when combined with a stubborn pride in one's ignorance. A willful ignoring of risk information may keep a lack of better information from being viewed as materially contributing to an injury. An example is a case that involved damage to a home from a fire, which originated in a prefabricated fireplace installed by a man who had only a sixth grade education and had read only the first page of the installation manual. Material on that page referred readers to instructions on page six that "were directly applicable." A metal strip was missing from the fireplace as it was delivered, but the installer "neither inquired further nor asked to be supplied with the missing . . . strip." He said that "because he had installed other similar fireplaces without an untoward event he did not need to rely on the manual." The court concluded that even if more specific warnings that appeared in an addendum to the installation instructions "had been available, such warnings would have been futile because [the installer] did not even read the instructions he had available."[147]

A subcategory of the injury law constitution thus includes several pockets of social judgment about information. Among these are judgments about when possessors of information about risk must provide it at all and about the quality of the information they must provide, including its comprehensibility. These judgments take into account the probable effect—or lack of effect—of hazard information on those who encounter products or situations that do not on their face present risks, including people whose general inclination is to ignore such information. They put some premium on common sense reading of cautionary statements, as in the case of the pneumatic tourniquet. But they make some room for lack of education, training, even intelligence.

145. Sollami v. Eaton, 747 N.E.2d 375, 381 (Ill. Ct. App. 2001).
146. Bantam Books, Inc. v. FTC, 275 F.2d 680, 684 n.2 (2d Cir. 1960) (Moore, J., concurring in the result).
147. Safeco Ins. Co. v. Baker, 515 So.2d 655, 657–58 (La. Ct. App. 1987).

We have been dealing with questions about access to information and communication of it. We turn now to issues that arise from uncertainties about information—about what the "facts" are. These issues run through both the private law of injuries and public regulation of safety.

Some of the fiercest arguments in tort law have occurred about allegations of injuries allegedly caused by so-called toxics—chemicals and fibers ranging from drugs to substances present in the workplace. We summarized the landmark *Daubert* case in chapter 5, noting its references to the testability of expert opinions and whether opinions had been published or peer reviewed. The Supreme Court said in *Daubert* that publication or peer review would "be a relevant, though not dispositive, consideration in assessing the scientific validity of a particular technique or methodology on which an opinion is premised."[148] Although emphasizing that the kind of "inquiry" that the relevant rule of evidence "envisioned" was "a flexible one," the court stressed that "[t]he focus . . . must be solely on principles and methodology, not on the conclusions that they generate."[149]

The concern with methodology came sharply into focus after *Daubert*. An important step was the Court's decision in *General Electric Co. v. Joiner*.[150] That case dealt with allegations that the plaintiff's exposure to polychlorinated biphenyls (PCBs) in the course of his employment as an electrician, which required him to work with transformers containing fluid laden with PCBs, had "promote[d]" his small cell lung cancer. The court of appeals had reversed a trial court holding that testimony of the plaintiff's experts on causation was inadmissible, but the Supreme Court reversed the court of appeals. Chief Justice Rehnquist premised in his opinion for the Court that "[a] court may conclude that there is simply too great an analytical gap between the data and the opinion proffered." Responding to the plaintiff's argument that the trial court's "disagreement was with the conclusion that the [plaintiff's] experts drew from the studies" they relied on, the Chief Justice declared that "conclusions and methodology are not entirely distinct from one another." He said a court did not have to "admit opinion evidence which is connected to existing data only by the *ipse dixit*"—essentially the "I say so"—"of the expert."[151] He sank the plaintiff's case with his

---

148. Daubert v. Merrell Dow Pharms., 509 U.S. 579, 594 (1993), summarized, chapter 5, text accompanying notes 20–21.
149. *Id.* at 594–95.
150. 522 U.S. 136 (1997).
151. *Id.* at 146.

conclusion that animal studies which the plaintiff's experts relied on to show a link between PCBs and deaths from lung cancer "were so dissimilar to the facts presented in [the] litigation that it was not an abuse of discretion for the District Court to have rejected the experts' reliance on them."[152]

There often is a gap in time between particular alleged causes and the occurrence of later events attributed to those causes, like disease. Sometimes the gap can be bridged by statistics, but those statistics require interpretation. We referred in a prior chapter to a difficult issue involving interpretation—the issue of how much increase in risk a plaintiff must show to convince a court that his illness was caused by exposure to a particular substance. Some courts have insisted that plaintiffs show a doubling of the risk and others have permitted evidence below one and one-half times the rate of contracting a disease in a population not exposed to the substance at issue.[153] These technical arguments fit into the overall injury constitution in their manifestation of attitudes toward risk. We can assume that judges who are generally averse to risk are likely to opt for a lesser standard of increased risk with respect to proof of causation of disease.

An interesting combination of elements on the causation issue appears in a case in which the plaintiff alleged that a tetanus toxoid vaccine had caused a cluster of serious neurological problems. Experts for both parties disagreed frontally. The plaintiff's expert, a board-certified neurologist, said he was "highly confident that, in the right individuals, a tetanus toxoid vaccination can cause" effects on the central nervous system, that the vaccine the plaintiff took "'probably' played a role in [the plaintiff's] illness," and that he could "ascertain no alternative causes." Witnesses for the government, which was defending the suit under the National Childhood Vaccine Act, which provides compensation for vaccine-related injuries, said they were not aware of medical data that would indicate a causal link between the vaccine the plaintiff took and her illnesses. A Special Master denied the plaintiff's claim. Relying on a particular "analytical framework" he had written himself, he said that the plaintiff had not measured up to an element of that framework, which required "confirmation from the relevant medical community" discerning a link between the vaccine and the plaintiff's injuries.[154]

But the Court of Federal Claims disagreed, saying that the Vaccine Act "did not preclude" proof of causation "from being established by a petitioner

152. *Id.* at 144–45.

153. See *supra*, chapter 5, text accompanying notes 25–27.

154. Summarized in Althen v. Sec'y of Dept. of Health & Human Servs., 58 Fed. Cl. 270, 279 (Fed Cl. 2003), aff'd, 418 F.3d 1274 (Fed. Cir. 2005).

in the absence of peer reviewed literature." Pointing to the short time period between the plaintiff's vaccination and the first symptom of her illness—eighteen days—the court found evidence of "a logical sequence of cause and effect," adding that there was no evidence of another cause.[155] This case emerged from a legislative decision, enacted in the Vaccine Act, to provide compensation to a small group of victims of a prophylactic public health measure. Motivating the statute was a concern that tort judgments were driving vaccine manufacturers from the field. One can also detect motives of social justice and compassion. In arriving at its judgment, which was affirmed by the Court of Appeals for the Federal Circuit, the Court of Federal Claims resolves an uncertainty created by conflicting testimony, pitting "probablies" against an insistence that there is no literature of proof by making a common sense judgment of probability. The decision is particularly interesting as a contribution to the injury law constitution because of the way it bundles a legislative compensation scheme with practical tort rules on proof of causation.

Quite as interesting are problems of uncertainty that arise when the question is whether government should take hold of safety problems, and if so, how. The subject of medical injuries has been a focal topic of law and politics for many years—the foundation of the large body of medical malpractice law in torts, and the centerpiece of various proposals for change in that law as well as for the passage of governmentally enforced preventive measures. This area, so fraught with political argument, presents a notable illustration of the range of statistical uncertainty about many large social problems. We have noted that the Institute of Medicine estimated that the range of fatalities attributable to medical errors was from 44,000 to 98,000.[156] Presumably even 44,000 would be enough to generate legislation and regulatory measures to reduce that toll. But the range is remarkable—an example of how even social statistics that are calculated with responsible modesty are sometimes pretty vague.

A stunning example of confessed ignorance about risk appears in an area now in a frontier process of development. This is the remarkable new technology known as nanotechnology, which builds "structures" at a level of "1/1000 the width of a human hair."[157] Some two-dimensional nanoparticles have been said to have "one hundred times the tensile strength of steel," an ability to conduct heat that is beyond all materials "but the purest

155. 58 Fed. Cl. at 284–86. The court of appeals in affirming said it saw "no 'objective confirmation' requirement in the Vaccine Act's preponderant evidence standard." 418 F.2d at 1279.
156. See *supra*, chapter 4, text accompanying note 10.
157. John Miller et al., A Realistic Assessment of the Commercialization of Nanotechnology: A Primer for Lawyers and Investors, 1 Nanotechnology L. & Bus. 10, 10 (2004).

diamond," and an ability to conduct current like that of copper but at much higher levels.[158] It has been predicted that nanoparticles in three dimensions will be useful—among other things—as "sensors to detect chemicals in the environment" and in medical uses including targeted delivery of drugs within the body.[159]

Despite proved and potential uses of this technology, concerns have been raised about the possible effects on the health of consumers who use products made from nanoparticles and workers exposed to them on the job. One reason nanotechnology is a particularly fascinating area in injury law is that so much of the anxiety about it has been about risks that are uncertain. In the first decade of this century, there were reports that nanoparticles have adverse effects, sometimes even fatal ones, on living things from fish to rats and mice and even water fleas.[160] One study, published in 2008, indicated that certain kinds of nanoparticles, known as long-fibered carbon nanotubes (CNTs), had a tendency to cause disease in mice similar to that caused by a well-established pathogen, namely asbestos.[161] Indicative of the uncertainties about risk was a comment by the authors of that study that "it remains unknown whether there will be sufficient exposure to such particles in the workplace or environment" to cause disease in human beings.[162] This very uncertainty led the authors to declare that the effects of carbon nanotubes "must be addressed with some urgency before the commercial use of long CNTs becomes widespread."[163]

Already there had occurred one episode of human illnesses, including a few serious ones, associated with a nanoproduct. This was an aerosol spray called "Magic Nano," used to confer water resistance on household fixtures like bathtubs and toilets or to make them repel dirt. In Germany, the product sent a few people to hospitals suffering from pulmonary edema, and reportedly had adverse effects on more than a hundred others.[164]

158. See Peter J. Tomasco, Manufactured Nanomaterials: Avoiding TSCA and OSHA Violations for Potentially Hazardous Substances, 33 B.C. Envtl. Aff. L. Rev. 205, 209–10 (2004), in part quoting Cientifica Report, Nanotubes 12.

159. The Royal Soc'y & The Royal Acad. of Eng'g, Nanoscience and Nanotechnologies: Opportunities and Uncertainties viii (2004), available at www.nanotec.org.uk/finalReport.htm.

160. See David V. Warheit, Nanoparticles: Health Impacts?, Materials Today, Feb. 2004, 32, 34–35; Emery E. Knowles III, Nanotechnology: Evolving Occupational Safety, Health and Environmental Issues, 52 Professional Safety 20, 23 (2006)(summarizing research studies).

161. Craig A. Poland et al., Carbon nanotubes introduced into the abdominal cavity of mice show asbestos-like pathogenicity in a pilot study, 3 Nature Nanotechnology 423, 423 (2008).

162. Id. at 427.

163. Id.

164. David Graber and Pat Phibbs, German Institute Working to Understand Why "Magic Nano" Cleaner Caused Ailments, 34 Prod. Safety & Liab. Rep. (BNA) 390–91 (Apr. 17, 2006).

The reaction to these events was of a piece with more general concerns about the health effects of nanoparticles. With various hypotheses being offered for the illnesses associated with Magic Nano, a spokesman for a German government agency said that these explanations underlined "the need for manufacturers to test not only chemical ingredients in products but also formulations of those chemicals under conditions that mimic how consumers use those products."[165]

This statement symbolized the fact that the more general concerns about nanotechnology were not about proved risk, but rather about uncertainty. Reflecting the lack of knowledge about hazards was a document published by the National Institute for Occupational Safety and Health (NIOSH) in 2005, titled a "Strategic Plan for NIOSH Nanotechnology Research." Among the strategic "goals" it identified were "understanding and prevent[ing] work-related injuries and illnesses possibly caused by nano-materials." The word "possibly" manifested the dearth of information. So did the authors' reference to the "need to determine the toxicity of nano-materials," to "identify possible health effects from the early uses of these materials," and to "monitor the ongoing health of individuals working with nanomaterials."[166] Among the "critical issues" mentioned in the Plan was the need to determine "the likelihood that current exposure-response data (human or animal) could be used in identifying and assessing hazards."[167]

The very next month, NIOSH co-issued a document called "Approaches to Safe Nanotechnology" with the Centers for Disease Control and Prevention. This "Approaches" document referred to an "information gap" that was "critical because of the unknown risk that nanomaterials pose to workers."[168] It said, in bold face, that "[i]n the case of nanomaterials, the uncertainties are great because the characteristics of nanomaterials may be different from those of the larger particles with the same chemical composition."[169] It declared that "[v]ery little is known about the safety risks that engineered nanomaterials might pose," and said specifically that "nanoscale combustible material could present a higher

---

165. *Id.*

166. National Inst. for Occupational Safety and Health, Strategic Plan for NIOSH, Nanotechnology Research: Filling the Knowledge Gaps, update from the Internet at http://www.cdc.gov/niosh/topics/nanotech/strat_plan.html (Feb. 26, 2008), which did not contain all the exact language quoted in the text. The original language is quoted in Marshall S. Shapo, Experimenting With the Consumer 192 (2009).

167. *Id.*

168. Natl. Inst. for Occupational Safety and Health and Centers for Disease Control & Prevention, Approaches to Safe Nanotechnology: An Information Exchange with NIOSH (distributed only for "pre-dissemination peer review") (Oct. 1, 2005), www.cdc.gov/niosh/topics/nanotech/pdfs/Approaches_to_Safe_Nanotechnolgy.pdf, at 3.

169. *Id.* at 4.

risk than a similar quantity of coarser material, given its unique properties."[170]

As more workers became exposed to nanoparticles, and as companies put more nano-products on the consumer market, the information gaps remained. At the end of 2006, the Health and Safety Laboratory in Buxton, England identified fundamental gaps in the very technology of measurement. It said that "[v]ery few studies have evaluated . . . instruments for the measurement of engineered nanoparticles in the workplace" and that there had been "very few assessments of exposure level to engineered nanoparticles in the workplace."[171] In mid-2007, the Swiss Federal Office for Environment and Federal Office of Public Health reportedly said that "[i]nformation on nanoparticles" was "insufficient to conduct risk assessments or craft regulations."[172]

Yet, moving through this fog of uncertainty, the development of the technology proceeded unregulated: laissez-faire with a vengeance. The lack of direct hands-on regulation was just one illustration of the elasticity of the injury law constitution, which parallels that of the Constitution itself. The injury law constitution includes an antipathy to interference with the use of innovative technologies. However, this attitude exists in constant tension with the potential for anger, even rage, that boils over when risk explodes in the reality of injury—for which the injury law constitution has plenty of after-the-fact remedies.

Safety Legislation

Information requirements. An extensive stack of safety statutes, dealing with many areas of risky activity and types of product hazards, reflects Congress' concern with the importance of information to consumers and workers. The implementation of these statutes by agencies demonstrates the particularity of consumer needs for such information, and litigation on both statutes and regulations has dealt with questions about when consumers can argue that specific types of risk information should be communicated to the public.

The 1969 cigarette legislation required that every package of cigarettes sold in this country contain a conspicuous statement, "Warning: The Surgeon General Has Determined That Cigarette Smoking Is Dangerous

170. *Id.* at 12.
171. Health & Safety Laboratory, Buxton, UK, Health & Safety Executive Nano Alert Serv., no. 1, at 5–6 (Dec. 2006).
172. Data Insufficient to Regulate Nanoparticles, But Management Possible, Swiss Report Says, 37 O.S.H. Rep. (BNA) 632 (July 12, 2007).

to Your Health."[173] The Federal Insecticide, Fungicide and Rodenticide Act (FIFRA), which regulates pesticides, condemns as "misbranded" not only a pesticide that has any "false or misleading" statements, but also one that "is contained in a package or other container or wrapping which does not conform to the standards established by the Administrator" of the EPA or which has a label that does not conform to directions for use or contain warnings, including directions and warnings that comply with requirements imposed by the administrator.[174] These statutes, therefore, not only provide general principles for the communication of information, but specify what type of information about risk shall be provided, or empower administrators to specify types of information. As explained below, these laws have generated thorny issues involving federal-state relations.

The degree of coercion that agencies exercise with respect to the provision of information, and the amount of publicity given to that information, has varied with the subject matter. On the more informal end of the scale, for example, the National Institutes of Health (NIH) put on the Internet a document of several pages called "Understanding Clinical Trials."[175] In the specific case of breast implants, the FDA released an "Information Update" that included a list of 15 "Breast Implant Risks," emphasized that "breast implants **are not lifetime devices**," and told women who were thinking about having implants, "[y]ou should understand there is a high chance that you will need to have additional surgery at some point to replace or remove your implant(s)," naming problems that included deflation, infection, and calcium deposits.[176]

The FDA also ventured an information solution in the case of hormone therapy. NIH had found the results of research on postmenopausal estrogens involving thousands of women to be of sufficient concern that over a period of two years it terminated two different studies—one on a combination of estrogens and progestins and the other on estrogen alone.[177] With respect to hormone therapy products remaining on the market, the FDA's solution appeared in a series of "draft guidances." In the one issued in 2005, it recommended the issuance of a "Patient Information Leaflet"

173. Public Health Cigarette Smoking Act of 1969, Pub. L. 91–222, 84 Stat. 88, §4 (1970).
174. 7 U.S.C.A. §136(q)(1)(2006).
175. Nat'l Inst. of Health, An Introduction to Clinical Trials, http://clinicaltrials.gov/ct/gui/c/w2b/info/whatis?JServeSessionIdzone_ct=xvasgu6spl, updated at and replaced by Understanding Clinical Trials, http://clinicaltrials.gov/ct2/info/understand, printed from the Internet, July 4, 2011.
176. Food and Drug Administration, Breast Implants, An Information Update (2000), at 19, 23.
177. For a summary of this history, see Marshall S. Shapo, Experimenting with the Consumer 158–72 (Praeger Publishers 2009).

featuring a boxed warning that included statements about the increased risk of several diseases as well as bullet-point references in the text of the leaflet to eight specific diseases.[178]

Higher on the scale of governmental compulsion are agency actions that effectively require the transmission of risk information. Illustrative of a seller's response to apparent pressure was a statement in 2005 by Pfizer, the maker of Viagra, that it would put warnings about sudden loss of vision on the label of the product—as its competitor Eli Lilly had done for Cialis. An "FDA Alert" that accompanied these events said that "[w]e do not know at this time if Viagra, Cialis" or the other erectile dysfunction drug Levitra "causes" sudden vision loss. However, it mentioned groups of men who were at relatively high risk for that kind of event, such as smokers and men with heart disease and high blood pressure. It included the rather obvious advice that if men lost their eyesight while taking one of those drugs, they should stop the drug immediately and "[g]et medical help right away."[179]

From time to time, the FDA uses the jawbone on sellers of medical products by requiring "Dear Doctor" letters to be sent to "physicians and others responsible for patient care." Agency regulations prescribe the content of these letters and even their form. The regulations say, for example, that "[w]hen the information concerns a significant hazard to health," the statement must appear in the "far left third" of a Number 10 envelope inside a rectangle with the words:

IMPORTANT
DRUG
WARNING

The agency specifies that those words "shall be in three lines, all capitals, and centered," with the word "Important" in 36 point Gothic Bold type and the words "Drug" and "Warning" in 36 point Gothic Condensed type, and that "the rectangle's border and the statement therein shall be red." The regulations require similar language and format for "important changes in drug package labeling," and "correction[s] of prescription drug advertising or labeling."[180]

---

178. Food and Drug Administration, Draft Guidance, Guidance for Industry: Non-contraceptive Estrogen Drug Products for the Treatment of Vasomotor Symptoms and Vulvar and Vaginal Atrophy Symptoms—Recommended Prescribing Information for Health Care Providers and Patient Labeling, Revision 4, at 21–25 (Nov. 2005), www.fda.gov/downloads/drugs/drugsafety/InformationbyDrugClass/ucm135336.pdf.

179. FDA Alert [7/2005], formerly at http://www.fda.gov/cder/consumerinfo/viagra/default.htm, summarized in Marshall S. Shapo, Experimenting With the Consumer, *supra*, at 122.

180. 21 C.F.R. §200.5 (current to 2010).

Safety regulation sometimes affects tort litigation. For example, "Dear Doctor" letters may prove advantageous to defendants as well as plaintiffs in private lawsuits. In a case involving a suicide attributed to the acne drug Accutane, the court noted that statements in one "Dear Doctor" letter "specifically warn[ed] that Accutane treatment may cause suicide" and that updated warnings in a later "Dear Healthcare Provider" letter as well as other documents including an "Informed Consent/Patient Agreement" had "specifically warned that some Accutane patients had ended their own lives despite a lack of depressive symptoms." In denying recovery to a plaintiff who sued the manufacturer, the court said that "[t]aken as a whole, the warnings clearly, accurately, and consistently conveyed" to the doctor of the plaintiff's decedent "that Accutane might cause suicide, with or without prior symptoms of depression."[181]

By comparison, there are cases where the failure to mention a particular risk in a "Dear Doctor" letter may help support a plaintiff's verdict. That was the situation in a case where the jury found for a smoker who claimed that an oral contraceptive had caused a stroke. In holding the evidence sufficient to support a verdict for the plaintiff, the court focused in part on evidence that the maker of the Pill the plaintiff took had "never warned of smoking, in conjunction with taking the pill, through its usual communications with the medical profession" including "Dear Doctor" letters. The court particularly instanced a colloquy between the plaintiffs' lawyer and the defendant's executive director for medical research who acknowledged that the company had not warned of the effects of smoking on stroke risk in Pill users.[182]

Preemption. A legal question involving risk information that has occupied a substantial amount of the litigation landscape in products liability cases is when safety agencies can reserve to themselves the decision on the kind of information that must be communicated to consumers. The central issue in these cases has been whether the existence of a regulatory scheme "pre-empts"—that is, bars—a civil action based on the failure to provide certain kinds of information. These skirmishes are part of a wider war over preemption in the safety area, a war that has involved more than twenty-five separate pieces of regulatory legislation.

The Supreme Court has issued decisions on preemption issues involving risk information in at least three different product areas. The Court's decision in *Cipollone v. Liggett Group, Inc.*[183] on cigarette labeling was

---

181. Snyder v. Hoffman-LaRoche, Inc. 2008 WL 4790666, at 6 (M.D.Fla. 2008).
182. Skill v. Martinez, 91 F.R.D. 498, 508–09 (D. N.J. 1981).
183. 505 U.S. 504 (1992).

complicated, involving two separate statutes on the subject and drawing several opinions by the justices. The Cigarette Labeling and Advertising Act of 1965 made it "unlawful" to sell any cigarettes in the United States unless the package had a conspicuous label with the words "Caution: Cigarette Smoking May Be Hazardous To Your Health." That law also said that "No statement relating to smoking and health, other than the statement" quoted above, "shall be required on any cigarette package" and that "[n]o statement relating to smoking and health shall be required in the advertising of any cigarettes the packages of which are labeled in conformity with the provisions of this Act."[184]

Six justices were willing to say that this 1965 law "only pre-empted state and federal rulemaking bodies from mandating particular cautionary statements on cigarette labels or in cigarette advertisements" but "did not pre-empt" products liability suits in state courts.[185] However, a plurality of four led by Justice Stevens had a different opinion about the 1969 legislation, which contained the stronger declaration that "The Surgeon General Has Determined That Cigarette Smoking Is Dangerous To Your Health,"[186] and which also amended the 1965 law with the words, "No requirement or prohibition based on smoking and health shall be imposed under State law with respect to the advertising or promotion of any cigarettes the packages of which are [lawfully] labeled."[187] That language, Justice Stevens said, preempted a claim that the defendant cigarette manufacturers had breached a duty to warn of the hazards of their products with regard to allegations that "post-1969 advertising or promotions should have included additional, or more clearly stated, warnings."[188]

A solid majority then coalesced on the view that there was no preemption of claims based on "intentional" misconduct, particularly fraud. Justice Stevens said that at a minimum, "the 1969 Act does not pre-empt petitioner's claims based on express warranty, intentional fraud and misrepresentation, or conspiracy."[189] Three other members of the Court, going further, declared that "the plain language of the 1969 Act fail[s] clearly to require pre-emption of petitioner's state common-law damages claims," and that indeed there was "no suggestion in the legislative history that Congress intended to expand the scope of the pre-emption provision in the drastic

184. Federal Cigarette Labeling and Advertising Act, Pub. L. 89–92, 79 Stat. 282, §§4, 5 (July 27, 1965).
185. See Cipollone, 505 U.S. at 519–20.
186. Pub.L. 91–222, 84 Stat. 87, §4, (Apr. 1, 1970).
187. Id. §5(b).
188. 505 U.S. at 524.
189. Id. at 530.

manner that the plurality attributes to it."[190] To the nonlawyer, or even the nonspecialist lawyer, these opinions taken together look like a dense thicket seeded by interpretation of statutory language and the sometimes uneasy relationship between federal safety laws and state tort law. But one must not lose sight of the most fundamental expression of the Congressional will: about the need for information concerning the risk of products used by millions of people, manifested in the cautionary "may" statement in the labeling requirement of the 1965 legislation and the much stronger warning in the 1969 law.

Another Supreme Court case concerning the preemptive effect of a safety statute that deals with the informational content accompanying a product focused on the Federal Insecticide, Fungicide and Rodenticide Act (FIFRA), the informational content of which is summarized above.[191] Perhaps even more than with the cigarettes decision, the Court had to cope with doctrinal complexity. The plaintiffs, peanut farmers, claimed that a herbicide had damaged their crops. The defendant tried to bar the action on the basis of statutory language that said a state "shall not impose or continue in effect any requirements for labeling or packaging in addition to or different from those required" under the legislation. Justice Stevens' majority opinion concluded that there was no preemption of claims for "defective design, defective manufacture" or "negligent testing," all of which seemed fairly obvious since none of those claims involved labeling or packaging.[192] However, the majority dug a little into legal doctrines focused on representations in also concluding that there was no preemption of claims for express warranty. Although Justice Stevens acknowledged that the defendant had put an express warranty on the label of the product, he employed that very fact in favor of the plaintiff. He pointed out that a claim based "on an express warranty asks only that a manufacturer make good on the contractual commitment that it voluntarily undertook by placing that warranty on its product"; the warranty was, in short, not "labeling or packaging required" by the statute.[193] The question was yet more subtle with respect to claims for fraud and negligent failure to warn. Justice Stevens did not flatly say these claims were preempted. Rather, he said that to avoid preemption, a plaintiff would have to show that his claims under those theories were "genuinely equivalent" to, and "fully consistent with" the misbranding provisions of FIFRA.[194]

---

190. *Id.* at 542 (Blackmun, J., concurring in part and dissenting in part).
191. See *supra*, text accompanying note 174.
192. Bates v. Dow AgroSciences LLC, 544 U.S. 431, 444 (2005).
193. *Id.* at 444–45.
194. See *id.* at 447, 452, 454.

Two cases involving medical products produced opposite results. In a decision that held for a maker of a medical device, the majority was at pains to specify the particular elements of the statute that led to its decision. Writing for the Court, Justice Scalia emphasized that as between two review processes for devices, the balloon catheter at issue had undergone a "premarket approval" process which was much more intense than the other method of review.[195] He said that "[s]tate tort law that requires a manufacturer's catheters to be safer, but hence less effective, than the model that FDA has approved disrupts the federal scheme no less than state regulatory law to the same effect." He contrasted jury verdicts with FDA decision making, saying that jurors would see "only the cost of a more dangerous design" and would not be "concerned with its benefits, noting that "the plaintiffs that reaped those benefits are not represented in court."[196] In a concurring opinion, Justice Stevens acknowledged that some "common law rules administered by judges" would "unquestionably qualify" as the kind of "requirements" under the preemption statute that would justify preemption.[197] Justice Ginsburg dissented, saying that it was "state premarket regulation of medical devices, not any design to suppress state tort suits," that "accounts for Congress' inclusion of a preemption clause in the" Medical Device Amendments.[198]

Justice Stevens returned to the preemption fray with an opinion for the Court in a case involving an antihistamine, used to treat nausea, which was administered intravenously to the plaintiff, Diana Levine, by the "IV-push" method, which involves direct injection.[199] A different, slower, method of administration is by "IV drip," from a hanging intravenous bag. A physician assistant's administration of the drug by IV-push somehow resulted in the drug getting into an artery, which caused gangrene leading to the amputation of the plaintiff's hand and later her entire forearm. The manufacturer's label, which the FDA had required, included the language "INADVERTENT INTRA-ARTERIAL INJECTION CAN RESULT IN GANGRENE OF THE AFFECTED EXTREMITY." Although the label complied with FDA requirements, the plaintiff argued, as Justice Stevens summarized it, that "the labeling was defective because it failed to instruct clinicians to use the IV-drip method . . . instead of the higher-risk IV-push method." A Vermont jury gave a special verdict that the product was defective "as a result of inadequate warnings and instructions," and awarded $7,400,000, a figure that

195. Riegel v. Medtronic, Inc., 552 U.S. 312, 322–23 (2008).
196. Id. at 324.
197. Id. at 332 (Stevens, J., concurring in part and concurring in the judgment).
198. Id. at 342 (Ginsburg, J., dissenting).
199. Wyeth v. Levine, 129 S. Ct. 1187 (2009).

was reduced by the amount of a prior settlement with the health center where the plaintiff was treated and a clinician.

Justice Stevens rejected the manufacturer's argument that it could not give a warning that would satisfy both the state law on warnings on which the jury had been instructed and also the misbranding provisions of the Food, Drug, and Cosmetic Act. He noted that a drug manufacturer did not have to wait for FDA approval of a change in the manufacturer's labeling. He strenuously opposed the contention that "the FDA, rather than the manufacturer, bears primary responsibility for drug labeling."[200] He concluded with a general rejection of the argument that "claims like Levine's obstruct the federal regulation of drug labeling."[201] Justice Alito's dissent stressed how the label of the drug "clearly warn[ed]" about the dangers of IV push.[202] In language echoing that of Justice Scalia's opinion for the Court in the balloon catheter case, he viewed the "real issue" as being "whether a state tort jury can countermand the FDA's considered judgment" that the warning label it had "mandated" rendered the IV use of the drug "safe."[203] He pointed out in this connection that the warning label for the drug had been "subject to the FDA's strict regulatory oversight since the 1950's."[204] He noted that the plaintiff's lawyer had told the jury during closing argument, "Thank God we don't rely on the FDA . . . to make the safe[ty] decision. You will make the decision."[205]

This case, the decision of which had been much anticipated, contains a powerful mixture of ingredients. One of these is the expertise of a safety agency, which has a broad perspective on the risks and benefits of drugs. Another is the ability of a jury of ordinary persons to determine the adequacy of a written warning. That kind of decision, made by people who are accustomed to deciphering warnings on a variety of consumer products, occurs in a legal context in which adequacy of warning is often found to be a jury question.[206] At base this is a simple issue of tort law, which is a large wedge of the basic law of injuries that is constantly applied in every state. The resolution of state law issues, however, takes place under the canopy of the broader law of injuries, which here includes federal safety statutes. Who is the better decision maker about whether information concerning risk is inadequate or misleading? In cases summarized above involving

200. See id. at 1196–97.
201. Id. at 1204.
202. Id. at 1227 (Alito, J., dissenting).
203. Id. at 1218.
204. Id. at 1222.
205. Id. at 1218.
206. See, e.g., 1 Marshall S. Shapo, The Law of Products Liability §19.12[1] (5th ed. 2010).

cigarettes and a pesticide as well as a prescription drug, the Supreme Court staked out a significant amount of territory in which juries could make that decision. The injury law constitution may thus be said to prioritize the judgment of members of the public at trench level whenever that can meaningfully be registered.

CHAPTER 8

Social and Individual Goods, Sometimes in Competition

O ur injury law encompasses a range of goods, both social and individual. One of the main functions of the constitution of injury law is to strike balances when these goods compete with one another. The articulation of these goods often takes on the character of mantras. As we analyze them, it will become apparent that they are sometimes more shibboleth than reality.

FREEDOM OF MOVEMENT VS. DIGNITARY INTERESTS

Injury law concerns itself in many ways with the dignity of the individual, a topic introduced in chapter 3. In practical terms, this good includes freedom to move about and freedom to express oneself, but also freedom from unwanted contact and from events that cause serious interferences with emotional tranquillity.

In a purely physical way, freedom of movement sometimes collides with the right to be free from unwanted contact. A classic tort case arose from a crippling injury inflicted by one schoolboy on another, through what may have been nothing more than a boyishly annoying kick across a schoolroom aisle. From the kicker's point of view, he was doing nothing more than exercising a right that young boys have exercised from time immemorial. However, at least in the setting of a schoolroom in which the order of the day forbade even mischievous kicks, the right to physical security of the boy who was kicked trumped whatever right the kicker had. The Wisconsin Supreme Court called this kick a battery.[1] Had the boy who was kicked

---

1. Vosburg v. Putney, 50 N.W. 403 (Wis. 1891).

retaliated with a kick of his own and hurt the kicker, the applicable law—the social moderator—would have been the self-defense rules, which often require judges and juries to apply a rule of reasonableness to a judgment of what the facts were.

In a very different arena, one which includes criminal activity, a striking example of the law's regard for physical dignity appears in the unique Iowa case *Katko v. Briney,*[2] which involved a clash between the right to physical security and property rights. The defendant, Edward Briney, had become sick and tired of break-ins in outbuildings on his farm property. Particularly concerned to protect some "old bottles and dated fruit jars" in one of those buildings, he set a spring gun in one of the rooms. The plaintiff, Marvin Katko, and a friend broke into the house to steal these objects, "which they considered antiques." When Katko started to open the door of a room where he thought the bottles and jars might be, the shotgun went off and blew away a good part of one of his legs. The jury may well have had some sympathy for the plight of a citizen essentially defenseless against thievery. But these Iowa jurors also followed the law, which as the trial court instructed them essentially banned the use of spring guns except for the protection of human life. They awarded $20,000 compensatory damages and $10,000 punitive damages to Katko, and the state supreme court affirmed, citing among other sources a treatise that said that "the law has always placed a higher value upon human safety than upon mere rights in property."[3]

The competition between social and individual goods intensifies with physical contact in sports and games. We want to be free from unwanted contacts, but we also value the benefits that come from athletic activity, including what are literally contact sports. Even where contact is not the name of the game, a paralyzing injury may not be grounds for liability. The Triple Crown winner Ron Turcotte learned that what is a foul under the rules of the sport may not be a tort. He sued Jeffrey Fell, another jockey, for paraplegia that resulted from a bumping of his horse. As the New York Court of Appeals described Turcotte's allegations, "only . . . as a result of carelessness," Fell had "failed to control his mount" as he literally jockeyed for position. The court referred to Turcotte's own testimony about the danger "inherent in" horse racing—the weight and swiftness of the animals, the frequent bumping that is a part of racing, and the "fine line between what is lawful and unlawful." It concluded, with a strong version of terminology shared by lawyer and layman alike, that Turcotte had assumed the risk of whatever foul Fell had committed: that Turcotte had "consented to

2. 183 N.W.2d 657 (Iowa 1971).
3. *Id.* at 660 (quoting William L. Prosser, Law of Torts 116 (3d ed. 1964)).

relieve ... Fell of the legal duty to use reasonable care to avoid crossing into his lane of travel."[4]

One might approve this judgment on the grounds that Turcotte, a veteran rider, was a sports professional who freely elected to accept the risks of a highly specialized, and often literally high-stakes activity. Yet courts have applied a similar principle even to pickup games where the stakes are no more than a highly informal tallying of scores or even success on a particular play. Kendra Knight found that out when she played in a touch football game on a dirt lot during the halftime of the 1987 Super Bowl. In this game, "[n]o rules were explicitly discussed." Ms. Knight claimed that Michael Jewett, another participant in a Super Bowl party, was playing too roughly, and that she told him so. He only remembered that she had asked him to "be careful." In any event, she kept playing. In an effort to intercept a pass, Jewett collided with Ms. Knight and knocked her over, then stepped backward on her hand. That caused an injury to her little finger that led to an amputation.

In parsing a somewhat technical body of California law, the state supreme court decided that the case was one of "primary assumption of risk" and that Ms. Knight could not even try to compare Jewett's negligence with any negligence of her own. The court referred to the idea that it would "chill[]" "vigorous participation" in "active sporting event[s]" to impose liability on a player for "his or her ordinary careless conduct."[5] Thus, in both very professional and very amateur sports arenas, both the social and individual interests in freedom of movement for athletes often outweigh the individual interest in bodily security. As we shall see below, more intense struggles occur in a workaday world far removed from the Belmont racetrack where Turcotte was hurt so badly—the world of factories and farms.

For the moment, though, we depart from physical bumpings, sometimes held torts and sometimes not, to examine a parallel clash of freedoms— where freedom of movement and of expression clash with the freedom to be free from jolting interferences with emotional security. A Wisconsin case that arose from an everyday situation nicely represents the tensions. The defendant, a contractor, started a renovation project on the plaintiff's storm windows, but did not reinstall windows as winter approached. As temperatures grew cold inside the house, the plaintiff complained. The defendant angrily responded that "she made him 'sick'" and slammed down the receiver. This prompted a suit for intentional infliction of emotional distress, but the Wisconsin Supreme Court—usually fairly liberal to tort

4. Turcotte v. Fell, 502 N.E.2d 964, 969–70 (N.Y. 1986).
5. Knight v. Jewett, 834 P.2d 696, 710 (Cal. 1992).

suits—rejected the action. It said that the defendant's conduct was not "extreme and outrageous," a requirement of the "intentional infliction" tort. It captured the competing interests in this simple situation by saying that "[a] person performing a personal service contract carries with him his own feelings of hostility and his own set of emotional pressures."[6]

The anti-"heartbalm" statutes, discussed in chapter 7, which bar such actions as seduction and alienation of affection, symbolize a thought shared by many people: when love and sex are the issue, there should be maximum freedom for people to act in ways that may adversely affect others, assuming that there is no unconsented physical imposition. The passage of those statutes by several states,[7] and the reluctance of some courts to underwrite such actions,[8] are representative of this corner of injury law.

Yet when the defendant's conduct moves from sweet nothings to physical activity, the law sometimes proves more sympathetic to plaintiffs. Stalking is now a crime, at least a misdemeanor, in several states. Wyoming, for example, makes it both a crime and grounds for a tort action to "engage[ ] in a course of conduct reasonably likely to harass" another. The legislature defined harassment to embrace conduct like "verbal threats" and "written threats" as well as "nonconsensual physical contact, directed at a specific person" or that person's family, and specified that the offense is not limited to that list. The culpability standard in the Wyoming statute, interestingly, is more one associated with negligence than with intentional torts. It is enough if the defendant "knew or should have known" that his conduct "would cause a reasonable person to suffer substantial emotional distress"—a lesser standard than the "severe emotional distress" required for the tort of intentional infliction of emotional distress—and if the conduct "does in fact seriously alarm" the victim.[9]

A tort when the goose does it may also be one when the offender is the gander. In a Texas case, a spurned woman followed her former lover all over town several days a week for several years—at work, at home, and even when he went with his wife and children to school and to restaurants. She kept up a stream of "unwanted letters, cards and gifts" and the plaintiff's family members and co-workers reported hearing her make "sexually vulgar remarks" to him. She defended on the basis that the plaintiff's brief prior

---

6. Alsteen v. Gehl, 124 N.W.2d 312, 319 (Wis. 1963).
7. See, e.g., William R. Corbett, A Somewhat Modest Proposal to Prevent Adultery and Save Families: Two Old Torts Looking for a New Career, 33 Ariz. St. L. J. 989, 1007–10 (2001).
8. See, e.g., id. at 1007 (judicial rejection of suits).
9. Wyo. Stat. §6-2-506.

affair with her made him unworthy of a tort remedy, but the court was unpersuaded.[10]

A high-profile example of judicial willingness to grant relief when a defendant's physical movements impinge on a plaintiff's emotional security without physical contact is the case, mentioned earlier, of the photographer who obnoxiously pursued Jacqueline Kennedy Onassis and her children.[11] The trial judge's unusual remedy of an injunction specified the distances the defendant must maintain from Ms. Onassis—distances of up to 100 yards. Although the appellate court modified that distance to as little as 25 feet, it rejected a defense based on "newsmen[']s" privilege and prohibited the defendant from "any act foreseeably or reasonably calculated to place the life and safety of [Ms. Onassis] in jeopardy" and "any conduct which would reasonably be foreseen to harass, alarm or frighten" her.[12]

Thus, there are warring strains in the law over freedoms, including what might broadly be defined as freedom of expression. Our prior discussion of defamation and privacy law[13] adds a set of calibrations to the stalking statutes and cases as they bump against the anti-heartbalm statutes and cases and against judicial refusals to give damages for emotional outbursts that upset their targets. The constitution of injury law, with its balances of freedoms, provides an overall framework for decisions on these skirmishes. The case of Jacqueline Onassis and the photographer briefly raises an issue involving the Constitution, but a defense based on the First Amendment loses.

AUTONOMY AND CHOICE OF RISKS

Closely linked to the element of personal freedom is the element—sometimes more of a will-o'-the-wisp—of personal autonomy, with its blood relative the concept of personal choice. An important legal issue, which arises in diverse factual contexts, is whether a plaintiff should be barred from recovery, or have his award reduced, because of his knowledge of a risk. The basic idea supporting a bar to liability or a reduction of damages is that free people confronted with the many alternatives available to them in many areas of life should be free to select the risky alternatives.

Choice is central to the issues that arise under a relative newcomer to tort jurisprudence, the doctrine of informed consent in medical cases.

10. Kramer v. Downey, 680 S.W.2d 524, 525–26 (Tex. Ct. App. 1984).
11. See *supra*, chapter 7, text accompanying note 91.
12. Galella v. Onassis, 487 F.2d 986, 994, 995, 998 (2d Cir. 1973).
13. See *supra*, chapter 7, text accompanying notes 87–94.

The basic elements of the doctrine are simple enough. A doctor must tell a patient about the nature of a course of treatment or procedure, its possible alternatives, and both its risks and benefits. Within that easy-to-state framework there reside a lot of complexities, involving the nature of the alternatives, the stakes for the patient, and the pressures of the moment.

A Wisconsin case presents a difficult problem in a setting of "excruciating" pain suffered by a woman in childbirth. This patient, who had had two children by Caesarean section, elected to try a vaginal birth. However, as her pain escalated, she told her doctor she wanted another C-section. She claimed that his answer "intimidated" her into continuing with the vaginal birth. After her painful labor continued for some time unproductively, the doctor performed an emergency C-section. The child was born a spastic quadriplegic, unable to move below the neck or speak, and the parties stipulated that she would have been born healthy if she had been delivered a half hour earlier. The doctor argued that the mother's informed consent had remained throughout the process, but the Wisconsin Supreme Court disagreed. Noting that it was "undisputed" that the plaintiff had told the defendant "on three separate occasions" that she wanted to stop the vaginal delivery and have a C-section, the court said that "[t]hough she never said the magic words, 'I revoke,' ... her repeated statements are a clear indication of her withdrawal of consent."[14] The court said it would not view the original informed consent discussion "as a solitary and blanketing event, a point on a timeline after which such discussions are no longer needed." By contrast, it said that the patient's withdrawal of her consent had put her and her doctor "in their original position—a physician, a patient, and a series of options for treatment," creating "a blank slate" for a new "diagram" of the treatment.[15]

Many other factual twists lie inside the question of how "informed" consents are, and how "consenting" the patient is. There is data indicating that within a day of signing a consent, many surgical patients do not remember even the most basic features of the consent they presumably have given.

There also exists a blend of factual and philosophical questions concerning how "free" choice is. We have noted a range of judicial responses to that question in cases involving workplace injuries and consumer products.[16] The complexity of choice is evident in the struggles that individuals may have in their own minds about whether to take a risk. Sometimes, beyond the desperate circumstances of the woman in childbirth or the patient with

14. Schreiber v. Physicians Ins. Co., 588 N.W.2d 26, 31 (Wis. 1999).
15. *Id.* at 32.
16. See *supra*, chapter 3, text accompanying notes 48–60.

advanced disease who must decide whether to have an experimental treatment, there exist competing attitudes within individuals. It is human to explore and to seek adventure. It is also human to be risk-averse. In employing doctrines like assumption of risk—both express and implied—courts seek to mediate among these conflicting personal attitudes as they affect particular situations. The competition between different goods—for example, desires for natural childbirth and for relief from pain—requires courts to mesh the facts with philosophical judgments about the nature and the social value of personal autonomy.

One constraint on choice in the area of compensation is the ban on tort litigation that is a standard part of workers' compensation, a system that covers many millions of employees. We have noted that the workers' compensation statutes effect a trade between workers and employers. The bargain is for a fairly certain recovery of some money by injured workers, without the need to show that employers were negligent, in exchange for a bar to the employee's ability to bring a possibly more lucrative civil action based on fault. The tort system gave the individual freedom to bring such an action, subject to defenses based on his conduct. In creating their historic compromise, the workers' compensation statutes took that freedom away. Generally, the principal exception that permits a tort action, and one that exists only in a minority of states, is for especially culpable conduct on the part of the employer, often cast in terms that describe intentional torts like fraud or battery.

One of the most interesting recent arguments involving autonomy and the freedom to choose in the law governing injuries—a dispute with constitutional and overtly political dimensions—concerns access to experimental medicines. Providing a good historical frame for the problem is the prescription list for drugs. It will surprise many people to learn that it has been only since 1952 that this list existed. In the end of the nineteenth century, access to what today are controlled substances was free and easy. One writer has mentioned a "great . . . cocaine taking epidemic in the [eighteen] eighties and nineties" in the United States, with recommendations for use including "hay fever, asthma, sciatica, tuberculosis" and "even . . . the common cold."[17] In fact, the syrup on which Coca-Cola was based contained cocaine until 1903, and we have noted that at that time drugstore customers could freely buy cocaine for nickels.[18] The "free and easy

17. Marshall S. Shapo, Freud, Cocaine, and Products Liability, 77 B.U. L.Rev 421, 423 (1997), quoting E.M. Thornton, The Freudian Fallacy: An Alternative View of Freudian Theory 127, 130 (1984).
18. See chapter 2, text accompanying note 11.

distribution of cocaine" began to end only with the passage of the Pure Food and Drug Act in 1906.[19]

Not until the Food, Drug, and Cosmetic Act of 1938 did the government require makers of new drugs to get approval by the FDA of the safety of those products. That legislation forced drug makers to inform the FDA about any new products that would be provided to human beings. It took another dozen years for the Durham-Humphrey Amendment to establish a prescription list.[20] Another decade passed before the New Drug Amendments of 1962 set up a system that required FDA approval— implemented by the agency in a three-phase process—for trials of investigational drugs. The 1962 amendments also required manufacturers to show that their drugs were effective.

An important judicial limitation on individual choice came in the 1979 decision of *United States v. Rutherford.*[21] Justice Marshall's opinion for a unanimous court dealt with a substance called laetrile, made from apricot pits, which desperate patients have used as a last-ditch remedy for cancer. The drug had not passed through the two principal checkpoints of drug law—safety and effectiveness. In concluding that the government could ban the interstate shipment of Laetrile, and rejecting the plaintiffs' argument that a ban on the drug did not apply to terminally ill patients, Justice Marshall said that "[t]o accept the proposition that the safety and efficacy standards of the [Food, Drug, and Cosmetic] Act have no relevance for terminal patients is to deny the [FDA's] authority over all drugs, however toxic or ineffectual, for such individuals." In recounting a history of quack cures for cancer, he declared that "this historical experience does suggest why Congress could reasonably have determined to protect the terminally ill, no less than other patients, from the vast range of self-styled panaceas that inventive minds can devise."[22]

The *Rutherford* decision sharply drew the line against total individual autonomy in the acquisition of scientifically unapproved medications. However, a dramatic challenge to the government's authority began in the late 1980s, centering on the demands of patients with AIDS for drugs that had not received FDA approval. A platform for the controversy was the "treatment IND," for which a patient who sought an experimental drug would have to show that he had "a serious or immediately life-threatening

19. See Shapo, *supra*, 77 B.U. L.Rev. at 424, quoting Richard Ashley, Cocaine: Its History, Uses and Effects 65.

20. 1951 Food, Drug, and Cosmetics Act Amendments, Pub. L. 82–215, 65 Stat. 648–49 (Oct. 26, 1951).

21. 442 U.S. 544 (1979).

22. *Id.* at 557–58.

disease" for which "no comparable or satisfactory alternative drug or other therapy is available."[23] The pivot of the argument was the FDA's preference for "controlled clinical trials," for which a principal control is the randomization of patients—half of whom get the experimental product under consideration and half of whom receive a placebo. The FDA's administration of this policy galvanized more than one thousand protestors, mainly AIDS sufferers, who trapped FDA staff members in their own headquarters.[24] Although the FDA acknowledged the "urgency associated with life-threatening illnesses," it insisted that there must be placebo testing "where no therapy has been shown to be effective," reasoning that "controlled clinical trials" would give better outcomes overall for society in the long run.[25]

The case for autonomy was a particularly persuasive one in the case of AIDS, where activists, although not themselves doctors, had steeped themselves with knowledge of pharmacology. Essentially, this relatively sophisticated group of patients was saying that it knew as much about risk as the regulators, and were ready to buy into that level of risk.

As the war over AIDS drugs went on, the Public Health Service issued policy statements, designed to increase the availability of "promising investigational drugs for AIDS and other HIV-related diseases," which favored "'parallel track' protocols while . . . controlled clinical trials essential to establish the safety and effectiveness of new drugs are carried out."[26] In order to be considered for the "parallel track," patients had to show their inability "to participate in . . . controlled clinical trials"—for example, because they were "too ill to participate," or because clinical trials were "fully enrolled," or because the patient could not "take standard treatment because it is contraindicated, cannot be tolerated, or is no longer effective."[27]

With the initial pressure for more access to experimental drugs having come from the community of persons with AIDS, Congress elaborated on the idea of "individual patient access" more generally in the FDA Modernization Act of 1997. That law incorporated both the idea of the treatment IND and an emergency IND, and also set up a "fast track" for new drugs. The treatment IND provisions of the Act required applicants to show "a serious or immediately life-threatening disease or condition," that

23. 52 Fed. Reg. 19466, at 19466 (May 22, 1987).

24. Larry Thompson, Experimental Treatments? Unapproved but Not Always Unavailable, FDA Consumer, Jan.–Feb. 2000.

25. See 53 Fed. Reg. 41516, 41517–20 (Oct. 21, 1988).

26. Public Health Service, Expanded Availability of Investigational New Drugs Through a Parallel Track Mechanism for People With AIDS and Other HIV-Related Disease, 57 Fed. Reg. 13250 (Apr. 15, 1992).

27. Id. at 13257.

there was no "comparable or satisfactory alternative therapy," that a "controlled clinical trial" was in existence, or that "all clinical trials necessary for approval" of the drug had "been completed." Moreover, evincing the concern that expanded access would compromise the so-called gold standard of clinical trials using randomization, an applicant would have to show that the treatment IND would "not interfere with the enrollment of patients" in clinical trials. Congress further required "sufficient evidence of safety and effectiveness to support" the uses for which the drugs were proposed, and a showing that the "available scientific evidence, taken as a whole," would provide "a reasonable basis to conclude" that the product "may be effective for its intended use and would not expose patients to an unreasonable or significant risk of illness or injury."[28]

The "fast track" part of the statute required that drugs be "intended for the treatment of a serious or life-threatening condition" and that they "demonstrate[] the potential to address unmet medical needs for such a condition."[29] Almost a decade later, the FDA proposed a rule for expanded access that drew on the ideas in the FDA Modernization Act—requiring patients to show a serious condition and "no comparable or satisfactory alternative therapy," potential benefits justifying potential risks, and no interference with clinical trials.[30] Both the push for autonomy, and the FDA's commitment to the idea that "good science" required randomized clinical tests, were evident in the agency's description of the rule as "attempt[ing] to reconcile individual patients' desires to make their own decisions about their health care with society's need for drugs to be developed for marketing."[31]

While the FDA was continuing its efforts to strike this balance, a court case provided the kind of focus for the issue that only litigation can offer. This case was *Abigail Alliance for Better Access to Developmental Drugs v. von Eschenbach*.[32] The Abigail Alliance was an advocacy group established by the father of Abigail Burroughs, whose frail condition had kept her out of research trials on an experimental drug for the head and neck cancer that claimed her life. The suit opposed the FDA's policy that prevented patients from getting drugs that had gone through Phase One trials, which essentially test out the basic pharmacological actions of drugs.

28. 21 U.S.C. 360bbb.
29. 21 U.S.C.A. §356(a)(1).
30. FDA, Proposed Rule, Expanded Access to Investigational Drugs for Treatment Use, 71 Fed. Reg. 75147, 75150-51 (Dec. 14, 2006).
31. *Id.* at 75150.
32. 445 F.3d 470 (D.C. Cir. 2006).

The Alliance prevailed before a three-judge panel of the D.C. Circuit, but eventually lost before the full court. The writer of the prevailing opinion for the panel, Judge Judith Rogers, favored what she called an approach based on the "concepts of individual rights to autonomy and self determination." Describing a "right to die" Supreme Court decision as holding that "an individual has a due process right to make an informed decision to engage in conduct, by withdrawing treatment, that will cause one's death," Judge Rogers found it a "logical corollary" "that an individual must also be free to decide for herself whether to assume any known or unknown risks of taking a medication that might prolong her life."[33] Dissenting, Judge Thomas Griffith said that what Justice Cardozo had called the "concept of ordered liberty" did "not contemplate that judges should resolve the scientific uncertainties presented by experimental drugs."[34]

Weighing in as this case progressed, Ezekiel Emanuel, a breast oncologist and then chief of the bioethics division of the National Institutes of Health, inveighed against the giving of experimental drugs on an ad hoc basis. He gave as an example of the downside of such expanded access the waste of "[p]recious time" that occurred because of "delayed enrollment" in clinical trials when political pressure forced insurers to pay for bone marrow transplants for metastatic breast cancer. Saying that hundreds of women died while getting these transplants, "often in isolation rooms separated from their families," he declared that it had cost "[m]illions, if not billions" for what had turned out to be a "substandard treatment."[35] He said that "maintaining hope should never be confused with delaying the research studies that could give hope to future patients or administering ever-more ineffective and unproven treatments."[36]

Judge Griffith, the dissenter to the panel decision, prevailed in the full court. He stressed that the drugs at issue in the case were "experimental and have not been shown to be safe, let alone effective at (or 'necessary' for) prolonging life."[37] Judge Rogers argued, now in dissent, that the Alliance was invoking a "fundamental" right. She said that right rested on "core" ideas of "personal autonomy, self-determination," and even "self-defense."[38] In reply, Judge Griffith rejected Judge Rogers' characterization of the "right" claimed by the Alliance as "fundamental," saying that the FDA's clinical

33. *Id.* at 476, 484, referring to Cruzan v. Director, Missouri Dept. of Health, 497 U.S. 661 (1990).

34. *Id.* at 498 (Griffith, J., dissenting).

35. Ezekiel J. Emanuel, Drug Addiction, New Republic, July 3, 2006, at 9–10.

36. *Id.* at 12.

37. Abigail Alliance for Better Access to Developmental Drugs v. von Eschenbach, 495 F.3d 695, 708 (D.C. Cir. 2007).

38. *Id.* at 717 (Rogers, J., dissenting).

testing process provided the "rational basis" for impingement on that claimed "right." He said that "the FDA's policy of limiting access to investigational drugs" was "rationally related to the legitimate state interest of protecting patients, including the terminally ill, from potentially unsafe drugs with unknown therapeutic effects."[39]

A particularly interesting statement in Judge Griffith's majority opinion indicated that a resolution of the conflict between personal autonomy and broad social benefits was ultimately for politics. He said that "[t]he Alliance's arguments about morality, quality of life, and acceptable levels of medical risk are certainly ones that can be aired in the democratic branches, without injecting the courts into unknown questions of science and medicine."[40]

INDIVIDUAL GOODS AND INDIVIDUALIZATION

Paralleling the thread of autonomy in injury law is the question of how much the law should individualize its responses to injury or the risk of injury. We discussed one aspect of this question under the heading of the definition of rights, particularly with reference to damage awards for the highly personalized category of pain and suffering. That class of tort damages, as distinguished from more definable categories like wage loss and medical bills, depends largely on the response of juries, reviewed by judges, to something that is not conventionally measurable. Even in an era where there are commissions or task forces for a multiplicity of subjects, it may come as a surprise to learn that there was a federal Commission on the Evaluation of Pain. That Commission underlined the subjectively individual nature of the subject in its declaration that "no one can know the pain of another person."[41] If this observation contradicts former President Clinton's famous insistence that he could feel the pain of others, it is a kind of common sense; and the Commission noted, more analytically, that "there is no direct external way to interpret" a person's response to pain stimuli "or to compare objectively one painful experience to the next or one person's pain to another's."[42]

It is often not easy to fit the rules of injury law into neat boxes, but the foggy realities of pain and suffering make it especially difficult to knit those rules into a coherent whole. This simply illustrates why we outline here a

39. See *id.* at 712–13.
40. *Id.* at 713.
41. Report of the Commission on the Evaluation of Pain, 50 Soc. Sec. Bulletin No. 1, 13, 22 (Jan. 1987).
42. *Id.* at 21.

constitution of injury law that depends on interpretation of broad principles, with many skirmishes on particulars and applications that depend on
the facts of specific cases. I once heard a leading plaintiffs' lawyer say that
having as clients identical twins who had suffered the same objectively
defined injury, he could "prove" to a jury that the pain of one was worth
a half million dollars but that the pain of the other should be valued at a
million.

A very different problem in the search for individualization in tort law,
one that spills over into safety regulation, relates to the subsets of the population that are statistically more than usually sensitive to particular stimuli,
for example, chemicals. We introduced above a small body of tort cases
which involves reactions to particular products that the sellers of those
goods claim arise from "hypersensitivity," or "allergy," or "idiosyncrasy."[43]

The first issue in such cases involves the data: what percentage of the
population has a particular type of reaction to a substance? The next issue is
how the law should treat various statistical profiles. Calling a reaction an
"allergic" reaction may not prevent the person who has it from suing a product maker if there are enough people in that class. For example, we noted
that the Wisconsin Supreme Court was prepared to entertain a case in
which latex gloves used by medical professionals could "cause allergic reactions in 5 to 17 percent" of users. But how to deal with a case where the
percentage of such reactions is very small? A New York court denied recovery against the maker of a deodorant for which there had been four reported
reactions out of 600,000 sales of the product. It cited precedents that
rejected claims for "an injury due solely to the rare allergic reaction or
unusual idiosyncrasy of a particular individual."[44]

We thus have an interesting pairing of results. On the one hand, juries are
permitted—within limits that may seem as arbitrary as the awards reduced
on the basis of those limits—to make exquisite determinations of what pain
is worth in particular individuals. On the other hand, if a reaction to stimuli
is unusual in the sense that few suffer it, sometimes courts will say that the
law cannot compensate for such highly individual responses. One reason
given for that outcome is that the seller had no notice that some people
were suffering unusual reactions and therefore could not be shown to be
negligent.[45] The most difficult case is the one where the seller in fact is aware
of a very small number of adverse reactions. Then the question may turn on

43. See chapter 3, text accompanying notes 110–114.
44. Kaempfe v. Lehn & Fink Prods. Corp., 249 N.Y.S.2d 840, 848 (App. Div. 1964).
45. Presbrey v. Gillette Co., 435 N.E.2d 513, 521 (Ill. App. Ct. 1982)("nothing in the
pre-marketing testing to show" that a deodorant "contained any ingredient which was injurious
to a number of people").

one's view of general fairness: Should the mass of consumers who do not have those reactions have to chip into the price of a product in order to provide a fund that will compensate their "idiosyncratic" cousins?

Workers' compensation, a system with more administrative efficiency than tort, gains much of that efficiency from a relative disregard for individuality. As we have noted, workers' compensation uses rigid schedules for awards that at best bundle intangible elements of loss into lump sums paid for specific types of injury. So much for loss of an arm at the shoulder, so much for loss of a leg below the knee, so much for a little finger, and don't take up valuable time by telling a jury how much it hurts *you.*

Undoubtedly workers' compensation more frequently provides funds for the relief of injured people than does tort law. Yet it is interesting that the creators of that unique compensation system, the September 11th Victim Compensation Fund, opted for various kinds of individualization. They tied compensation for economic loss to earnings, and they wholeheartedly adopted a list of highly individualized categories for the valuation of non-economic loss, including "mental anguish" and "hedonic damages" as well as pain and suffering.

Necessarily, legislation setting up safety regulation tends to ignore the individual case—necessarily, because it builds its regulatory structures upon statistics of injuries in the fields it covers. However, as we have observed, different agencies have placed very different values on life. Moreover, when disputes arise, regulation or the interpretation of regulatory rules sometimes turn to various levels of individualization. One example is references to small numbers of specific injuries in the determination of whether a risk of harm is "unreasonable" (one decision refers to such evidence about lawn darts).[46] Another illustration involves the issue of whether a specific workplace environment presents an "imminent danger" to employees that can be remedied only by refusing to do a job.[47] In another connection, we noted above the FDA's struggles to create categories that would allow individual patients access to experimental drugs. The agency has undertaken to do this in the face of its dedication to randomized clinical trials, which in a sense are the epitome of deindividualization—the use of medications and placebos on people who do not know which they are receiving.

---

46. R.B. Jarts v. Richardson, 438 F.2d 846, e.g., at 851 nn. 6–7 (2d Cir. 1971).

47. See, e.g., Whirlpool Corp. v. Marshall, 445 U.S. 1, 12 n.16 (1980)(citing legislative history that "contains numerous references to" the "preventive purpose" of the Occupational Safety and Health Act "and to the tragedy of each individual death or accident").

It has been said that statistics don't cry,[48] but people do. The jagged edges of legislative choices about when to regulate and how to value lives, and the specificity of application when courts must apply legislation to particular cases, reflect the balance that the law strikes between general categories of injuries and their particular impacts. The injury law constitution houses the processes that produce these balancing acts and the apparent anomalies they sometimes generate.

COMMUNITARIANISM

Running alongside concepts of autonomy and individuality, and often bumping into them, is the idea of communitarianism. Often, in order to serve the greater good, the law minimizes the space it provides for individual interests. This process sometimes creates paradoxes. They may be illustrated in this way:

Moral emphasis	Economic emphasis
Individualism	*Communitarianism*
Personal dignity	Overall social utility
Communitarianism	*Individualism*
Sense of social unity	Personal choice

The analyst who places a priority on a moral view of injuries begins with the dignity of the individual, which is opposed to the economic analyst's idea of achieving the greatest benefit for the greatest number, which in turn, somewhat ironically, is an idea with a community emphasis. At the same time, the moralist emphasizes a community-centered view of injuries because it promotes a sense of social unity. And, to complete the paradox, the economic analyst stresses the freest possible range of movement for the individual. Thus two cells that appear opposed when we read them horizontally seem in harmony when we read them diagonally.

The idea of communitarianism has received some interesting elaborations. In their excellent book on communitarianism that centers on tort law, Robert Cochran and Robert Ackerman posit that "tort law should protect intermediate communities," which they define as "the communities that fall between the individual and the community-at-large—including families,

---

48. See, e.g., Mark Shields, in Colloquy with Jim Lehrer (PBS NewsHour broadcast Mar. 20, 2009), transcript available at http://www.pbs.org/newshour/bb/politics/jan-june09/politi-calwrap_03-20.html.

friendships, religious congregations, neighborhoods, unions, companies, and schools."[49] Just one example of the difficult problems on which they focus is the case of "failure to provide medical care to children for religious reasons." They sympathetically note that parents who do not provide care for a child with an illness that would be fatal if not treated "believe that spiritual care is the best means of care for the child" and indeed "are doing what they think will cure the child." However, they argue that "this is one of the unusual cases in which the state should intervene in the intermediate community." They say that "[t]he interest of the child and the value of life are so great and the efficacy of medical treatment is so clearly established that the intervention of the larger community through tort (and perhaps criminal) law is justified"—the tort intervention consisting of the award of damages for a child's death.[50]

In another contested area of tort law, Cochran and Ackerman declare that for "[t]hose who trade in firearms," "[i]t is not enough to say, 'Our product is inherently dangerous, and therefore we cannot be responsible.'" Rather, they assert that gun sellers' "products *are* inherently dangerous, and therefore they *do* share responsibility."[51] At the same time, they inveigh against "coddling those who exercise too little responsibility for their own well-being," giving as an example the fact that "the failure to wear seat belts and motorcycle helmets exacts a toll, not on the immediate victim, but upon those entrusted to his care and upon a society in which we are all interdependent."[52] Yet, they acknowledge the "fine line" that society must walk, "resisting the impulse to coddle but also resisting a return to a 'classical theory' of contract in which hard bargains are enforced against powerless or unknowing parties."[53]

Another commentator, Robert Bush, advanced a theory of "group responsibility" that covered both multiple producers and multiple claimants in products liability cases. In cases where it was impossible for a claimant to identify which of several firms made a product that injured him, Bush suggested that imposing some liability on each firm would "require an individual producer . . . to attend to the safety practices of fellow producers making similar products and to expect them to attend to his safety practices, because each stands to be affected by what the others do or fail

49. Robert F. Cochran Jr. & Robert M. Ackerman, Law and Community: The Case of Torts 11 (Rowman & Littlefield 2004).
50. See *id*. at 114–17.
51. *Id*. at 251.
52. *Id*.
53. *Id*. at 251–52.

to do."[54] He drew a parallel for classes of victims—for example groups of people injured by the same product. In such situations, "A victim often will recover less than his full damages, while others injured by unrelated causes will get a windfall." Drawing on a decision by Judge Jack Weinstein in a case involving Agent Orange, a defoliant to which Vietnam veterans attributed illnesses, he posited that "the individual is asked to feel compensated by benefits that go to others in the group." If this result seemed "unfair and cruel to the individual victim," yet it "encourages him—actually forces him—to view himself not as an individual victim at all, but as a member of a suffering group, in which his pain is shared by others and eased by the alleviation of their pain." Although the "expanded self-understanding" fostered by uneven distributions of compensation might seem impossibly idealistic, Bush argued that it would "combine[] with the incentives of group recovery to encourage actual and potential victims of injury to solidify the links between them by forming actual associations or communities to defend their common health and well-being."[55]

An area of great tension between the rights of individuals and of the community exists in controversies over whether federal safety legislation preempts common law suits for injury. In my study of products liability, I have identified an alphabet-full of statutes under which that question has arisen—from motor vehicle design and flammable fabrics to locomotives and diseased meat products. We have discussed two Supreme Court decisions handed down in consecutive years that show how the specific language of statutes may affect the outcome of cases. One is the 2008 case of *Riegel v. Medtronic*,[56] in which the Court held that a plaintiff claiming injury from a balloon catheter could not sue the manufacturer because the comprehensive review of that product by the FDA occupied the field of safety regulation for the product. A strong contrast appeared the next year, when the Court upheld a multimillion dollar award to a woman who lost an arm to gangrene that occurred from an injection of the defendant's drug. In his opinion for the Court in *Wyeth v. Levine*,[57] Justice Stevens pointed out that although the section of the law governing medical products had an express preemption clause for devices like Riegel's balloon catheter, it did not have "such a provision for prescription drugs." This, he said,

---

54. Robert A. Baruch Bush, Between Two Worlds: The Shift from Individual to Group Responsibility in the Law of Causation of Injury, 33 U.C.L.A. L. Rev. 1473, 1546 (1986).

55. *Id.* at 1547–48.

56. 552 U.S. 312 (2008), discussed *supra* chapter 7, text accompanying notes 195–198.

57. 129 S.Ct. 1187 (2009), other language of which is discussed in chapter 7, text accompanying notes 199–206.

was "powerful evidence that Congress did not intend FDA oversight to be the exclusive means of ensuring drug safety and effectiveness."[58]

The tensions between individuals' right to sue and the preemptive power of safety legislation will not disappear. Capturing those tensions is the declaration by Cochran and Ackerman that "[t]he standard by which communities, of whatever size, should be judged and the standard by which law, as well, should be judged is whether they serve the good of persons." The community, they say, "is primarily an instrumental value that serves persons."[59] If abstract, this formulation focuses the question on how narrowly the law should define the "persons" it serves—as injured individuals, or as beneficiaries of systems of regulation designed to assure the most efficient trade-offs between risks and benefits in the nation at large.

INNOVATION

A vital engine in the modern economic world is innovation. Social critics will have their innings about the dubious benefits of many newfangled products or ways of doing things. There is also room for argument about just how new some "new" products are: medical critics will point out that many products marketed as new achieve very little advantage over those already on the market.

The computer has spawned innumerable beneficial shoots and blooms. Just one example is the e-mail a great majority of the population uses for professional and personal reasons. Yet the computer and its massive sibling, the Internet, have also made possible the infliction of new varieties of harms traditionally recognized as injuries. We have noted that Congress sought to strike a balance in one area, that of defamations anonymously posted on electronic bulletin boards, by immunizing Internet service providers for material provided by others.[60] Very few people who possess motor vehicles would want to do without them. Yet an enormous ledger of injuries arose from the invention of the motor car; the national figure on vehicle fatalities stayed for many years in the low forty thousands, dipping by several thousand only recently. Medical products provide relief from suffering, improvements in health, and often save lives outright. But many such products cause harm to some, often a relatively small number of people.

58. *Id.* at 1200.
59. Cochran & Ackerman, *supra* note 49, at 247.
60. Communications Decency Act §230, 47 U.S.C. §230(c)(1), see chapter 7, text accompanying note 87.

Innovation thus produces casualties. Society strives through all its injury law mechanisms to minimize the number of them. Through tort law, while spreading losses as well as compensating for them, sometimes it also reduces losses from injury as a by-product.[61] Through workers' compensation, it compensates large numbers of victims, although as we briefly noted earlier, the results on risk-taking by both employers and employees are subject to debate.[62]

Through safety statutes, the law may give a push to technology that reduces risk, but it may also increase the costs of innovation. We have long since passed the days when untrammeled markets permitted sellers of many types of risky products to have their way entirely with consumer safety. Still, sometimes regulation may damp innovation, as well as inflicting directly on sellers the costs of injury. There comes a time when some product sellers will not wish to subject themselves to the burdens of regulation nor to the risk of civil liability for the consequences of product failure. The different branches of injury law affect the level of casualties, at least in a general way, as the law incorporates into itself a balance between innovation and rights to physical and emotional integrity. Within the framework of the injury law constitution, it resolves many conflicts through its various mechanisms for the application of general social attitudes and for the arbitration of policy disagreements.

EQUALITY

One of the great continuing conversations in American law emerges from the proposition that all persons are equal before the law. Translating that lofty idea into results in concrete environments presents many challenges. For the workplace, every American legislature has enacted the grand

---

61. Some data indicates that when no-fault regimes for auto accidents replace the fault-based tort system, vehicle fatalities increase. See, e.g., Alma Cohen & Rajeev Deheija, The Effect of Automobile Insurance and Accident Liability Laws on Traffic Fatalities, 47 J. L. & Econ. 357 (2004).

62. See, e.g., Linda Darling-Hammond & Thomas J. Kniesner, The Law and Economics of Workers' Compensation 59 (Rand R-2716-IC 1980) ("we still do not know whether imposing workers' compensation reduces" the systematic underestimation of job hazards by employees, or "leaves it unchanged, or reduces it"); Richard B. Victor, Linda R. Cohen, and Charles Phelps, Workers' Compensation and Workplace Safety: Some Lessons From Economic Theory 50 (Rand R-2918-ICJ 1982) (while it is "generally true" that increases in workers' compensation benefits produce greater investments in safety, there are several situations in which they are "likely to reduce or have no effect" on such investments—situations including "periods of relatively rapid inflation in safety input prices" and "the use of engineering controls rather than personal protective equipment 'in hazardous industries where the demand for labor is very responsive to changing labor costs,'" as in situations involving "significant foreign competition").

compromise of workers' compensation laws. The legislative bargain represented by workers' compensation significantly levels the field of financial responsibility for workplace injuries. It assures at least some compensation for many injured employees who previously went without it because of the inequality, inherent in disproportionate power of control, imposed by doctrines like assumption of risk.

Various regulatory systems aim to reduce the inequality of information between sellers and consumers and the resultant constraints on meaningful free choice of goods and services. The Federal Trade Commission Act, originally passed in 1914, condemns not only outright deceptive advertising but "unfair" "acts or practices."[63] Since the 1930s, securities laws have provided at least some protection against fraudulent or misleading statements and omissions in the sale of securities, prohibiting seller misconduct in language as broad as "any manipulative, deceptive or other fraudulent device or contrivance"—terms used, for example, in various parts of the Securities Exchange Act.[64]

The food and drug legislation imposes limitations on sellers of drugs and devices with respect to the representations they make. Every television viewer exposed to public advertising for prescription drugs is familiar with lists of warnings hurriedly spoken and ending with catchall advice to "talk with your doctor."

Laws of this kind redress imbalances not only of information but of sophistication. The lay patient knows very little about the biochemical effects of the drugs she takes. The occasional purchaser of stock lacks the know-how of the professional trader. Various other statutes protect, at least to some extent, the "ignorant" and the "credulous." A provision in the Uniform Commercial Code (UCC), legislation adopted in every state that in part codifies many years of common law decisions, provides remedies for "unconscionable" conduct by sellers of consumer goods, remedies that take into consideration the disadvantaged position of many buyers. Only illustrative of judicial interpretation of this provision is a South Dakota case involving a herbicide that did not work. The court says that purchasers like the farmer who bought the product "are not in a position to bargain with

63. 15 USCA §45(a). A 1994 amendment adds a restrictive clause to this broad language. It requires that to show that an act is "unfair," the Commission must establish that it "causes or is likely to cause substantial injury to consumers which is not reasonably avoidable by consumers themselves and not outweighed by countervailing benefits to consumers or to competition." The amendment also says that "[i]n determining whether an act or practice is unfair, the Commission may consider established public policies as evidence to be considered with all other evidence," although "[s]uch public policy considerations may not serve as a primary basis for such determination." Id. §45(n).

64. See, e.g., 15 U.S.C.A. §78o(c)(as amended through 2010).

chemical manufacturers for contract terms more favorable than those listed on the preprinted label, nor are they in a position to test the effectiveness" of the product before they buy it.[65]

Paralleling judicial interpretation of statutes like the UCC, inequalities of information and sophistication trigger continuing battles in the common law. A poignant illustration of such disagreements is a case in which a foundry employee sued for disease caused by silica products. Reversing the plaintiff's judgment against a supplier of the products, a majority of the Texas Supreme Court concluded that it was wrong for the trial court to exclude evidence that the plaintiff "had an eighth grade education, had difficulty reading, and thus did not pay attention to warning labels," as well as evidence that he "seldom used a mask or respirator." The majority said that this evidence would have been enough to "rebut any presumption that [the plaintiff] would have heeded a warning" by the defendant "and that the absence of such a warning was at least *a* cause, if not the only cause, of [the plaintiff's] injury."[66]

This opinion drew a sharp dissent from Justice Lloyd Doggett. Pointing out that "more than one million adult Texans" had "less than a ninth grade education," he said that the majority had rewritten "the product safety law of Texas to deny protection to those who have 'only an eighth grade education' by assuming that such people would 'not pay attention to warning labels.'"[67] Justice Doggett went on to a career in Congress, and this opinion, among others, is symbolic of the political content of the branch of private law called torts.

An interesting set of variations on inequality appears in the application of the rationale that favors spreading of the risk of injury to those who reap the benefits of risky activities or products. Typical language in judicial opinions that invoke this rationale appears in a case in which the Eighth Circuit used the term "spreading" in designating General Motors as "the party financially best able to afford the cost of injuries."[68] Yet, judicial sympathy for parties lacking in relative power may extend to businesses. In another case, the Third Circuit said that the fact that "a corporation the size of General Motors may be able to spread the cost" of strict liability "does not mean that a machine shop employing five or ten individuals has similar capabilities." It added that "General Motors' ability to self-insure if no liability policies are available does not aid the machine shop when its

---

65. Durham v. Ciba-Geigy Corp., 315 N.W.2d 696, 700 (S.D. 1982).
66. Dresser Indus., Inc. v. Lee, 880 S.W.2d 750, 754 (Tex. 1993).
67. *Id.* at 755 (Doggett, J., dissenting).
68. Passwaters v. General Motors Corp., 454 F.2d 1270, 1277 (8th Cir. 1972).

premium for a policy (assuming it can get one) rises to confiscatory heights."[69]

The law of tort damages enforces one kind of inequality while at the same time providing an important equalizer. Economic damages largely reflect the inequalities in income between high-salaried and low-wage employees. The executive disabled by a tortious injury can expect much more compensation for his lost earnings than the laborer. As we have noted, the September 11th Fund in large measure perpetuated this set of inequalities, with tables that tied compensation awards to amounts of earnings. Most workers' compensation statutes give awards based largely on percentages of average weekly wages, but generally those amounts will be substantially lower than those provided by the September 11th Fund. Moreover, the rules devised for that Fund set rather generous minimums for awards—$500,000 where a victim who died had a spouse or dependent and $300,000 where the victim had no spouse or dependents.[70] At the same time, Congress included an unusual leveling provision that required those getting awards from the Fund to deduct "collateral sources" like payments from insurance policies and various other programs that would otherwise provide funds for injuries and deaths.[71]

One place where tort law evens out inequalities is the category of noneconomic losses like pain and suffering. Courts have not established hard-and-fast dollar limits on those items of damages, which do not involve losses that can be measured like lost earnings and medical bills. Although courts frequently reduce pain and suffering awards as being excessive, those awards embody a recognition that the poor person feels pain in the same way as her rich boss. Even here, though, we find an interplay between courts and legislatures that epitomizes the room for argument provided by the injury law constitution. Many state legislatures have passed dollar "caps" on noneconomic damages, particularly for medical malpractice cases. This in turn has generated litigation on the constitutionality of such limits, with varying results. Some courts have found statutory "caps" invalid as a violation of equal protection, while others have upheld those laws.

69. Polius v. Clark Equip. Co., 802 F.2d 75, 81 (3d Cir. 1986).
70. 28 CFR §104.41.
71. September 11th Victim Compensation Fund of 2001, Pub. L. 107–42, tit. IV §§405(b)(6), 402(4), codified at 49 U.S.C.A. §40101, also discussed *supra*, chapter 3, text accompanying notes 131–133; infra, chapter 10, text accompanying notes 19–20.

We referred earlier to one of the great mantras of American life, importing theological overtones into politics and law: the idea of individual responsibility.[72] This notion has economic as well as moral features, for it suggests that the law can provide useful incentives for people to govern their conduct. In tort law, the idea becomes specifically incorporated into doctrines governing both the conduct of potential injurers and that of potential victims. A person who engages in risky activity must take responsibility for the safety of others; but those exposed to risk have a responsibility for their own safety.

In tort law, a plaintiff's knowledge of a risk imposes a significant degree of responsibility on him to avoid injury. Fixed in doctrinal concrete in such defenses as contributory negligence and assumption of risk, victim knowledge may sometimes be so specific that it will bar any recovery at all. Thus, we referred earlier to the case of a man who "walked out from between two parked cars in the middle of [a] block," in the middle of the night wearing dark clothing, and "stepped immediately into the path of [an] oncoming car." He behaved so unreasonably that a judge said that a jury would have to find him contributorily negligent and therefore barred from recovery in a suit against the driver.[73] At least as foolhardy is a driver who sees a pedestrian aiming a rifle at his car, bypasses a police car and turns back to the man wielding the rifle, then leaves his car and shouts obscenities at that individual. When the armed man fatally shoots the driver, a court "must conclude that decedent was contributorily negligent" in a suit against a hospital from which the shooter eloped.[74]

One case indicates that actual knowledge of a danger may translate into assumed risk for professional tennis players as well as for laborers in more traditional workplaces. In a Wightman Cup match between the United States and Great Britain, the American Julie Heldman sued for injuries she attributed to bubbles in a synthetic tennis court that were created by moisture. Where there was testimony from her own team captain and a British star that players in the Cup matches were afraid of injury, the court said that given the plaintiff's professional status, there was enough evidence for the jury to decide whether she "knew that the bubbles created a dangerous condition."[75]

72. See *supra*, chapter 3, text accompanying notes 72–84.
73. Garcia v. Bynum, 635 F.Supp. 745, 747 (D.D.C. 1986), discussed chapter 3, text accompanying note 73.
74. Voss v. United States, 423 F.Supp. 751, 754 (E.D. Mo. 1976).
75. Heldman v. Uniroyal, Inc, 371 N.E.2d 557, 567 (Ohio Ct. App. 1977).

In fact, a plaintiff's very appearance of taking extreme care may shift the responsibility for accidents onto him. This is evident in a Pennsylvania case in which an experienced bulldozer operator, using the machine on a steep slope, drove it "in a slow, deliberate and systematic fashion . . . for more than one-half hour before" a rollover that killed him. The court said that his conduct had "rais[ed] the logical inference that he knew what he was doing was very dangerous."[76] The same result occurred in a case in which the plaintiff—a "careful, conscientious, experienced . . . worker" recently promoted to foreman—tried to "troubleshoot [a] problem" with a pressurized gas tank instead of sending it for repairs. Noting not only that the plaintiff's decedent in this case was violating an employer safety rule, but also general knowledge about the dangers of such tanks, the court concluded that a jury should decide whether the decedent "made a deliberate decision to encounter a known risk or had a willingness to take a chance."[77]

At some point, however, courts will decide that knowledge does not impose responsibility on injury victims. Here, the law shuttles from economic incentives to ideas of fairness. A tragic example is a case in which a worker fell to his death while trying to remove planking over an unguarded elevator shaft. This normally was a two-man job, but he kept working alone in the absence of his coworker. In circumstances where the plaintiff apparently felt that he might lose his job "if he stood idle," a federal judge characterized the situation as one of "economic duress," and concluded that the plaintiff "was neither contributorily negligent nor voluntarily or unreasonably assumed the risk."[78] And if there is no assumption of risk when a worker has at least a minute or two to consider a danger, courts may be even more reluctant to impose responsibility on a worker for her own safety when she is in a hurry. In a case in which a fifteen year old girl made a "split-second" decision to remove paper towels from a meat-slicing machine without turning off the power, the court said that she had not made the "considered choice" that would support an "assumption of risk" defense.[79]

At the very edge of the knowledge category is the case where the plaintiff knows of a danger in the general sense but not of a very specific aspect of the hazard, at least at the moment he gets hurt. Judge Breyer, then of the First Circuit, drew a fine distinction in a case where the plaintiff failed to remove his finger from under a clamping cylinder on a machine, which crushed the finger. Judge Breyer acknowledged that the plaintiff had admitted that he knew the machine "had no warning signs or barriers, and that

76. Kupetz v. Deere Co., 644 A.2d 1213, 1222 (Pa. Super. Ct. 1994).
77. Hanlon v. Airco Indus. Gases, 579 N.E.2d 1136, 1141–42 (Ill. Ct. App. 1991).
78. DiSalvatore v. United States, 499 F.Supp. 338, 339, 344–46 (E.D. Pa. 1980).
79. Coty v. U.S. Slicing Mach. Co., 373 N.E.2d 1371, 1378 (Ill. Ct. App. 1978).

those facts made the machine dangerous"; indeed, the jury found that he had "used the machine unreasonably." However, Judge Breyer posited that the plaintiff might have "thought his hand was outside the 'danger area' but he unintentionally let his hand slip within it." This could have meant, Judge Breyer suggested, that "he 'unreasonably' but 'unknowingly' ran the risk" and that thus "a jury might conclude that he did not 'voluntarily' put his hand in the danger zone."[80]

Another First Circuit decision pushed at least as far the requirement that defendants must show that plaintiffs had very specific knowledge of a hazard. This case involved a power roof sweeper that the plaintiff had used many times, knowing that it had a tendency to buck. A warning label on the machine said, "DO NOT OPERATE WITHIN TEN FEET OF EDGE OF ROOF," but the plaintiff said he had not read the label and had not been given instructions on how to operate the machine safely. After he added fuel to the machine, he restarted it about two to five feet from the edge of the roof and it bucked back against him, causing him to lose his balance and fall from the roof. On this evidence, the court said there was "at least a reasonable inference that [the plaintiff] did not appreciate the risk involved in starting the sweeper." It thus affirmed the denial of a motion for directed verdict by the defendant, saying that the question of assumption of risk was for the jury.[81]

The choice of legal doctrine in this area may have significant consequences. Some doctrines—like assumption of risk and "no duty"—provide a complete bar against claims by injury victims. For a long time, the doctrine of contributory negligence was also a total bar to recovery, but a large majority of the states now have adopted doctrines of comparative fault or comparative negligence. These defenses, to one extent or another, allow plaintiffs some recovery in injury cases, although that recovery will be reduced by their own negligent contribution to the accident. An economic reason for comparative fault posits that the doctrine will inspire greater care by both those who create risk to others and those who take risk unto themselves. However, the rationale that many courts favor is one based on fairness rather than economic incentives. The Illinois Supreme Court, for example, said that comparative negligence "produces a more just and socially desirable distribution of loss" than a rule that imposes all responsibility on negligent plaintiffs.[82]

80. Venturelli v. Cincinnati, Inc., 850 F.2d 825, 830–31 (1st Cir. 1988).
81. Austin v. Lincoln Equip. Assocs., Inc., 888 F.2d 934, 937 (1st Cir. 1989).
82. Alvis v. Ribar, 421 N.E.2d 886, 893 (Ill. 1981). The Illinois legislature subsequently adopted a modified version of comparative fault, under which claimants could recover part of

Workers' compensation takes the onus of responsibility away from workers, except in such cases as injury caused by substance abuse, and places all financial responsibility on employers. In the other great system of injury law, that of safety regulation, legislators have made a sweeping determination that imposes responsibility for safety on risk-taking industries. Such legal regimes do not impose individual responsibility on persons subject to risk, which generally would be difficult to do in the kinds of areas they regulate. Moreover, even if that were possible, those areas often are ones where those at risk lack either knowledge about the existence of risk or the ability to protect themselves against it.

SOCIAL RESPONSIBILITY

It is part of the capitalist ethic that enterprise managers are responsible only to their shareholders for the bottom line, and that forays into the realm of social responsibility—although companies may make them for various reasons—must be subordinated to managers' obligations to their owners. Yet, Congress and state legislators in enacting various kinds of safety legislation have undertaken to impose responsibility on businesses on behalf of society. Moreover, the workers' compensation laws manifest the view of legislators that it is the obligation of employers to "ameliorat[e] the economic plight of an employee injured in the course of and on account of his employment, or of his dependents if death ensues from his injury."[83]

The courts, operating under the sharp focus of individual cases, have developed a kind of a common law of social responsibility in their decisions on punitive damages. This body of law is a wedge of the injury law constitution that checks the power of private actors, mostly businesses that otherwise feel allegiance only to their shareholders. The verbal formulas for the kind of conduct required for punitive damages, previously discussed, negatively imply the minimum standard for social responsibility that businesses must meet. We mentioned terms like "outrageous," and "intentional, reckless, willful, wanton, gross and fraudulent,"[84] language from a Wisconsin decision, which suggest the level of conduct at which courts will impose on behalf of a society a form of financial responsibility beyond ordinary civil liability. The Wisconsin legislature has elevated this standard for plaintiffs,

their damages only if their contributory fault was "not more than 50% of the proximate cause of the injury or damage." 735 ICLS 5/2-1116.

83. See Charon's Case, 75 N.E.2d 511, 513 (Mass. 1947).

84. See Wangen v. Ford Motor Co., 294 N.W.2d 437, 458, 462 (Wis. 1980).

requiring that they show that defendants "acted maliciously toward the plaintiff or in an intentional disregard of the rights of the plaintiff."[85]

The Supreme Court has fixed on several elements of defendants' conduct in reviewing the amounts of punitive awards. One element that Justice Stevens said is "[p]erhaps the most important indicium of a punitive damages award is the degree of reprehensibility" of that behavior.[86] A state decision referring to the "level of reprehensibility" of the defendant's conduct affirmed a $31 million punitive award that was almost eighteen times the amount of compensatory damages. In this asbestos case, a Florida appellate court said that the defendant, knowing of the risk of the product, had "consciously made a purely economic decision not to warn its consumers" or to remove the product from the market.[87] The Supreme Court has identified a number of other factors for review of the amount of punitive damages, including the profitability of the defendant's conduct, its "financial position" and "all the costs of litigation."[88]

Although it has been pointed out that focusing on the making of profits does not make much sense, since all businesses exist to make a profit, several decisions have spotlighted profits in upholding punitive awards. In one case, in which the maker of a modular knee concealed a manufacturing error, the court said that this concealment was "for the sole purpose of protecting [the defendant's] profits."[89] And in a cigarette case, a federal judge angrily mentioned evidence that the defendant had "knowingly caused" suffering to smokers "for the sake of profit."[90]

The moral judgments that courts make in punitive damages cases include the responsibilities that arise from knowledge of hazards and also from the deliberate character of the conduct of defendants. In a case in which the defendant used a silicone sealant in installing windshield retention systems in vehicles, which was a much quicker method of installation then one that used urethane, the court said that a jury could have decided that this method of installation "was purposefully performed with an awareness of risk and

85. Wis. Stat. §895.043(3).

86. BMW of N. Am. v. Gore, 517 U.S. 559, 575 (1996), discussed further in chapter 11, text accompanying notes 65–66.

87. Owens-Corning Fiberglas Corp. v. Ballard, 739 So.2d 603, 607 (Fla. Dist. Ct. App. 1998), decision approved, 749 So.2d 483 (Fla. 1999).

88. Pacific Mut. Ins. Co. v. Haslip, 499 U.S. 1, 21–22 (1991), discussed further, chapter 11, text accompanying note 61.

89. Vossler v. Richards Mfg. Co., 192 Cal. Rptr. 219, 227 (Cal. Ct. App. 1983), disapproved in Adams v. Murakami, 813 P.2d 1348 (Cal. 1991), on grounds that in reviewing punitive awards, there must be consideration of defendant's financial condition.

90. Burton v. R.J. Reynolds Tobacco Co., 205 F.Supp.2d 1253, 1263 (D.Kan. 2002).

disregard of the consequences so as to constitute 'wanton and reckless conduct.'"[91]

Although judges generally adhere to a loose code that discourages moral pronouncements, opinions involving conduct justifying punitive damages do exhibit a tendency toward moralisms. In one case, a California appellate court described as "despicable" the conduct of a manufacturer in designing a vehicle "with a known propensity to roll over" while "giving the vehicle the appearance of sturdiness."[92] Courts also weigh in with moral judgments that exonerate companies. In a case involving a tie-down system used on trailers that transported automobiles—a system that was "standard in the industry" at the time the plaintiff was injured—the Eighth Circuit said it was not suggesting "that a manufacturer may ignore safety concerns based on customer demand," but that there was "simply . . . not the evidence of evil motive or reckless disregard . . . necessary to support a punitive damages award."[93]

The constitution of injury law thus reflects a constant set of tensions about social goods. On the one hand we find the notion that maximum freedom of action promotes innovation and resulting social benefits. On the other, we find the idea that the corporate ethic of obligation only to shareholders must be checked by the law, which imposes principles of social responsibility on otherwise free actors. A century ago American legislators placed financial responsibilities on employers through the workers' compensation acts. Over the course of a full century, Congress increasingly has required businesses to meet safety standards in the workplace and in the production of a myriad of consumer goods. And courts have fashioned a morally tinted body of law on punitive damages that communicates society's condemnation of the exceptional wrongfulness of those who quite irresponsibly impose risks on others.

ACCOUNTABILITY AND DECENTRALIZED DECISION MAKING

Generally, we think it's a good thing to hold people accountable for their actions. In tort law, defensive doctrines like contributory negligence and

91. Miller v. Solaglas Cal., Inc., 870 P.2d 559, 569 (Colo. Ct. App. 1993).

92. Romo v. Ford Motor Co., 122 Cal.Rptr.2d 139, 158–59 (Ct. App. 2002). The Supreme Court vacated the state court decision, which had upheld a $290 million award, although the Court did not discuss the propriety of giving a punitive award at all in the case. Ford Motor Co. v. Romo, 538 U.S. 1028 (2003) (vacating for reconsideration in light of State Farm Mut. Ins. Co. v. Campbell, 538 U.S. 408 (2003)).

93. Ford v. GACS, Inc., 265 F.3d 670, 678 (8th Cir. 2001).

assumption of risk seek to achieve this goal with respect to injury victims. With respect to defendants, rules of agency law that hold corporations responsible for the culpable acts of employees push in that direction. Legal rules that "pierce the corporate veil" help to assure that firms cannot hide behind legal structures created for the purpose of avoiding liability. One variation on rules that overcome hurdles to suing corporations is an Eighth Circuit case establishing jurisdiction over a French firm with a wholly owned subsidiary in Arkansas when the firms employed a "unified marketing strategy," which included the "highlighting" of the activities of the Arkansas firm that completed products initially fashioned in France.[94]

The pursuit of defendants that exercise significant degrees of control over processes and distribution systems that expose others to risk occurs in a variety of ways. Courts have imposed liability for products injuries on a wide range of firms in the distributional chain, ranging from manufacturers of completed products through component makers, on down through wholesalers, retailers and in a few cases importers. In some cases they even have extended liability to trademark owners and franchisors for injuries caused by products or services made or provided by their licensees.

The search for parties on whom liability for defective goods can be imposed both efficiently and fairly has sometimes identified corporate successors. Special targets of successor liability have been firms that have expressly or impliedly assumed the liability of prior corporations and firms that have merged with other companies. Some courts have imposed liability where there is a basic "continuity of enterprise" between a predecessor and a successor, and a few have held firms liable when they have simply continued the "product line" of a prior firm.

One limitation of tort law with respect to accountability is that it often takes a long time to fix responsibility on creators of risks that cause injury, with the result that, as one report observed, the people "who made the original risky decisions have long departed from the scene by the time the risks they took materialize . . . in the form of disability, death, and litigation."[95] This sometimes happens because of the delayed effects of toxic products, but it is also is a result of delay in the litigation process itself. However, delayed accountability is a built-in part of the injury problem, and presumably is preferable to no accountability at all. Moreover, the successors of firms whose officials made risky decisions—and later purchasers of corporate stock—can often be fairly said to expose themselves to liabilities growing out of those risks. When successors at least should have known of those

94. Anderson v. Dassault Aviation, 361 F.3d 449, 454–55 (8th Cir. 2004).
95. 1 Am. Law. Inst., Reporters' Study, Enterprise Liability for Personal Injury 27 (1991).

risks, delayed findings of accountability are arguably not unjust, and are meaningful even if their impact is attenuated over time.

A parallel point is that courts frequently blend opportunities to control risk into rules that apportion liability between or among multiple defendants. We describe this set of rules in a later chapter.[96] All of these principles developed for assigning liability—from making employers responsible for the torts of employees to rules on successor liability and apportionment of damages among defendants—serve the goal of making accountable the party that is in fact most responsible for an injury.

We also pay some homage to the general idea, one that effectively provides a clause in the injury law constitution, that it is usually desirable to decentralize decision making, and therefore responsibility. Controversies over the law on preemption by federal regulatory schemes of tort actions, discussed above, exemplify the tensions in this area of tort actions. The Supreme Court's decisions in successive years in *Riegel v. Medtronic*, the balloon catheter case, and *Wyeth v. Levine*, the drug case involving gangrene caused by arterial leakage from an intravenous injection, are especially illustrative of those tensions. A specific preemption clause saved the manufacturer in *Riegel*, but despite Justice Alito's dissenting complaint in *Levine* that one Vermont jury was able to overrule a system of FDA regulation, that state's tort law dominated the federal agency's oversight of prescription drug safety.[97] The perceived virtues and vices of decentralization often depend on whose ox is being gored.

One author has identified, as an interesting category of litigation that effectively aims to decentralize responsibility, suits that "single out high level government officials because of the policies that they make and try to implement."[98] This is the so-called *Bivens* litigation—suits against federal officials for violations of constitutional rights. Drawing on recent literature, the author suggests that this kind of case is "really a form of impact litigation,"[99] which "disaggregate[s] . . . government defendants to the individual level."[100] Although noting that such "high profile tort suit[s] seem[] to offer a difficult and unlikely effort to constrain government policy through a weak alternative means,"[101] he suggests that they are

96. See chapter 10, text accompanying notes 14–16.
97. See chapter 7, text accompanying notes 195–206.
98. David Zaring, Three Models of Constitutional Torts, 2 J. Tort Law, Issue 1, 1, at 3 (Bepress 2008).
99. *Id.* at 23.
100. *Id.* at 28.
101. *Id.* at 25.

representative of a concept of "decentralized government" that has attracted interest.[102]

We have summarized a group of social and individual goods, some of which embody conceptions of the "good" in the philosophical sense. Because of the competition that takes place between and among these goods, the law often must deal in tradeoffs, including tradeoffs among values. It must reconcile individuality and communitarianism, preferences for risk against risk aversion, and values linked to the desire for innovation when those values conflict with personal interests in physical integrity and emotional tranquillity.

Sometimes the law chooses among conflicting goods by adopting social preferences that manifest themselves over time. A good example of this in judge-made law, which has responded to changes in values over time, is the tort of intentional infliction of emotional distress. Advocacy for tort liability for emotional distress began to find its way into academic literature by as early as the 1920s.[103] By 1939, William L. Prosser had discovered a basis for such liability in a diverse group of prior cases, at least where the defendant's conduct was intentional.[104] Before those developments, judges influenced by a relatively hardened perspective on human relations relegated emotional tranquillity to the back seat behind a more rough and tumble view of the world that emphasizes freedom of movement and of speech even when they prove abusive to others.

Now, every American court recognizes a tort of intentional infliction of emotional distress under one label or another—some jurisdictions call it the tort of "outrage." However, the competition between values that adoption of this tort has resolved for intentional acts or statements continues in an adjoining compartment of the law: in the controversy over whether to allow an action for negligent infliction of emotional distress. A substantial number of courts have refused to recognize that tort, preferring to give running room to people who carelessly risk psychological harm to others.

A striking pair of Texas cases illustrates the cultural and legal tensions that infect this topic. In *St. Elizabeth Hospital v. Garrard*[105] the plaintiffs sued the hospital and a doctor for grief, uncertainty, and worry resulting from

---

102. See *id.* at 26–27.

103. See, e.g., Herbert Goodrich, Emotional Disturbance as Legal Damage, 20 Mich. L. Rev. 497 (1922) (saying, at 513, that "the law has already recognized the possession of a peaceful mental state as a subject for protection"). A later, landmark article is Calvert Magruder, Mental and Emotional Disturbance in the Law of Torts, 49 Harv. L. Rev. 1033 (1936) (saying, at 1067, that "the courts have already given extensive protection to feelings and emotions").

104. William L. Prosser, Intentional Infliction of Mental Suffering: A New Tort, 37 Mich. L. Rev. 874 (1939).

105. 730 S.W.2d 649 (Tex. 1987).

the delivery of a stillborn infant. They alleged that although the plaintiff father and an attending physician had agreed to have an autopsy done, it was not performed. They claimed that the child's body had been delivered to a mortuary and then disposed of in an "unmarked, common grave." In this 1987 case, a majority of the Texas court held that plaintiffs suing for "negligent infliction of mental anguish" did not have to present "proof of physical injury resulting" from that anguish. Rejecting the argument that "false claims" of this kind might "lead[] to arbitrary results," the majority said that "[j]urors are best suited to determine whether and to what extent the defendant's conduct caused compensable mental anguish by referring to their own experience." Referring to "an established trend in American jurisprudence," the court said that "[t]he distinction between physical injury and emotional distress is no longer defensible."[106]

Just six years later, though, in *Boyles v. Kerr*,[107] a new majority of the Texas court explicitly overruled *Garrard* "to the extent that it recognizes an independent right to recover for negligently inflicted emotional distress."[108] This case involved an unusual situation—a suit by a young woman against a young man for videotaping a consensual act of sexual intercourse between them and then showing the tape to friends, with a resultant spread of gossip among others. On the surface, the plaintiff's pleading of negligent infliction of emotional distress seemed odd, since it appeared that the better description of the defendant's conduct would have been intentional rather than negligent, but that apparently was a choice the plaintiff's lawyer made to take advantage of the terms of the defendant's insurance policy.

Having indicated in an original opinion in the case that it viewed the defendant's conduct as "**truly egregious**,"[109] the majority quoted precedent on the idea that foreseeability of injury did not provide a sufficient limitation on liability in negligence for an "intangible injury." The precedent, a California case, had emphasized the need "to avoid limitless liability out of all proportion to the degree of a defendant's negligence," a liability "against which it is impossible to insure without imposing unacceptable costs on those among whom the risk is spread."[110] Despite the *Garrard* majority's discerning of a "trend" in favor of its holding, the *Boyles* majority said that "[m]ost other jurisdictions do not recognize a general duty not to negligently inflict emotional distress," that many others "limit recovery by requiring proof of a physical manifestation," and that

---

106. *Id.* at 654.
107. 855 S.W.2d 593 (Tex. 1993).
108. *Id.* at 595–96.
109. *Id.* at 602.
110. *Id.* at 599 (quoting Thing v. La Chusa, 771 P.2d 814, 826–27 (Cal. 1989)).

only "a few . . . recognize a general right to recover for negligently inflicted emotional distress."[111]

This pair of Texas cases provides an especially sharp example of the tradeoff between running room to be careless and breathing room for the interest in being free from serious emotional disturbance. These are goods both social and individual. It is desirable for each person to have both kinds of room for maximum use of his or her talents and abilities, as it is desirable for society that each person possess both opportunities for self-expression and a zone for preservation of emotional tranquillity. The one allows for both personal growth and legitimate catharsis, while the other provides a basis for people to contribute to society without overwhelming, and counterproductive, interference by others.

111. *Id.* at 598–99.

CHAPTER 9

The Rationales of Injury Law

I focus in this chapter on the rationales, goals and purposes of injury law. In part, this analysis elaborates on several factors, discussed in chapter 3, that are foundation blocks for the concept of rights.

Safety. A principal concern of decision makers is the promotion and maintenance of safety. Proponents of regulatory statutes announce this goal in forthright language. One of the most direct pronouncements on this point is a remark of Senator Yarborough, a sponsor of the Senate bill that became the Occupational Safety and Health Act, who said, "[w]e are talking about assuring the men and women who work in our plants and factories that they will go home after a day's work with their bodies intact."[1] This language of assurance from legislative history is particularly emphatic, but the terminology in various statutes is also very strong, often unqualified, on the point of providing safety to the classes of persons who the legislation is designed to protect.[2] As courts began to apply the theory of strict liability to cases involving product injuries, the idea of providing "maximum protection" to consumers became a mantra.[3] A 1965 Illinois decision adopting strict liability for products presented a very strong version of this philosophy: "The public interest in human life and health demands all the protection the law can give."[4] Statutes and decisions that use this kind of language aim to reduce injuries to the minimum achievable level.

---

1. Whirlpool Corp. v. Marshall, 445 U.S. 1, n.16.
2. The general duty clause of the Occupational Safety and Health Act, for example, says that "[e]ach employer . . . shall furnish to his employees employment and a place of employment which are free from recognized hazards that are causing or likely to cause death or serious physical harm to his employees." 29 U.S.C. §654(a)(1).
3. See, e.g., Jimenez v. Superior Court, 29 Cal.4th 473, 478, 58 P.3d 450, 453, 127 Cal.Rptr.2d 614, 618 (2002) (quoting language from California precedents going back to 1964).
4. Suvada v. White Motor Co., 210 N.E.2d 182, 186 (1965).

This risk-averse philosophy, whether reflected in legislation designed to prevent injuries or in judicial decisions in injury cases, is very much at odds with the idea of law as a tribune of economic efficiency. A set of rationales that cut against, or at least moderate, a thoroughgoing commitment to safety has its roots in economic theory. A varied set of economic approaches to safety emphasize the idea of efficiency. In tort law, a favorite creature of professors is the so-called Learned Hand Test, created by a famous judge. Using an algebraic formula, Judge Hand said, in essence, that the question of whether a party had been negligent would depend on whether a combination of the probability of an injury and its severity was greater or less than the cost of preventing it.[5] This approach can be condensed into the issue of whether accident costs exceed accident avoidance costs. Another formula, adopted in a comment to a section of the Third Restatement of Torts, is "a 'risk-benefit' test . . ., where the 'risk' is the overall level of the foreseeable risk created by the actor's conduct and the 'benefit' is the advantages that the actor or others gain if the actor refrains from taking precautions." The drafters of this comment said that this test could "also be called a 'cost-benefit test' where 'cost' signifies the cost of precautions and the 'benefit' is the reduction in risk those precautions would achieve."[6]

Yet another formula uses the concept of comparing risk and utility. The Second Restatement of Torts took the position that an act was negligent if its risk "outweigh[ed] what the law regards as the utility of the act or of the particular manner in which it is done."[7] Interestingly, the drafters of that Restatement section indicated that the measuring rod for the determination of utility was not a neat numerical one. As we noted in the chapter on doctrine, they focused on "[t]he social value which the law attaches to the interest which is to be advanced or protected by" the defendant's conduct and the probability that the conduct at issue would further that interest or that "another and less dangerous course of conduct" would do so.[8] Another formulation, a theological starting point for scholars who do economic analysis of law, suggests that when one party's conduct causes injury to another, determinative factors on the liability issue include the ability of parties to acquire information about risk and ultimately their comparative abilities to avoid injury.[9]

---

5. United States v. Carroll Towing Co., 159 F.2d 169, 173 (2d Cir. 1947).
6. Restatement (Third) of Torts: Liability for Physical Harm §3, cmt. e (2010).
7. Restatement (Second) of Torts §291 (1965).
8. Id. §292.
9. These are principal by-products of the much-cited article by Ronald Coase, The Problem of Social Cost, 3 J. L. & Econ. 1 (1960).

A common goal of various economic analysis formulas is the creation of incentives for people to adjust their risk-taking in a way that leads to efficient results—efficiency in one sense being defined as the package of risks and benefits that people would buy at specific prices. This emphasis on pricing and costs contrasts with the view of those who wish to minimize the risk of accidents without regard to technical efficiency considerations. These two ways of looking at the world of injuries have led to all-out battles in both the law of torts and the field of public regulation of safety. In the law of products liability, in particular, a substantial battle arose over the question of whether the definition of a defect was exclusively one based on "risk-utility balancing"[10] or whether that definition should include other factors, notably that of consumer expectations.[11]

In the public law arena, arguments have raged about whether a cost-benefit test should be the primary standard for government agencies dealing with safety. Just one example of the complex nature of the argument appears in John Graham's analysis of the proposition that there should be "special protection for those at the highest individual risk." Graham points out that although there is evidence that "low-income populations incur disproportionate risks from hazardous exposures to some products, technologies, and production facilities," "there is also a literature suggesting that low-income households bear disproportionate shares of the costs of environmental regulation."[12] In early 2009, with the coming of the Obama administration, there were reports of concern among environmentalists about the appointment to the post of director of the Office of Information and Regulatory Affairs—a position tagged by the media as a "regulatory czar"—of Cass Sunstein, a law professor whose writings had stressed the advantages of cost-benefit analysis.[13] Illustratively, the president of Clean Air Watch said that "if a Republican nominee had" Sunstein's views on

10. Restatement (Third) of Torts: Products Liability §2, cmt. d (1997).
11. See, e.g., my critique of an exclusive emphasis on risk-utility in Marshall S. Shapo, In Search of the Law of Products Liability: The ALI Restatement Project, 48 Vand. L. Rev. 631, 660–68 (1995).
12. John D. Graham, Saving Lives through Administrative Law and Economics, 157 U. Pa. L. Rev. 395, 520–22 (2008).
13. See, e.g., Cass R. Sunstein, The Cost-Benefit State: The Future of Regulatory Protection (Am. Bar Ass'n 2002) concluding that generally, "government should perform cost-benefit calculations for all major regulations and that agencies should be required to show that the benefits justify the costs," id. at 138, although urging that the argument on behalf of cost-benefit analysis "is presumptive only, and that in certain contexts agencies have good reasons for embarking on a different course," id. at 86. Sunstein identifies two places for regulators to bend in setting out "refined versions" of the so-called precautionary principle in his article Irreversible and Catastrophic, 91 Corn. L. Rev. 841 (2006) (summarizing the "Irreversible Harm Precautionary Principle" and the "Catastrophic Harm Precautionary Principle" at 845–46).

cost-benefit analysis, "the environmental community would be screaming for his scalp."[14]

Freedom. Implicitly and explicitly, judges and lawmakers view freedom as a principal goal. This includes freedom of movement and freedom to engage in moneymaking activities, and free expression—in print and electronically, as well as in various graphic forms, for example in film. In injury law, the problem arises when these freedoms conflict with freedom from invasions of physical and emotional integrity and from injury to reputation. In the common law, the law of defamation places limits on the kinds of lies people may tell about others; and a few decisions in the tort law of privacy even impose liability for the publication of truthful but damaging images of others or facts about their private lives. Safety legislation that people generally take for granted imposes many limits on the ability of people and corporations to act as they wish—speed limits, the design of automobiles with regard to crash protection, and the kinds of drugs one may sell or buy as well as the way sellers may advertise them. In the case of conduct that exposes others to physical risk, the war between freedoms corresponds with the clash between those who favor safety at all costs and those who focus on cost-benefit tradeoffs. It is often difficult to pigeonhole such problems involving physical risk into cost-benefit categories; and in the area of defamation and privacy, one is often at a loss to discover the efficient level of lying or truth-telling.

Corrective justice. An idea that contrasts sharply with an efficiency approach to injury law is that of corrective justice. This idea goes back to a brief passage in the writings of Aristotle, of which there are several translations. In one that I often use, Aristotle writes of corrective justice as "the intermediate between loss and gain"—that is, the loss of an injured person and the gain of the one who inflicts the injury. When an injury dispute goes a judge, he says, the parties assume "that if they get what is intermediate they will get what is just."[15] This language has been the subject of commentary by many scholars, who differ on some of the most basic aspects of the concept. Indeed, Allan Beever has referred to the work of other commentators who view it as "mysterious."[16] Beever criticizes others for the close linkage they discern between the idea of corrective justice and notions

---

14. Tom Hamburger and Christi Parsons, "Obama's Nominee for Regulatory Czar Faces Scrutiny," *Los Angeles Times,* January 26, 2009, http://articles.latimes.com/2009/jan/26/nation/na-sunstein26.

15. 2 Jonathan Barnes, The Complete Works of Aristotle 1786–87 (1984) (hereafter Aristotle).

16. See, e.g., Allan Beever, Corrective Justice and Personal Responsibility in Tort Law, 28 Oxf. J. L. Stud. 475, 500 (2008) (summarizing commentary on this position).

of personal responsibility. He stresses that in tort law, "personal responsibility focuses primarily on the defendant, while corrective justice looks at the
relationship between the parties."[17] For him, the central question is one of
what is fair between the parties, whether or not the defendant is held to be
personally responsible.[18] What seems to be common to all scholars is the
idea that corrective justice narrowly focuses on the question of what is just
between the parties, rather than on the implications that a decision in one
case might have for society as a whole—for example, whether holding
for one party or the other would achieve efficiency. This idea of corrective
justice, although it has inspired a lot of academic commentary, is at odds
with the view that probably dominates the minds of American judges in
tort cases. That view is that in deciding tough cases, judges should focus on
"instrumental" factors—what the impact of a decision one way or the other
would be on society.

Even if one prefers an efficiency rationale to corrective justice, damages
in tort personal injury cases are focused on individual loss. Most tort awards
are for compensatory damages, and there are several explanations about
what they are intended to compensate for. The diversity of these explanations reflects the difficulty of defining the value of tort damages to society.
Geoffrey MacCormack, analyzing the rules of the Twelve Tables, published
in the Roman Republic around 450 B.C., says that the law embodied in these
documents "is commonly thought have reached a stage of development
between revenge and compensation." He notes that over time, "custom
began to impose limits upon the extent to which vengeance might be
exacted" by one person or kin group against another, with compensation
evolving "as a means of buying off revenge, as a sort of ransom." After that,
the state began to "impose limits upon the degree of revenge to be exacted."
It would "exclude the possibility of revenge in certain cases and provide
instead a financial penalty," and where revenge was "still permitted," it might
"make exaction depend upon a decision by a court."[19] The German scholar
Ulrich Magnus, noting that the goals that prevailed in the Code
of Hammurabi were "revenge, punishment, and sanctions," has said that
Roman law at the time of the Lex Aquilia—adopted around 287 B.C.—
included "penal elements" as well as compensatory ones, although at the

17. See, e.g., *id.* at 483, 491.
18. See *id.* at 491.
19. Geoffrey MacCormick, Revenge and Compensation in Early Law, 21 Am. J. Comparative
L. 69, 73–74 (1973).

time of the Corpus Juris, in 533 A.D., "the goal of compensation of damage began to prevail over the goal of punishment and sanction."[20]

MacCormack has also said that in "modern primitive societies," "acts of revenge and procedures for the payment of compensation co-exist." He points out that in such societies revenge of certain kinds "imports an element of compensation," one that "may be described as negative compensation in the sense that the loss is made good through the infliction of a similar loss on the killer's group."[21] Emily Sherwin has suggested that even modern tort damages involve a "pursuit of compensation" that "is closely akin to ordinary nonretributive revenge" and that indeed "[c]orrective justice, despite the high moral ground often claimed for it, is a close companion to revenge."[22]

Where some rationales for compensatory damages focus on their value to society, others are centered on the victim; sometimes, the line between those categories is a blurry one. Certainly, "[c]ondemnation serves a social function," one that communicat[es] to members of society that we don't do that . . ., that we abhor that act, that way of thinking, and that lack of feeling that may have lead to the transgression." And "[c]ondemnation can also be assaultive," making a wrongdoer "squirm or show some other sign of suffering." In general, it "binds people in a society together in common healing when a boundary has been crossed." Condemnation, "in a culture that has an ambivalent relation to the emotion of anger," gives "authoritative approval to the expression of anger, vindictive feelings and moral superiority" in situations where "in ordinary social relations," these emotions "are often kept under wraps."[23]

With all of these explanations on the table, it seems reasonable to assume that the idea of fairness—that is fairness between the parties—is central to the thinking of many ordinary people about awards of damages. One writer identifies "assumptions underlying a principle of compensating for losses" as being that "[s]uch awards are *fair* to the plaintiff," who "receives his losses," and that they are also "*fair* to the defendant," because "he was at fault but is not penalized for his actions."[24]

The general social symbolism of tort damages appears in an observation by Professor Sherwin that noneconomic damages in particular, for example

---

20. Ulrich Magnus, International Torts, A Comparative Study, 39 Washburn Law Journal 347, 348–349 (2000).

21. MacCormick, *supra*, at 79–81.

22. Emily Sherwin, Compensation and Revenge, 40 San D. L. Rev. 1387, 1412–13 (2003).

23. Sharon Lamb, The Psychology of Condemnation: Underlying Emotions and Their Symbolic Expression in Condemning and Shaming, 68 Brooklyn L. Rev. 929, 931–32 (2003).

24. Robert J. Nordstrom, Damages as Compensation for Loss, 5 North Carolina Central L. Rev. 15, 19 (1974).

awards for pain and suffering, "can be seen as vehicles for a transfer of wealth—a mark of status in modern society—from wrongdoers to victims." She says that "the victim enjoys the symbolic satisfaction of asserting a public demand for payment."[25] And Professor Pryor has suggested that a "rehabilitative lens" provides a way in which "tort compensation may have the effect (even if unintended) of signaling that money is commensurable with deeply personal losses, such as losses of cognition or the loss of a child."[26] A general observation on the public message sent by tort compensation is that it "can symbolize public respect for rights and public recognition of the transgressor's fault by requiring something important to be given up on one side and received on the other, even if there is no equivalence of value possible."[27]

There is a substantial catalog of victim-centered rationales for compensatory damages. A traditional formulation focuses on the restoration of the injured person to his or her life before the injury—the usual phrase is "making whole." One rather idealistic application of this idea focuses on the notion of human "flourishing." An advocate of the view of "wholeness as flourishing" points to the award by some courts of damages for loss of enjoyment of life to persons whose injuries have left them comatose. She says that the idea "does not pretend that tort damages literally return plaintiffs to their pre-accident conditions," but "focuses on how the injury inflicted by the defendant has impaired the plaintiff's pre-accident capacity to flourish and directs our attention to the ways in which financial compensation can restore it."[28] Another writer has said that punitive damages in particular "help[] restore the plaintiff's emotional equilibrium" and indeed "may also restore the emotional equilibrium of society as a whole."[29] Yet another rationale stresses the idea of money payments as reducing the "'sense of continuing outrage'" of "'one who has suffered a violation of his bodily integrity.'"[30]

25. Sherwin, *supra* note 22, at 1401–02.

26. Ellen Pryor, Rehabilitating Tort Compensation, 91 Geo. L. J. 659, 692–93 (2003).

27. Margaret Jane Radin, Compensation and Commensurability, 43 Duke L. J. 56, 69 (1993).

28. Heidi Li Feldman, Harm and Money: Against the Insurance Theory of Tort Compensation, 75 Texas L. Rev. 1567, e.g., at 1586–94 (1997).

29. David G. Owen, Punitive Damages in Products Liability Litigation, 74 Mich. L. Rev. 1257, 1279–80 (1976).

30. Radin, *supra* note 27, at 73, quoting Louis L. Jaffe, Damages for Personal Injury: The Impact of Insurance, 18 L. & Contemp. Probs. 219, 224 (1953). See also Daniel J. Shuman, The Psychology of Compensation in Tort Law, 43 U. Kan. L. Rev. 39, 50–51 (1994), quoting J. C. Flugel, Man, Morals, and Society: A Psycho-Analytical Study 145 (1945) on the proposition that "punishment of wrongdoers 'tends to relieve the outraged feelings of those who have been hurt; after its infliction their anger abates, and they tend to regard the incident as closed.'"

There have been some powerful criticisms of tort damages, particularly those that are awarded in a lump sum. One critic has pointed out that even damages awards for tangible economic loss require "impossible predictions about future earnings . . . and medical care." He says that "[w]e fail to compensate disabled victims for losing the intrinsic satisfactions of work but also fail to deduct their opportunity benefits from not working." Noting the standard requirement that judgments for compensatory damages have "to be discounted to present value," he says this involves "another impossible, decades long prediction of interest rates." From an avowed socialist perspective, he attacks economic damages for "reproduc[ing] inequality," especially because damages for lost earnings are related directly to income. Among other things, he criticizes such damages because "victims, their families, and other audiences see the award as an official declaration of the victim's worth." As to noneconomic loss, he criticizes the goals of that form of damages as being "ambiguous, incoherent, and contradictory."[31]

We have introduced the idea of corrective justice, and noted some of the many meanings that have been given to that phrase. The roller-coaster nature of this series of arguments is evident in an essay by Richard Posner that placed corrective justice in the framework of economic analysis of law. Stressing that "[t]here is nothing in Aristotle to suggest" that "corrective justice imposes duties regardless of cost," Posner wrote that "[c]orrective justice is an instrument for maximizing wealth" and that in the "normative economic theory of the state" that Posner favors, "wealth maximization is the ultimate objective of the just state."[32]

Various observers have stressed that an important part of tort litigation is the belief by injured persons that they have had an opportunity to be heard, whatever the result.[33] The opportunity to be heard itself contributes to the dignity of the victim.

The compensatory damages remedy reflects within itself various tensions about the just desserts of victims. As we have noted, damages for economic loss generally are linked to income and thus effectively perpetuate inequality. By contrast, damages for noneconomic loss assume, at least in theory, that the pain of the poor person is no different than that felt by the wealthy plaintiff. In practice, this ideal is not fully honored, given that

---

31. Richard Abel, General Damages are Incoherent, Incalculable, Incommensurable, and Inegalitarian (but otherwise a great idea), 55 DeP. L. Rev. 253, 255–258 (2006).

32. Richard A. Posner, The Concept of Corrective Justice in Recent Theories of Tort Law, 10 J. L. Studies 187, 206 (1981).

33. Shuman, supra, at 74, "[a]t its restorative best, the tort system offers plaintiffs the opportunity to be heard in a dignified and culturally meaningful proceeding that conveys a message that society cares what happened and to have a judgment of responsibility made by a trusted decision maker who helps reshape the balance of power between the plaintiff and defendant."

insurance companies often calculate offers of settlement based on a multiplier of "hard" special economic damages, in particular, "traditional" medical expenses and "wages lost during the acute phase of the injury."[34] However, at least in theory American law does not distinguish among social and economic classes for the purposes of deciding compensation for intangible losses. Modern readers may find it interesting that the laws of Hammurabi did make distinctions of that sort with respect to penalties for various kinds of offences. A defendant of higher status faced "a very harsh penalty of 60 lashes with an ox hide whip" for a slap, while the same "insult among commoners entailed a penalty of only 10 shekels."[35]

One other potential element of the case for compensation is need. Tort law does not recognize need as grounds for a compensation award. However, there are social programs that provide an often thin cushion of money awards for those who injury has put in need. The Social Security disability system does this for disabled people who have paid premiums for the required time for eligibility, however their disability was caused—including but not limited to tortiously caused injuries. The Supplemental Security Income program provides monetary transfers to needy disabled persons regardless of the cause of their disability. Finally, a remarkable marriage of a need category to a compensation system that includes many terms used in conventional tort law appears in a rule mentioned earlier that was promulgated for the September 11th Victim Compensation Fund. This rule says that the Special Master should "take into consideration" circumstances that "may include the financial needs or financial resources of the claimant or the victim's dependents and beneficiaries."[36]

Compensation, therefore, is a many-splendored thing, with advocates who identify a flock of rationales.

The apology. We should note in connection with damages the remedy of the apology, which bridges the fault of the defendant and the loss of the plaintiff. As Daniel Shuman has explained it, "[a]n apology simultaneously explicates the injurer's role in causing the harm and responds to the indignity of the harmful conduct by offering the injured an important showing of respect."[37] The apology in Japan "is an indication of an individual's wish to maintain or restore a positive relationship with another person who has been harmed by the individual's acts." In Japan, "[w]hen compensation or damages are to be paid . . ., it is extremely important that the person

---

34. See, e.g., John Chandler, Handling Motor Vehicle Accident Cases, Treatises & Forms 2d §6.19 (database updated Sept. 2009).

35. Andrew R. Simmonds, 17 St. Thomas L. Rev. 123, 126–27 (2004).

36. 28 CFR §104.41 (2011).

37. Shuman, *supra* note 30, at 68.

responsible expresses to the victim his feeling of deep regret and apologizes, in addition to paying an appropriate sum."[38] By contrast, "[a]n American who is found to have wronged another is likely to consider that paying the damages or accepting punishment ends further responsibility and that there is no need for personal contrition or apology to the injured individual."[39]

Vindication. Paralleling the goals of giving injury victims the right to be heard and providing public respect for them is the idea of vindication. Used fairly often in legal literature but not frequently defined, the term vindication signifies both individual and public consequences. In injury cases, it confirms for the victim her belief in the rightness of her cause, while at the same time signaling that judgment to the community at large.

Punishment. We have adverted to the historical role of punishment as a rationale for injury law. Today, tort law slots the goal of punishment primarily under the remedy of punitive damages.[40] There are a number of subgoals for punishment. One of these goals, deterrence, overlaps with one purpose of compensatory damages. An Alabama lawyer, Betty Love, gave a classic presentation of this rationale. Justifying the imposition of punitive damages on corporations, she said, "a corporation has no soul, no heart, and no fear of God, hell or damnation, since it exists only for the one purpose of making money."[41] Moreover, although compensatory awards will often influence conduct, there is an especially stinging message in punitive awards. They tell a very culpable party—and others who might learn from the example— that society disapproves the type of behavior at issue so strongly that wrong-doers must pay more than would compensate the victim—whether that is defined as "making whole" or otherwise.

Another reason for punishing is retributive. A recent analyst of punitive damages defines "retributive punishment" as "an authorized coercive condemnatory setback to the defendant's interests on account of an offense against the legal order," one that "create[s] a message that the offender's behavior is prohibited."[42] This definition may be too narrow in one sense, for even a judgment of compensatory damages based on a finding of negligence tells people that the defendant should not have engaged in that conduct. Indeed, in teaching the first-year torts course, in any year I will

---

38. Hiroshi Wagatsuma and Arthur Rosett, The Implication of Apology: Law and Culture in Japan and the United States, 20 Law & Soc. Rev. 461, 472 (1986).

39. *Id.* at 462.

40. See, e.g., chapter 3, text accompanying notes 78–81.

41. Report of remarks of Betty Love at meeting of Tort Law Section, annual convention of Association of Trial Lawyers of America, 50 U.S. L.W. 2088 (Aug. 11, 1981).

42. Dan Merkel, Retributive Damages: A Theory of Punitive Damages as Intermediate Sanction, 94 Cornell L. Rev. 239, 242 (2009).

hear more than once a student refer to a defendant held liable for compensatory damages as being "guilty," although that language technically belongs in criminal law territory. Moreover, such an award is coercive, since the power of the state stands behind collections of compensatory damages as well as punitive damages. Condemnation, by comparison, is more a creature of punishment. More than a half century ago, the great English scholar Arthur Goodhart wrote that

> Without a sense of retribution we may lose our sense of wrong. Retribution in punishment is an expression of the community's disapproval of crime, and if this retribution is not given recognition then the disapproval may also disappear.[43]

The very term retribution, it should be noted, connotes a sense of getting back at a wrongdoer. Thus, although scholars may technically distinguish retribution from vengeance, the line between retributive punishment and revenge seems a thin one.

While tort law provides punishment through punitive damages, some critics have expressed uneasiness, even downright opposition, to that feature of civil litigation. An important objection is that punitive damage awards are not imposed under the safeguards afforded by the criminal law, including the requirement of proof of guilt beyond a reasonable doubt and the protections for criminal defendants provided by the Constitution. Although a few states do not allow punitive awards in civil cases, most do, and thus the majority of states reject this basic objection.

The most powerful social signal for punishment is indeed the one sent by the criminal law. Occasionally public prosecutors do convict those alleged to have been responsible for the type of personal injuries that are the routine business of tort law. But these prosecutions are not the norm. In fact, the best publicized convictions in tort-like cases have come in prosecutions for various kinds of economic fraud rather than activities that pose physical risks, as witness the plea bargain for Bernard Madoff for a Ponzi scheme that fleeced thousands of victims out of many billions of dollars.

As is implied by the quotation above from Betty Love on punitive damages, the law imposes "special responsibilit[ies]" on certain kinds of actors, and the view of these responsibilities held by some observers extends to tort damages generally and not only punitive damages. A comment to the section on strict products liability of the Second Restatement of Torts used that language with respect to product sellers' obligation to "any member of

43. Arthur Goodhart, English Law and the Moral Law 92–93 (1953).

the consuming public who may be injured by" their goods.[44] Some commentaries have gone further in articulating critical views that some people in society, and some judges, have had of corporations. Robert Morris wrote in 1961 that tort awards based on "enterprise liability" "may even satisfy a deep felt desire for revenge" against corporate entities.[45] Disapproving confirmation of the point appears in a 1991 study by scholars who took a dim view of "[t]he populist view of tort litigation" "that allows ordinary people to put 'authority in the dock' and hold it accountable" for injury and illness that affect large numbers of people.[46]

Social justice. Many people think the law should be a tool for social justice, one that raises up the disadvantaged, if necessary taking money from those who are well off to do so. Generally, we tend to think of this as a task for legislatures. In the area of prevention of injuries and compensation for them, Congress and state legislatures have undertaken this job in many ways. Congress has enacted a great variety of statutes that aim to reduce injuries, in many kinds of activities and with respect to a vast catalog of products. State legislatures, and Congress as well, have passed many statutes directed at assuring compensation to injury victims who otherwise would not receive money for their injuries. The principal system providing this kind of compensation is for employees injured on the job. State workers' compensation laws cover a large proportion of employees, and Congress has passed such laws covering government employees as well as other groups of workers, statutes that include the Longshoreman and Harbor Workers Compensation Act. A Congressionally enacted liability statute is the Federal Employers' Liability Act. That law articulates several standards for determining liability to injured railroad workers, including a basic negligence standard, although the Supreme Court's liberal interpretation of it has drawn criticism as achieving results that come close to making it a workers' compensation law embodying liability without fault.

The legislators who enacted this diverse group of safety and compensation statutes had as principal purposes either the minimization of injuries or the provision of financial aid to injury victims, on grounds that it was unjust to maintain the unsafe conditions that caused injuries or to fail to compensate for them. However, it has been noted that some laws or judicial decisions aimed at redressing the disproportionate results of injuries may not achieve the justice at which they aim. Observers have pointed out, for example, that regulations designed to decrease illnesses caused by pollution

44. Restatement (Second) of Torts §402A, cmt. c. (1965).
45. Robert Morris, Enterprise Liability and the Actuarial Process—The Insignificance of Foresight, 70 Yale L.J. 554, 599 (1961).
46. 1 Reporters' Study, Enterprise Liability for Personal Injury 26–27 (ALI 1991).

may have the effect of reducing employment for low-income workers, who would prefer jobs to unemployment even if toxic chemicals connected with production could cause adverse health effects.

Although we do tend to regard social justice as the province of the legislature, courts have sometimes opted for a form of that kind of justice when they decide individual cases, reasoning that it is fair to distribute losses among certain classes of people. Aristotle described this as "the justice which distributes common possessions," to which he contrasted the "justice in transactions"[47]—the "corrective justice" that is much talked about by academic writers on tort law.

One justification for achieving a broader form of justice through tort decisions is that such decisions spread the losses from injuries by distributing them among large populations—typically, groups of people who benefit from activities or products that cause injury. The justice of spreading lies in its ability to provide money for what may be an overwhelming misfortune to one or a few persons by transferring the loss to the broader group. A principal mechanism for this spreading is insurance, which initially achieves its results before accidents happen. By setting premiums on the basis of predicted accident rates, insurance spreads risk, so that it may later spread loss. Critics attack the use of the spreading rationale by courts as permitting judicial legislation, and criticize it as particularly unfair when it is used to justify liability against relatively small enterprises that cannot afford insurance. However, though controversial, it is presented matter-of-factly in such places as a list of rationales for strict liability for manufacturing defects provided by the drafters of the Restatement of Products Liability.[48]

Uniformity. A point of high tension in our injury law concerns the desire for uniformity and regularity. Most people would at least accept those goals as important procedural bases for law. A consistent application of uniform principles helps people to plan their lives—not just business people but those going about every facet of their everyday existence. It also appeals to our sense of fairness. We recoil at the idea that in similar situations, different people will be treated differently. Yet, believing in the value of a federal system, we are prepared to tolerate—at least to an extent—opposing rules adopted by different states. When that tolerance frays, Congress may try to enact one set of rules on a particular subject, or turn over to administrative agencies the task of making rules for the whole country. Yet, on many

47. See Aristotle, *supra* note 15.
48. See Restatement (Third) of Torts: Products Liability §2, cmt. a, at 41 (justification on "fairness grounds because it arguably causes the financial burden of accidents to be borne by those who benefit directly from the product and do not suffer harm").

occasions, such efforts at national uniformity have generated litigation on the breadth of "preemption" that Congress intended. The injury law constitution moderates these tensions in various ways, for example through a sifting process involving different levels of federal and state courts and by judicial interpretations of federal legislation and the Constitution.

Rationality. A great premise underlying all our efforts to adopt rules that are efficient or just, and capable of application to all without bias, is a commitment to rationality. On occasion, pursuit of this goal provokes arguments about the desirability of safety regulation, with battles occurring over choices made by government agencies. Cost-benefit analysis may compel a finding that regulation is irrational. Professor Sunstein provided two examples. In one case, a regulation costing $200 million is expected to save 80 lives, valued at $6 million each. In the other, a regulation costing $400 million would save only four lives. In the latter case, he says, "ordinarily" an agency "would be barred from issuing" the regulation.[49] Yet even people who advocate a broad adoption of a numbers-based approach acknowledge that there are reasons to depart from it, for example on grounds of fairness or the difficulty of controlling a risk.[50]

Moreover, sometimes the statistics on the benefits in a cost-benefit comparison may be quite uncertain. And there are always controversies about how to value injuries for the purpose of calculating costs. It is difficult enough in tort litigation to place a value on an individual's suffering. So what value should officials place on suffering—and on life itself—in formulating safety regulations? Such questions place a considerable strain on the definition of rationality. They force people with very different premises about what is rational to justify their views. Consider just one case in the torts area, discussed earlier, which involved a suit by a woman whose husband of thirty years died from a negligent act. Was it rational to award $414,000 for loss of his "counseling and guidance and love and affection"?[51] About all courts can do in reviewing such awards is to say what is irrational—as I noted in another chapter, the Seventh Circuit said it had the "uncomfortable feeling" that the jury's award in that case was "too high"— but on this "amorphous question" it thought it would "exceed[] the limits of our authority if we were to disturb it."[52] Rationality depends partly on

49. Sunstein, The Cost-Benefit State, *supra* note 13, at 21.

50. See, e.g., *id.* at 22 ("regulators might reasonably decide that the numbers are not decisive if, for example, children are mostly at risk, or if the relevant hazard is faced mostly by poor people, or if the hazard at issue is involuntarily incurred or extremely difficult to control").

51. See Huff v. White Motor Corp., 609 F.2d 286 (7th Cir. 1979), discussed chapter 3 *supra*, text accompanying note 125.

52. *Id.* at 296–97.

what system of law we are dealing with, and at what point in the process the review of rationality takes place.

The injury law constitution turns out to be capacious in the same way as the great Constitution. It houses the tensions that arise from what are often opposed commitments which many people hold in mind at the same time: commitments to an efficiency-oriented society and a just one; to individualized justice between disputants and a judicial system that takes into account the effects of its decisions on society generally; to freedom of action and the right to be free from invasions of physical and emotional security.

Perspectives: How we argue. The variety of rationales for injury law is only one set of strata of this topic. Layered on top of the rationales we have discussed are a group of approaches to the subject that largely have been discussed by professors, but which now and then find their way into judicial decisions. The way that we argue about solutions to injury problems often controls not only the discourse, but what the solutions will be. The foundations of these arguments range from traditional legal doctrine to various kinds of ideological perspectives.

Legal doctrines. Once a factual foundation has been established for litigation, practicing lawyers must deal with legal doctrine—with theories of liability. We have noted that the basic theories of liability in tort law span a spectrum of culpability. On one end are acts harmful to others that are deliberate wrongs, which blur into a category of wanton, willful, and reckless conduct, with the spectrum continuing on down through the categories of gross negligence, negligence, and strict liability. Crosscutting these doctrines are theories applied to various kinds of representations that turn out not to be accurate, and here the liability map reproduces itself in shades of intentionality, negligence, and strict liability. Torts related to various kinds of invasions of land often draw on the terminology of nuisance, which also includes a spectrum of culpability that mimics the general one. A catalog of torts covers communications that damage the reputation or upset the emotional tranquillity of persons about whom lies—sometimes even truths—are told. For false statements, defamation law has also used culpability terminology; and sometimes the degree of culpability, or the lack of it, has constitutional implications that will affect judicial decisions. In the area where truth-telling is injurious, or verges on communicating false images of people, the law has developed a number of categories under the label of "privacy."

Philosophy of judging. Much has been written about the philosophy of judging and the responsibility of judging. Judge Learned Hand captured an important ideal in a gemlike tribute to Justice Cardozo. Extolling Cardozo's "wisdom," but acknowledging that he did not know "of what it is composed," Judge Hand identified "[o]ne ingredient I think I do know: The wise man is the detached man." He said that the "wise man is one exempt from the handicap" of a "past" that shapes "[o]ur convictions, our outlook, the whole make-up of our thinking," a past into which has "been woven all sorts of frustrated ambitions with their envies, and of hopes of preferment with their corruptions."[53]

A variation on this model of dispassionate judgment appears in an essay by Hans Linde, who served as a judge for more than a dozen years on the Oregon Supreme Court.[54] Linde sharply criticized judges who adopted what he called the "policy style" of judging—that is, "opinions that choose a basis for decision not because it is fair, or old, or logically consistent, but on grounds that it will effectively serve a social end that is more valuable or important than some other end."[55] This "policy reasoning," "[c]ompressed in the phrase 'cost-benefit analysis,'" demanded "knowledge of the present situation, identifying goals and values, setting priorities among them, determining whether a proposed policy will promote the preferred goals, with what likelihood of success, with what side effects, and . . . at what cost compared to alternative solutions."[56] Linde sharply distinguished the appropriate role of judges from that of legislators—"[t]he decisive difference between the two forms of lawmaking is that legislation is legitimately political and judging is not."[57] He pointed out that "[v]alue premises asserted for a legal rule . . . can have consequences," with impact on questions like whether courts should require proof of a particular fact.[58] He insisted that judicial opinions "should not invoke public policy unless" they "can cite a source for it"[59]—for example, legislation that bears on the issue being decided. In this connection, he quoted a remark by Justice Ginsburg in her Senate confirmation hearing on the urgent need for "a clear recognition by all branches of government that in a representative democracy important policy questions should be confronted, debated and resolved by elected officials."[60]

Procedural rules. Paralleling this constrained view of the judge's role in injury cases is the procedural and evidentiary framework of injury litigation.

---

53. Learned Hand, Mr. Justice Cardozo, 39 Colum. L. Rev. 9, 10–11, 52 Harv. L. Rev. 361, 362–63, 48 Yale L. J. 379, 380–81 (1939).

54. Hans A. Linde, Courts and Torts: "Public Policy" Without Public Politics?, 28 Valp. U. L. Rev. 821 (1994).

55. *Id.* at 824.

56. *Id.*

57. *Id.* at 834.

58. *Id.* at 829.

59. *Id.* at 824.

60. *Id.* at 854, quoting Laurie Asseo, "High Court Nominee Reports Net Worth," The Oregonian (Portland), July 7, 1993, at A8.

Those rules require parties to follow a prescribed obstacle course for sorting out the legal validity of allegations and the strength of evidence. In large part they are designed to require parties to stay within the bounds of relevancy and, generally, to prove their cases. In the end, ideally, they point toward just results.

Economics-based approach. An overlay on legal doctrine and basic approaches to judging, as well as on the procedural framework of litigation, is the view that law reflects economic realities. Crucially, this idea emphasizes the impact of legal rules on incentives, and in injury law it often utilizes a comparison of costs and benefits. Often, in application to specific questions, it focuses on the "least cost avoider"—the party that can most cheaply avoid an injury. Its concern with costs often fixes on transaction costs, which may include the expense of parties getting together to work things out and the cost of getting information about risky activities or products.

Feminism. An approach to law that has developed an important niche in the literature is that of feminism. The flowering of feminism in law has occurred in legislation, followed by judicial decisions. A foundation for feminism in legislation has been Title VII of the Civil Rights Act of 1964, which triggered a series of judicial decisions on sexual harassment. Those decisions have not been limited to abusive conduct against women, but that category has been the largest group of cases. An analyst of judicial decisions predating anti-discrimination legislation—decisions going back to the nineteenth century—described the law as "act[ing] like a scoring handicap in a round of golf," under which "the unequal were made equal." This writer, Barbara Welke, described "a balance," under which "[m]en had to consider women's situation, but women themselves were also required to consider it." The result was that "courts refused to impose solely on women the risk of what would have been ordinary acts for a man and seemed inclined to 'understand' women's failings." Welke sums up decisions in "cases involving injury to women" as "suggest[ing] that courts constrained women to act within the acceptable bounds of ladylike conduct, as defined by men."[61]

A modern application of feminist theory to injury law, by Leslie Bender, did not limit itself to the impact of law on women. Focusing on mass tort litigation, Bender emphasized imbalances in power between parties, differentiating the "masculinist model" of "'overpowering or controlling/protecting'" from a "feminist model" rooted in "'empowering or power-balancing.'"[62] Bender criticized current tort law as "weighted down by a

---

61. Barbara Welke, Unreasonable Women: Gender and the Law of Accidental Injury, 19 Law and Social Inquiry 369, 398 (1994).
62. Leslie Bender, Changing the Values in Tort Law, 25 Tulsa L. Rev. 759, 763 (1990).

language and value system that privileges economics and costs." She declared that "[a]s harms for mass tort have become more widespread, legal analysis in tort law has become desensitized to the individuals and groups of people harmed," "dehumaniz[ing] people generally," "see[ing] them as statistics, or see[ing] their injuries as costs of economic growth and progress."[63] One of Bender's principal suggestions was that "we use feminist theory to change the meaning of responsibility in tort—which now means primarily an obligation to make monetary reparations for harms caused— to a meaning rooted in a concept of care."[64] Opposing the idea of judicial detachment that Judge Hand extolled in his tribute to Cardozo, Bender quoted feminist authors on the idea that "detachment, which is the mark of mature moral judgment in the justice perspective, becomes *the* moral problem in the care perspective—the failure to attend to need."[65] A secondary, provocative suggestion, if one with some unrealistic features, was that an effective incentive to safer behavior by corporations would be to force corporate officials to spend time in caregiving—which might range from actual nursing care to personal transportation of victims to the doctor.[66]

Pragmatism. American judges generally begin their analysis of cases by resorting to hardscrabble legal doctrine, and they do not usually engage in philosophical speculation. It is true that from time to time, often without knowing it, they will import various perspectives from other disciplines, for example economics. However, most American judges are probably pragmatists most of the time. The redoubtable Judge Posner, who has written extensively on pragmatism in judging, has said that "[p]ragmatism . . . is a devil to define," "because it's not one thing, one body of ideas, but at least three and maybe . . . five."[67] As Posner ranges across various definitions of pragmatism, he identifies "the core of pragmatic adjudication or, more broadly, of legal pragmatism" as "a heightened concern with consequences," or—quoting himself—as "a disposition to ground policy judgments on facts and consequences rather than conceptualisms and generalities."[68] Posner writes of an attitude "that predisposes Americans to judge proposals by the criterion of what works, to demand, in William James's apt phrase,

63. *Id.* at 767. See also chapter 2, text accompanying notes 39–40.
64. *Id.* at 768.
65. *Id.* at 769 n.21, quoting Carol Gilligan and Jane Attanucci, Two Moral Orientations in Mapping the Moral Domain; A Contribution of Women's Thinking to Psychological Theory and Education at 82 (Harvard University Press 1988).
66. See *id.* at 769.
67. Richard A. Posner, Law, Pragmatism, and Democracy 24 (Harvard University Press, 1st Paperback ed. 2005).
68. *Id.* at 59, quoting Richard A. Posner, The Problematics of Moral and Legal Theory 227 (1999).

the 'cash value' of particular beliefs, to judge issues on the basis of their concrete consequences for a person's happiness and prosperity."[69] Symbolizing the complexity of pragmatism as a method, if not a philosophy, is the fact that Posner offers no fewer than a dozen "generalizations" that "may be useful" about pragmatism.[70]

The tradition of judge-made law in America is inherently pragmatic in the sense that it follows the common law method of deciding cases, in the process building up structures of precedent. Precedents develop from the response of judges to concrete cases—very much a pragmatic way of doing things—and emerges from a combination of specific facts, common sense, and some attention to the social impact of decisions. Although the common law is said to be incremental, sometimes it takes leaps, which judges often justify by asserting that they are simply taking the next logical step in a path that precedent has plowed. In the area of tort law, a classic example is Judge Cardozo's decision in the 1916 case of *MacPherson v. Buick Motor Co.*[71] In that case, Cardozo fashioned a theory of liability for negligence that eliminated the requirement that product consumers could sue only the seller from which they directly bought a product, rather than a company removed in the chain of distribution—typically, the manufacturer. He reached back to American and English decisions from the nineteenth century to build a case for a more liberal rule, but although he presented it as representing a synthesis, it was a new rule. Some forty-five years later, Justice Traynor announced a theory of "strict liability in tort" for products that could be applied against manufacturers as well as retailers. He too put together a number of precedents, from his state of California and other jurisdictions, describing them as cases in which "strict liability has usually been based on the theory of an express or implied warranty running from the manufacturer to the plaintiff," as a foundation for his straight-out adoption of a tort theory of strict liability.[72]

Even a new nuance in a decision jolts the seismograph of the law a little bit. And the law does not move in straight lines. Courts construct limitations on new forms of liability as they have developed these doctrines. Illustrative is the refusal of several courts to apply the strict liability theory for products to makers of product components. One example is a case involving a suit against the Ford Motor Company, which made truck cabs and chassis that another firm converted into garbage trucks. The court refused to hold Ford strictly liable for not installing backup warning devices

---

69. *Id.* at 50.
70. See *id.* at 59–60.
71. 111 N.E. 1050 (N.Y. 1916).
72. Greenman v. Yuba Power Prods., Inc., 377 P.2d 897, e.g., at 899–901 (Cal. 1963).

on its chassis where there was evidence that the other firm was more expert at designing garbage trucks and that it would be more practical for it to install the warning devices.[73] There is a group of similar decisions on truck components,[74] and one may find analogies concerning other products. One decision, for example, rejects a suit against a maker of a golf cart, when an intermediate distributor had installed a chassis cover and a carriage latch to make the cart "suitable for golf course maintenance work." The court in that case says it is "significantly guided" by the opinion in the garbage truck case. It mentions, among factors influencing its decision, "relative expertise— which party is best acquainted with the design problems of the product as modified" and what it describes as "practical considerations—which party is in the better position to remedy or warn of the defect."[75]

We should note that while courts often rather delicately shape and trim the principles they develop in common law fashion, occasionally after the engine has jerked forward, it will jerk back. We have discussed a remarkable tort law example of this: the Texas Supreme Court's adoption of the tort of negligent infliction of emotional distress, followed six years later by a turnaround decision that rejected that theory.[76]

In practice, courts employ different modes of argument, even if they do not specifically identify them. Generally constrained by the idea that making policy is the job of legislatures, they yet continue to make policy in relatively narrow ways—as well as to fill in gaps in legislation by their own views of what is socially useful. Undoubtedly they respond to basic economic principles, including the incentives generated by the imposition of or refusal to impose tort liability. At the same time, they have referred to considerations of social justice. And we have noted that conflicting political and social views of the role of women have contributed to the way the law deals with injuries to women.

As courts respond to various modes of argument about the content of justice in injury cases, they are sending messages about right and wrong— sometimes, for example, what is economically right, but sometimes what is morally wrong. The progression of liability theories in cases of product injury from the elimination of a requirement that claimants show a direct contractual relationship under negligence law to the destruction of that hurdle under strict liability appears to embody moral components, including components related to imbalances of power.

---

73. Verge v. Ford Motor Co., 581 F.2d 384 (3d Cir. 1978).
74. See, e.g., 1 Marshall S. Shapo, The Law of Products Liability §12.03 [7][a][iii], note 69 (5th ed. 2010).
75. Trevino v. Yamaha Motor Corp., U.S.A., 882 F.2d 182, 185 (5th Cir. 1989).
76. See *supra*, chapter 8, text accompanying notes 105–111.

One can describe judicial responses to those modes of argument, and to the rationales to which they are tied, as pragmatic. It also may be useful to describe these responses as a pluralistic approach—a selection process for ideas that recognizes the "complexity of the human universe" with which injury law must deal.[77] It is part of the genius of the injury law constitution that it situates these arguments in a supple discourse that bends with attitudes and societal needs.

77. See, e.g., Am. Bar Ass'n, Special Committee on the Tort Liability System, Towards a Jurisprudence of Injury: The Continuing Creation of a System of Substantive Justice in American Tort Law (M. Shapo Rptr. 1984), e.g., at 4–1 ("pluralistic nature of tort law"), 11–9 ("plurality of rationales" of tort law and "its conceptual flexibility").

CHAPTER 10
Remedies and Sanctions

For injured people, those who fear injury, and those engaged in conduct that creates risk of injury, the bottom line is the remedy. The law provides remedial tools and sanctions designed not only to compensate for injury, but to minimize injury risks.

Prevention. In the realm of prevention, safety regulation is the first line of defense. It is both broad—ideally, comprehensive—and by design, prophylactic. Sometimes it imposes direct prohibitions on conduct. Don't run stop signs. Don't use this chemical in your workplace, or in the consumer product you distribute. Don't ship new drugs in interstate commerce if they have not gone through the FDA's approval process. In other cases, regulation tells you what you have to do, although backing up its rules for conduct are prohibitory remedies. On the prescriptive side, the FDA requires submission of applications for investigational new drugs as part of its process for ensuring the safety and effectiveness of drugs. Just one example of prohibitory rules in the workplace is the statement, "Makeshift devices, such as but not limited to boxes and barrels, shall not be used on top of scaffold platforms to increase the working level height of employees."[1] And that is not the half of it—not nearly the tenth of it. Page upon page of workplace regulations provide details on the positioning of stairway type ladders, the construction of scaffolds and methods of access to them, and protection against falling objects (there's a lot more to that than hardhats). Rules of this kind may be enforced through civil or criminal sanctions.

Tort law has preventive consequences. Courts possess the prophylactic tool of the injunction. They will use it on occasion in environmental cases, sometimes tailoring it to specific levels of pollutants and, very infrequently,

1. 29 C.F.R. §1926.451(f)(14).

to shut down a plant. Now and then, they may tell a stalker to desist. That is what federal courts did to the photographer who made himself a nuisance to Jacqueline Kennedy Onassis.[2] Whether under the heading of tort or other labels, courts have prescribed the distances that anti-abortion protesters must keep from clinics where abortions are performed.[3]

Damages: prevention. But the main grist of the tort mill is the suit for damages, and the damages remedy itself may have substantial impact on conduct. This is economic common sense. Imposing liability on a particular activity is likely to keep people from participating in it as much as before, or even at all. The Supreme Court has recognized this in some cases where the issue is whether the existence of a federal regulatory program preempts state tort suits. A prime example is the Court's decision imposing preemption against a plaintiff who claimed that a car should have had an airbag, when federal regulations gave automakers a choice of systems for protecting passengers from collisions, for example various types of safety belts. Justice Breyer, in his opinion for the majority, viewed the effect of the plaintiff's suit as being that of "a rule of state tort law" that "would have required manufacturers of all similar cars to install airbags rather than other passive restraint systems."[4] And in Justice Alito's dissent in a case where the majority concluded that there was no preemption when a jury found that a warning on a drug was inadequate, he suggested that the jury's verdict "second-guess[ed]" the FDA's determination of the safety of the drug's label.[5] He said that the majority's "result cannot be reconciled with" the Court's decision in the airbag case. In language paralleling that of Justice Breyer in the airbag case, he said that the Supremacy Clause—which makes the Constitution, "and the laws of the United States which shall be made in pursuance thereof," as well as treaties, "the supreme Law of the Land"— "applies with equal force to a state tort law that merely countermands a federal safety determination and to a state law that altogether prohibits car manufacturers from selling cars without airbags."[6]

Compensation in money. The remedy of cash payments comes after the fact of injury. The simplest form of money transfers occurs under workers'

2. See *supra*, chapter 7, text accompanying note 94.
3. See Madsen v. Women's Health Ctr., Inc., 512 U.S. 753 (1994) (upholding injunction establishing a 36-foot buffer zone at clinic entrances and driveway, although finding 36-foot zone unconstitutional as applied to adjoining private property, and rejecting other elements of injunction).
4. Geier v. Am. Honda Motor Co., 529 U.S. 861, 881 (2000).
5. See Wyeth v. Levine, 129 S. Ct. 1187, 1220, 1229 (2009)(Alito, J., dissenting). *Levine* is discussed *supra*, chapter 7, text accompanying notes 199–206.
6. *Id.* at 1217, 1227.

compensation—flat payments, based on schedules, for disability and various specific kinds of injuries.

Tort presents a much more complex profile. We have just referred to the effects of tort awards on behavior, and we do not ignore the psychological importance to injury victims of having their day in court. Crucially, though, tort law provides money payments. The most straightforward category of damages compensates for economic loss that can more or less be quantified. Hospital and doctor bills are literally hard copy. The proper figure for lost earnings may be much less clear, because of the uncertainty of future earnings both for living injury victims and in death cases. One cannot be sure whether a living victim or a decedent would have kept her job, or how much she would have earned in the future—and indeed whether illness or some injury other than that caused by the defendant would have ended her life before the average life span of the mortality tables. Still, plaintiffs can present wage or salary checks from the past as predictors of an earnings record in the future.

The case of intangible harms, now often referred to as noneconomic damages, presents even more difficulties. The problem lies not only in the uncertainty of future events—including the length of life—but in the fact that we have no objective measuring rod for things like pain, suffering, and loss of the capacity to enjoy life. One thing that is pretty certain is that courts will not allow plaintiffs' lawyers to ask jurors how much they would take to endure the pain undergone by a claimant.[7] There are deep moral and common sense intuitions behind this rule. At the extreme, the opposite result would validate masochism as a productive activity. More practically, we have noted a judicial declaration in a mesothelioma case that reasonable people would not accept any amount of money for a prolonged period of unendurable agony.[8]

One of the most difficult tasks for judges in tort cases is to establish and apply principles of review to the amount of damages. Sometimes courts may refer to the amounts that prior decisions have approved in cases with similar injury profiles. In the mesothelioma case just mentioned, where the jury awarded $12 million for pain and suffering, the appellate court did just that. Adducing awards given by a trial judge who had presided over all the federal asbestos litigation in New York, and using rough arithmetical averaging, the appeals court came up with a figure of $3.5 million for the

---

7. See, e.g., Beagle v. Vasold, 417 P.2d 673, 182 n.11 (Cal. 1966) (indicating that court does not approve "golden rule" argument).

8. See the discussion of Consorti v. Armstrong World Indus., Inc., 72 F.3d 1003, 1009 (2d Cir. 1995), chapter 4, text accompanying note 32.

plaintiff in the case before it.[9] This is an acceptable practical solution to a problem for which it is difficult to state the major premise of the solution. Yet, when judges compare the plaintiff before them with prior claimants, they must face up to the reference by a federal commission to the adage that no one can know the pain of another.[10] In making comparisons about intangibles, courts confront a doubled problem—comparing the pain of a present litigant, which it is said they cannot know, with that of prior claimants, about which they could know even less. A foggy subcompartment of our injury law constitution consigns these decisions to a ping-pong match, with few crisp rules, between judges and jurors as reflectors of community sentiment bearing on dollar evaluations of intangibles. Interested spectators may be legislators, who become participants in the match when they impose dollar limits on such damages.

We may compare another difficult issue, but one that is at least binary in nature, and is a more substantive one. This is the question, previously discussed, of whether to allow actions for negligent infliction of emotional distress. Here, the court may assume that there is a significant degree of harm, but before deciding on the amount of remedy must decide whether remedy should be given at all. This, as we have explained, represents a judgment about culture—what people believe, or at any rate how they feel, about the validity of certain kinds of injuries.[11]

A notable recent example of the remedy problem appears in Congress' response to the terrible events of September 11th. In authorizing a fund for victims, to be paid from the general revenues, Congress set up a lengthy list of categories of both "economic" and "noneconomic" loss. Although, as we have noted, the awards for economic loss were rather closely tied to income, the Rules adopted by the Justice Department and applied by the Special Master set minimums—up to $500,000—for the amount of total compensation that would be paid to claimants. They also established flat, uniform numbers for noneconomic loss, a choice the Special Master explained was made because he "could not justifiably conclude that one deceased victim or one victim's family suffered more than another."[12]

Even in a day of trillion-dollar deficits, it is worth noting that the Victim Compensation Fund did not deal in small change. Ultimately it paid approximately seven billion dollars to claimants. Putting aside the amounts of

9. See 72 F.3d at 1015.

10. See *supra*, chapter 8, text accompanying note 41.

11. See *supra*, chapter 4, text accompanying notes 17–20; chapter 8, text accompanying notes 105–111.

12. Kenneth Feinberg et al., Final Report of the Special Master for the September 11th Victim Compensation Fund of 2001, at 9.

the payouts, the Fund presents some fundamental questions. A principal issue is whether, given the many misfortunes people suffer without compensation—from the government or anyone else—Congress should have acted at all to provide a remedy for these terrible injuries, inflicted by evil persons an ocean away who were beyond the reach of the American legal system.[13]

Assignment of burdens. Courts or legislatures that decide to provide a remedy for injuries must allocate the burden of responsibility, sometimes between and among injurers and sometimes between injurers and victims.

Worker's compensation assigns burdens quite straightforwardly. It is the employer that must get insurance. The employee does not pay premiums, although presumably the cost of workers' compensation insurance comes at least in part out of the employee's wage rate.

As is so with the quantification of money payments, tort law assigns burdens in a more complex way than workers' compensation. Where claimants as well as injurers have contributed to a harm, many states divide financial responsibility according to the degree of fault of both parties or of the proportionate contribution of a product defect and the plaintiff's fault. A few jurisdictions impose all of the burden on a negligent plaintiff. In those states, even if a plaintiff's negligence only contributed in a small way to the injury, he or she recovers nothing.

Other divisions of responsibility occur when there is more than one defendant. In some cases, the law will allow one defendant to recover fully—that is, to get indemnity—against another defendant who can effectively be shown to be fully responsible for an injury. One distinction that courts use when they shift loss entirely from one defendant to another pins the entire liability on the party that was "actively" negligent when the other party was only "passively" negligent. Sometimes courts divide liability equally between or among parties that have contributed to an accident, even though in percentage terms one may have been more contributory than another. The most nuanced type of division of responsibility allows the jury to break down the contribution of multiple parties by percentages. Readers may find remarkable the ability of one Illinois jury to determine that a diver who broke his neck had "assumed the risk" of injury in an above ground swimming pool "to the extent of 96%" and that the strict liability for failure to warn of the maker of the pool was four percent.[14] They may find

---

13. My own commentary on this question appears in Marshall S. Shapo, *Compensation for Victims of Terrorism,* e.g., at 230–62 (Oceana/Oxford University Press 2005).

14. Erickson v. Muskin Corp., 535 N.E.2d 475 (Ill. Ct. App. 1989).

even more remarkable a Mississippi jury's conclusion that one of several defendants was three-quarters of one percent responsible for an injury.[15]

The search for justice has thus produced many different approaches to the division of financial responsibility for injuries. In tort cases, courts apparently try to allocate financial burdens according to a party's ability to exercise control over levels of safety and frequency of accidents. However, they may also be blending conceptions of fault and causation. One party may be very negligent but a relatively small assignment of responsibility may indicate that its negligence did not contribute as much to an injury as the acts of another negligent party that did not behave as culpably.

A controversial set of issues arises from the application of so-called joint liability theories, under which more than one party that contributes to an accident may be held liable for the entire damages, although it may be able to recover part of that amount from other parties held liable. Weighing in favor of the joint liability rule is the idea that if one of several defendants contributed to an accident in a way that cannot be separated out from the contributions of others, it is arguably just, in the scheme of things, to make that defendant pay everything so the plaintiff can be fully compensated. However, there is an evident injustice in making a party who was only one of several contributors to an injury pay the entire damages when, for example, the other parties might be insolvent or unreachable. Some legislatures have abolished the joint liability doctrine, with at least one statute eliminating it when a defendant's fault is "less than 25% of the total fault attributable" to all parties, including the plaintiff.[16]

A particularly knotty set of questions arises from the imposition of a form of liability sometimes called "market share liability." We noted earlier that particularly where it is impossible to identify the manufacturer of a product that injured a particular claimant when several firms have made that kind of product, some courts have said that each of the major firms in the field must pay according to its percentage of the market for that product. Variations on the arguments about joint and several liability are played here. Market share liability provides a measure of justice for the injured consumer, who otherwise would go without any compensation since she cannot prove which defendant made the product that injured her. However, there is a special twist of injustice noted by opponents of market share-type liability—it removes from the plaintiff the burden of proof on the issue of whether the defendant's product or negligence caused an injury.[17]

15. See Mack Trucks, Inc. v. Tackett, 841 So.2d 1107 (Miss. 2003).
16. 735 ILCS 5/2-1117.
17. See chapter 3, text accompanying notes 90–93.

We can see that even when injuries have been clearly established, the question of rights frequently remains in dispute. This often occurs when the question of rights becomes linked to the issue of how burdens should be assessed. We noted the special difficulty in distributing the financial burden of injuries that arises when tort law collides with workers' compensation.[18] Tort law is the principal user of various devices in the legal toolbox to distribute the burden of liability between and among parties that have contributed to accidents. A contrast appears in government programs that provide money for people injured by many kinds of causes, including but not limited to the culpable acts of others. As we have noted, the Social Security disability program transfers to disabled people money accumulated from taxes paid by both employers and employees, without inquiring into whether a disability has occurred from an injury caused by a tort or otherwise. The Supplemental Security Income program, funded by general tax revenues, provides cash payments for needy disabled people—also without regard to how they have become disabled.

Once again, the September 11th Victim Compensation Fund has generated arresting questions about the distribution of injury burdens. That fund, which came from the general revenues, was not dependent on premiums paid by anyone. One of its provisions that is particularly relevant here is Congress's requirement that the Special Master should reduce compensation paid from the Fund "by the amount of the collateral source compensation" received by a claimant. It defined that category to mean "all collateral sources, including life insurance, pension funds, death benefit programs, and payments by Federal, State or local governments" related to the attacks of September 11th.[19]

This is a notable exception in a statute that otherwise is pretty generous to claimants. It differs sharply from the traditional tort law rule in the United States—which itself contrasts with the law in most of the rest of the world—that permits tort claimants to keep collateral payments. The traditional American rule has been controversial, because—putting to one side the fees that claimants must pay their lawyers—it allows claimants to receive what amounts to a double recovery for the same items of damages. Under the American rule, a tort claimant does not have to deduct from a jury award items of damage for which she has been reimbursed by her own insurer—although often insurers have clauses in their policies that effectively allow them to recover such payments. It is particularly interesting that

18. See *supra*, chapter 6, 114–16.
19. September 11th Victim Compensation Fund of 2001, 49 USCA §40101, Pub. L. 107–42 §§405 (b)(6), 402(4).

the drafters of the Fund statute required a deduction for life insurance, which has tended to be a sacred cow among claimants' collateral sources. That protected status has existed, in part, because of the images that surround life insurance—I have referred elsewhere to "the image of the family that has scrimped and saved to pay premiums for a policy that will at least enable it to subsist if the breadwinner dies."[20] The collateral source issue is just one part of the larger question we have mentioned concerning the September 11th Fund—why Congress decided to use general federal revenues in creating this unique set of rights.

We have reviewed a group of methods by which the law constructs remedies and sanctions for injuries. One straightforward method, workers' compensation, wanders into a legal thicket when it bumps up against another remedial system, tort law, which itself has developed a diverse set of ways to apportion the costs of injuries. Paralleling these systems are the direct requirements and prohibitions, backed by sanctions, of diverse systems of safety regulation. Layered alongside the principal modes of injury compensation are two differently funded government disability programs that include injury-caused disability within the much broader category of disabilities generally. Finally, we have noted the unique compensation scheme devised by Congress for victims of the September 11th attacks. These different methods of remedying the financial burdens of injuries, and preventing or minimizing injuries, illustrate the complexity of the injury law constitution. Taken together, they exhibit the brokering that constitution provides among elements of causal impact, moral responsibility, dispassionate accounting related to control of risk, and humanitarian concerns.

---

20. Marshall S. Shapo, *Compensation for Victims of Terrorism*, 120 (Oceana 2005).

CHAPTER 11

The Supreme Court and Injury Law

Our injury law has three main pillars—common law, compensation legislation, and safety regulation. I have suggested that one can view this system of law as governed by a kind of constitution, which provides an overall guide to proper conduct and ultimately to the definition of justice. The Supreme Court is a leading arbiter of this injury law constitution, sometimes articulating and sometimes implying its governing principles.

There is a large number of cases in which the Court has performed this role. To fully analyze that body of cases requires an extended separate treatment, a project I am developing. In this chapter, I focus on a relatively small set of cases, some of which I have mentioned in earlier chapters, in a preliminary effort to outline the principal ideas that have guided the Court's contributions to the overall basis for our law of injuries. I stress that my selection of these cases is only a sampling. It is, in fact, remarkable that in an area of litigation largely dominated by the development of common law by state courts, the Supreme Court has painted in so many wedges of substantive federal jurisprudence and in a number of cases has constructed an overlay of federal law on state law.

It is not surprising that most of the Court's decisions in this area have related to the interpretation of federal statutes or to the way the Constitution applies to common law. Federal statutes, and the Constitution itself, are peculiarly the province of the Court. However, in some decisions of interest, the Court effectively sits as a common law court.

Misrepresentations. A notable common law decision by the Court dates to the year 1839. It involved the sale to an out-of-state buyer of a mine that the owner said was "rich in gold," specifying a formation as much as 12-feet wide, with "veins . . . disseminated throughout the whole formation, in threads of from two to six inches wide.["] The defendant seller claimed that he had explicitly declared that he sold the mine "for what it is, gold or snow-balls," and he argued that the doctrine of *caveat emptor*, which he contended required buyers to show "actual fraud and intentional misrepresentation," protected him when the mine turned out to have very little gold. Rejecting this argument, and pointing out that the seller's statements came "up to the standard of mathematical certainty,"[1] a majority of the Court said that "that wherever a sale is made of property not present, but at a remote distance, which the seller knows the purchaser has never seen, but which he buys upon the representation of the seller, relying on its truth, then the representation, in effect, amounts to a warranty; at least, that the seller is bound to make good the representation."[2] The majority said this principle applied to cases "in which the one party places a known trust and confidence in the other." It stressed that the plaintiff appellee "had never seen the mine, and the appellant knew it; the appellee had seen the letter of description and specimens, and the appellant knew that he had; the appellee confided in the truth of the appellant's representation, and his skill in mines, and in mining operations, and the appellant knew that he did."[3] The majority declared that "[i]f under these circumstances, the seller were not bound by his representation, we know not in what cases we ought to apply the well-known and excellent maxim, 'fides servanda est'"[4]—that is, "faith must be kept." As to the argument that the defendant had not made an intentional misrepresentation, the majority said,

> Whether the party thus misrepresenting a fact, knew it to be false, or made the assertion without knowing whether it were true or false, is wholly immaterial; for the affirmation of what one does not know, or believe to be true, is equally in morals and law, as unjustifiable as the affirmation of what is known to be positively false. And even if the party innocently misrepresents a fact by mistake, it is equally conclusive; for it operates as a surprise and imposition on the other party.[5]

Here, from a rough and ready America, is a lesson in basic honesty. There is also a lesson in the basic economics of transaction costs; the Court noted that in theory the purchaser could "have traveled some hundreds of miles to ... examine the mine," but makes it clear that it was not necessary for him to do so, given his reliance on the representation of the seller.[6]

1. Smith v. Richards, 38 U.S. (13 Pet.) 26, 43 (1839).
2. *Id.* at 42 (1839).
3. *Id.* at 39–40.
4. *Id.* at 42–43.
5. *Id.* at 36.
6. See *id.* at 42.

Economic loss. Decisions of the Court have identified boundaries between major areas of common law as well as between common law and statutory compensation schemes. The Court focused on common law categories in a case involving supertankers, discussed earlier, which turned on a distinction in the law of products liability that roughly classifies "property damage" together with personal injury as a category for which tort liability may be sought as contrasted with "economic loss." The Court concluded that internal damage to turbines on the tankers was "economic loss" for which a tort-type recovery could not be granted under admiralty law. The Court specifically agreed with prior appellate court decisions "in recognizing products liability, including strict liability, as part of the general maritime law."[7] But reasoning from products liability law that the damage to the turbines was "injury to a product itself,"[8] to which tort liability would not apply, the Court identified as one concern the uncertainty that a liability rule would cause for manufacturers trying "to structure their business behavior."[9]

However, in a later case, the Court found a distinction with respect to the question of whether property that was lost was the purchased "product itself" or "other property." This case involved the sinking of a fishing vessel that allegedly was defectively designed by the defendant, a craft to which the initial purchaser had added extra equipment, including "a skiff, a seine net, and various spare parts." The first purchaser had resold the ship to the plaintiff, which sued for the loss of the added equipment. Justice Breyer's opinion for the majority concluded that the extra equipment was "not part of the product that itself caused physical harm" but rather was "other property."[10] No human person was injured in the case, but this characterization placed the case in the category of damage to property, for which tort recovery could be had, rather than "economic loss." Although in the supertanker case the Court had operated on a model in which buyers and sellers could allocate risks between themselves, Justice Breyer said that this idea did not apply as satisfactorily "in the context of resale after an initial use" in the fishing vessel case, because the second purchaser "does not contract directly with the manufacturer (or distributor)."[11]

The technical distinction the Court made between "the product itself" and "other property" is part of a continuing war in injury law between

7. East River S.S. Corp. v. Transamerica Delaval, Inc., 476 U.S. 858, 865 (1986), see also *supra*, chapter 4, text accompanying notes 21–22.
8. See *id.* at 872, 874, 876.
9. *Id.* at 870.
10. Saratoga Fishing Co. v. J. M. Martinac and Co., 520 U.S. 875, 884 (1997).
11. *Id.* at 882.

the needs of commerce and the dictates of compensatory justice. This distinction—as arcane as it may seem to lay persons—helps to define the boundaries of injury law, and therefore of the injury law constitution, as contrasted with contract law.

We noted above an area in which the Court became the arbiter of a collision zone between the common law and a legislatively created compensation system. In the Lockheed case, the Court concluded that the exclusivity of the federal workers' compensation statute did not bar a suit by a products liability defendant against a workers' compensation employer.[12]

Defamation. We briefly referred earlier to the Supreme Court's incursion into a body of injury law that historically had been state territory—the law of defamation. The first case in a train of decisions by the Court on defamation involved an advertisement in the *New York Times* that, in a racially charged context, allegedly libeled the police commissioner of Montgomery, Alabama. The Court reversed a judgment by the Alabama Supreme Court upholding a jury verdict for the plaintiff. Speaking through Justice Brennan, the Court rejected the argument that the Fourteenth Amendment to the federal Constitution, being "directed against State action," did not apply through the First Amendment to the plaintiff's civil lawsuit, although the litigation was "between private parties." Justice Brennan said that in upholding the substantial judgment against the Times, "the Alabama courts . . . applied a state rule of law" that the defendants said violated their First Amendment rights.[13] In this case, the Court constitutionalized the law of defamation, saying that a public official who alleged libel "relating to his official conduct" would have to show that the defamation was published with what the court insisted on calling "actual malice"—that is, knowledge that the statement "was false or with reckless disregard of whether it was false or not."[14]

This decision was unanimous as to result, with two different concurring opinions. A fragmented Court later applied its "actual malice test" to "public figures."[15] Several years after that, a majority of the Court refined its views on defamation in cases where the plaintiff was a private individual. In *Gertz v. Robert Welch, Inc.,*[16] the Court restricted state actions for defamation to

12. See *supra*, chapter 6, text accompanying note 68.
13. New York Times Co. v. Sullivan, 376 U.S. 254, 265 (1964).
14. *Id.* at 279–80.
15. See Curtis Pub'g Co. v. Butts and Associated Press v. Walker, 388 U.S. 130 (1967).
16. 418 U.S. 323 (1974).

cases in which the plaintiff showed at least negligence.[17] The Court also put some constraints on the ability of state courts to award "presumed damages"—a somewhat vague category it distinguished from "actual injury." The Court said that for "presumed" damages and punitive damages as well, a private individual would have to show "the actual malice" that it had defined in the Alabama case to mean knowledge of falsity or reckless disregard.[18]

At this point, however, the Court's takeover of state tort law did not go unchallenged. In a scathing dissent, Justice White said that the Court's "deep-seeded antipathy to 'liability without fault'" employed a "catch-phrase" with "no talismanic significance."[19] He attacked the majority's requirement that the plaintiffs prove "actual injury" to avoid the application of the "actual malice" standard, pointing out that certain kinds of defamations had "traditionally" been subject to suit "without proof of fault . . . or of the damaging impact" of such publications.[20] He declared that "[t]he Court's consistent view prior to" the Alabama case involving the *New York Times* "was that defamatory utterances were wholly unprotected by the First Amendment."[21] He ridiculed the argument that the threat of libel suits was "causing the press to refrain from publishing the truth," saying that the majority had given no evidence of that.[22] He said it was "difficult . . . to understand why the ordinary citizen should himself carry the risk of damage and suffer . . . injury in order to vindicate First Amendment values by protecting the press and others from liability for circulating false information."[23]

The cases we have summarized here are just part of a group of decisions in which the Court has put constitutional limitations on defamation suits. They provide an interesting parallel to the decisions on economic loss, which feature a boxing match between the requirements of commerce and the demands of justice for injured parties. In the area of untrue statements about individuals, where injury can be harder to value than economic loss from defective products, the tensions are even higher. Here the fisticuffs occur between what Justice Brennan in the *New York Times* case called the social value of "debate on public issues" that is "uninhibited, robust, and

---

17. *Id.* at 346–47 ("so long as they do not impose liability without fault, the States may define for themselves the appropriate standard of liability for a publisher or broadcaster of defamatory falsehood injurious to a private individual").

18. See *id.* at 348–50.

19. *Id.* at 389 (White, J. dissenting).

20. See *id.* at 376.

21. *Id.* at 384–85.

22. *Id.* at 390.

23. *Id.* at 392.

wide-open"[24] and the injustices suffered by those who are the targets of false statements that injure reputation.

*** ***

Section 1983. A substantial amount of the Supreme Court's business in the area of injury law deals with 42 United States Code section 1983, a major channel into the great bundle of rights provided by the Constitution. We discussed earlier the landmark case of *Monroe v. Pape*,[25] in which the Court made it clear that citizens could sue officers for breaking the law, as well as for using it. The law under section 1983 as the Court has developed it is a particularly significant part of the injury law constitution, because it draws directly on the federal Constitution. Indeed, that body of law is a unique combination of statute, constitutional rights, and tort ideas. The Court has been at pains to point out that not every tort committed by officials is a violation of constitutional rights, but as we previously noted, Justice Douglas declared in his majority opinion in the *Monroe* case that the statute "should be read against the background of tort liability that makes a man responsible for the natural consequences of his actions."[26]

The *Monroe* case itself exhibits the difficulties inherent in drawing the line as to where official behavior violates the civil rights of Americans—even the rights of noncitizens who are in the country. As summarized earlier, the allegations in the case described a raw episode of police brutality. More broadly speaking, though, the tensions the case contains arise from the requirements of law enforcement. It is symbolic that the defendant, Frank Pape, a Chicago police captain, was a fearsome officer who one police lieutenant described as "the Babe Ruth of the Police Department." During the twenty years he ran the robbery detail for the department, Pape "was known to have shot and killed at least nine criminals" and "was in 16 cops-and-robbers shootouts." The good news, from the point of view of his associates, was that "[h]e had the reputation that when criminals heard that he was looking for them, they'd turn themselves in. He was the kind of guy we all wanted to work for."[27]

Monroe is just illustrative of the fact that a substantial part of the Court's business under section 1983 has involved violent acts by police officers and prison employees. We noted earlier a case in which Chief Justice Rehnquist held in favor of a victim of police brutality. In that case, he confronted the

24. See 376 U.S. at 270.
25. 365 U.S. 167 (1961), discussed in chapter 7, text accompanying notes 9–14.
26. 365 U.S. at 187.
27. Ann Keegan, Toughest Cop in Town, Chicago Tribune, Feb. 9, 1994, §5, at 1 & 2.

need for a "careful balancing" of individual and governmental interests, saying that "[t]he 'reasonableness' of a particular use of force must be judged from the perspective of a reasonable officer on the scene, rather than with the 20/20 vision of hindsight." Using that standard, he vacated a judgment for a defendant that had been rendered under a test that required section 1983 plaintiffs to show that officers had acted "maliciously and sadistically." Instead, he said that the case must be reconsidered under an "objective" standard that balanced the "'Fourth Amendment interests'" of individuals "against the countervailing governmental interests at stake."[28]

As the author of the first major article on the application of section 1983, I have come to believe that the *Monroe* case was the case of the century about our everyday rights as Americans. The Supreme Court has in fact pushed the application of section 1983 well beyond cases involving physical force. Although the statute is not always in the spotlight of media reports about its application, it has been the main pathway for plaintiffs complaining about such diverse injustices as the malapportionment of state legislatures, segregated schools, and awful conditions in prisons.

An important supplement to the avenue that *Monroe* opened up for suits against individual officials was the Court's decision in the *Monell* case, which rejected a limitation in *Monroe* that had blocked plaintiffs from bringing section 1983 suits against municipalities. After an exhaustive review of the legislative history of the 1871 statute that became section 1983, Justice Brennan concluded that there were grounds for suit against the City of New York for an "official policy" that "compelled pregnant employees to take unpaid leaves of absence before such leaves were required for medical reasons." He said the history of the legislation indicated that Congress "*did* intend municipalities and other local government units" to be the subjects of suit where, as in the pregnancy leave case, a government's action "that is alleged to be unconstitutional implements or executes a policy statement, ordinance, regulation, or decision officially adopted or promulgated by that body's officers." Indeed, he declared that local governments could be sued "for constitutional deprivations visited pursuant to governmental 'custom' even though such a custom has not received formal approval through the body's official decision-making channels."[29] This was very much in line with the circumstances of the passage of section 1983—which has been titled the Ku Klux Act, and which Congress enacted in the context of widespread brutality against blacks in parts of the South where law and order had

---

28. See Graham v. Connor, 490 U.S. 386, 396–99 (1989), discussed *supra*, chapter 7, text accompanying notes 15–17.
29. Monell v. Dept. of Social Services of City of New York, 436 U.S. 658, 690–91 (1978).

virtually broken down. Justice Brennan emphasized that this liability of local governments was not to be imposed simply because their "employees or agents" had violated constitutional rights but only on occasions "when execution of a government's policy or custom, whether made by its lawmakers or by those whose edicts or acts may fairly be said to represent official policy."[30] That statement distinguishes the "constitutional tort" body of law under section 1983 from ordinary tort law, which imposes liability on employers for the culpable acts of an employees even though an employer was not negligent in the hiring or retention of an employee or in supervision of an employee's behavior. In a setting where the Court must decide what a violation of a constitutional right is under section 1983, the *Monell* doctrine illustrates the complex nature of the injury law constitution.

In the decade following *Monell*, the Court manifested increasing reluctance and then outright opposition to the application of section 1983 to negligent conduct. First it temporized, calling the question "more elusive than it appears at first blush,"[31] and then saying that nothing in the language of the statute or its legislative history limited it "solely to intentional deprivations of constitutional rights."[32] However, while continuing to insist in a later decision that section 1983 "contains no state-of-mind requirement independent of that necessary to state a violation of the underlying constitutional right,"[33] the Court flatly declared that "the Due Process clause is simply not implicated by a *negligent* act of an official causing unintended loss of or injury to life, liberty, or property."[34] Without "rul[ling] out the possibility that there are other constitutional provisions that would be violated by mere lack of care,"[35] the Court declared that "lack of due care suggests no more than a failure to measure up to the conduct of a reasonable person." This provided the basis for its pronouncement that "[t]o hold that injury caused by such conduct is a deprivation within the meaning of the Fourteenth Amendment would trivialize the centuries-old principle of due process of law."[36]

Governmental duty to act. In the refinements that the Court has fashioned on section 1983, a subgroup of tragic cases has presented a particularly difficult challenge: the issue of whether the statute applies to allegations that government officers failed to act to protect someone against threatened harm. Supreme Court majorities denied recovery in two cases that involved

30. *Id.* at 694.
31. Baker v. McCollan, 443 U.S. 137, 139 (1979).
32. Parratt v. Taylor, 451 U.S. 527, 534 (1981).
33. Daniels v. Williams, 474 U.S. 327, 330 (1986).
34. *Id.* at 328.
35. *Id.* at 334.
36. *Id.* at 332.

that issue. In the *DeShaney* case,[37] social workers and county officials alleg-edly failed to remove a little boy from the custody of his father, who had been abusing the child. Although a "child protection team" had decided there was not enough evidence of abuse to retain the boy in the custody of the court, a social worker testified that "I just knew the phone would ring some day and Joshua would be dead." In fact, a particularly brutal beating caused such severe brain damage to the boy, then four, that it appeared he would have to spend the rest of his life in an institution for profoundly retarded persons. Although Chief Justice Rehnquist acknowledged that the facts were "undeniably tragic,"[38] he concluded that the boy's rights under the due process clause of the Constitution had not been violated. He said it was important to "remember ... that the harm was inflicted not by the State of Wisconsin, but by Joshua's father."

The common law background of the *DeShaney* case lay in the well-established rule of English and American law that there is no liability for a failure to act to protect another from harm. The Chief Justice observed that "[t]he people of Wisconsin may well prefer a system of liability which would place upon the State and its officials the responsibility for failure to act" in such situations. However, he said that the adoption of such a rule was up to state lawmakers and was not a job for the Court by "expansion of the Due Process Clause of the Fourteenth Amendment."[39] Justice Brennan in his dissent stressed that the State was not a passive bystander to Joshua DeShaney's peril, because "[t]hrough its child-protection program," it had "actively intervened" in the boy's life and thus "acquired ever more certain knowledge that Joshua was in grave danger."[40] Adding a famously emotional addition to the legal discourse on injuries, Justice Blackmun's dissent con-cluded with the lament, "poor Joshua." In a counterpoint to the traditional emphasis that judges should be dispassionate, he declared that "compas-sion need not be exiled from the province of judging."[41]

In a case briefly mentioned earlier that was even more wrenching, if pos-sible, a Colorado plaintiff had obtained a restraining order against her hus-band that said he was not to "molest or disturb [her] peace" or that "of any child." A preprinted text on the back of the restraining order had a "**NOTICE TO LAW ENFORCEMENT OFFICIALS**," that said "YOU SHALL USE EVERY REASONABLE MEANS TO ENFORCE THIS RESTRAINING ORDER" and told officials that "YOU SHALL ARREST,

37. DeShaney v. Winnebago County Dept. of Soc. Servs., 489 U.S. 489 (1989).
38. *Id.* at 191.
39. *Id.* at 203.
40. *Id.* at 210 (Brennan, J., dissenting).
41. *Id.* at 213 (Blackmun, J., dissenting).

OR, IF AN ARREST WOULD BE IMPRACTICAL UNDER THE CIRCUMSTANCES, SEEK A WARRANT FOR THE ARREST OF THE RESTRAINED PERSON" when there existed "INFORMATION AMOUNTING TO PROBABLE CAUSE THAT THE RESTRAINED PERSON HAS VIOLATED OR ATTEMPTED TO VIOLATE ANY PROVISION OF THIS ORDER." Although the order required the husband to stay at least a hundred yards from the family home at all times, one day he took the couple's three daughters while they were playing outside the home without having made any advance arrangements. The plaintiff repeatedly called the police department, showed officers who came to her house a copy of the restraining order, "and requested that it be enforced and the three children be returned to her immediately." Over a period of five hours, she repeatedly appealed to the police and got no response. More than seven hours after her first call, her husband came to the police station and "opened fire with a semi-automatic handgun." After the police, shooting back, had killed him, they found in his truck the murdered bodies of all three of his daughters.[42]

Justice Scalia's opinion for the Court, rejecting liability under section 1983, emphasized the discretion that he believed resided in the police. Saying that "a benefit is not a protected entitlement if government officials may grant or deny it in their discretion,"[43] he referred to "[t]he deep-rooted nature of law-enforcement discretion, even in the presence of seemingly mandatory legislative commands."[44] Opposing the plaintiff's argument that she had what he characterized as "a constitutionally protected property interest in having the police enforce the restraining order," he rejected what he called "[t]he creation of a personal entitlement to something as vague and novel as enforcement of restraining orders."[45] He emphasized, quoting precedent, what he described as the Court's "continuing reluctance to treat the Fourteenth Amendment as a 'a font of tort law.'"[46] He thus underlined the distinction between tort and constitutional tort, placing that distinction within the broad framework of the federal Constitution. Echoing the majority opinion in the *DeShaney* case, he said that the court's decision did "not mean States are powerless to provide victims with personally enforceable remedies," but rather that "the people of Colorado are free

42. Town of Castle Rock v. Gonzalez, 545 U.S. 748 (2005).
43. *Id.* at 756.
44. *Id.* at 761.
45. *Id.* at 751, 766.
46. *Id.* at 768, quoting Parratt v. Taylor, 451 U.S. 527, 544 (1981), quoting Paul v. Davis, 424 U.S. 693, 701 (1976).

to craft" a "system by which police departments are generally held financially accountable for crimes."[47]

Justice Stevens in his dissent vigorously took issue with the idea that the word "shall" in the "notice to law enforcement officials" that "you shall use every reasonable means to enforce" restraining orders left room for police discretion. Referring to the "specific purpose" of mandatory arrest provisions for domestic violence, and the history of statutes with that purpose, he said that the plaintiff "had a 'legitimate claim of entitlement' to enforcement." He declared that "[p]olice enforcement of a restraining order is a government service that is no less concrete and no less valuable than other government services, such as education." Indeed, he went so far as to say that "Colorado law *guaranteed* the provision of a certain service, in certain defined circumstances, to a certain class of beneficiaries" and that the plaintiff had "reasonably relied on that guarantee." Creating the hypothetical case of a contract that the plaintiff might have made "with a private security firm to provide her and her daughters with protection from her husband," Justice Stevens said that in that case "it would be apparent that she possessed a property interest in such a contract."[48]

The result the majority reached in this case does line up with the common law rule that denies the existence of a duty to act to save another person in peril. However, featuring interpretive warfare over the meaning of a state statute with strong protective language, the case presents a struggle involving elements of the injury law constitution. These include a relatively limited definition of rights under the federal Constitution and well-recognized rights to physical security that could literally be privatized when there is insufficient public enforcement.

The opposing opinions in the restraining order case have an interesting parallel in a state court case in which the well-regarded New York state judge Charles Breitel rejected a claim by a plaintiff who repeatedly asked for police protection against a rejected suitor who had "reportedly threatened to have [her] killed or maimed if she did not yield to him." In the end, the police refused a final cry for help after the plaintiff had received a "phone call warning her that it was her 'last chance,'" which was followed the next day by a hired thug throwing lye in her face. Judge Breitel summarized the case for immunizing police discretion by saying that even in cases involving "particular seekers of protection based on specific hazards," "[t]he amount of protection that may be provided is limited by the resources

47. *Id.* at 768–69.
48. *Id.* at 781–84, 789–91 (Stevens, J., dissenting).

of the community and by a considered legislative-executive decision as to how those resources may be deployed."[49]

Judge Breitel's opinion for the court drew a dissent from Judge Kenneth Keating that revealed the mighty policy forces that oppose each other in this territory under the injury law constitution. Judge Keating, who had been a United States Senator before he became a state judge, responded directly to Judge Breitel's point about allocation of public funds—specifically, what Keating characterized as the argument that imposing "liability for inadequate police protection will make the courts the arbiters of decisions taken by the Police Commissioner in allocating his manpower and his resources." He said that the case before the court was not one "where the injury or loss occurred as a result of a conscious choice of policy made by those exercising high administrative responsibility after a complete and thorough deliberation of various alternatives." Rather, he said the case involved only "plain negligence on the part of" the police officers to whom the plaintiff made her pleas for protection. A former politician's point of view was evident in his broad, practical description of "two alternatives" for public officials without "sufficient funds and resources to meet a minimum standard of public administration": "either improve public administration or accept the cost of compensating injured persons." Judge Keating declared that under decisions like the majority's, cities were "able to engage in a sort of a false bookkeeping in which the real costs of inadequate or incompetent police protection have been hidden by charging the expenditures to the individuals who have sustained often catastrophic losses rather than to the community where it belongs."[50]

These cases on the duty of officials to provide protection to threatened persons provide a cameo of a controversy that runs on alongside the battles in the socially less explosive area of tort liability for economic loss and in the more volatile area of defamation law over the boundaries of media freedom. Here it is the concept of discretion, in its respectable academic garb, that collides with a right to physical security whose proponent claims that officials have an obligation to protect her. Case by case, the injury law constitution oversees that struggle, with its mixture of law, history, and ideology.

Sexual harassment. The Supreme Court's ventures into injury law have gone beyond its choice of common law doctrines for products liability, its imposition of an overlay of constitutional limitations on state defamation law, and its creation of a large edifice of "constitutional tort" law. We have

49. Riss v. City of New York, 240 N.E.2d 860, 860–61 (N.Y. 1968).
50. *Id.* at 864–65 (Keating, J., dissenting).

noted also its construction of a broad foundation for a law of sexual harassment based on Title VII of the Civil Rights Act of 1961. In her opinion for the Court in one case in that area, Justice O'Connor used balancing language reminiscent of that used by state courts concerning tort claims for intentional infliction of emotional distress. She defined "a middle path between making actionable any conduct that is merely offensive and requiring the conduct to cause a tangible psychological injury." Employing language from a prior opinion on the "hostile environment" concept, she said that "'mere utterance of an . . . epithet which engenders offensive feelings in a employee' . . . does not sufficiently affect the conditions of employment to implicate Title VII." She added that "[c]onduct that is not severe or pervasive enough to create an objectively hostile or abusive work environment—an environment that a reasonable person would find hostile or abusive—is beyond Title VII's purview." However, with a reference to "severity" of conduct, she eventually concluded that the plaintiff merited a reversal of an adverse judgment below on the basis of conduct summarized in chapter 7.[51] Thus, interpreting a federal statute that targets discriminatory behavior, Justice O'Connor uses language—including "severity" terminology—that echoes common law concepts. In this area, the injury law constitution bridges the boundaries of two systems of law.

Preemption revisited. An assignment that has naturally fallen to the Court is to define the boundary between state tort law and federal regulatory schemes. This is the area of preemption. We have reviewed in some detail a decision in which the Court ruled that federal regulation of drugs did not bar a state tort action,[52] noting by contrast another case in which the Court imposed preemption on a claim involving a medical device.[53] Another set of opinions reached diverse results on tort claims for cigarette caused illness.[54] We also noted that the Court refused preemption with respect to some theories of liability in a case involving a herbicide, but imposed a more restrictive standard on claims based on other theories.[55] And we briefly referred to the issue of whether state claims based on the lack of air bags in motor vehicles were preempted, an issue on which a narrow majority held for preemption.[56]

51. Harris v. Forklift Sys., 510 U.S. 17, 21–23 (1993). See also chapter 7, text accompanying note 42.
52. See *supra*, chapter 7, text accompanying notes 199–205.
53. See *supra*, chapter 7, text accompanying notes 195–197.
54. See *supra*, chapter 7, text accompanying notes 183–190.
55. See *supra*, chapter 7, text accompanying notes 191–194.
56. See *supra*, chapter 10, text accompanying note 4.

The Justices' opinions on preemption have wrestled with practical judgments about safety and the desirability of uniform standards. It is hard to generalize about the Court's decisions in this area, precisely because they have dealt with areas of human activity and products that are so different, and with statutes that are often so specifically related to those areas.

Self-medication. Although there is significant variation in the results of the preemption decisions, often related to diversity of subject matter, the Court has spoken rather definitively on the government's ability to constrain personal choices to confront risk. The occasion was a suit by terminally ill cancer patients trying to procure a drug called Laetrile, which the FDA had prohibited from shipment in interstate commerce on grounds that under the governing statutory language it was "not generally recognized" by experts as "safe and effective" for use. The court of appeals had concluded, as Justice Marshall summarized it for the Supreme Court, that there was an implied exemption in the statute that applied to the plaintiffs because "the safety and effectiveness standards" of the statute "could have 'no reasonable application to terminally ill patients.'"[57] In an opinion for a unanimous Court that reversed the court of appeals, partly summarized earlier, Justice Marshall said, "we have no license to depart from the plain language of the Act, for Congress could reasonably have intended to shield terminally ill patients from ineffectual or unsafe drugs." He noted, among other things, the "special sense in which the relationship between drug effectiveness and safety has meaning in the context of incurable illnesses"—namely, that "[a]n otherwise harmless drug can be dangerous to any patient if it does not produce its purported therapeutic effect."[58]

Punitive damages. The Supreme Court's ventures into injury law, particularly those where it sounds constitutional themes in areas of the law previously reserved to common law decision making, sometimes have an almost operatic quality. In particular, the Court has written a long-running act, in several scenes, on punitive damages, an area where it has gradually discovered grounds in the Constitution for imposing limitations on state tort judgments. This part of the story is particularly dramatic because of the way it weaves together complex elements of human passion and judicial activism, because of the very fact that it involves conduct allegedly so blameworthy that it inspires juries to want to punish culpable actors, and perhaps not least, because of the way that justices who frequently are ideological opponents sometimes join one another in interesting harmonies.

---

57. Rutherford v. United States, 442 U.S. 544, 554–55 (1979).
58. *Id.* at 555–56. For an earlier summary that includes other language from Justice Marshall's opinion, see chapter 8, text accompanying notes 21–22.

The Court entered the arena of punitive damages in a somewhat tentative way in 1989 in a case involving business torts—alleged predatory pricing and interference with contractual relations. That case, in which the Court ultimately allowed to stand a jury's punitive award that was more than one hundred times the compensatory damages award—drew several separate opinions from the justices. While one might ordinarily expect that the "liberal" justices would be quite sympathetic to a punitive damages award, two of the most liberal justices took a preliminary critical view of the whole subject. Justice Brennan, in a brief opinion joined by Justice Marshall, was censorious about awards of punitive damages "by juries guided by little more than an admonition to do what they think is best."[59] And Justice O'Connor, viewed ideologically as a "centrist"—joined by Justice Stevens, usually associated with the "liberal" wing of the court—indicated she was ready to think about challenges to punitive damage awards as a violation of due process.[60]

In two cases after that, the Court continued to sustain very substantial punitive awards. In a 1991 case, where the award was for "more than four times the amount of compensatory damages" and "more than 200 times the out-of-pocket expenses" of the plaintiff, Justice Blackmun said that the instructions given to an Alabama jury had appropriately restricted its discretion so that it was not unlimited. He referred also to a group of criteria that the Alabama Supreme Court had used, which he suggested provided some "objective" standards for the amount of punitive damages.[61] Two years later, in a slander of title case, the Court affirmed a $10 million punitive award that was 526 times the "actual damages" of $19,000. Justice Stevens' plurality opinion could not find the award "grossly excessive" despite this "dramatic disparity," because of the "bad faith" of the defendant and "the fact that the scheme employed . . . was part of a larger pattern of fraud, trickery and deceit."[62]

Then, the year 1994 saw the Court begin to tighten the screws on punitive awards. One case dealt with the unusual Oregon law on the subject. A state statute named seven specific criteria for juries to consider with respect to punitive damages, but the fact that there was no judicial review of punitive awards in the state caused a seven member majority of the Court to hold that the Oregon procedures violated due process.[63] An interesting

59. Browning-Ferris Indus. of Vermont, Inc. v. Kelco Disposal, Inc., 492 U.S. 257, 281 (1989) (Brennan, J., concurring).
60. See, e.g., id. at 283 (O'Connor, J., concurring and dissenting).
61. Pacific Mut. Ins. Co. v. Haslip, 499 U.S. 1, 23 (1991).
62. TXO Production Corp. v. Alliance Resources Corp., 509 U.S. 443, 462 (1993).
63. Honda Motor Co. v. Oberg, 512 U.S. 415 (1994).

pairing of judges dissented. Justice Ginsburg, who was joined by Chief Justice Rehnquist, said that the criteria in the Oregon statute, which included the likelihood of serious harm that could come from the defendant's conduct, the "profitability" of its "misconduct," and the "total deterrent effect of other punishment," had actually "channeled the jury's discretion more tightly" than in cases in which the Court had upheld punitive awards.[64]

Two years later, Justice Stevens spoke for the Court in reducing an award of $2 million, which already had been cut down by the Alabama Supreme Court from $4 million in a case in which the compensatory award was only $4,000. In this case the jury punished the defendant, the automaker BMW, for its repainting of a car that had minor damage without telling the dealer about the repairs it had made. Justice Stevens fixed on the "degree of reprehensibility of the defendant's conduct" as "the most important indicium of a punitive damages award." He said there was no evidence of "indifference to or reckless disregard for the health and safety of others" by the defendant or of "deliberate false statements, acts of affirmative misconduct, or concealment of evidence of improper motive," which had been the case in prior decisions in which the Court had approved large awards.[65] And now Justice Stevens introduced into the conversation the question of the "ratio" of punitive damages to compensatory awards, noting that in this case—even with the reduction of the award by the state supreme court—the ratio was "a breathtaking 500 to 1."[66]

Several years after that, in 2003, the Court zeroed in on punitive damage ratios to compensatory damages, as well as the rationales for punitive awards. In this case, *State Farm Mutual Insurance Company v. Campbell,* the jury had awarded $145 million in punitive damages against the defendant for "bad faith" and "fraud" in the way it handled an auto liability claim. Justice Kennedy's opinion for the majority not only asserted that there was "a presumption against an award that has a 145-to-1 ratio"—the compensatory award was for $1 million—but suggested that "[s]ingle-digit multipliers are more likely to comport with due process, while still achieving the State's goals of deterrence and retribution, than awards with ratios in range of 500 to 1."[67] Justice Kennedy loosed another arrow at the employment of "evidence of out-of-state conduct to punish a defendant for action that was lawful in the jurisdiction where it occurred," noting the plaintiff's use of the

64. See *id.* at 438–46 (Ginsburg, J., dissenting).
65. See BMW of N. Am. v. Gore, 517 U.S. 559, 575–79 (1996).
66. *Id.* at 583.
67. 538 U.S. 408, 425–26 (2003).

case "as a platform to expose, and punish, the perceived deficiencies of State Farm's operations throughout the country."[68]

Now the Court produced a remarkable set of disagreements, in a case involving a death from cigarette-caused lung cancer. The Oregon appellate court and the state supreme court upheld a punitive award of $79.5 million where the jury had given $21,485 in economic damages and $800,000 in noneconomic damages—the latter figure having been reduced by the trial court to $500,000. As I have noted elsewhere, both levels of the state reviewing courts conveyed a "tone of moral outrage" at the behavior of the defendant cigarette manufacturer.[69] The appellate court said it was "difficult to conceive of more reprehensible misconduct for a longer period of time on the part of a supplier of consumer products to the Oregon public than what occurred in this case."[70] The Oregon Supreme Court labeled the defendant's behavior "extraordinarily reprehensible" at two different points in its opinion.[71] Among other things, the state supreme court said that the defendant had "harmed a much broader class of Oregonians" than smokers who suffered from cigarette caused illness—"even those who never got ill." That court said that "every one of those smokers *risked* serious illness or death for as long as they remained deceived" by the defendant's efforts "to spread false and misleading information"—"for nearly half a century"—in an effort to raise doubts about whether cigarettes caused disease.[72]

The Supreme Court reversed the punitive award, with a most interesting lineup of Justices. Justice Breyer's opinion for the majority made quite a fine distinction with reference to the possibility that the jury might have based its punitive award partly on the harm that the defendant's cigarettes had caused to people other than the plaintiff. Adding a page to the condemnation by the *State Farm* majority of the use of evidence of out-of-state conduct, Justice Breyer declared that the "Due Process Clause forbids a State to use a punitive damages award to punish a defendant for injury that it inflicts upon nonparties or those who they directly represent." The distinction he drew was that the plaintiffs could "show harm to others in order to demonstrate reprehensibility"; indeed, he said that "[e]vidence of actual harm to nonparties can help to show that the conduct that harmed the plaintiff also

68. *Id.* at 420–22.
69. 2 Marshall S. Shapo, The Law of Products Liability ¶29.10[4][a], text accompanying note 229.15.8.1 (5th ed. 2010).
70. Williams v. Philip Morris Inc., 92 P.3d 126, 145 (Or. App. Ct. 2004).
71. 127 P.3d 1165, 1177, 1181 (Or. 2006).
72. *Id.* at 1177.

posed a substantial risk of harm to the general public, and so was particularly reprehensible."[73]

Justice Stevens found this distinction a "nuance" that "elude[d]" him. He
said that "[w]hen a jury increases a punitive damages award because injuries to third parties enhanced the reprehensibility of the defendant's conduct, the jury is by definition punishing the defendant—directly—for a
third party harm."[74] Another dissent, by Justice Ginsburg, demonstrated
that the Court does not always break down into ideological squads. Joined
by Justices Scalia and Thomas, she referred to a jury instruction offered by
the defendant that the trial court had refused to give. That instruction had
said that the jury could "consider the extent of harm suffered by others in
determining" the "reasonable relationship" between the punishment
achieved by punitive damages and the harm to the plaintiff "by the defendant's punishable misconduct," but that the jury could not "punish the
defendant for the impact of its alleged misconduct on other persons."
Paralleling Justice Stevens' quizzical response to the majority, Justice
Ginsburg asked, "[u]nder that charge, just what use could the jury properly
make of 'extent of harm suffered by others.'?" She said, "[t]he answer slips
from my grasp."[75] Justice Thomas in a brief separate dissent pursued a line of
historical argument he had previously used: that "the Constitution does
not constrain the size of punitive damages awards."[76]

The Court sent the case back to the Oregon Supreme Court, but that
tribunal refused to budge, saying that a jury instruction proposed by the
defendant had "misstated the law."[77] Then the case ended, not with a bang
but with a whimper, with the Supreme Court ultimately dismissing a
petition by the manufacturer for further review of the case.[78]

It was ratios that formed the pivot of a continuing disagreement in the
Court on punitive damages in the 2008 case of *Exxon Shipping Co. v. Baker*,[79]
which arose from the spill of 11 million gallons of oil from the tanker *Exxon
Valdez* in Prince William Sound in Alaska. The jury in this case awarded
$5 billion in punitive damages against Exxon for the spill, which occurred
after its drunk captain left the bridge of the ship shortly before it ran aground
on a reef. The jury also had calculated compensatory damages of
$507.5 million. Justice Souter, writing for the Court, viewed the "fair upper

73. Philip Morris USA v. Williams, 549 U.S. 346, 353–55 (2007).
74. *Id.* at 360 (Stevens, J., dissenting).
75. *Id.* at 363 (Ginsburg, J., dissenting).
76. *Id.* at 361 (Thomas, J., dissenting) (quoting prior opinions).
77. See Williams v. Philip Morris USA Inc., 176 P.3d 1255, 1262–63 (2008).
78. Philip Morris USA Inc. v. Williams, 556 U.S. 178 (Mem.) (2009).
79. 554 U.S. 471 (2008).

limit" for punitive damages in maritime cases as one with a ratio of 1:1 between compensatory and punitive damages.[80] Speaking of the "stark unpredictability of punitive awards,"[81] he said that in "a well-functioning system," awards at a ratio of 1:1 "or lower" "would roughly express jurors' sense of reasonable penalties in cases with no earmarks of exceptional blameworthiness . . . (cases like this, without intentional or malicious conduct, and without behavior driven primarily by desire for gain, for example)."[82] Although the decision was technically limited to the fact that the Exxon case was governed by maritime law, Justice Souter's reference to a 1:1 ratio as proper indicated that the Court had traveled a very long road on ratios.

Justice Stevens lodged a partial dissent which at least implicitly took exception to the idea that there was not "exceptional blameworthiness" in the case. He described Exxon's conduct as a "decision to permit a lapsed alcoholic to command a supertanker carrying tens of millions of gallons of crude oil through the treacherous waters of Prince William Sound, thereby endangering all of the individuals who depended upon the Sound for their livelihoods." He argued that "the jury could reasonably have given expression to its 'moral condemnation' of Exxon's conduct in the form of this award."[83] In one of several other separate opinions, Justice Breyer, partially dissenting, noted the trial court's statement that it had given an "exacting review" of the $5 billion award and that the court of appeals had ultimately decided that a $2.5 billion award was appropriate and had "specifically noted the 'egregious' nature of Exxon's conduct."[84]

The Court's excursion into the area of punitive damages—an expedition of more than two decades thus far—has been an especially interesting act in the little opera score it has written within the injury law constitution. It takes its legal as well as human drama from the use of civil litigation to punish, when ordinarily the main thrust of tort law is to compensate for injury. This saga also has occurred in the context of the fact that compensatory damages themselves have effects on behavior. The topic raises empirical questions about the amounts of awards that are necessary to achieve the particular effects on conduct that are in part a purpose of the punitive damages remedy. The preoccupation of some Justices at various times with ratios, and in particular the focus in State Farm on single-digit multipliers, forces us to ask what the magic of that kind of ratio is. I suggest

80. See id. at 513.
81. Id. at 499.
82. Id. at 512–13.
83. Id. at 522 (Stevens, J., concurring in part and dissenting in part).
84. Id. at 526 (Breyer, J., concurring in part and dissenting in part).

that it is unclear that single-digit multipliers are less arbitrary than a wide range of ratios above nine to one.

A particular, if obvious, feature of the operation of punitive damages is the very fact that jurors become stirred up enough to award them. Many will consider laughable the monumental award of $145 billion by a Florida jury in a cigarette class action. The reviewing courts reversed this award,[85] but the very extravagance of it provides a lesson in the multifaceted landscapes of the civil justice system and of the injury law constitution more generally. Clearly, at some point judges must constrain the passions of jurors, but even the reins that the Supreme Court has put on punitive damages cannot obscure the way that these awards represent moral judgments. While history and common sense both counsel prudence about the amount of leeway given for expression of those judgments, they are part of the fiber of our injury law constitution to which the Court's intramural arguments contribute.

85. See Liggett Group, Inc. v. Engel, 853 So.2d 434 (Fla. Dist. Ct. App. 2003); Engel v. Liggett Group, Inc., 945 So.2d 1246 (Fla. 2006).

Conclusion

Consumers of any media are aware of the breadth of concern about, and interest in, the problem of injuries. I offer an evocative set of examples from front pages of *The New York Times*. One front page included three stories that covered a wide spectrum of injury law territory. One of those stories analyzed the way that New York City settles lawsuits on police brutality.[1] Another reported a proposal of President Clinton on tobacco policy which included giving the FDA authority "to regulate nicotine as an addictive drug," "fundamental changes in the way cigarettes are made and sold," and "rapid disclosure of documents" on the behavior of tobacco companies.[2] A third front-page article reported on voter anger in New Jersey about rates for automobile liability insurance.[3] Moreover, a story inside the same edition of the paper bore the headline, "U.S. Survey Clears Implants of Role in Breast Cancer."[4]

Two months later, a *Times* front page featured a story on the ongoing investigation into the explosion of TWA Flight 800 that split the plane apart and killed all 230 passengers.[5] The same front page included a three-paragraph summary of an article inside the paper on recommendations by officials of several health-focused agencies that people who had taken two kinds of diet pills should have medical examinations,[6] and a squib item

1. Deborah Sontag and Dan Berry, Using Settlements to Gauge Police Abuse, N.Y. Times, Sept. 17, 1997, at A1.
2. Clinton Will Seek Tougher Proposal to Rein in Smoking, N.Y. Times, Sept. 17, 1997, at A1.
3. Whitman Faces Anger of Voters Over Insurance, N.Y. Times, Sept. 17, 1997, at A1.
4. N.Y. Times, Sept. 17, 1997, at A19.
5. FBI Inquiry Over, Safety Board Seeks Flaw in Flight 800, N.Y. Times, Nov. 14, 1997, at A1.
6. Medical Exams Used for Diet Pill Users, N.Y. Times, Nov. 14, 1997, at A1.

about an inside story on an expert committee that declined to endorse as safe a pill to reduce baldness.[7]

This especially striking collection of front-page stories appeared in *Times* pages in the fall of 1997, but it is representative of items that daily appear in national media today. Those stories span a range of products and activities, with impacts on millions of consumers, which are subject to varying intensities of regulation. Many of those products and activities have become the focus of lawsuits. These few articles simply illustrate the continuing conflicts that underlie the development of a constitution of injury law in this country. The law that constitution arbitrates is a living, breathing cauldron of controversy, in a state of constant flux that includes elements of culture, ideology, and politics. New ideas constantly challenge established ones, and defenders of orthodoxies hit back.

This ongoing process takes place in battles in courts and legislatures— and in fact sometimes in battles between courts and legislatures. From those struggles over legal policy, we derive a special meaning of that great phrase that introduces the Constitution of the United States: "We the People." This book has focused not only on the principles but also on the controversies in the area of injury law that are constitutive. Analogously to the great Constitutional debates of 1787—and reflecting contemporary arguments among American judges and in legislatures—the injury law constitution encompasses a vast cluster of personal and social dramas involving attitudes toward injury, including the definition of injury. The actors in these dramas—all comprised within the body of "We the People"—include large numbers of individual claimants and defendants in tort cases, as well as many classes of entrepreneurs and consumers involved in wars over regulation and the scope of compensation systems. They also include various stripes of politicians, including those who call themselves advocates of "consumer protection" and those who view themselves as defenders of the "free market." At any one time, the overall product of these many battles between persons and groups has the quality of a constitution.

The social institutions that work on injury law issues—courts, legislatures, and regulatory agencies—sometimes do so in complementary ways but also sometimes act in competition with one another. Congress and state legislatures have passed dozens of laws designed to affect the risk of injuries, or the consequences of injuries. Yet, every year many proposals to change tort law or to institute new schemes of safety regulation fail in Congress. One controversial bill that failed would have adopted a national

7. No Decision on Baldness Pill, N.Y. Times, Nov. 14, 1997, at A1.

system of no-fault insurance for automobile injuries.[8] A bill passed by Congress that would have nationalized the law of products liability was vetoed by President Clinton.[9]

Specialized grounds of dueling between state courts and legislatures have featured arguments over the constitutionality of legislation to place dollar limits on the amount of damages recoverable in tort actions. Also a subject of state-centered constitutional litigation have been statutes that completely cut off the ability of injury victims to sue, even when they could not have discovered the cause of their injuries before the expiration of the statutory period allowed for suits. Another battleground, which we analyzed earlier, has generated the varied Supreme Court decisions on whether federal systems of safety regulation bar injury victims from bringing tort suits.[10]

Sometimes competition over injury law occurs between parties that casual observers might see as natural allies. One example is proposals for no-fault compensation plans for people injured by products. That idea would stir intense opposition from product makers but might be congenial to insurance companies that now provide products liability insurance to those manufacturers but could view no-fault insurance in that area as a profitable source of business.

An assortment of conflicts arises between individuals and the broader society. One argument against expansions of products liability and medical liability law is that such expansions would reduce the amounts of useful products and medical services available to members of the public generally, especially to low-income people. In some dramatic cases, the conflict between individual and society occurs between particular sufferers and government agencies. We gave as one example the *Abigail Alliance* case, in which the Court of Appeals for the District of Columbia Circuit ruled against a suit on behalf of a patient who sought access to an experimental drug not shown to meet FDA safety and efficacy standards.

One result of these various competitions—among institutions and between individuals and institutions—is the evolution of what I have called the jagged frontier of injury law. Laypersons apprised of the differences in amounts of compensation paid to injury victims with similar injuries,

8. See, e.g., P. John Kozyris, No-Fault Insurance and the Conflict of Laws—An Interim Update, 1973 Duke L.J. 1009, 1010 n.2 (noting 49–46 vote in the Senate in 1972 that effectively shelved bill).

9. Veto message of May 2, 1996, of Product Liability Fairness Act of 1995, reported, e.g., in Mark A. Hofmann, Liability reform vetoed, Bus. Ins., May 6, 1996, at 1.

10. See *supra*, chapter 7, text accompanying notes 183–206, chapter 10, text accompanying notes 4–6.

and of the different valuations to human life given by government agencies, might express puzzlement. These variations exist in part as a result of some of the rivalries we have mentioned, and also because of the different systems of injury law—regulation, tort, and compensation schemes—that govern us. They also exist because of the great variety of human activities, and the large number of conflicting views held throughout society about the nature of rights and the definition of injuries.

A by-product of a terrible event—the September 11th Victim Compensation Fund—was a hurried attempt to collate many rules that have developed over the years in tort law and in statutory compensation systems. But the statute and rules that created the Fund only spotlighted the question of what the rationales are for providing compensation for injuries. Some observers asked why taxes paid by Americans generally should go to September 11th victims in particular. Others wondered why, if such a fund was created for a terrorist atrocity, payments should not be provided for those who were injured or lost relatives in the Oklahoma City bombing—or for the widow of the *Wall Street Journal* reporter who was beheaded in Pakistan.

Philosophical and ideological clashes swirl around the topic of how society should respond to injuries, with respect to both compensation and prevention. One camp includes people whose basic views draw on the notion of survival of the fittest. People who take this position often tend to support the idea that the benefits to society from innovation usually are greater than the harms that innovations may cause to those they injure. These views can take an exaggerated form. Some might argue that there actually is a humanitarian strain in a Darwinian approach—at the most extreme position, that eugenic improvement achieved by eliminating from the population those whose vulnerabilities cause them to fall victim to certain kinds of innovation is an overall benefit to humanity. Thus, it would be contended that our awareness of the steepness and slipperiness of the Darwinian slope, and of the moral difficulties thereby raised, does not overcome the desirability of improving the genetic lot of future generations.

A contrasting set of ideas is Biblical in nature. It emphasizes our obligations to feed the hungry and to help the unfortunate in general. A common sense modern variation on this point lies in recognition of a simple truth. We may easily acknowledge that society benefits from technical improvement and the intense personal effect that often produces it, effort that often is associated with high social and economic standing. Yet we must recognize that in many ways, one's position in society is often a matter of luck. That is, fortune frequently is a result of good fortune.

Many dialectics contribute to the constitution of injury law. We have reviewed a number of ways in which the complex relationships between courts and legislatures provide such interplays. Just one example is the changes in the vector of law related to the question of immunity of tobacco companies from products liability suits. We have noted that this issue includes a dialectic between different institutions of government.[11] The everyday problem of tort suits for injuries that occur when a worker is ordered to do something exceptionally dangerous illustrates a different kind of dialectic, one involving competing freedoms—employers' freedom to assign tasks and employees' right to be free from injury.

We have noted the complicated nature of our injury law constitution with respect to various aspects of the availability of information about risk. These include not only comparative advantages in the acquisition and comprehension of information, but also the problem that arises where there is uncertainty about what the data are. A particularly difficult aspect of the problem relates to people's sophistication in assessing information about potential injury—often, the ability to understand what data about risk mean and to comprehend the kind of choice that uncertainty often requires. Economic theorists talk about "perfect information," but in practical terms the question is usually one of whether information is adequate to the decision that must be made. Frequently an issue of fairness threads its way into these questions: When is it fair to impose risks on people who, even if they understand a risk, as a practical matter are within the power of the creator of the risk?

Drawing on materials from both within and without the legal system, the injury law constitution offers tools for defining the boundaries of personal privacy against intrusions of various kinds. In this regard it can draw on different strains of the contributions to American law of Louis D. Brandeis during his distinguished career as an attorney: his early efforts to define the concept of privacy, and his creation of advocacy documents that employed behavioral data. Angular to Brandeis's landmark arguments for the protection of privacy interests might be data indicating that many people accept impingements on those interests as part of the realities of modern life.

In cases where the issue is whether to compensate for injuries to psychological interests, elements of this constitution force decision makers to mediate among competing views, often held simultaneously by individuals. These include both beliefs about the reality of psychic injury and ideas about the need for a certain degree of toughness when one lives in society—as well as a sense that life requires us to absorb a certain amount of punishment without recompense.

---

11. See *supra*, chapter 6, text accompanying notes 48–56.

More generally, the injury law constitution helps us to define the role of judges as moral arbiters, in a legal system that tends to push large-scale decisions about rights and wrongs into the legislative arena.

*** ***

We now seek to summarize some basic elements of the practical constitution of injury law of the United States. In presenting this summary, we note that there always is a tension between pragmatism and principle. Cynics will suggest that principle is a will-o'-the-wisp, but there is much to be said for the effort to dig for principles and to try to ascertain them.

OVERALL PRINCIPLES

The dignity of individual human beings deserves the primary respect of society, especially as it inheres in physical and emotional security and in the economic and financial foundations of dignitary interests.

Individuals should have maximum freedom for the exercise of personal autonomy, and the law should foster people's ability to make choices that materially affect their lives.

Responsibility for injury should be assessed, as much as possible, on the basis of control of risk, with moral culpability ordinarily being a significant factor in the assessment, and decisions on responsibility should take into account the risks and costs of the activity or product at issue, and its benefits and social utility. Responsibility should be allocated in as precise a way as possible in the context of existing institutional structures, including corporate forms of organization.

The award of compensation for injury should be determined in an individualized way whenever possible. When practical circumstances require mass treatment of injuries, as much respect as possible should be given to individual dignitary interests.

INTERESTS AND RIGHTS

People should have maximum freedom of physical action and speech, consistent with the interests of others described below. They must bear without compensation harms ordinarily inherent in everyday contacts with others.

Generally, the legally protected interests of persons include those things that are pertinent to the maintenance and advancement of individual lives. These things include individuals' physical security and emotional tranquillity, their property, both tangible and intangible, and their ability to make informed choices concerning benefits and risks of injury associated with activities and products.

Identifiable bodily harm is compensable. Intangible harms consequent on identifiable physical injury, including pain and suffering, are compensable. Compensation should be awarded for harms to emotional interests without physical invasions of the person when those harms are very serious, as when an actor's conduct inspires fear or terror or causes significant effects on a person's ability to function. There are no firm dividing lines among types of protectable property interest, although the law should take into account of the importance of those interests in the maintenance and advancement of individual lives.

On matters involving risks of injury, government decision makers should take into account the amount of information that is available about risk, and the availability of that information to both parties who create risk and those who are exposed to it, as well as the ability of parties exposed to risk to comprehend that information. When information about risk is uncertain, decisions on whether to permit the creation of potential risks to individuals or to the public, or to require compensation for injuries, should take into account the social benefits from risky activities and products. Decision makers also should make judgments of fairness about the exposure to risk of injured persons or those potentially subject to risk.

INJURIES

The decision on whether a harm is legally cognizable should depend not on arbitrary classifications of the nature of the harm, but rather on the importance of the individual interests harmed and the impact on society of designating a particular harm as legally cognizable.

The determination of whether there is a legally cognizable harm, or the need for public regulation of activities or products, may be made on the basis of the culpability of the alleged injurer or risk creator, as objectively determined from the circumstances. However, decisions on compensation or regulation shall not be limited to culpability.

Decisions on whether a harm is legally cognizable should take into account: the risk creator's level of knowledge of the risk; the ability of the person harmed or subject to risk to comprehend the risk; the ability of risk creators or those subject to risk to control the level of risk; and the relationship of the parties, including the risk creator's power to require the person harmed to undergo the risk and the inability of persons subject to risk to avoid or minimize it.

Where a small class of persons is particularly vulnerable to a risk of injury that they cannot avoid or significantly minimize, courts should be relatively liberal in decisions on whether to award compensation, either when judging lawsuits for civil liability or interpreting compensation legislation. However, when the power to order exposure to risk and the inability of those subject to risk to avoid or minimize risk are taken into account, ordinarily one can impose a risk on others without being held legally responsible for injuries if one specifically identifies that risk, clearly communicating it to the persons who will be exposed to the risk.

Where members of a particularly vulnerable class suffer injury from activities or products that substantially benefit the community and risk creators cannot be identified or cannot make payment, legislatures should provide basic compensation for their injuries.

DECISION MAKERS

Since many useful activities and products pose risks to others, the law should establish processes to decide the level of risk that is socially acceptable, where people do not define that level by private agreement fairly arrived at.

Decisions on controversies concerning injuries should be as decentralized as possible.

Because individualized determination of disputes involving risk is desirable, courts and alternative dispute resolution tribunals are generally the best resolvers of controversy where a dispute concerns a specific injury.

The legislature is superior to individuals and to courts and tribunals for the resolution of injury law controversies when: Disputed issues of policy are pervasive within an area of law, typically when recurrent problems of risk and injury affect significant numbers of people, and particularly when such issues require normative judgments that define community values; there are conflicts about the desirable level of risk within large classes of people, for example between or within consumer groups or business groups.

The criminal law is the principal legal process for inflicting penalties on persons who deserve punishment for causing injury, but in cases involving egregious conduct, generally it also is appropriate for a court to award punishment damages in civil litigation. Courts that approve such awards should identify their rationales for doing so, and it is desirable that they state their assumptions about the behavioral effect of such awards.

Ordinarily, legislatures should be the decision makers on issues of injury law involving elements of social compassion, including compassionate moral principles. Where there is a clear benefit to the community from activities or products that impose significant risks on a few, legislatures should refer to compassionate considerations both in setting levels of safety for activities and products and in devising compensation programs. Moreover, it is appropriate for courts to take into account those considerations in establishing principles to govern civil litigation.

DECISION MAKING

It is appropriate for judges to announce moral judgments about conduct that strains the bonds of community trust or constitutes a serious breach of moral codes of conduct, although this should be done only sparingly. Courts may also employ moral judgments as reinforcing elements in decisions that involve manifest imbalances in the ability of parties to make decisions on risks of injury.

When a legislative compensation system is based significantly on compassionate rationales, ordinarily courts should interpret its coverage broadly.

When a conflict exists between legal institutions about the proper system of injury law to apply to a case, ordinarily it is best to choose the most decentralized decision-making system.

When a choice must be made between exclusivity of a regulatory system and the ability to bring civil lawsuits, ordinarily the law should not exclude civil lawsuits, given the desirability of individualized justice, unless the regulatory statute explicitly bars such suits. However, the relative comprehensiveness of a regulatory system and the particularity of its requirements as applied in a specific case should be taken into account in deciding whether the system should be found to be exclusive.

When significant ideological controversies underlie crucial issues in litigation, judges should be especially careful to identify and consider their own ideological presuppositions in order to achieve as impartial a decision as possible.

Decision makers on issues of injury law should identify and consider their own definitions of rationality and take into account the range of behaviors that might be considered rational.

In disputed areas of fact and policy, decision-makers should regard truth as provisional and open to argument.

*** ***

A signal declaration about the purpose of American law, as well as the vocation of American lawyering, was John Adams' rhetorical question to a friend, written early in Adams' career:

> Now to what higher object, to what greater character, can any mortal aspire than to be possessed of all this knowledge, well digested and ready at command, to assist the feeble and friendless, to discountenance the haughty and lawless, to procure redress to wrongs, the advancement of right, to assert and maintain liberty and virtue, to discourage and abolish tyranny and vice?[12]

What is "the advancement of right"? And what, indeed, are rights? The concept of rights, tied to the collateral concept of injuries, has a complex heritage in our history. A most profound progenitor was the Civil War, a struggle for the rights of an enslaved population encased in a struggle to preserve the Union. Ideas of rights, and protectable rights, have ebbed and flowed. During World War II, more than eight decades after the Dred Scott decision reflected an acceptance of the institution of slavery, the Supreme Court effectively upheld the internment of more than 100,000 Japanese Americans living on the West Coast. Yet two decades later, Congress passed a series of rights-protecting laws, including at one swoop a law prohibiting discrimination in public accommodations and a law prohibiting discrimination in employment, including discrimination on the basis of race and sex. A generation after that, there followed legislation designed to protect an especially vulnerable group in the population: the Americans With Disabilities Act. The concept of justice is a slippery one, and the question of what is just presents many difficult issues. But as the injury law constitution responds to those issues, it parallels the way that people in general live their lives: It stumbles toward justice.

12. John Adams to Jonathan Sewall, 1 L.H. Butterfield (ed.), Diary and Autobiography of John Adams 124, quoted in David McCullough, John Adams 53 (Simon & Schuster paperback trade ed. 2008).

INDEX

ABA (American Bar Association), xvii
Abel, Richard, 34
*Abigail Alliance for Better Access to
  Developmental Drugs v. von Eschenbach*
  (2006), 188–90, 265
Abzug, Bella, 118
Accountability for injuries, xv, 206–11
Accutane, 172
Ackerman, Robert, 193–94, 196
"Actual malice" test for defamation, 246–47
Adams, John, 7, 11, 272
Advertisements, 153, 198, 246
Agency law, 207
Agent Orange, 195
Agriculture and Forestry Committee, 117
AIDS drugs, 186–87
Aid to the Permanently and Totally
  Disabled, 68
ALI (American Law Institute), xviii
Alito, Samuel, 176, 208, 236
Allergic reactions, 63, 191
Allison, J. W. F., 14, 16–17
Altruism, 67
Alzheimer's patients, 60–61
American Bar Association (ABA), xvii
American Law Institute (ALI), xviii
Americans with Disabilities Act, 35, 64, 272
Anti-heartbalm statutes, 130–31, 182–83
Apologies, 221–22
"Approaches to Safe Nanotechnology"
  (NIOSH), 168–69
Archonship of Eucleides, 3–4
Aristotle, xvi, 2, 3–4, 40, 216, 220, 225
Artificial hearts, xii
Asbestos suits
  bankruptcies and, 58
  colon cancer and, 97
  costs of, 58n89

damages in, 205, 237–38
pain and suffering and, 82
"Snowmen of Grand Central" and, 77
warnings and, 150–51, 156–57, 158
workers' compensation exclusivity rule
  and, 115
Assumption of risk doctrine
  accountability and, 207
  Alzheimer's patients and, 60
  autonomy and freedom and, 48–51
  burdens, assignment of, 239
  compensation, bar to, xvii
  individual responsibility and, 201,
    202–3
  personal autonomy and, 185
  sports activities and, 48, 180–81, 202
  workers' compensation and, 136–37
Autonomy, 47–52, 131n36, 183–90, 211, 256,
  268. *See also* Choice; Movement,
  freedom of

Bad faith torts in insurance, 30
Bankruptcies, 58
Battery, 102, 103, 179–80
Beever, Allan, 216–17
Bender, Leslie, 34, 229–30
Bernstein, Anita, 44
Berryman, Jeffrey, 45, 47
Bivens litigation, 208–9
Blackburn, Justice Colin, 107
Blackmun, Harry, 78–79, 251, 257
BMW, 258
Bork, Robert, 52
Boyles v. Kerr (1993), 210
BP oil spill, 89, 136
Brandeis, Louis D., 267
Breast implants, 95–96, 159–60, 170, 263
Breitel, Charles, 253–54

Brennan, William J., 51, 246, 247–48,
    249–50, 251, 257
Breyer, Stephen, 202–3, 236, 245, 259–60, 261
Bridgestone, 144
British Constitution, 12–18
Burchell, Jonathan, 45–46
Burroughs, Abigail, 188
Bush, Robert, 194–95
Business torts, 257

Cairns, Lord, 107
Calabresi, Steven, 9
Cancers
    cigarettes and, 111
    cure for, 65
    experimental drugs for, 186, 189
    hormonal drugs and, xiii
    information in litigation process and,
        164–65
    mesothelioma, 82, 237
    relative risk of, 97
Cardozo, Benjamin N.
    on consumer remedies for product
        injuries, 29
    Learned Hand tribute to, 227, 230
    on individual responsibility, 54
    liability theory of, 231
    on ordered liberty concept, 189
    on rescue, 67
    on rights, 48
    on self-determination, 37
Caregivers, conduct of, 60–61
Catlin, George, 13, 14–15
Causes of injuries, 73–75
Caveat emptor doctrine, 244
Centers for Disease Control and
    Prevention, 168
Chapman, Bruce, 45
Child abuse, 251
Children, medical care for, 194
Child trespasser doctrine, 66
Choice, question of freedom, 50, 184–90
Cialis, 171
Cigarette cases
    assumption of risk, 49
    health dangers and, 110–11
    preemption and, 172–74, 177
    punitive damages and, 259, 262
    safety legislation and, 169–70
    social responsibility and, 205
    tobacco companies, immunity of, 267

tort suits, 110–11
    warnings and, 160–61
Cigarette Labeling and Advertising Act of
    1965, 173–74
Cipollone v. Liggett Group, Inc. (1992), 172–73
Civil Rights Act of 1866, 9
Civil Rights Act of 1964, 35, 131–32, 229, 255
Civil War, 272
Class actions, 57–58, 89, 90, 262
Clean Air Watch, 215
Clinical trials, randomized, 187–88, 192
Clinton, Bill
    on pain, 190
    products liability bill and, 265
    alleged sexual imposition, 130
CNTs (long-fibered carbon nanotubes), 167
Cocaine, 27–28, 185–86
Cochran, Robert, 193–94, 196
Code of Hammurabi, 217
Coke, Edward, 14
Collectivism, 52
Commission on the Evaluation of Pain, 190
Common law, 7–8, 14, 16, 38
The Common Law (Holmes), 53, 107
Communitarianism, 193–96, 209
Comparative fault doctrine, 203, 203–4n82
Comparative negligence doctrine, 203
Consent. *See also* Informed consent
    in sports, 48
Constitution, British, 12–18
Constitution, U.S. *See also specific amendments*
    Due Process clause, 250, 251, 259
    injury law constitution and, 1, 10
    interpretations of, 39–40
    living Constitution metaphor, 11n67
    meaning of, 11–12
    privileges and immunities clause, 8
    punitive damages and, 260
    Supremacy Clause, 236
    "We the People" phrase, 264
Constitutional torts, xxi, 23, 31, 38, 128–29,
    250. *See also* Section 1983 actions,
The Constitution of Athens (Aristotle), 3
Consumer knowledge, 154–57, 162–63
Consumer Product Safety Act (CPSA), 118
Consumer Product Safety Commission,
    98, 118
Consumer protection statutes, 28, 64–65.
    See also specific statutes, e.g., Food,
    Drug and Cosmetic Act, Consumer
    Product Safety Act

in ancient Greece, 4
Contract law, 42, 78–79, 86, 112–13, 194, 246
Contributory negligence
    accountability and, 206–7
    individual responsibility and, 53, 201,
        202, 203
    as matter of law, 54
    mental illness and, 62
    product defects and, 49
Control of risk, 269
Corpus Juris, 218
Corrective justice, xvi, 40, 56, 216–21,
    220n33, 225
Cost-benefit analysis, 214–16, 226, 228
Court of Cassation (Italy), xxi, 18
Courts
    Case-by-case growth of law, 231
    Judge and jury, 90
    Moral judgmemts, 232, 271
    Punitive damages, 270–71
    Legislatures, relation to, 87–88, 92–93,
        265–66
    Reversals of decisions, 209–11, 232
    Value of judicial decisions, 12
CPSA (Consumer Product Safety Act), 118
Cranworth, Lord, 107
Criminal law, 223, 270–71
Crisci v. Security Insurance Company
    (1967), 30
Culpability, 38, 268, 269
Customs and Border Patrol, 98

Damages. See also Punitive damages
    apologies and, 221–22
    calculation of, 80–84, 265
    caps on, 93
    compensatory, 217–23, 236–39
    criticisms, 220
    existential, 18, 19–20, 20n125, 21n130
    individual loss as focus, 217–19
    inequalities in income and, 200
    for medical malpractice, 87
    leeway for juries, 66–67
    money transfers and, 236–38
    need, 221
    non-economic, xviii, 18–22, 19n117,
        20n125, 21–22n132, 81–82, 200,
        218–19. See also pain and suffering,
        this category
    pain and suffering, 190, 200, 237–38
    presumed, 247

prevention and, 236
    regularization of amounts in, 91
    September 11th Fund, 68–69
Darwinian approach to injuries, 266
Daubert v. Merrell Dow Pharmaceuticals, Inc.
    (1993), 95, 164
"Dear Doctor" letters, 171–72
Deaths, statistics on numbers of, 73–74
Decency, 46
Decentralized decision-making, 208, 270, 271
Deepwater Horizon, 89, 136
Defamation, 51, 146–48, 182, 196, 216, 227,
    246–48. See also Libel
Defects in product design. See Design defects
Democracy, 85–86, 93–94
DES (diethylstilbestrol), 59
DeShaney, Joshua, 251
DeShaney v. Winnebago County Dept. of Soc.
    Servs. (1989), 251, 252
Design defects, 110, 137–43, 158
Deterrence, 222
Dicey, A. V., 13
Diethylstilbestrol (DES), 59
Dignity of human beings, 44–47, 179–83, 268
Dikasterion (jury court), 2
Disabled people, 221, 241
Discretionary acts by government officials,
    32–33
Distributive justice, 67, 68
Doggett, Lloyd, 199
Domestic violence, 253
Double compensation, 20–21, 241–47
Douglas, William O., 55, 125–26, 128, 248
Draco, 3
Drug Amendments of 1962, 33
Drugs. See also specific drugs
    advertising for, 198
    banned, 186
    experimental, xiii, 185–90, 192, 256, 265
    legislation on, 64
    safety and, 124, 235
    warnings and, 150, 153, 155, 157–59,
        170–72, 175–77
Due process clause, 250, 251, 259
Dunham, William, 15
DuPont, 151
Duty,
    breaches of, 104–5
    limitation of liability, 89–90
    to act, governmental, 250–54
Dworkin, Ronald, 44, 80

Easterbrook, Frank H., 154
East River S.S. Corp. v. Transamerica Delaval (1986), 78–79
Economic theory, injury law and, 193, 197, 214–16, 229, 268. *See also* Risk-utility balancing
Economic loss doctrine, 78–80, 192, 245–46
Eggshell skull concept, 63
Eighth Amendment, 128
Eleusis, 3–4
Eli Lilly, 171
Emanuel, Ezekiel, 189
Emergency Medical Treatment and Active Labor Act, 26
Emotional distress, infliction of. *See* Intentional infliction of emotional distress; Negligent infliction of emotional distress
Employment, scope of, 134–36
Employment contracts, 19, 19n118
English language, 91–92
Enterprise liability, 224
Environmental Protection Agency (EPA), 97, 98, 117, 170
Environmental regulations, 215–16
Equality before the law, 197–200
Equal protection, 87
Essentiality standards, 117–18
European Convention on Human Rights, 16, 18, 21
European Court of Human Rights, xxi, 15
European Court of Justice, 15
Exclusivity rule, 114–16
Exculpations, 112–14
Expectations,
    and injury law, 42–43
    products liability, 109
Existential damages, 18, 19–20, 20n125, 21n130
Express warranty theory, 43, 145, 174
Exxon Shipping Co. v. Baker (2008), 260–61
Exxon Valdez oil tanker spill, 260–61

"Failure to act," 105, 251
Fault, 101–2, 106. *See also* Comparative fault doctrine; No-fault compensation
FDA. *See* Food and Drug Administration
FDA Modernization Act of 1997, 187–88
Federal Employees' Compensation Act (FECA), 116
Federal Employers' Liability Act, 77

Federal Hazardous Substances Act, 91–92, 97–98
Federal Insecticide, Fungicide and Rodenticide Act (FIFRA), 117, 170, 174
Federal Office for Environment (Switzerland), 169
Federal Office of Public Health (Switzerland), 169
Federal Tort Claims Act, 28, 32
Federal Trade Commission (FTC), 163
Federal Trade Commission Act, 198, 198n63
Fell, Jeffrey, 180–81
Feminism, 34, 229–30
Fides servanda est maxim, 244
FIFRA. *See* Federal Insecticide, Fungicide and Rodenticide Act
Finley, Lucinda, xviii
First Amendment, 183, 246, 247
Fletcher, George, 40–41
Food, Drug, and Cosmetic Act, 28, 94, 120, 123–24, 176, 186
Food and Drug Administration (FDA)
    drug approvals and, 186–88, 189–90, 192, 235, 256
    hormone therapy and, 170–71
    labeling and, 94, 153, 175–76
    nicotine regulation and, 263
    safety regulation and, xiv, 195–96, 208, 236, 265
Ford Motor Company, xiii, 231–32
Fourteenth Amendment, 8–9, 246, 249, 250, 251, 252
Fourth Amendment, 127
Frankfurter, Felix, 125
Fraud, xv, 43, 173, 257–58
Freedom. *See also* Autonomy, Choice
    in injury law rationales, 47–52, 216
    of movement, 179–83
FTC (Federal Trade Commission), 163
Funding of injury compensation, 241–42

General Electric Co. v. Joiner (1997), 164–65
General Motors, xi, 199–200
German language, 153
Germany
    nanoparticle injuries in, 167–68
    Supreme Court in, 6–7
Gertz v. Robert Welch, Inc. (1974), 246–47
Ginsburg, Ruth Bader, 175, 228, 258, 260

Glasbeek, H. J., 45
Goffman, Erving, 47
Goodhart, Arthur, 223
Good Samaritan laws, 25–26
Gore-Tex, 151
Government officials and immunity, 31–33
Graham, John, 215
Green, Leon, xiv
Grey, Tom, 11
Griffith, Thomas, 189–90
Gross negligence, 104
Grotius, Hugo, 6
Group responsibility theory, 194–95
Guilt. *See* Culpability
Gurney, Edward, 119
Gusfield, Joseph, 46–47

Hammurabi, 221
Hand, Learned, 214, 227–28, 230
Harms not injuries, 76–80
Haynsworth, Clement, 79
HC (Hitachi Cable), 144
Health and Safety Laboratory (Buxton, England), 169
"Heeding presumptions," 156–57
Heldman, Julie, 201
He liaia (prospective jurors), 2
History of the American Revolution (Ramsay), 7
Hitachi Cable (HC), 144
Hitcachi Shin Din Cable (HSD), 144–45
Holmes, Oliver Wendell, 37, 53, 54, 61, 90, 107
Hoplites, 2–3
Hormone therapies, 170–71
Hospital and medical costs, 80
Hostile environment test, 131–32, 255
Howard, A. E. Dick, 4–5
Howard, Philip, xix–xx
HPV (Human papillomavirus), 129–30
HSD (Hitcachi Shin Din Cable), 144–45
Humanitarian considerations, 65–69. *See also* Social justice
Human lives
costs per statistical, 83
dignity of, 44–47, 179–83, 268
quantifying of, 98–99
Human papillomavirus (HPV), 129–30
Human rights, 15–16, 18
Human Rights Act 1998 (UK), xxi, 15–17

Ignorance of law. *See* Uncertainties
Immunity, government, 32–33
Implied warranty theory, 43
"The Inconvenient Public" (Fischoff & Merz), 75
Individual goods. *See* Social and individual goods
Individualism, 52–53. *See also* Autonomy
Individualization
individual goods and, 190–93
of injury compensation, 268
of justice, xx, 56–61, 93, 270–71
power and, 136
rights and, 56–61
Individual knowledge, 62. *See also* Information
Individual responsibility. *See* Personal responsibility
Information, 143–77. *See also* Labeling; Warnings
communication and, 143–49
cost of providing, 154
duties to provide, 149–63
gaps in, 168–69
in litigation and regulation, 164–69
"perfect information," 267
quality of, 157–58
risks of injuries and, 267, 269
safety legislation, 123, 169–77
specificity of, 158–63, 202–3
Informed consent, 114, 172, 183–84
Injuries, 71–84. *See also* Injury law and power; Injury law constitution; Injury law rationales
behavioral causes of, 74–76
disproportionate effects, 41–43
harms not recognized as, 76–80
loss, calculation of, 80–84
risk, sources of, 71–73
statistics of, 73–74, 84
Injury law and power, 25–35
judicial decisions and, 28–33, 35
preventing harm, 25–27
products of liability, 28–29
regulatory law development and, 27–28, 35
scholarship on, 33–34
Injury law constitution, generally, 1–24
Basic components and elements, xx–xxi, 121, 264–65, 266
Defined, 1–2, 12, 22–24

Injury law constitution, generally
  (*Continued*)
  Principles, 268–71
  Resolution of controversies, 22, 113–14,
      183, 197, 227, 233, 242, 264, 267
  Social mores, 39
Injury law constitution, comparisons,
  British constitution and, 12–18
  Italian injury law and, 18–22
  U.S. Constitution and, 1, 8–12
Injury law rationales, 213–33
  apology, remedy of, 221–22
  corrective justice and, 216–21, 220n33
  economics-based approaches and, 229
  feminism and, 229–30
  freedom and, 216
  legal doctrines and, 227
  philosophy of judging and, 227–28
  pragmatism and, 230–33
  procedural rules and, 228–29
  punishment and, 222–24
  rationality and, 226–27
  safety and, 213–16
  social justice and, 224–25, 232
  uniformity and, 225–26
  vindication and, 222
Innovations, 196–97, 209
Insane individuals, 60, 60n97, 62
Institute of Medicine, 74, 166
Institutional analysis of injuries, xviii
Insults, non-compensability of, 77
Insurance
  Bad faith torts, 30
Insurance policies and claims, 29–31, 225,
      242, 265
Intangible harms, 66–67, 80, 81, 210, 237,
      269. *See also* Non-economic damages
Intentional infliction of emotional distress
  cognizable injuries and, 77–78
  development of law of, 29, 209–11,
      209n103
  sexual relationships and, 130, 131
  social tensions and, 181–82
Intentional infliction of nervous shock, 46
Intentional torts, 44, 46, 102–4
Interests, group and individual, 265, 269
Internet, 144–46, 196
Internet service providers, 146, 196
*Introduction to the Study of the Law of the
      Constitution* (Dicey), 13
Intrusion, actions for, 147–48

Irvine, Lord, 17
Italian Civil Code, 18
Italian constitution, 18–22

James, William, 230–31
Japan, apologies in, 221–22
Jefferson, Thomas, 8, 10
Joint liability theories, 240
Jones, Paula, 130, 131
Judging, philosophy of, 227–28.
      See also Courts
Judicial administration, 93
Juries, 67–68, 90, 93, 94, 262
Jurisdiction issues, 143–45, 207
Justice, individualization of, xx, 56–61, 93,
      270–71. *See also* Corrective justice;
      Distributive justice; Social justice

Kant, Immanuel, 6–7, 44
Katko v. Briney (1971), 180
Keating, Kenneth, 254
Kennedy, Anthony, 258–59
Kennedy Onassis, Jacqueline, 148, 182, 236
Kent, James, 8
King, Anthony, 13, 17
Kissinger, Henry, 32
Knowledge, individual, 62. *See also* Information
Ku Klux Act, 38, 55, 125–28, 249–50.
      See also Section 1983 actions
Kyl, John Henry, 117

Labeling, 94, 153, 158, 175–76. *See
      also* Warnings
Laetrile, 186, 256
"Law of ancient lights," 53
Learned Hand Test, 214
Learned intermediary doctrine, 94, 153, 159
Least cost avoiders, 229
Legal doctrines, 101–21. *See also specific
      theories of liability*
  exculpations and limitations on liability,
      112–14
  fault, 101–2
  intentional torts, 102–4
  negligence, 104–6
  strict liability for activities, 106–8
  strict liability for products, 108–11
Legislative histories, 88, 213
Legislatures,
  Relation to courts, 87–88, 92–93, 270,
      271n273

Leval, Pierre N., 82
Levitra, 171
Lex Aquilia, 217–18
Liability without fault, 106. *See also* No-fault
    compensation; Strict liability; *specific*
    theories of liability (e.g., Strict liability)
Libel, 146, 246–47. *See also* Defamation
Life, human. *See* Human lives
Linde, Hans, 228
Living Constitution metaphor, 11*n*67
Locke, John, 6, 10*n*60
Lockerbie disaster, xii
Long-fibered carbon nanotubes (CNTs), 167
Longshore and Harbor Workers'
    Compensation Act, 224
Love, Betty, 222, 223
Low-income populations, 215, 225, 265
Lump sums, 192, 220

MacCormack, Geoffrey, 217–18
MacPherson v. Buick Motor Co. (1916), 231
Madison, James, 10
Madoff, Bernard, 223
Magic Nano, 167–68
Magna Carta, xxi, 4–5, 7, 23, 87
Magnus, Ulrich, 217–18
Malpractice. *See* Medical malpractice
Manufacturing defects, 109–10
Marbury v. Madison (1803), 88
Marketing defect claims, 49
Market share liability, 59, 240
Marshall, John, 88, 186, 256, 257
Massachusetts Constitution of 1780, 7
Mass tort suits, 89, 229–30
Master-servant relationships, 135
Material Safety Data Sheets (MSDS), 158
McDonald's, 54
Medical and hospital costs, 80
Medical care, failure to provide, 194
Medical Device Amendments, 123, 175.
    See also medical devises
Medical devices, 152–54, 158, 159–60,
    175–76. *See also* Drugs;
    Products liability
Medical malpractice, 60, 87, 166
Medicines. *See* Drugs
Menschenbild (personhood) concept, 7*n*33
Mental illness, 62. *See also* Insane individuals
Mesothelioma, 82, 237. *See also* Asbestos suits
Minimum contacts test, 143–44
Misrepresentation, suits for, 157, 243–44

Monell v. Dept. of Social Services of City of
    New York (1978), 127–28, 249, 250
Monroe, James and Flossie, 125–26
Monroe v. Pape (1961), 125–26, 128,
    248–49
Montoya, Joseph, 119
Moral content of rights, 37, 193–94, 244, 266
Morgan, Nichole, 25
Morris, Robert, 224
Movement, freedom of, 179–83
MSDS (Material Safety Data Sheets), 158
Multi-district litigation, 89
Multiple parties in tort litigation, 88–89,
    239–40

Nader, Ralph, xi
Nanotechnology, 166–69
National Center for Health Statistics, 73
National Childhood Vaccine Act, 165–66
National Institute for Occupational Safety
    and Health (NIOSH), 168
National Institute of Medicine, 74, 166
National Institute of Mental Health, 74, 166
National Institutes of Health (NIH),
    170, 189
National Security Council, 32
National Traffic and Motor Vehicle Safety
    Act, 123
Natural rights, 6–10, 39. *See also* Kant,
    Emanuel; Locke, John
Negligence. *See also* Contributory negligence
    burdens, assignment of, 239–40
    comparative, 203
    culpability and, 38
    gross, 104
    as legal doctrine, 104–6
    Section 1983 actions and, 250
    standard of care and, 105–6
    workers' compensation and, 114, 115
Negligent infliction of emotional distress,
    xvii, 232, 238. *See also* Intentional
    infliction of emotional distress
Nervous shock, intentional infliction of, 46
New Drug Amendments of 1962, 186
New York Times
    defamation case against, 246, 247
    injuries examples, 263–64
New Zealand, tort law in, xix
NIH (National Institutes of Health), 170, 189
NIOSH (National Institute for Occupational
    Safety and Health), 168

Nixon, Richard, defendant in whistleblowing case, 31
"No duty" doctrine, 203
No-fault compensation, xvii, 47, 57, 92–93, 114–16, 264–65. *See also* workers' compensation
Non-economic damages, xviii, 18–22, 19*n*117, 20*n*125, 21–22*n*132, 81–82, 200, 218–19, 269. *See also* Intangible harms

Obvious risks, 155–56, 162–63
Occupation, deprivation of, 80–81
Occupational Safety and Health Act of 1970
  fairness and, 35
  language of, 123
  safety and, 27, 47, 213, 213*n*2
  workplace power and, 28, 132–34, 137
Occupational Safety and Health Administration (OSHA), 83, 97, 103, 132–34
O'Connor, Sandra Day, 128, 132, 255, 257
Ohio constitution, open courts provision in, 5, 87
Oil spills
  BP Deepwater Horizon spill, 89, 136
  Exxon Valdez tanker spill, 260–61
Oklahoma City bombing, 266
Open and obvious risks, 155–56, 162–63
Open courts provisions, 5, 87–88
Oral contraceptives, 172
OSHA. *See* Occupational Safety and Health Administration
Oxford English Dictionary, 14

Packaging of products. *See* Labeling; Warnings
Pain and suffering, 66, 81–82, 87, 190–92, 200, 237–38
Pan American World Airways, xii
Pape, Frank, 125–26, 248
Parliamentary sovereignty, 14
Patient information leaflet (FDA), 170–71
PCBs (polychlorinated biphenyls), 164–65
Peel, Robert, 13
Peltzman, Sam, 33
Penn, William, 8
Percy, Charles, 119
Personal autonomy. *See* Autonomy
Personalization of justice. *See* Individualization

Personal responsibility, 54–56, 62–63, 201–4, 217, 268
Pesticides, 117–18, 170, 177
Peters, Justice Raymond E., 41–42
Pfizer, 171
Pharmaceuticals. *See* Drugs
Piercing the corporate veil, 207
Poison Prevention Packaging Act, 98
Police brutality, 55, 125–28, 248–50, 263. *See also* Section 1983 actions
Police protection, 253–54
Politics (Aristotle), 3
Polychlorinated biphenyls (PCBs), 164–65
Ponzi schemes, 223
Posner, Richard, 220, 230–31
Post, Robert, 46–47
Pound, Roscoe, 44
Poverty, 67
Powell, H. Jefferson, 12
Powell, Lewis, 116
Power, 125–43. *See also* Injury law and power
  police behavior and, 31–32, 125–29
  products and, 137–43
  sex and, 129–32
  workers' compensation and, 27, 134–36
  in workplace, 28, 132–37
Pragmatism, 230–33, 268
Preemption, 93–94, 172–77, 195–96, 255–56, 271
  decentralization and, 208
  democracy and, 85–86, 93–94
  federal, xiii–xiv
  prevention and, 236
  risk information and, 172–77
  uniformity and, 225–26
Pregnancy leaves, 127–28, 249
Prevention of injuries, xvii, 25–27, 235–36. *See also* Safety
Prisoners' rights, 39
Privacy, 46–47, 182, 216, 227, 267
Privileges and immunities clauses, 8–9
Procedural rules, 228–29
Productivity costs, 74, 84
Products liability
  accountability and, 207
  communitarianism and, 194–96
  courts' role, 92
  design, 138–43
  economic loss and, 245
  exculpatory clauses and, 113
  individualization of justice and, 59

information, failure to provide, 75,
    143–45, 149–63
nationalization of law of, bill vetoed, 265
power and, 137–43
preemption and, 93–94
risk-utility balancing and, 215
scientific uncertainty and, 95–97
strict liability and, 108–11, 231–32
warnings and, 149–63
warranty in, 43, 78–79
workers' compensation and, 116, 246
Property damage, 42, 245
Property rights, 180
Prosser, William L., 29, 209
Proximate cause of injuries, 89, 137,
    155, 160
Pryor, Ellen, 219
Psychic injuries, 29, 209–11, 267
Public disclosure of private facts, tort of, 148
Public figures, 146–47, 246
Public Health Service, 187
Public policy, and tort law, xiv, 228
Punishment. *See also* Punitive damages
    cruel and unusual, 128
    damages and, 271
    injury law rationales and, 222–24
    revenge, 223
    retribution, 222–23
Punitive damages
    auto manufacturers and, 75
    emotional equilibrium and, 219
    individualization of justice and, 61
    individual responsibility and, 55–56
    injury to nonparties, 259–60
    intentional torts and, 103–4
    moral judgments, 205–6
    punishment and, 222–23
    ratio to compensatory damages, 257,
        260–61
    reprehensibility standard, 258
    social responsibility and, 204–6
    Supreme Court and, 205, 256–62
Pure Food and Drugs Act, 27–28, 186

Qualified immunity defense, 129
Quality of information, 157–58
Quid pro quo sexual favors, 131

Ramsay, David, 7
Rationality in injury law, 226–27
Reaume, Denise, 46

Reckless disregard standard, in defamation,
    146–47
Regulation,
    effects, 33
    element of injury law constitution, xx–xxi
    rationales, 116–21
Rehnquist, William, 127, 164–65, 248–49,
    251, 258
Religious beliefs, 194
Remedies and sanctions, 235–42. *See also*
    Punitive damages
    apologies and, 221–22
    burdens, assignment of, 239–42
    compensation in money, 236–39
    damages and, 236
    prevention and, 235–36
Representations, and injury law, 43
Restatements of Torts
    intentional infliction of emotional
        distress, 29
    intentionality, definition, 102–3
    non-negligent activities, 108
    post-sale warnings, 150
    risk-benefit test in, 214
    strict liability, 109, 223–25
    tobacco cases, 110, 111
Restraining orders, 251–53
Retributive punishment, 222–23
Revenge, 217–18, 223, 224
Ribicoff, Abraham, 118–19
Riegel v. Medtronic (2008), 195, 208
Rights, 37–69
    autonomy and freedom, 47–52
    dignity and, 44–47
    expectations and, 42–43
    historical development, 272
    humanitarian considerations and, 65–69
    individualism and, 52–53
    individualization and, 56–61
    individual responsibility and, 54–56
    individual victims and, 62–65
    injuries, effects of, 40–42
    injuries, relation to, 84
    representations and, 43
    right to die, 189
    rights-creating language, 39
Risk. *See also* Assumption of risk doctrine;
        Open and obvious risks
    Basis for tort liability, 101
    Quantitative standards, 97–99
    Sources, 71–73

Risk-benefit test, 214
Risk-utility balancing, 215
Rogers, Judith, 189
Rollover protective structure (ROPS), 141
Roman law, 45
Rule of law, 14, 16–17
Rutherford, United States v. (1979), 186
Ryan White Comprehensive AIDS
    Resources Emergency Act, 120
Rylands v. Fletcher (1868), 107, 111

Safety. *See also* Prevention of injuries
  drugs and, 124, 235
  information and, 169–77
  injury law rationale, 213–16
  legal doctrine and, 116–21
  workers' compensation and, 33
St. Elizabeth Hospital v. Garrard (1987),
    209–10
Sanctions. *See* Remedies and sanctions
Sarokin, H. Lee, 160
Scalia, Antonin, 147, 175, 252–53, 260
Scientific uncertainty, 95–97, 164–69
Second Treatise on Government (Locke), 6
Section 1983 actions, 125–28, 248–53
Securities Exchange Act, 198
Securities laws, 198
Seduction suits, 130–31. *See also* Anti-
    heartbalm statutes,
Self-defense, 61, 180
Sensitivities, 62–64
September 11th Victims
    Compensation Fund
  compensation and, xiv, 81, 266
  creation of, 40
  distribution of burdens, 241–42
  economic and non-economic losses and,
    68, 192, 238–39
  individualization and, 192
  inequalities in income and, 200
  injuries, recognition of, 84
  need and, 82, 221
  victims' suits, 89–90
Sexual autonomy misappropriation, 131n36
Sexual harassment, 44, 130–32, 229, 254–55
Sexually transmitted diseases, 129–30, 131
Shari'a, 104
Sherwin, Emily, 218–19
Shuman, Daniel, 221–22
Sic utere tuo ut alienum non laedas maxim, 53
Silicone implants. *See* Breast implants

Silicosis cases, 151–52
Sindell v. Abbott Laboratories (1980), 59
Smoking. *See* Cigarette cases
"Snowmen of Grand Central" case, 77
Social and individual goods, 179–211.
    See also Social mechanisms of law
  accountability and decision making,
    206–11
  autonomy and choice of risks, 183–90
  communitarianism and, 193–96, 209
  equality and, 197–200
  freedom of movement vs. dignitary
    interests, 179–83
  individualization and, 190–93
  individual responsibility and, 201–4
  innovation and, 196–97, 209
  social responsibility and, 204–6
Social contract, 10
Social justice, 224–25, 232
Social mechanisms of law, 85–99
  court-legislature battles and, 87–99
  duty as limitation on liability, 89–90
  multiple parties, 88–89
  patterns and particularities and, 90–92
  preemption and democracy and, 85–86,
    93–94
  private contract and, 86
  quantifying lives and, 98–99
  quantitative standards and, 97–98
  scientific uncertainty and, 95–97
  statutory terms, interpretation of, 88
  uncertainty or ignorance about law, 94–95
Social responsibility, 204–6. *See also*
    Personal responsibility, Punitive
    damages
Social Security, 67–68, 221, 241
Solon, 2–3
Sophisticated users of products, 151
Souter, David, 260–61
Spanish language, 91–92
Specificity of information, 158–63
Sports activities, 180–81, 201
Spouses, loss of, 66–67
Stalin, Joseph, 52
Stalking, 147, 182–83
Standards of care, 60, 93, 105–6, 111, 192
Standing to sue, 93
Starr, Kenneth, 147
State constitutions, 9–10
State Farm Mutual Insurance Co. v. Campbell
    (2003), 258–59, 261

Statistics on injuries, 73–74, 84
Stevens, John Paul
  on preemption, 174, 175–76, 195–96
  on punitive damages, 204, 257, 258,
    260, 261
  on restraining orders, 253
  on warnings, 173
"Stigma plus" concept, 128, 129
"Strategic Plan for NIOSH Nanotechnology
  Research" (NIOSH), 168
Strict liability
  for activities, 106–8
  burdens, assignment of, 239
  precedent and, 92–93n18
  for products, 29, 41, 108–11
  safety and, 139, 213
  spreading costs and, 199
  warnings and, 158
  workplace injuries and, 50
"Substantial certainty" concept in intentional
  torts, 102–4
Successor corporations' liability, 207–8
Sugarman, Stephen D., xixn22
Suicides, 74, 153, 172
Sunstein, Cass, 83, 215–16, 215n13, 226
Supplemental Security Income program,
  221, 241
Supremacy Clause, 236
Supreme Court, 243–62
  defamation and, 246–48
  economic loss and, 245–46
  government duty to act and, 250–55
  misrepresentations and, 243–44
  preemption and, 172–77, 255–56
  punitive damages and, 256–62
  Section 1983 and, 125–29, 248–50
  self-medication and, 256

Temporary Assistance for Needy Families
  (TANF), 68
Thomas, Clarence, 260
Title VII of Civil Rights Act of 1964, 131–32,
  229, 255
Tobacco policy, 263. See also Cigarette cases
Tort law
  Criticized, xix–xx, 33
  Difficulty of receiving compensation,
    xvii–xviii
  Doctrines, 101–14, 227
  Effects, 199–200, 235–36
  Element of injury law constitution, xx

Workers' compensation and, xvii
Trade secrets, 151
Traynor, Roger, 29, 41, 108, 231
Treatment IND, 186–88
Truth, Finding and publishing, 147–49
Tribe, Laurence H., 12
Turcotte, Ron, 180–81
TWA Flight 800 explosion, 263
Twelve Tables, rules of, 217
Tyvek, 151

Uncertainties
  about law, 94–95
  scientific, 95–97, 164–69
"Understanding Clinical Trials" (NIH), 170
Uniform Commercial Code (UCC), 113,
  113n63, 198–99
Uniformity as goal of injury law, 225–26
Unsophisticated consumers, 198–200

Vaccinations, 165–66
Vaughan v. Menlove (1837), 56, 60
Viagra, 159, 171
Vindication in injury law, 222
Virginia, colonial charter of, 5–6
Virginia State Bar Association, 7
Vulnerability of persons, 270

Warnings. See also Labeling
  asbestos suits and, 150–51, 156–57, 158
  on drugs, 150, 153, 155, 157–59, 170–72,
    175–77
  on products, 75, 91–92, 94, 149–63,
    199, 203
Warranty
  express warranty theory, 145, 157–58, 174
  implied warranty theory, 43
  strict liability, historical background, 108
Washington, Bushrod, 8
Weinstein, Jack, 195
Welke, Barbara, 229
Whistleblowing, 31–32
White, Byron, 247
Wiedeman v. Keller (1897), 109n42
Will of the people, 10
Wightman Cup, 201
Williams, Stephen F., 154
Wood, Gordon, 10–11
Workers' compensation. See also Workplaces
  burdens, assignment of, 239, 241, 242
  damages in, 76, 83

Workers' compensation. *See also* Workplaces
(*Continued*)
    equality and, 197–98
    exclusive remedy, 185
    history, 27
    humanitarian considerations and, 67
    individualization and, 192
    individual responsibility and, 204
    innovation and, 197
    intentional wrongs and, 103, 114
    Legal standards, 123
    money transfers and, 38–39, 236–37
    no-fault compensation and, 92, 114–16
    personal autonomy and, 185
    products liability and, 116
    rationales, 114
    remedies in, 90–91
    risk-taking and, 33, 197, 197n62
    safety and, 33
    schedules in, 83, 91, 121, 192, 237
    social justice and, 224–25
    social responsibility and, 204
    tort law and, xvii, 115–16
    weekly wages and, 200
    workplace power and, 27, 134–36
Workplaces. *See also* Workers' compensation
    heeding presumptions in, 157
    power in, 28, 132–37
    sex in, 131–32. *See also* sexual harassment
World War II, 272
World Wide Web. *See* Internet
Wyeth v. Levine (2009), 195–96, 208

Yarborough, Ralph, 47, 213

Printed in the USA/Agawam, MA
January 22, 2013

572142.008